TAKING SIDES

Clashing Views on Controversial

Issues in Mass Media and Society

SIXTH EDITION

Clashing Views on Controversial

Issues in Mass Media and Society

SIXTH EDITION

Selected, Edited, and with Introductions by

Alison Alexander
University of Georgia

and

Jarice Hanson
University of Massachusetts–Amherst

McGraw-Hill/Dushkin
A Division of The McGraw-Hill Companies

Photo Acknowledgment
Cover image: © 2001 by PhotoDisc, Inc.

Cover Art Acknowledgment
Charles Vitelli

Library of Congress Cataloging-in-Publication Data
Main entry under title:
Taking sides: clashing views on controversial issues in mass media and society/selected, edited,
and with introductions by Alison Alexander and Jarice Hanson.—6th ed.
Includes bibliographical references and index.
1. Mass media. 2. Information services. I. Alexander, Alison, *comp.* II. Hanson, Jarice, *comp.*
302.23
0-07-242254-8
94-31766

Printed on Recycled Paper

Preface

Comprehension without critical evaluation is impossible.

— Friedrich Hegel (1770–1831)
German philosopher

Mass communication is one of the most popular college majors in the country, which perhaps reflects a belief in the importance of communications systems as well as a desire to work within the communications industry. This book, which contains 36 selections presented in a pro and con format, addresses 18 different controversial issues in mass communications and society. The purpose of this volume, and indeed of any course that deals with the social impact of media, is to create a literate consumer of media—someone who can walk the fine line between a naive acceptance of all media and a cynical disregard for any positive benefits that they may offer.

The media today reflect the evolution of a nation that has increasingly seized on the need and desire for more leisure time. Technological developments have increased our range of choices—from the number of broadcast or cable channels we can select to the publications we can read that cater specifically to our individual interests and needs. New and improving technologies allow us to choose when and where to see a film (through the magic of the VCR), to create our preferred acoustical environment (by stereo, CD, or portable headphones), and to communicate over distances instantly (by means of computers and electronic mail). Because these many forms of media extend our capacities to consume media content, the study of mass media and society is the investigation of some of our most common daily activities. Since many of the issues in this volume are often in the news (or even *are* the news!), you may already have opinions on them. We encourage you to read the selections and discuss the issues with an open mind. Even if you do not initially agree with a position or do not even understand how it is possible to make the opposing argument, give it a try. We believe that thinking seriously about mass media is an important goal.

Plan of the book   This book is primarily designed for students in an introductory course in mass communication (sometimes called introduction to mass media or introduction to mass media and society). The issues are such that they can be easily incorporated into any media course regardless of how it is organized—thematically, chronologically, or by medium. The 36 selections have been taken from a variety of sources and were chosen because of their usefulness in defending a position and for their accessibility to students.

Each issue in this volume has an issue *introduction,* which sets the stage for the debate as it is argued in the YES and NO selections. Each issue concludes with a *postscript* that makes some final observations about the selections, points the way to other questions related to the issue, and offers suggestions for further reading on the issue. The introductions and postscripts do not preempt what is the reader's own task: to achieve a critical and informed view of the issues at stake. In reading an issue and forming your own opinion you should not feel confined to adopt one or the other of the positions presented. Some readers may see important points on both sides of an issue and may construct for themselves a new and creative approach. Such an approach might incorporate the best of both sides, or it might provide an entirely new vantage point for understanding. Relevant Internet site addresses (URLs) that may prove useful as starting points for further research are provided on the *On the Internet* page that accompanies each part opener. At the back of the book is a listing of all the *contributors to this volume,* which will give you additional information on the communication scholars, practitioners, policymakers, and media critics whose views are debated here.

Changes to this edition This sixth edition represents a considerable revision. There are 11 completely new issues: *Is Television Harmful for Children?* (Issue 2); *Is the First Amendment Working?* (Issue 8); *Is Negative Campaigning Bad for the American Political Process?* (Issue 9); *Has Democracy Been Transformed by New Uses of Media?* (Issue 10); *Should Internet Access Be Regulated?* (Issue 11); *Do Ratings Work?* (Issue 12); *Shold the FCC Be Abolished?* (Issue 13); *Should the Internet Facilitate a Free Exchange of Information?* (Issue 15); *Do Public Relations Practitioners Provide a Valuable Service to the Public?* (Issue 16); *Can Privacy Be Protected in the Information Age?* (Issue 17); *Does the Internet Have the Power to Transform Culture?* (Issue 18). In addition, for Issue 1 (*Are American Values Shaped by the Mass Media?*) the issue question has been retained but the No-side selection has been replaced to bring a fresh perspective to the debate. Issue 14 (*Media Monopolies: Are the Dangers of Concentration Overstated?*) contains a new issue question and a new No-side selection. In all, there are 24 new readings.

A word to the instructor An *Instructor's Manual With Test Questions* (multiple-choice and essay) is available through the publisher for the instructor using *Taking Sides* in the classroom. And a general guidebook, *Using Taking Sides in the Classroom,* which discusses methods and techniques for integrating the pro-con approach into any classroom setting, is also available. An online version of *Using Taking Sides in the Classroom* and a correspondence service for *Taking Sides* adopters can be found at http://www.dushkin.com/usingts/.

   Taking Sides: Clashing Views on Controversial Issues in Mass Media and Society is only one title in the Taking Sides series. If you are interested in seeing the table of contents for any of the other titles, please visit the Taking Sides Web site at http://www.dushkin.com/takingsides.

Acknowledgments We wish to acknowledge the encouragement, support, and detail given to this project. We are particularly grateful to Theodore Knight, list manager for the Taking Sides series. We are extremely thankful for the care given to the project by all of the staff at McGraw-Hill/Dushkin, and in particular Rose Gleich, administrative assistant, and Juliana Gribbins, developmental editor. We would also like to extend our appreciation to the many professors who reviewed our fifth edition, and we are grateful for the advice they have provided in the preparation of this edition. To them, and their students, thank you.

Our thanks go to the following individuals:

Ty Adams
University of Arkansas-Monticello

Charles Aust
Kennesaw State University

Janice Barrett
Boston University

Mike Basil
University of Denver

Barbara Burke
University of Minnesota-Morris

Gary D. Christenson
Elgin Community College

Robert Finney
California State University-Long Beach

Paul Gates
Appalachian State University

Gloria Hurh
Western Illinois University

Barbara Irwin
Canisius College

Cristine Kahn-Egan
Florida State University

Jin Kim
State University of New York at Plattsburgh

Mary Loporcaro
St. John Fisher College

Trevy McDonald
North Carolina Central University

Harold Moses
Daytona Beach Community College

Carol M. Parker
University of Central Oklahoma

Jeff Ritter
La Roche College

William J. Ryan
Rockhurst College

Kathryn Segnar
Temple University

Glenda Treadaway
Appalachian State University

Tommy Thomason
Texas Christian University

We would also like to thank Todd Fraley and Cheryl Christopher at the University of Georgia, and Kristine Fortini and Janna Goodwin at the University of Massachusetts, for their valuable assistance. Finally, we would like to thank our families (David, James, Katie, Jaime, and Torie) for their patience and understanding during the period in which we prepared this book.

Alison Alexander
University of Georgia

Jarice Hanson
University of Massachusetts-Amherst

Contents In Brief

Contents

Professor of media studies Neil Postman argues that television promotes triviality by speaking in only one voice—the voice of entertainment. Thus, he maintains that television is transforming American culture into show business, to the detriment of rational public discourse. Professors of communication Horace Newcomb and Paul M. Hirsch counter that television serves as a site of negotiation for cultural issues, images, and ideas. Viewer selection from among institutional choices is a negotiation process as viewers select from a wide set of approaches to issues and ideas.

W. James Potter, a professor of communication, examines existing research in the area of children and television violence. Such research is extensive and covers a variety of theoretical and methodological areas. He examines the nature of the impact of television on children and concludes that strong evidence exists for harmful effects. Jib Fowles, a professor of communication, finds the research on children and television violence less convincing. Despite the number of studies, he believes that the overall conclusions are unwarranted. Fowles finds that the influence is small, lab results are artificial, and fieldwork is inconclusive. In short he finds television violence research flawed and unable to prove a linkage between violent images and harm to children.

Marketing professors Mary C. Martin and James W. Gentry address the literature dealing with advertising images and the formation of body identity for preadolescent and adolescent females. They report a study to explore how social comparison theory influences young women. *Washington Monthly* editor Michelle Cottle takes the perspective that females are not the only ones influenced by media image. She cites polls and magazine advertising that indicate that males are exposed to images of idealized body type as well, and she argues that these images also have an impact on the male psyche.

Ruth Shalit, a reporter for *The New Republic*, argues that inaccurate coverage of minority news and the treatment of minority news staff at some places are a form of racism. She focuses on the *Washington Post* as an extreme example of this activity. Executive editor Leonard Downie, Jr., and publisher Donald Graham of the *Washington Post* respond to Shalit's charges. They argue that their newspaper has achieved a higher standard of minority reporting and employment than Shalit claims.

PART 2　MEDIA ETHICS　85

President of NBC News Michael Gartner argues that identifying accusers in rape cases will destroy many of society's wrongly held impressions and stereotypes about the crime of rape. Katha Pollitt, journalist and social critic, argues that the decision to reveal victims' identities without their consent cannot be justified.

Doctor Joseph R. DiFranza and his colleagues report a national study that examines the possibility of children being tempted to smoke because of the tobacco industry's use of images that appeal to and are remembered

Larry J. Sabato, professor of government, Mark Stencel, politics editor for Washingtonpost.com, and S. Robert Lichter, president of the Center for Media and Public Affairs, assert that the line dividing public life and private life is more blurred than ever. The authors state that this is creating an age of scandal. They conclude that this focus on politics-by-scandal results in disaffected voters, discouraged political candidates, and news devoid of analysis of policy issues and substantive debate. William G. Mayer, assistant professor of political science, defends negative campaigning as a necessity in political decision making. He argues that society must provide the public with the substantive information needed to make informed decisions at the polls and insists that this must occur during political campaigns. Therefore negative campaigns are needed so that citizens can make intelligent choices concerning their leaders.

Professor Dale Herbeck discusses the traditional model of the New England town meeting and how it has been used by television since 1992 to get the political candidate's campaign message to as many people as possible in an intimate setting. He states that this type of event has transformed a portion of direct democracy, and he discusses what happens in a mediated environment. Elizabeth Weise, a writer for *USA Today,* addresses the New England town meeting facilitated by the Internet. She cites a number of studies and issues that support her view that the Internet is not yet an appropriate venue for this type of democratic interaction, largely because key individuals have not yet learned how to use it effectively.

PART 4 REGULATION 209

Author Michael A. Banks explains that as more people turn to libraries for Internet access, libraries and communities have been forced to come to grips with the conflict between freedom of speech and objectional material on the World Wide Web and in Usenet newsgroups. He adds that software filters are tools that help librarians keep inappropriate materials out of the library. The American Civil Liberties Union (ACLU) concludes that mandatory blocking software in libraries is both inappropriate and unconstitutional. Blocking censors valuable speech and gives librarians,

Professors Eli M. Noam and Robert N. Freeman contend that there will be more competition in the future among U.S. media markets, not less. Using U.S. Department of Justice procedures for identifying overly concentrated markets, they demonstrate that media industries are only moderately concentrated and advise that such concern should focus on local, not national, media. Ben H. Bagdikian, a Pulitzer Prize-winning journalist states that the public needs to be aware of the control that international conglomerates like General Electric and Rupert Murdoch have over the media. One should not assume that technology will be the savior, since it too is subject to the domination of the same conglomerates.

Journalist Andrew Sullivan argues that the Internet makes instant communication between citizens easier than ever before. He presents his argument in Marxist terms, stating that Marx's primary complaint about capitalism was that it reduced everything to money. However, the Internet does not have money at its core, and therefore, can link users to each other without a profit motive. Attorneys for the plaintiffs Russell J. Frackman et al., writing the Motion on behalf of members of the Recording Industry Association of America (RIAA), argue that peer-to-peer programs, like Napster, infringe upon copyright and also subvert sales and royalties to performers and those in the record distribution chain. Therefore, they argue that it should be illegal for Napster to distribute music via the Internet.

James E. Lukaszewski is a public relations practitioner who, in a commencement address to the 1999 Summer Institute on Public Relations Program at New York University (NYU), outlines the practical skills necessary for a successful career in public relations. Professor Stuart Ewen traces the evolution of the profession and practice of public relations, and cites events in which the field of public relations did not operate in the best interest of the public.

Journalist Simson Garfinkel discusses how today's technology has the potential to destroy our privacy. He makes the case that the government and individuals could take steps to protect themselves against privacy abuse, particularly by returning to the groundwork set by the government in the 1970s and by educating people on how to avoid privacy traps. *Forbes* reporter Adam L. Penenberg discusses his own experiences with an Internet detective agency, and he explains how easy it is for companies to get unauthorized access to personal information. He specifically describes how much, and where, personal information is kept and the lack of safeguards in our current system.

Professor Peter F. Drucker outlines a history of social organization in relation to technology in order to put the "information revolution" into perspective. He compares the changes in our present and future lives to the introduction of the Industrial Revolution and reminds us that while social change often takes much longer than the term revolution suggests, the real impact of social change is often accompanied by more subtle shifts in our institutions. Professors Kevin A. Hill and John E. Hughes discuss the utopian and dystopian visions of the future and find, based upon empirical evidence, that neither scenario of the future is likely to occur. Instead, the actual practices involved with the Internet point to a future in which different social groups may influence the Internet's ability to effect change.

Introduction

Ways of Thinking About Mass Media and Society

Alison Alexander

Jarice Hanson

The media are often scapegoats for the problems of society. Sometimes the relationships between social issues and media seem too obvious *not* to have some connection. For example, violence in the media may be a reflection of society, or, as some critics claim, violence in the media makes it seem that violence in society is the norm. But, in reality, one important reason that the media are so often blamed for social problems is that the media are so pervasive. Their very ubiquity makes them seem more influential than they actually are. If one were to look at the statistics on violence in the United States, one would see that there are fewer violent acts performed today than in recent history—but the presence of this violence in the media, through reportage or fictional representation, makes it appear more prevalent.

There are many approaches to investigating the relationships that are suggested by media and society. From an organizational perspective, the producers of media must find content and distribution forms that will be profitable. They therefore have a unique outlook on the audience as consumers. From the perspective of the creative artist, the profit motive may be important, but the exploration of the unique communicative power of the media may be paramount. The audience, too, has different use patterns and desires for information or entertainment, and consumers demonstrate a variety of choices in content offered to them as well as what they take from the media. Whether the media reflect society or shape society has a lot to do with the dynamic interaction of many of these different components.

To complicate matters, the "mass" media have changed in recent years. Not long ago, "mass" media referred to messages that were created by large organizations for broad, heterogeneous audiences. This concept no longer suffices for contemporary media environments. While the "mass" media still exist in the forms of radio, television, film, and general interest newspapers and magazines, many media forms today are hybrids of "mass" and "personal" media technologies that open a new realm of understanding about how audiences process the meaning of the messages. Digital technologies and distribution forms have created many opportunities for merging (or converging) media. The Internet, for example, has the capacity to transmit traditional voice, mail, text, and image-based content in a unique form of instant communication while the senders of the messages may be, or appear to be, anonymous. Time-shifting, memory, storage of information, and truth all play important roles in the use of Internet communication, and call our attention to aspects of the communicative process that need fresh examination.

Still, most of the new services and forms of media rely, in part, on the major mass media distribution forms and technologies of television, radio, film, and print. The challenge, then, is to understand how individuals in society use media in a variety of formats and contexts and how they make sense of the messages they take from the content of those media forms.

Historically, almost every form of media in the United States was first subject to some type of regulation by the government or by the media industry itself. This has changed over the years; there is now a virtually unregulated media environment in which the responsibility for the content of media no longer rests with higher authorities. We, as consumers, are asked to be critical of the media that we consume. This requires that we be educated consumers, rather than rely on standards and practices of industry or on government intervention into situations involving questionable content. Although this may not seem like a big problem for most adults, the questions become more difficult when we consider how children use the media to form judgments or seek information.

The growing media landscape is changing our habits. The average American still spends over three hours a day viewing television, which is on in the average home for over seven hours a day. Politics and political processes have changed, in part, due to the way politicians use the media to reach voters. A proliferation of television channels has resulted from the popularity of cable, but does cable offer anything different from broadcast television? Videocassettes deliver feature-length films to the home, changing the traditional practices of viewing films in a public place and video distribution via the Internet is now a practical option for anyone who has transmission lines with the capacity to download large files. The recording industry is still reeling over the impact of MP3 and free software that allows consumers to sample, buy, or download music online. Communications is now a multibillion-dollar industry and the third fastest-growing industry in America. One can see that the media have changed American society, but our understanding of how and why remains incomplete.

Dynamics of Interaction

In recent years, the proliferation of new forms of media has changed on a global scale. In the United States, 98 percent of homes have at least one telephone, though there are places in the world where phone lines may be limited or where telephones do not exist at all. Over 98 percent of the United States population has access to at least one television set, but in some parts of the world televisions are still viewed communally, or viewed only at certain hours of the day. The use of home computers and the Internet grows annually in the United States by leaps and bounds, but still, only one third of the world has access to the Web. These figures demonstrate that the global media environment is still far from equitable, and they suggest that different cultures may use the media in different ways.

But apart from questions of access and availability, many fundamental questions about the power of media in any society remain the same. How do audiences use the media available to them? How do message senders produce meaning? How much of the meaning of any message is produced by the audience? Increasingly important is, how do additional uses of media change our interpersonal environments and human interactions?

Within the same framework for discussion, we must examine the power and potential of any media organization to merge and control more of what is seen and heard through the media. Once, there were more than 20 major competing media companies in the United States spanning from print to television broadcasting. Now, as one of the selection authors in this volume suggests, there are only nine companies worldwide that produce the greatest amount of media content and utilize all forms of distribution. What then, is the impact of this type of control over content?

As we begin a new century with new forms of communication, many of the institutions we have come to depend upon are undergoing massive changes. The recording industry is perhaps one of the most rapidly changing fields, with microradio and webstreaming offering different alternatives for message distribution. It is not surprising that the CD industry recently lowered prices in order to save sales at the same time that the group Metallica has entered into a lawsuit against the firm Napster.com, which has allowed free downloads of music files from one personal computer to another. We can expect to continue to see threats and challenges to our traditional media systems in the future. Even the ubiquitous personal computer could become obsolete with personal desk assistant (PDAs) offering cheaper, more portable forms of computing, and, in particular, linkage to the Internet.

Progress in Media Research

Much of media research has been in search of theory. Theory is an organized, commonsense refinement of everyday thinking; it is an attempt to establish a systematic view of a phenomenon in order to better understand that phenomenon. Theory is tested against reality to establish whether or not it is a good explanation. So, for example, a researcher might notice that what is covered by news outlets is very similar to what citizens say are the important issues of the day. From such observation came agenda setting (the notion that media confers importance on the topics it covers, directing public attention to what is considered important).

Much early media research comes from the impact and effect of print media, because print has long been regarded as a permanent record of history and events. The ability of newspapers and books to shape and influence public opinion was regarded as necessary to the founding of new forms of governments—including the United States government. But the bias of the medium carried certain restrictions with it. Print media was necessarily limited to those individuals who could read. The relationships of information control and the power of these forms of communication to influence readers contributed to the belief that reporting should be objective and fair and that a multiple number of views should be available.

The principles that emerged from this relationship were addressed in an often-quoted statement attributed to Thomas Jefferson, who wrote, "Were it left to me to decide whether we should have a government without newspapers, or newspapers without a government, I should not hesitate a moment to prefer the latter." But the next sentence in Jefferson's statement is equally as important: "But I should mean that every man should receive those papers and be capable of reading them."

Today media research on the relationships of media senders, the channels of communication, and the receivers of messages is not enough. Consumers must realize that "media literacy" is an important concept. People can no longer take for granted that the media exist primarily to provide news, information, and entertainment. They must be more attuned to what media content says about them as individuals and as members of a society. By integrating these various cultural components, the public can better criticize the regulations or lack of regulation that permits media industries to function the way they do. People must realize that individuals may read media content differently.

The use of social science data to explore the effects of media on audiences strongly emphasized psychological and sociological schools of thought. It did not take long to move from the "magic bullet theory"—which proposed that media had a major direct effect on the receivers of the message and that the message intended by the senders was indeed injected into the passive receiver—to theories of limited and indirect effects.

Media research has shifted from addressing specifically effects-oriented paradigms to exploring the nature of the institutions of media production themselves as well as examining the unique characteristics of each form of media. What most researchers agree upon today, is that the best way to understand the power and impact of media is to look at context-specific situations to better understand the dynamics involved in the use of media and the importance of the content.

Still, there are many approaches to media research from a variety of interdisciplinary fields: psychology, sociology, linguistics, art, comparative literature, economics, political science, and more. What each of these avenues of inquiry have in common is that they all tend to focus attention on individuals, families or other social groups, society in general, and culture in the broad sense. All of the interpretations frame meaning and investigate their subjects within institutional frameworks that are specific to any nation and/or culture.

Today researchers question the notions of past theories and models as well as definitions of *mass* and *society* and now place much of the emphasis of media dynamics in the perspective of global information exchange. A major controversy erupted in the early 1970s when many Third World countries disagreed with principles that sought to reify the industrialized nations' media. The New World Information Order perspective advanced the importance of media in carrying out developmental tasks within nations that have not had the economic and social benefits of industrialized countries, and it noted that emerging nations had different priorities that reflected indigenous cultures, which would sometimes be at odds with Western notions of a free press. The Third World countries' concerns dealt with power as imposed upon a nation from outside, using media as a vehicle for cultural dependency and imperialism.

Many of the questions for media researchers in the twenty-first century will deal with the continued fragmentation of the audience, caused by greater choice of channels and technologies for traditional and new communication purposes. The power of some of these technologies to reach virtually any place on the globe within fractions of a second will continue to pose questions of access to media and the meaning of the messages transmitted. As individuals become more dependent upon the Internet for communication purposes, the sense of audience will further be changed as individual users choose what they want to receive, pay for, and keep. For all of these reasons, the field of media research is rich, growing, and challenging.

Questions for Consideration

In addressing the issues in this book, it is important to consider some recurring questions:

important

1. Are the media unifying or fragmenting? Does media content help the socialization process, or does it create anxiety or inaccurate portrayals of the world? Do people feel powerless because they have little ability to shape the messages of media?
2. How are basic institutions changing as we use media in new and different ways? Do media support or undermine our political processes? Do they change what we think of when we claim that we live in a democracy? Does media operate in the public interest, or does media serve the rich and powerful corporations' quest for profit? Can the media do both simultaneously?
3. Whose interests do the media represent? Do audiences actively work toward integrating media messages with their own experiences? How do new media technologies change our traditional ways of communicating? Are they leading us to a world in which interpersonal communication is radically altered because we rely on information systems to replace many traditional behaviors?

Summary

We live in a media-rich environment where almost everybody has access to some form of media and some choices in content. As new technologies and services are developed, are they responding to the problems that previous media researchers and the public have detected? Over time, individuals have improved their ability to unravel the complex set of interactions that ties the media and society together, but they need to continue to question past results, new practices and technologies, and their own evaluative measures. When people critically examine the world around them—a world often presented by the media—they can more fully understand and enjoy the way they relate as individuals, as members of groups, and as members of a society.

The Center for Media Education

The Center for Media Education (CME) is a national, nonprofit organization dedicated to improving the quality of electronic media, especially on the behalf of children and families. This site discusses such topics as the effect of television violence, online advertising, media images, and new technologies.

http://www.cme.org

Communication Studies: General Communication Resources

An encyclopedic resource related to a host of mass communication issues, this site is maintained by the University of Iowa's Department of Communication Studies. It provides excellent links covering advertising, cultural studies, digital media, film, gender issues, and media studies.

http://www.uiowa.edu/~commstud/resources/general.html

Kaiser Family Foundation

The Kaiser Family Foundation site provides articles on a broad range of television topics, including the V-chip, sexual messages, and programs about AIDS. From the home page, go to "select a topic" and choose television.

http://www.kff.org

National Coalition on Television Violence

The National Coalition on Television Violence addresses the problem of television violence. It also explains how violence affects people and offers suggestions as to preventing violence in everyday life. This site includes extensive analysis of children's shows, a bibliography, and information about related organizations.

http://www.nctvv.org

Writers Guild of America

The Writer's Guild of America is the union for media entertainment writers. The nonmember areas of this site offer useful information for aspiring writers. There is also an excellent links section.

http://www.wga.org

PART 1

Mass Media's Role in Society

*H*ow *powerful are the media? Do media merely reflect the social at-titudes and concerns of our times, or are they also able to construct, legitimate, and reinforce the social realities, behaviors, attitudes, and images of others? The ways media help us to shape a sense of reality are complex. Should concern be directed toward vulnerable populations such as children? If we truly have a variety of information sources and content to choose from, perhaps we can assume that distorted images are balanced with realistic ones. But is this truly the media scenario in which we live? How media is influenced by the social environment can-not be ignored. Media is both a place for displaying culture and a force for cultural change. Questions about the place of media within society—and within what many call the Information Age—cannot be ignored.*

- Are American Values Shaped by the Mass Media?

- Is Television Harmful for Children?

- Is Emphasis on Body Image in the Media Harmful to Females Only?

- Are Newspapers Insensitive to Minorities?

ISSUE 1

Are American Values Shaped by the Mass Media?

YES: Neil Postman, from *Amusing Ourselves to Death* (Viking Penguin, 1985)

NO: Horace Newcomb and Paul M. Hirsch, from "Television as a Cultural Forum: Implications for Research," *Quarterly Review of Film Studies* (Summer 1983)

ISSUE SUMMARY

YES: Professor of media studies Neil Postman argues that television promotes triviality by speaking in only one voice—the voice of entertainment. Thus, he maintains that television is transforming American culture into show business, to the detriment of rational public discourse.

NO: Professors of communication Horace Newcomb and Paul M. Hirsch counter that television serves as a site of negotiation for cultural issues, images, and ideas. Viewer selection from among institutional choices is a negotiation process as viewers select from a wide set of approaches to issues and ideas.

Can the media fundamentally reshape a culture? Americans are now part of a culture in which information and ideas are disseminated predominantly by television, not by print. This shift from print to electronic media has dramatically and irreversibly altered the content and meaning of public discourse, according to Neil Postman. Postman, however, strongly believes that the epistemology (the way of knowing) created by television is inferior to that of print for truth telling and rational public discourse. He is not alone in his concern that electronic media are negatively reshaping culture in the United States. Others argue that popular culture is not culture at all and that mass-produced popular culture is destroying the individuality of folk and high arts. Some suggest that the power of the media to shape attitude and opinions, paired with the power of media organizations to craft messages, will inevitably result in homogeneity. This homogenization is the logical consequence of a socialization process whereby values are assaulted year in and year out with consistent and limited messages. These are the conclusions of many who find the benefits of television to be overwhelmed by its attendant perils.

Horace Newcomb and Paul M. Hirsch offer the opposite interpretation. They assert that television operates as a cultural forum and is central to the process of public thinking. In part, the effects of mass media on American values may be explained by examining the limits and effectiveness of popular pluralism and the processes by which that pluralism is created and maintained. Communication, according to Newcomb and Hirsch, is dependent on shared meaning. Television is dependent upon pluralism more than many other forms of discourse. So one must consider how television is implicated in the creation of patterns of interpretation and the maintenance of sharing that defines pluralism as an effective cultural norm.

The media are so pervasive that it is hard to believe they do not have important effects. Alternatively, many people do not believe that the media have personally influenced them to buy products or have harmed them, nor do they believe that the media hold a place of "prime importance" in shaping their lives. In everyday experience, many people do not consider the media as having an observable impact on them or on those around them. However, to attempt to understand how the media may shape the attitudes of individuals and of society, and how they may shape culture itself, requires that the reader stand back from his or her personal experiences in order to analyze the arguments presented on each side of this debate.

In the following selection, Postman argues that Americans are "amusing [them]selves to death." Americans have become literate in the forms and features of television systems. Because the medium of television has become the dominant factor in the creation of social images, what we know and how we know it comes out of television, rather than print, literacy. The consequences of becoming a show business culture, according to Postman, are dire.

In the second selection, Newcomb and Hirsch advance a cultural forum model to understand the place of television in American society. Multiple meanings are key in understanding how television operates to provide a forum for the featuring of issues and ideas. Therefore, they provide a forum wherein those issues become a focus of cultural concern. Rather than concentrating on the fears of media's influence upon society, Newcomb and Hirsch push us to examine its functions.

Neil Postman  **YES**

The Age of Show Business

Adedicated graduate student I know returned to his small apartment the night before a major examination only to discover that his solitary lamp was broken beyond repair. After a whiff of panic, he was able to restore both his equanimity and his chances for a satisfactory grade by turning on the television set, turning off the sound, and with his back to the set, using its light to read important passages on which he was to be tested. This is one use of television—as a source of illuminating the printed page. . . .

I bring forward [this] quixotic [use] of television to ridicule the hope harbored by some that television can be used to support the literate tradition. Such a hope represents exactly what Marshall McLuhan used to call "rear-view mirror" thinking: the assumption that a new medium is merely an extension or amplification of an older one; that an automobile, for example, is only a fast horse, or an electric light a powerful candle. To make such a mistake in the matter at hand is to misconstrue entirely how television redefines the meaning of public discourse. Television does not extend or amplify literate culture. It attacks it. If television is a continuation of anything, it is of a tradition begun by the telegraph and photograph in the mid-nineteenth century, not by the printing press in the fifteenth.

What is television? What kinds of conversations does it permit? What are the intellectual tendencies it encourages? What sort of culture does it produce?

These are the questions, . . . and to approach them with a minimum of confusion, I must begin by making a distinction between a technology and a medium. We might say that a technology is to a medium as the brain is to the mind. Like the brain, a technology is a physical apparatus. Like the mind, a medium is a use to which a physical apparatus is put. A technology becomes a medium as it employs a particular symbolic code, as it finds its place in a particular social setting, as it insinuates itself into economic and political contexts. A technology, in other words, is merely a machine. A medium is the social and intellectual environment a machine creates.

Of course, like the brain itself, every technology has an inherent bias. It has within its physical form a predisposition toward being used in certain ways and not others. Only those who know nothing of the history of technology believe that a technology is entirely neutral. There is an old joke that mocks that naive belief. Thomas Edison, it goes, would have revealed his discovery of the electric light much sooner than he did except for the fact that every time he turned it on, he held it to his mouth and said, "Hello? Hello?"

Not very likely. Each technology has an agenda of its own. It is, as I have suggested, a metaphor waiting to unfold. The printing press, for example, had a clear bias toward being used as a linguistic medium. It is *conceivable* to use it exclusively for the reproduction of pictures. And, one imagines, the Roman Catholic Church would not have objected to its being so used in the sixteenth century. Had that been the case, the Protestant Reformation might not have occurred, for as Luther contended, with the word of God on every family's kitchen table, Christians do not require the Papacy to interpret it for them. But in fact there never was much chance that the press would be used solely, or even very much, for the duplication of icons. From its beginning in the fifteenth century, the press was perceived as an extraordinary opportunity for the display and mass distribution of written language. Everything about its technical possibilities led in that direction. One might even say it was invented for that purpose.

The technology of television has a bias, as well. It is conceivable to use television as a lamp, a surface for texts, a bookcase, even as radio. But it has not been so used and will not be so used, at least in America. Thus, in answering the question, What is television?, we must understand as a first point that we are not talking about television as a technology but television as a medium. There are many places in the world where television, though the same technology as it is in America, is an entirely different medium from that which we know. I refer to places where the majority of people do not have television sets, and those who do have only one; where only one station is available; where television does not operate around the clock; where most programs have as their purpose the direct furtherance of government ideology and policy; where commercials are unknown, and "talking heads" are the principal image; where television is mostly used as if it were radio. For these reasons and more television will not have the same meaning or power as it does in America, which is to say, it is possible for a technology to be so used that its potentialities are prevented from developing and its social consequences kept to a minimum.

But in America, this has not been the case. Television has found in liberal democracy and a relatively free market economy a nurturing climate in which its full potentialities as a technology of images could be exploited. One result of this has been that American television programs are in demand all over the world. The total estimate of U.S. television program exports is approximately 100,000 to 200,000 hours, equally divided among Latin America, Asia and Europe. Over the years, programs like "Gunsmoke," "Bonanza," "Mission: Impossible," "Star Trek," "Kojak," and more recently, "Dallas" and "Dynasty" have been as popular in England, Japan, Israel and Norway as in Omaha, Nebraska. I have heard (but not verified) that some years ago the Lapps postponed for several days their annual and, one supposes, essential migratory journey so that they could find out who shot J.R. All of this has occurred simultaneously with the decline of America's moral and political prestige, worldwide.

American television programs are in demand not because America is loved but because American television is loved.

We need not be detained too long in figuring out why. In watching American television, one is reminded of George Bernard Shaw's remark on his first seeing the glittering neon signs of Broadway and 42nd Street at night. It must be beautiful, he said, if you cannot read. American television is, indeed, a beautiful spectacle, a visual delight, pouring forth thousands of images on any given day. The average length of a shot on network television is only 3.5 seconds, so that the eye never rests, always has something new to see. Moreover, television offers viewers a variety of subject matter, requires minimal skills to comprehend it, and is largely aimed at emotional gratification. Even commercials, which some regard as an annoyance, are exquisitely crafted, always pleasing to the eye and accompanied by exciting music. There is no question but that the best photography in the world is presently seen on television commercials. American television, in other words, is devoted entirely to supplying its audience with entertainment.

Of course, to say that television is entertaining is merely banal. Such a fact is hardly threatening to a culture, not even worth writing a book about. It may even be a reason for rejoicing. Life, as we like to say, is not a highway strewn with flowers. The sight of a few blossoms here and there may make our journey a trifle more endurable. The Lapps undoubtedly thought so. We may surmise that the ninety million Americans who watch television every night also think so. But what I am claiming here is not that television is entertaining but that it has made entertainment itself the natural format for the representation of all experience. Our television set keeps us in constant communion with the world, but it does so with a face whose smiling countenance is unalterable. The problem is not that television presents us with entertaining subject matter but that all subject matter is presented as entertaining, which is another issue altogether.

To say it still another way: Entertainment is the supra-ideology of all discourse on television. No matter what is depicted or from what point of view, the overarching presumption is that it is there for our amusement and pleasure. That is why even on news shows which provide us daily with fragments of tragedy and barbarism, we are urged by the newscasters to "join them tomorrow." What for? One would think that several minutes of murder and mayhem would suffice as material for a month of sleepless nights. We accept the newscasters' invitation because we know that the "news" is not to be taken seriously, that it is all in fun, so to say. Everything about a news show tells us this—the good looks and amiability of the cast, their pleasant banter, the exciting music that opens and closes the show, the vivid film footage, the attractive commercials—all these and more suggest that what we have just seen is no cause for weeping. A news show, to put it plainly, is a format for entertainment, not for education, reflection or catharsis. And we must not judge too harshly those who have framed it in this way. They are not assembling the news to be read, or broadcasting it to be heard. They are televising the news to be seen. They must follow where their medium leads. There is no conspiracy here, no lack of intelligence, only a straightforward recognition that "good television" has little to do with what is "good" about exposition or other forms of verbal communication but everything to do with what the pictorial images look like.

... When a television show is in process, it is very nearly impermissible to say, "Let me think about that" or "I don't know" or "What do you mean when you say...?" or "From what sources does your information come?" This type of discourse not only slows down the tempo of the show but creates the impression of uncertainty or lack of finish. It tends to reveal people in the *act of thinking,* which is as disconcerting and boring on television as it is on a Las Vegas stage. Thinking does not play well on television, a fact that television directors discovered long ago. There is not much to *see* in it. It is, in a phrase, not a performing art....

I do not say categorically that it is impossible to use television as a carrier of coherent language or thought in process. William Buckley's own program, "Firing Line," occasionally shows people in the act of thinking but who also happen to have television cameras pointed at them. There are other programs, such as "Meet the Press" or "The Open Mind," which clearly strive to maintain a sense of intellectual decorum and typographic tradition, but they are scheduled so that they do not compete with programs of great visual interest, since otherwise, they will not be watched. After all, it is not unheard of that a format will occasionally go against the bias of its medium. For example, the most popular radio program of the early 1940's featured a ventriloquist, and in those days, I heard more than once the feet of a tap dancer on the "Major Bowes' Amateur Hour." (Indeed, if I am not mistaken, he even once featured a pantomimist.) But ventriloquism, dancing and mime do not play well on radio, just as sustained, complex talk does not play well on television. It can be made to play tolerably well if only one camera is used and the visual image is kept constant—as when the President gives a speech. But this is not television at its best, and it is not television that most people will choose to watch. The single most important fact about television is that people *watch* it, which is why it is called "tele*vision.*" And what they watch, and like to watch, are moving pictures —millions of them, of short duration and dynamic variety. It is in the nature of the medium that it must suppress the content of ideas in order to accommodate the requirements of visual interest; that is to say, to accommodate the values of show business.

Film, records and radio (now that it is an adjunct of the music industry) are, of course, equally devoted to entertaining the culture, and their effects in altering the style of American discourse are not insignificant. But television is different because it encompasses all forms of discourse. No one goes to a movie to find out about government policy or the latest scientific advances. No one buys a record to find out the baseball scores or the weather or the latest murder. No one turns on radio anymore for soap operas or a presidential address (if a television set is at hand). But everyone goes to television for all these things and more, which is why television resonates so powerfully throughout the culture. Television is our culture's principal mode of knowing about itself. Therefore —and this is the critical point—how television stages the world becomes the model for how the world is properly to be staged. It is not merely that on the television screen entertainment is the metaphor for all discourse. It is that off the screen the same metaphor prevails. As typography once dictated the style of conducting politics, religion, business, education, law and other important social matters, television now takes command. In courtrooms, classrooms, operating rooms, board rooms, churches and even airplanes, Americans no longer talk to each other, they entertain each other. They do not exchange ideas; they exchange images. They do not argue with propositions; they argue with good looks, celebrities and commercials. For the message of television as metaphor is not only that all the world is a stage but that the stage is located in Las Vegas, Nevada....

Prior to the 1984 presidential elections, the two candidates [Ronald Reagan and Walter Mondale] confronted each other on television in what were called "debates." These events were not in the least like the Lincoln-Douglas debates or anything else that goes by the name. Each candidate was given five minutes to address such questions as, What is (or would be) your policy in Central America? His opposite number was then given one minute for a rebuttal. In such circumstances, complexity, documentation and logic can play no role, and, indeed, on several occasions syntax itself was abandoned entirely. It is no matter. The men were less concerned with giving arguments than with "giving off" impressions, which is what television does best. Post-debate commentary largely avoided any evaluation of the candidates' ideas, since there were none to evaluate. Instead, the debates were conceived as boxing matches, the relevant question being, Who KO'd whom? The answer was determined by the "style" of the men—how they looked, fixed their gaze, smiled, and delivered one-liners. In the second debate, President Reagan got off a swell one-liner when asked a question about his age. The following day, several newspapers indicated that Ron had KO'd Fritz with his joke. Thus, the leader of the free world is chosen by the people in the Age of Television.

What all of this means is that our culture has moved toward a new way of conducting its business, especially its important business. The nature of its discourse is changing as the demarcation line between what is show business and what is not becomes harder to see with each passing day. Our priests and presidents, our surgeons and lawyers, our educators and newscasters need worry less about satisfying the demands of their discipline than the demands of good showmanship. Had Irving Berlin changed one word in the title of his celebrated song, he would have been as prophetic, albeit more terse, as Aldous Huxley. He need only have written, There's No Business But Show Business.

Horace Newcomb and Paul M. Hirsch

Television as a Cultural Forum

Acultural basis for the analysis and criticism of television is, for us, the bridge between a concern for television as a communications medium, central to contemporary society, and television as aesthetic object, the expressive medium that, through its storytelling functions, unites and examines a culture. The shortcomings of each of these approaches taken alone are manifold.

The first is based primarily in a concern for understanding specific messages that may have specific effects, and grounds its analysis in "communication" narrowly defined. Complexities of image, style, resonance, narrativity, history, metaphor, and so on are reduced in favor of that content that can be more precisely, some say more objectively, described. The content categories are not allowed to emerge from the text, as is the case in naturalistic observation and in textual analysis. Rather they are predefined in order to be measured more easily. The incidence of certain content categories may be cited as significant, or their "effects" more clearly correlated with some behavior. This concern for measuring is, of course, the result of conceiving television in one way rather than another, as "communication" rather than as "art."

The narrowest versions of this form of analysis need not concern us here. It is to the best versions that we must look, to those that do admit to a range of aesthetic expression and something of a variety of reception. Even when we examine these closely, however, we see that they often assume a monolithic "meaning" in television content. The concern is for "dominant" messages embedded in the pleasant disguise of fictional entertainment, and the concern of the researcher is often that the control of these messages is, more than anything else, a complex sort of political control. The critique that emerges, then, is consciously or unconsciously a critique of the society that is transmitting and maintaining the dominant ideology with the assistance, again conscious or unconscious, of those who control communications technologies and businesses. (Ironically, this perspective does not depend on political perspective or persuasion. It is held by groups on the "right" who see American values being subverted, as well as by those on the "left" who see American values being imposed.)

Such a position assumes that the audience shares or "gets" the same messages and their meanings as the researcher finds. At times, like the literary critic, the researcher assumes this on the basis of superior insight, technique, or sensibility. In a more "scientific" manner the researcher may seek to establish a correlation between the discovered messages and the understanding of the audience. Rarely, however, does the message analyst allow for the possibility that the audience, while sharing this one meaning, may create many others that have not been examined, asked about, or controlled for.

The television "critic" on the other hand, often basing his work on the analysis of literature or film, succeeds in calling attention to the distinctive qualities of the medium, to the special nature of television fiction. But this approach all too often ignores important questions of production and reception. Intent on correcting what it takes to be a skewed interest in such matters, it often avoids the "business" of television and its "technology." These critics, much like their counterparts in the social sciences, usually assume that viewers should understand programs in the way the critic does, or that the audience is incapable of properly evaluating the entertaining work and should accept the critic's superior judgment.

The differences between the two views of what television is and does rest, in part, on the now familiar distinction between transportation and ritual views of communication processes. The social scientific, or communication theory model outlined above (and we do not claim that it is an exhaustive description) rests most thoroughly on the transportation view. As articulated by James Carey, this model holds that communication is a "process of transmitting messages at a distance for the purpose of control. The archetypal case of communication then is persuasion, attitude change, behavior modification, socialization through the transmission of information, influence, or conditioning."[1]

The more "literary" or "aesthetically based" approach leans toward, but hardly comes to terms with, ritual models of communication. As put by Carey, the ritual view sees communication "not directed toward the extension of messages in space but the maintenance of society in time; not the act of imparting information but the representation of shared beliefs."[2]

Carey also cuts through the middle of these definitions with a more succinct one of his own: "Communication is a symbolic process whereby reality is produced, maintained, repaired, and transformed."[3] It is in the attempt to amplify this basic observation that we present a cultural basis for the analysis of television. We hardly suggest that such an approach is entirely new, or that others are unaware of or do not share many of our assumptions. On the contrary, we find a growing awareness in many disciplines of the nature of symbolic thought, communication, and action, and we see attempts to understand television emerging rapidly from this body of shared concerns.[4]

◦◦◉◦◦

Our own model for television is grounded in an examination of the cultural role of entertainment and parallels this with a close analysis of television program content in all its various textual levels and forms. We focus on the collective, cultural view of the social construction and negotiation of reality, on the creation of what Carey refers to as "public thought."[5] It is not difficult to see television as central to this process of public thinking. As Hirsch has pointed out,[6] it is now our national medium, replacing those media—film, radio, picture magazines, newspapers—that once served a similar function. Those who create for such media are, in the words of anthropologist Marshall Sahlins, "hucksters of the symbol."[7] They are cultural *bricoleurs,* seeking and creating new meaning in the combination of cultural elements with embedded significance. They respond to real events, changes in social structure and organization, and to shifts in attitude and value. They also respond to technological shift, the coming of cable or the use of videotape recorders. We think it is clear that the television producer should be added to Sahlins's list of "hucksters." They work in precisely the manner he describes, as do television writers and, to a lesser extent, directors and actors. So too do programmers and network executives who must make decisions about the programs they purchase, develop, and air. At each step of this complicated process they function as cultural interpreters.

Similar notions have often been outlined by scholars of popular culture focusing on the formal characteristics of popular entertainment.[8] To those insights cultural theory adds the possibility of matching formal analysis with cultural and social practice. The best theoretical explanation for this link is suggested to us in the continuing work of anthropologist Victor Turner. This work focuses on cultural ritual and reminds us that ritual must be seen as process rather than as product, a notion not often applied to the study of television, yet crucial to an adequate understanding of the medium.

Specifically we make use of one aspect of Turner's analysis, his view of the *liminal* stage of the ritual process. This is the "inbetween" stage, when one is neither totally in nor out of society. It is a stage of license, when rules may be broken or bent, when roles may be reversed, when categories may be overturned. Its essence, suggests Turner,

> is to be found in its release from normal constraints, making possible the deconstruction of the "uninteresting" constructions of common sense, the "meaningfulness of ordinary life," ... into cultural units which may then be reconstructed in novel ways, some of them bizarre to the point of monstrosity.... Liminality is the domain of the "interesting" or of "uncommon sense."[9]

Turner does not limit this observation to traditional societies engaged in the *practice* of ritual. He also applies his views to postindustrial, complex societies. In doing so he finds the liminal domain in the arts—all of them.[10] "The dismemberment of ritual has ... provided the opportunity of theatre in the high culture and carnival at the folk level. A multiplicity of desacralized performative genres have assumed, prismatically, the task of plural cultural reflexivity."[11] In short, contemporary cultures examine themselves through their arts, much as traditional societies do via the experience of ritual. Ritual and the arts offer a metalanguage, a way of understanding who and what we are, how values and attitudes are adjusted, how meaning shifts.

In contributing to this process, particularly in American society, where its role is central, television fulfills what Fiske and Hartley refer to as the "bardic function" of contemporary societies.[12] In its role as central cultural medium it presents a multiplicity of meanings rather than a monolithic dominant point of view. It often focuses on our most prevalent concerns, our deepest dilemmas. Our most traditional views, those that are repressive and reactionary, as well as those that are subversive and emancipatory, are upheld, examined, maintained, and transformed. The emphasis is on process rather than product, on discussion rather than indoctrination, on contradiction and confusion rather than coherence. It is with this view that we turn to an analysis of the texts of television that demonstrates and supports the conception of television as a cultural forum.

❧❦❧

This new perspective requires that we revise some of our notions regarding television analysis, criticism, and research. The function of the creator as *bricoleur*, taken from Sahlins, is again indicated and clarified. The focus on "uncommon sense," on the freedom afforded by the idea of television as a liminal realm helps us to understand the reliance on and interest in forms, plots, and character types that are not at all familiar in our lived experience. The skewed demography of the world of television is not quite so bizarre and repressive once we admit that it is the realm in which we allow our monsters to come out and play, our dreams to be wrought into pictures, our fantasies transformed into plot structures. Cowboys, detectives, bionic men, and great green hulks; fatherly physicians, glamorous female detectives, and tightly knit families living out the pain of the Great Depression; all these become part of the dramatic logic of public thought.

Shows such as *Fantasy Island* and *Love Boat,* difficult to account for within traditional critical systems except as examples of trivia and romance, are easily understood. Islands and boats are among the most fitting liminal metaphors, as Homer, Bacon, Shakespeare, and Melville, among others, have recognized. So, too, are the worlds of the Western and the detective story. With this view we can see the "bizarre" world of situation comedy as a means of deconstructing the world of "common sense" in which all, or most, of us live and work. It also enables us to explain such strange phenomena as game shows and late night talk fests. In short, almost any version of the television text functions as a forum in which important cultural topics may be considered. We illustrate this not with a contemporary program where problems almost always appear on the surface of the show, but with an episode of *Father Knows Best* from the early 1960s. We begin by noting that *FKB* is often cited as an innocuous series, constructed around unstinting paeans to American middle-class virtues and blissfully ignorant of social conflict. In short, it is precisely the sort of television program that reproduces dominant ideology by lulling its audience into a dream world where the status quo is the only status.

In the episode in question Betty Anderson, the older daughter in the family, breaks a great many rules by deciding that she will become an engineer. Over great protest, she is given an internship with a surveying crew as part of a high school "career education" program. But the head of the surveying crew, a young college student, drives her away with taunts and insensitivity. She walks off the job on the first day. Later in the week the young man comes to the Anderson home where Jim Anderson chides him with fatherly anger. The young man apologizes and Betty, overhearing him from the other room, runs upstairs, changes clothes, and comes down. The show ends with their flirtation underway.

Traditional ideological criticism, conducted from the communications or the textual analysis perspective, would remark on the way in which social conflict is ultimately subordinated in this dramatic structure to the personal, the emotional. Commentary would focus on the way in which the questioning of the role structure is shifted away from the world of work to the domestic arena. The emphasis would be on the conclusion of the episode in which Betty's real problem of identity and sex-role, and society's problem of sex-role discrimination, is bound by a more traditional conflict and thereby defused, contained, and redirected. Such a reading is possible, indeed accurate.

We would point out, however, that our emotional sympathy is with Betty throughout this episode. Nowhere does the text instruct the viewer that her concerns are unnatural, no matter how unnaturally they may be framed by other members of the cast. Every argument that can be made for a strong feminist perspective is condensed into the brief, half-hour presentation. The concept of the cultural forum, then, offers a different interpretation. We suggest that in popular culture generally, in television specifically, the raising of questions is as important as the answering of them. That is, it is equally important that an audience be introduced to the problems surrounding sex-role discrimination as it is to conclude the episode in a traditional manner. Indeed, it would be startling to think that mainstream texts in mass society would overtly challenge dominant ideas. But this hardly prevents the oppositional ideas from appearing. Put another way, we argue that television does not present firm ideological conclusions—despite its *formal* conclusions—so much as it *comments on* ideological problems. The conflicts we see in television drama, embedded in familiar and nonthreatening frames, are conflicts ongoing in American social experience and cultural history. In a few cases we might see strong perspectives that argue for the absolute correctness of one point of view or another. But for the most part the rhetoric of television drama is a rhetoric of discussion. Shows such as *All in the Family,* or *The Defenders,* or *Gunsmoke,* which raise the forum/ discussion to an intense and obvious level, often make best use of the medium and become highly successful. We see statements *about* the issues and it should be clear that ideological positions can be balanced within the forum by others from a different perspective.

We recognize, of course, that this variety works for the most part within the limits of American monopoly-capitalism and within the range of American pluralism. It is an effective pluralistic forum only insofar as American political pluralism is or can be.[13] We also note, however, that one of the primary functions of the popular culture forum, the television forum, is to monitor the limits and the effectiveness of this pluralism, perhaps the only "public" forum in which this role is performed. As content shifts and attracts the attention of groups and individuals, criticism and reform can be initiated. We will have more to say on this topic shortly.

Our intention here is hardly to argue for the richness of *Father Knows Best* as a television text or as social commentary. Indeed, in our view, any emphasis on individual episodes, series, or even genres, misses the central point of the forum concept. While each of these units can and does present its audiences with incredibly mixed ideas, it is television as a whole system that presents a mass audience with the range and variety of ideas and ideologies inherent in American culture. In order to fully understand the role of television in that culture, we must examine a variety of analytical foci and, finally, see them as parts of a greater whole.

We can, for instance, concentrate on a single episode of television content, as we have done in our example. In our view most television shows offer something of this range of complexity. Not every one of them treats social problems of such immediacy, but submerged in any episode are assumptions about who and what we are. Conflicting viewpoints of social issues are, in fact, the elements that structure most television programs.

At the series level this complexity is heightened. In spite of notions to the contrary, most television shows do change over time. Stanley Cavell has recently suggested that this serial nature of television is perhaps its defining characteristic.[14] By contrast we see that feature only as a primary aspect of the rhetoric of television, one that shifts meaning and shades ideology as series develop. Even a series such as *The Brady Bunch* dealt with ever more complex issues merely because the children, on whom the show focused, grew older. In other cases, shows such as *The Waltons* shifted in content and meaning because they represented shifts in historical time. As the series moved out of the period of the Great Depression, through World War II, and into the postwar period, its tone and emphasis shifted too. In some cases, of course, this sort of change is structured into the show from the beginning, even when the appearance is that of static, undeveloping nature. In *All in the Family* the possibility of change and Archie's resistance to it form the central dramatic problem and offer the central opportunity for dramatic richness, a richness that has developed over many years until the character we now see bears little resemblance to the one we met in the beginning. This is also true of *M*A*S*H*, although there the structured conflicts have more to do with framing than with character development. In *M*A*S*H* we are caught in an anti-war rhetoric that cannot end a war. A truly radical alternative, a desertion or an insurrection, would end the series. But it would also end the "discussion" of this issue. We remain trapped, like American culture in its historical reality, with a dream and the rhetoric of peace and with a bitter experience that denies them.

The model of the forum extends beyond the use of the series with attention to genre. One tendency of genre studies has been to focus on similarities within forms, to indicate the ways in which all Westerns, situation comedies, detective shows, and so on are alike. Clearly, however, it is in the economic interests of producers to build on audience familiarity with generic patterns and instill novelty into those generically based presentations. Truly innovative forms that use the generic base as a foundation are likely to be among the more successful shows. This also means that the shows, despite generic similarity, will carry individual rhetorical slants. As a result, while shows like *M*A*S*H, The*

Mary Tyler Moore Show, and *All in the Family* may all treat similar issues, those issues will have different meanings because of the variations in character, tone, history, style, and so on, despite a general "liberal" tone. Other shows, minus that tone, will clash in varying degrees. The notion that they are all, in some sense, "situation comedies" does not adequately explain the treatment of ideas within them.

This hardly diminishes the strength of generic variation as yet another version of differences within the forum. The rhetoric of the soap opera *pattern* is different from that of the situation comedy and that of the detective show. Thus, when similar topics are treated within different generic frames another level of "discussion" is at work.

It is for this reason that we find it important to examine strips of television programming, "flow" as Raymond Williams refers to it.[15] Within these flow strips we may find opposing ideas abutting one another. We may find opposing treatments of the same ideas. And we will certainly find a viewing behavior that is more akin to actual experience than that found when concentrating on the individual show, the series, or the genre. The forum model, then, has led us into a new exploration of the definition of the television text. We are now examining the "viewing strip" as a potential text and are discovering that in the range of options offered by any given evening's television, the forum is indeed a more accurate model of what goes on *within* television than any other that we know of. By taping entire weeks of television content, and tracing various potential strips in the body of that week, we can construct a huge range of potential "texts" that may have been seen by individual viewers.

Each level of text—the strip as text, the television week, the television day —is compounded yet again by the history of the medium. Our hypothesis is that we might track the history of America's social discussions of the past three decades by examining the multiple rhetorics of television during that period. Given the problematic state of television archiving, a careful study of that hypothesis presents an enormous difficulty. It is, nevertheless, an exciting prospect.

ꞏ⧁ꞏ

Clearly, our emphasis is on the treatment of issues, on rhetoric. We recognize the validity of analytical structures that emphasize television's skewed demographic patterns, its particular social aberrations, or other "unrealistic distortions" of the world of experience. But we also recognize that in order to make sense of those structures and patterns researchers return again and again to the "meaning" of that television world, to the processes and problems of interpretation. In our view this practice is hardly limited to those of us who study television. It is also open to audiences who view it each evening and to professionals who create for the medium.

The goal of every producer is to create the difference that makes a difference, to maintain an audience with sufficient reference to the known and recognized, but to move ahead into something that distinguishes his show for the program buyer, the scheduler, and most importantly, for the mass audience.

As recent work by Newcomb and Alley shows,[16] the goal of many producers, the most successful and powerful ones, is also to include personal ideas in their work, to use television as all artists use their media, as means of personal expression. Given this goal it is possible to examine the work of individual producers as other units of analysis and to compare the work of different producers as expressions within the forum. We need only think of the work of Quinn Martin and Jack Webb, or to contrast their work with that of Norman Lear or Gary Marshall, to recognize the individuality at work within television making. Choices by producers to work in certain generic forms, to express certain political, moral, and ethical attitudes, to explore certain sociocultural topics, all affect the nature of the ultimate "flow text" of television seen by viewers and assure a range of variations within that text.

The existence of this variation is borne out by varying responses among those who view television. A degree of this variance occurs among professional television critics who like and dislike shows for different reasons. But because television critics, certainly in American journalistic situations, are more alike than different in many ways, a more important indicator of the range of responses is that found among "ordinary" viewers, or the disagreements implied by audience acceptance and enthusiasm for program material soundly disavowed by professional critics. Work by Himmleweit in England[17] and Neuman in America[18] indicates that individual viewers do function as "critics," do make important distinctions, and are able, under certain circumstances, to articulate the bases for their judgments. While this work is just beginning, it is still possible to suggest from anecdotal evidence that people agree and disagree with television for a variety of reasons. They find in television texts representations of and challenges to their own ideas, and must somehow come to terms with what is there.

If disagreements cut too deeply into the value structure of the individual, if television threatens the sense of cultural security, the individual may take steps to engage the medium at the level of personal action. Most often this occurs in the form of letters to the network or to local stations, and again, the pattern is not new to television. It has occurred with every other mass medium in modern industrial society.

Nor is it merely the formation of groups or the expression of personal points of view that indicates the working of a forum. It is the *range* of response, the directly contradictory readings of the medium, that cue us to its multiple meanings. Groups may object to the same programs, for example, for entirely opposing reasons. In *Charlie's Angels* feminists may find yet another example of sexist repression, while fundamentalist religious groups may find examples of moral decay expressed in the sexual freedom, the personal appearance, or the "unfeminine" behavior of the protagonists. Other viewers doubtless find the expression of meaningful liberation of women. At this level, the point is hardly that one group is "right" and another "wrong," much less that one is "right" while the other is "left." Individuals and groups are, for many reasons, involved in making their own meanings from the television text.

This variation in interpretive strategies can be related to suggestions made by Stuart Hall in his influential essay, "Encoding and Decoding in the Television Discourse."[19] There he suggests three basic modes of interpretation, corresponding to the interpreter's political stance within the social structure. The interpretation may be "dominant," accepting the prevailing ideological structure. It may be "oppositional," rejecting the basic aspects of the structure. Or it may be "negotiated," creating a sort of personal synthesis. As later work by some of Hall's colleagues suggests, however, it quickly becomes necessary to expand the range of possible interpretations.[20] Following these suggestions to a radical extreme it might be possible to argue that every individual interpretation of television content could, in some way, be "different." Clearly, however, communication is dependent on a greater degree of shared meanings, and expressions of popular entertainment are perhaps even more dependent on the shared level than many other forms of discourse. Our concern then is for the ways in which interpretation is negotiated in society. Special interest groups that focus, at times, on television provide us with readily available resources for the study of interpretive practices.

We see these groups as representative of metaphoric "fault lines" in American society. Television is the terrain in which the faults are expressed and worked out. In studying the groups, their rhetoric, the issues on which they focus, their tactics, their forms of organization, we hope to demonstrate that the idea of the "forum" is more than a metaphor in its own right. In forming special interest groups, or in using such groups to speak about television, citizens actually enter the forum. Television shoves them toward action, toward expression of ideas and values. At this level the model of "television as a cultural forum" enables us to examine "the sociology of interpretation."

Here much attention needs to be given to the historical aspects of this form of activity. How has the definition of issues changed over time? How has that change correlated with change in the television texts? These are important questions which, while difficult to study, are crucial to a full understanding of the role of television in culture. It is primarily through this sort of study that we will be able to define much more precisely the limits of the forum, for groups form monitoring devices that alert us to shortcomings not only in the world of television representation, but to the world of political experience as well. We know, for example, that because of heightened concern on the part of special interest groups, and responses from the creative and institutional communities of television industries, the "fictional" population of black citizens now roughly equals that of the actual population. Regardless of whether such a match is "good" or "necessary," regardless of the nature of the depiction of blacks on television, this indicates that the forum extends beyond the screen. The issue of violence, also deserving close study, is more mixed, varying from year to year. The influence of groups, of individuals, of studies, of the terrible consequences of murder and assassination, however, cannot be denied. Television does not exist in a realm of its own, cut off from the influence of citizens. Our aim is to discover, as precisely as possible, the ways in which the varied worlds interact.

Throughout this kind of analysis, then, it is necessary to cite a range of varied responses to the texts of television. Using the viewing "strip" as the appropriate text of television, and recognizing that it is filled with varied topics and approaches to those topics, we begin to think of the television viewer as a *bricoleur* who matches the creator in the making of meanings. Bringing values and attitudes, a universe of personal experiences and concerns, to the texts, the viewer selects, examines, acknowledges, and makes texts of his or her own.[21] If we conceive of special interest groups as representatives of *patterns* of cultural attitude and response, we have a potent source of study.

On the production end of this process, in addition to the work of individual producers, we must examine the role of network executives who must purchase and program television content. They, too, are cultural interpreters, intent on "reading" the culture through its relation to the "market." Executives who head and staff the internal censor agencies of each network, the offices of Broadcast Standards or Standards and Practices, are in a similar position. Perhaps as much as any individual or group they present us with a source of rich material for analysis. They are actively engaged in gauging cultural values. Their own research, the assumptions and the findings, needs to be re-analyzed for cultural implications, as does the work of the programmers. In determining who is doing what, with whom, at what times, they are interpreting social behavior in America and assigning it meaning. They are using television as a cultural litmus that can be applied in defining such problematic concepts as "childhood," "family," "maturity," and "appropriate." With the Standards and Practices offices, they interpret *and* define the permissible and the "normal." But their interpretations of behavior open to us as many questions as answers, and an appropriate overview, a new model of television is necessary in order to best understand their work and ours.

⋆◈⋆

This new model of "television as a cultural forum" fits the experience of television more accurately than others we have seen applied. Our assumption is that it opens a range of new questions and calls for re-analysis of older findings from both the textual-critical approach and the mass communications research perspective. Ultimately the new model is a simple one. It recognizes the range of interpretation of television content that is now admitted even by those analysts most concerned with television's presentation and maintenance of dominant ideological messages and meanings. But it differs from those perspectives because it does not see this as surprising or unusual. For the most part, that is what central storytelling systems do in all societies. We are far more concerned with the ways in which television contributes to change than with mapping the obvious ways in which it maintains dominant viewpoints. Most research on television, most textual analysis, has assumed that the medium is thin, repetitive, similar, nearly identical in textual formation, easily defined, described, and explained. The variety of response on the part of audiences has been received, as a result of this view, as extraordinary, an astonishing "discovery."

We begin with the observation, based on careful textual analysis, that television is dense, rich, and complex rather than impoverished. Any selection, any cut, any set of questions that is extracted from that text must somehow account for that density, must account for what is *not* studied or measured, for the opposing meanings, for the answering images and symbols. Audiences appear to make meaning by selecting that which touches experience and personal history. The range of responses then should be taken as commonplace rather than as unexpected. But research and critical analysis cannot afford so personal a view. Rather, they must somehow define and describe the inventory that makes possible the multiple meanings extracted by audiences, creators, and network decision makers.

Our model is based on the assumption and observation that only so rich a text could attract a mass audience in a complex culture. The forum offers a perspective that is as complex, as contradictory and confused, as much in process as American culture is in experience. Its texture matches that of our daily experiences. If we can understand it better, then perhaps we will better understand the world we live in, the actions that we must take in order to live there.

Notes

1. James Carey, "A Cultural Approach to Communications," *Communications* 2 (December 1975).

2. Ibid.

3. James Carey, "Culture and Communications," *Communications Research* (April 1975).

4. See Roger Silverstone, *The Message of Television: Myth and Narrative in Contemporary Culture* (London: Heinemann, 1981), on structural and narrative analysis; John Fiske and John Hartley, *Reading Television* (London: Methuen, 1978), on the semiotic and cultural bases for the analysis of television; David Thorburn, *The Story Machine* (Oxford University Press: forthcoming), on the aesthetics of television; Himmleweit, Hilda et al., "The Audience as Critic: An Approach to the Study of Entertainment," in *The Entertainment Functions of Television,* ed. Percy Tannenbaum (New York: Lawrence Eribaum Associates, 1980) and W. Russel Neuman, "Television and American Culture: The Mass Medium and the Pluralist Audience," *Public Opinion Quarterly,* 46: 4 (Winter 1982), pp. 471–87, on the role of the audience as critic; Todd Gitlin, "Prime Time Ideology: The Hegemonic Process in Television Entertainment," *Social Problems* 26:3 (1979), and Douglas Kelnner, "TV, Ideology, and Emancipatory Popular Culture," *Socialist Review* 45 (May–June, 1979), on hegemony and new applications of critical theory; James T. Lull, "The Social Uses of Television," *Human Communications Research* 7:3 (1980), and "Family Communication Patterns and the Social Uses of Television," *Communications Research* 7: 3 (1979), and Tim Meyer, Paul Traudt, and James Anderson, Non-Traditional Mass Communication Research Methods: Observational Case Studies of Media Use in Natural Settings, *Communication Yearbook IV,* ed. Dan Nimmo (New Brunswick, N.J.: Transaction Books), on audience ethnography and symbolic interactionism; and, most importantly, the ongoing work of The Center for Contemporary Cultural Studies at Birmingham University, England, most recently published in *Culture, Media, Language,* ed. Stuart Hall et al. (London: Hutchinson, in association with The Center for Contemporary Cultural Studies, 1980), on the interaction of culture and textual analysis from a thoughtful political perspective.

5. Carey, 1976.

6. Paul Hirsch, "The Role of Popular Culture and Television in Contemporary Society," *Television: The Critical View*, ed. Horace Newcomb (New York: Oxford University Press, 1979, 1982).

7. Marshall Sahlins, *Culture and Practical Reason* (Chicago: University of Chicago Press, 1976), p. 217.

8. John Cawelti, *Adventure, Mystery, and Romance* (Chicago: University of Chicago Press, 1976), and David Thorburn, "Television Melodrama," *Television: The Critical View* (New York: Oxford University Press, 1979, 1982).

9. Victor Turner, "Process, System, and Symbol: A New Anthropological Synthesis," *Daedalus* (Summer 1977), p. 68.

10. In various works Turner uses both the terms "liminal" and "liminoid" to refer to works of imagination and entertainment in contemporary culture. The latter term is used to clearly mark the distinction between events that have distinct behavioral consequences and those that do not. As Turner suggests, the consequences of entertainment in contemporary culture are hardly as profound as those of the liminal stage of ritual in traditional culture. We are aware of this basic distinction but use the former term in order to avoid a fuller explanation of the neologism. See Turner, "Afterword," to *The Reversible World*, Barbara Babcock, ed. (Ithaca: Cornell University Press, 1979), and "Liminal to Liminoid, in Play, Flow, and Ritual: An Essay in Comparative Symbology," *Rice University Studies*, 60:3 (1974).

11. Turner, 1977, p. 73.

12. Fiske and Hartley, 1978, p. 85.

13. We are indebted to Prof. Mary Douglas for encouraging this observation. At the presentation of these ideas at the New York Institute for the Humanities seminar on "The Mass Production of Mythology," she checked our enthusiasm for a pluralistic model of television by stating accurately and succinctly, "there are pluralisms and pluralisms." This comment led us to consider more thoroughly the means by which the forum and responses to it function as a tool with which to monitor the quality of pluralism in American social life, including its entertainments. The observation added a much needed component to our planned historical analysis.

14. Stanley Cavell, "The Fact of Television," *Daedalus* 3: 4 (Fall 1982).

15. Raymond Williams, *Television, Technology and Cultural Form* (New York: Schocken, 1971), p. 86 ff.

16. Horace Newcomb and Robert Alley, *The Television Producer as Artist in American Commercial Television* (New York: Oxford University Press, 1983).

17. Ibid.

18. Ibid.

19. Stuart Hall, "Encoding and Decoding in the Television Discourse," *Culture, Media, Language* (London: Hutchinson, in association with The Center for Contemporary Cultural Studies, 1980).

20. See Dave Morley and Charlotte Brunsdon, *Everyday Television: "Nationwide"* (London: British Film Institute, 1978), and Morley, "Subjects, Readers, Texts," in *Culture, Media, Language*.

21. We are indebted to Louis Black and Eric Michaels of the Radio-TV-Film department of the University of Texas-Austin for calling this aspect of televiewing to Newcomb's attention. It creates a much desired balance to Sahlin's view of the creator as *bricoleur* and indicates yet another matter in which the forum model enhances our ability to account for more aspects of the television experience. See, especially, Eric Michaels, *TV Tribes*, unpublished Ph.D. dissertation, University of Texas-Austin. 1982.

POSTSCRIPT

Are American Values Shaped by the Mass Media?

Television is pervasive in American life. Yet the influence of television on society is difficult to ascertain. For example, a number of things have changed drastically since television was introduced in the 1950s: the election process, drug use, crime rates and patterns, civil rights for minorities, and the influx of women into the workforce. Did television cause all that? Probably not, but was it a contributing factor in these changes? How much influence did it have, and, most important, how can one measure television or media influence?

One school of thought argues that television's primary effect is to reinforce the status quo. Does television contribute to the homogenization of society and promote middle-class values? Or can it reveal problems with the status quo and thus encourage constructive public discourse? Although television has certainly become a shared experience for many, its role in maintaining or changing the country's laws or norms remains to be established.

Yet some effects of television have been dramatically illustrated. For example, television is now the primary source of news for most Americans. Television's ability to bring events to millions of viewers may mean that television itself is a factor in determining the events. Television has reshaped American politics, but it may have little influence on how people actually vote. It has also altered the ways in which Americans spend their time, ranking third behind sleep and work. Yet these influences may be only a prelude to larger social changes that will emerge as technology becomes even more pervasive.

Denis McQuail, in *Mass Communication Theory: An Introduction,* 3rd ed. (Sage Publications, 1994), provides an insightful review of mass communication theory, with particular emphasis on the usefulness of theories of society for understanding the influence of mass communication. Editors John Downing, Ali Mohammadi, and Annabelle Sreberny-Mohammadi, in *Questioning the Media: A Critical Introduction* (Sage Publications, 1990), provides a readable introduction to critical social issues as they relate to media, particularly media and identity.

For more from Horace Newcomb, see his edited book, *Television: The Critical View,* 6th ed. (Oxford University Press, 2000). Jon Katz has written a very entertaining volume that argues that media is less important than we tend to think. It is entitled, *Media Rants: Postpolitics in the Digital nation* (Wired Books, 1997). Another different view is found in David Marc, *Bonfire of the Humanities: Television, Subliteracy, and Long-Term Memory Loss* (Syracuse University Press, 1995).

ISSUE 2

Is Television Harmful for Children?

YES: W. James Potter, from *On Media Violence* (Sage Publications, 1999)

NO: Jib Fowles, from *The Case for Television Violence* (Sage Publications, 1999)

ISSUE SUMMARY

YES: W. James Potter, a professor of communication, examines existing research in the area of children and television violence. Such research is extensive and covers a variety of theoretical and methodological areas. He examines the nature of the impact of television on children and concludes that strong evidence exists for harmful effects.

NO: Jib Fowles, a professor of communication, finds the research on children and television violence less convincing. Despite the number of studies, he believes that the overall conclusions are unwarranted. Fowles finds that the influence is small, lab results are artificial, and fieldwork is inconclusive. In short he finds television violence research flawed and unable to prove a linkage between violent images and harm to children.

Youths now have access to more violent images than at any other time in United States history, and these images are available in a diverse array of electronic sources: television, movies, video games, and music. Does such graphic, immediate, and pervasive imagery influence children's behavior and ultimately the level of violence in society? Is media a powerful force that can no longer be considered mere entertainment? Or, are Americans as a society overreacting, using media as a scapegoat for the concern over seemingly hopeless social problems?

In April 1999, after a series of similar school shootings, Columbine High School in Littleton, Colorado, was forever etched in our memory. The shootings there raised, in the most dramatic way possible, questions of how America had come to this tragedy. Did media play a role? Many would argue yes and would point to reenactments of video games, fashion choices from recent movies, imitative behaviors, and Internet discussions. Others would point to the long history of mental illness and social isolation of the perpetrators as more proximate causes.

Is media violence a threat to society? Those who would answer affirmatively might point to the content of children's viewing, arguing that it is a significant part of the socialization process and decrying the stereotypes, violence, and mindlessness of much of television fare. Others might argue that there are other negative consequences intrinsic to television viewing: the common daily fare of television themes, particularly a perception of the world as a scary place. Many would maintain that there are millions of people who watch television with no discernable negative consequences. Furthermore, they might say that there is a constellation of negative influences that seem to appear in violent individuals, a lack of proof, and an absurdity of thinking that television entertainment harms people.

Researchers began to study the impact of television on children early in television history by asking who watches, how much, and why. They analyzed what children see on television and how the content influences their cognitive development, school achievement, family interaction, social behaviors, and general attitudes and opinions. This is a large and complex social issue, so even extensive research has not provided final answers to all the questions that concerned parents and educators, professional mass communicators, and legislators have raised.

W. James Potter asserts that decades of research have led to several strong conclusions: violence is a public health problem and evidence is there to support the risks of exposure and discern the most susceptible individuals. Moreover, violent portrayals are pervasive; exposure leads to negative effects, both immediately and over the long term; and certain types of portrayals and certain types of viewers maximize the probability of negative effects. Jib Fowles disagrees. The evidence just is not that strong, he asserts, and the impact is very small when it does occur. He criticizes the methods of laboratory, field, and correlational research. Why, he asks, are such small effects considered so worthy of concern? His suspicion is that the scapegoating of media allows politicians, businesspeople, and society in general to feel they are tackling a problem without really taking any of the steps necessary to promote fundamental change.

W. James Potter  **YES**

On Media Violence

Overview and Introduction

Violence in American society is a public health problem. Although most people have never witnessed an act of serious violence in person, we are all constantly reminded of its presence by the media. The media constantly report news about individual violent crimes. The media also use violence as a staple in telling fictional stories to entertain us. Thus, the media amplify and reconfigure the violence in real life and continuously pump these messages into our culture.

The culture is responding with a range of negative effects. Each year about 25,000 people are murdered, and more than 2 million are injured in assaults. On the highways, aggressive behavior such as tailgating, weaving through busy lanes, honking or screaming at other drivers, exchanging insults, and even engaging in gunfire is a factor in nearly 28,000 traffic deaths annually, and the problem is getting worse at a rate of 7% per year. Gun-related deaths increased more than 60% from 1968 to 1994, to about 40,000 annually, and this problem is now considered a public health epidemic by 87% of surgeons and 94% of internists across the United States. Meanwhile, the number of pistols manufactured in the United States continues to increase—up 92% from 1985 to 1992.

Teenagers are living in fear. A Harris poll of 2,000 U.S. teenagers found that most of them fear violence and crime and that this fear is affecting their everyday behavior. About 46% of respondents said they have changed their daily behavior because of a fear of crime and violence; 12% said they carry a weapon to school for protection; 12% have altered their route to school; 20% said they have avoided particular parks or playgrounds; 20% said they have changed their circle of friends; and 33% have stayed away from school at times because of fear of violence. In addition, 25% said they did not feel safe in their own neighborhood, and 33% said they fear being a victim of a drive-by shooting. Nearly twice as many teenagers reported gangs in their school in 1995 compared to 1989, and this increase is seen in all types of neighborhoods; violent crime in schools increased 23.5% during the same period.

This problem has far-reaching economic implications. The U.S. Department of Justice estimates the total cost of crime and violence (such as child abuse and domestic violence, in addition to crimes such as murder, rape, and robbery) to be $500 billion per year, or about twice the annual budget of the Defense Department. The cost includes real expenses (such as legal fees, the cost of lost time from work, the cost of police work, and the cost of running the nation's prisons and parole systems) and intangibles (such as loss of affection from murdered family members). Violent crime is responsible for 14% of injury-related medical spending and up to 20% of mental health care expenditures.

The problem of violence in our culture has many apparent causes, including poverty, breakdown of the nuclear family, shift away from traditional morality to a situational pluralism, and the mass media. The media are especially interesting as a source of the problem. Because they are so visible, the media are an easy target for blame. In addition, they keep reminding us of the problem in their news stories. But there is also a more subtle and likely more powerful reason why the media should be regarded as a major cause of this public health problem: They manufacture a steady stream of fictional messages that convey to all of us in this culture what life is about. Media stories tell us how we should deal with conflict, how we should treat other people, what is risky, and what it means to be powerful. The media need to share the blame for this serious public health problem.

How do we address the problem? The path to remedies begins with a solid knowledge base. It is the task of social scientists to generate much of this knowledge. For the past five decades, social scientists and other scholars have been studying the topic of media violence. This topic has attracted researchers from many different disciplines, especially psychology, sociology, mental health science, cultural studies, law, and public policy. This research addresses questions such as these: How much media violence is there? What are the meanings conveyed in the way violence is portrayed? and What effect does violence have on viewers as individuals, as members of particular groups, and as members of society? Estimates of the number of studies conducted to answer these questions range as high as 3,000 and even 3,500....

Effects of Exposure to Media Violence

Does exposure to violence in the media lead to effects? With each passing year, the answer is a stronger yes. The general finding from a great deal of research is that exposure to violent portrayals in the media increases the probability of an effect. The most often tested effect is referred to as *learning to behave aggressively.* This effect is also referred to as direct imitation of violence, instigation or triggering of aggressive impulses, and disinhibition of socialization against aggressive behavior. Two other negative effects—desensitization and fear—are also becoming prevalent in the literature.

Exposure to certain violent portrayals can lead to positive or prosocial effects. Intervention studies, especially with children, have shown that when a media-literate person talks through the action and asks questions of the viewer during the exposure, the viewer will be able to develop a counterreading of the violence; that is, the viewer may learn that violent actions are wrong even though those actions are shown as successful in the media portrayal.

The effects have been documented to occur immediately or over the long term. Immediate effects happen during exposure or shortly after the exposure (within about an hour). They might last only several minutes, or they might last weeks. Long-term effects do not occur after one or several exposures; they begin to show up only after an accumulation of exposures over weeks or years. Once a long-term effect eventually occurs, it usually lasts a very long period of time.

This [selection] focuses on the issues of both immediate effects and long-term effects of exposure to media violence....

From the large body of effects research, I have assembled 10 major findings. These are the findings that consistently appear in quantitative meta-analyses and narrative reviews of this literature. Because these findings are so widespread in the literature and because they are so rarely disputed by scholars, they can be regarded as empirically established laws.

Immediate Effects of Violent Content

The first six laws illuminate the major findings of research into the immediate effects of exposure to media violence. Immediate effects occur during exposure or within several hours afterward.

1. Exposure to violent portrayals in the media can lead to subsequent viewer aggression through disinhibition.

This conclusion is found in most of the early reviews. For example, Stein and Friedrich closely analyzed 49 studies of the effects of antisocial and prosocial television content on people 3 to 18 years of age in the United States. They concluded that the correlational studies showed generally significant relationships ($r = .10$ to $.32$) and that the experiments generally showed an increase in aggression resulting from exposure to television violence across all age groups.

This conclusion gained major visibility in the 1972 Surgeon General's Report which stated that there was an influence, but this conclusion was softened by the industry members on the panel....

Some of the early reviewers disagreed with this conclusion....

In the two decades since this early disagreement, a great deal more empirical research has helped overcome these shortcomings, so most (but not all) of these critics have been convinced of the general finding that exposure to media violence can lead to an immediate disinhibition effect. All narrative reviews since 1980 have concluded that viewing of violence is consistently related to subsequent aggressiveness. This finding holds in surveys, laboratory experiments, and naturalistic experiments. For example, Roberts and Maccoby concluded that "the overwhelming proportion of results point to a causal relationship between exposure to mass communication portrayals of violence and an increased probability that viewers will behave violently at some subsequent time." Also, Friedrich-Cofer and Huston concluded that "the weight of the evidence from different methods of investigation supports the hypothesis that television violence affects aggression."

Meta-analytical studies that have reexamined the data quantitatively across sets of studies have also consistently concluded that viewing of aggression is likely to lead to antisocial behavior. For example, Paik and Comstock conducted a meta-analysis of 217 studies of the effects of television violence on antisocial behavior and reported finding a positive and significant correlation. They concluded that "regardless of age—whether nursery school, elementary school, college, or adult—results remain positive at a high significance level." Andison looked at 67 studies involving 30,000 participants (including 31 laboratory experiments) and found a relationship between viewing and subsequent aggression, with more than half of the studies showing a correlation (r) between .31 and .70. Hearold looked at 230 studies involving 100,000 participants to determine the effect of viewing violence on a wide range of antisocial behaviors in addition to aggression (including rule breaking, materialism, and perceiving oneself as powerless in society). Hearold concluded that for all ages and all measures, the majority of studies reported an association between exposure to violence and antisocial behavior. . . .

On balance, it is prudent to conclude that media portrayals of violence can lead to the immediate effect of aggressive behavior, that this can happen in response to as little as a single exposure, and that this effect can last up to several weeks. Furthermore, the effect is causal, with exposure leading to aggression. However, this causal link is part of a reciprocal process; that is, people with aggressive tendencies seek out violent portrayals in the media.

> *2. The immediate disinhibition effect is influenced by viewer demographics, viewer traits, viewer states, characteristics in the portrayals, and situational cues.*

Each human is a complex being who brings to each exposure situation a unique set of motivations, traits, predispositions, exposure history, and personality factors. These characteristics work together incrementally to increase or decrease the probability of the person's being affected.

2.1 Viewer Demographics
The key characteristics of the viewer that have been found to be related to a disinhibition effect are age and gender, but social class and ethnic background have also been found to play a part.

Demographics of age and gender.   Boys and younger children are more affected. Part of the reason is that boys pay more attention to violence. Moreover, younger children have more trouble following story plots, so they are more likely to be drawn into high-action episodes without considering motives or consequences. Age by itself is not as good an explanation as is ability for cognitive processing.

Socioeconomic status.   Lower-class youth watch more television and therefore more violence.

Ethnicity.   Children from minority and immigrant groups are vulnerable because they are heavy viewers of television.

2.2 Viewer Traits

The key characteristics of viewer traits are socialization against aggression, ... cognitive processing, and personality type.

Socialization against aggression.   Family life is an important contributing factor. Children in households with strong norms against violence are not likely to experience enough disinhibition to exhibit aggressive behavior. The disinhibition effect is stronger in children living in households in which... children are abused by parents, watch more violence, and identify more with violent heroes; and in families that have high-stress environments.

Peer and adult role models have a strong effect in this socialization process. Male peers have the most immediate influence in shaping children's aggressive behaviors in the short term; adult males have the most lasting effect 6 months later....

Cognitive processing.   Viewers' reactions depend on their individual interpretations of the aggression. Rule and Ferguson (1986) said that viewers first must form a representation or cognitive structure consisting of general social knowledge about the positive value that can be attached to aggression. The process of developing such a structure requires that viewers attend to the material (depending on the salience and complexity of the program). Then viewers make attributions and form moral evaluations in the comprehension stage. Then they store their comprehension in memory.

Cognitive processing is related to age. Developmental psychologists have shown that children's minds mature cognitively and that in some early stages they are unable to process certain types of television content well....[U]ntil age 5, they are especially attracted to and influenced by vivid production features, such as rapid movement of characters, rapid changes of scenes, and unexpected sights and sounds. Children seek out and pay attention to cartoon violence, not because of the violence, but because of the vivid production features. By ages 6 to 11, children have developed the ability to lengthen their attention spans and make sense of continuous plots....

Personality type.   The more aggressive the person is, the more influence viewing of violence will have on that person's subsequent aggressive behavior (Comstock et al., 1978; Stein & Friedrich, 1972). And children who are emotionally disturbed are more susceptible to a disinhibition effect (Sprafkin et al., 1992)....

2.3. Viewer States

The degrees of physiological arousal, anger, and frustration have all been found to increase the probability of a negative effect.

Aroused state.   Portrayals (even if they are not violent) that leave viewers in an aroused state are more likely to lead to aggressive behavior (Berkowitz & Geen, 1966; Donnerstein & Berkowitz, 1981; Tannenbaum, 1972; Zillman, 1971).

Emotional reaction.   Viewers who are upset by the media exposure (negative hedonic value stimuli) are more likely to aggress (Rule & Ferguson, 1986; Zillmann et al., 1981). Such aggression is especially likely when people are left in a state of unresolved excitement (Comstock, 1985).... In his meta-analysis of 1,043 effects of television on social behavior, Hearold (1986) concluded that frustration... is not a necessary condition, but rather a contributory condition....

Degree of identity.   It has been well established that the more a person, especially a child, identifies with a character, the more likely the person will be influenced by that character's behavior.

Identity seems to be a multifaceted construct composed of similarity, attractiveness, and hero status. If the perpetrator of violence is perceived as *similar* to the viewer, the likelihood of learning to behave aggressively increases (Lieberman Research, 1975; Rosekrans & Hartup, 1967). When violence is performed by an *attractive* character, the probability of aggression increases (Comstock et al., 1978; Hearold, 1986). Attractiveness of a villain is also an important consideration (Health et al., 1989)....

2.4 Characteristics in the Portrayals

Reviews of the literature are clear on the point that people interpret the meaning of violent portrayals and use contextual information to construct that meaning.

In the media effects literature, there appear to be five notable contextual variables: rewards and punishments, consequences, justification, realism, and production techniques....

Rewards and punishments.   Rewards and punishments to perpetrators of violence provide important information to viewers about which actions are acceptable. However, there is reason to believe that the effect does not work with children younger than 10, who usually have difficulty linking violence presented early in a program with its punishment rendered later (Collins, 1973).

In repeated experiments, viewers who watch a model rewarded for performing violently in the media are more likely to experience a disinhibition effect and behave in a similar manner. But when violence is punished in the media portrayal, the aggressiveness of viewers is likely to be inhibited (Comstock et al., 1978). In addition, when nonaggressive characters are rewarded, viewers' levels of aggression can be reduced.

The absence of punishment also leads to disinhibition. That is, the perpetrators need not be rewarded in order for the disinhibition effect to occur....

Consequences.   The way in which the consequences of violence are portrayed influences the disinhibition effect.... For example, Goranson showed people a film of a prize fight in which either there were no consequences or the loser of the fight received a bad beating and later died. The participants who did not see the negative consequences were more likely to behave aggressively after the viewing.

A key element in the consequences is whether the victim shows pain, because pain cues inhibit subsequent aggression. Moreover, Swart and Berkowitz (1976) showed that viewers could generalize pain cues to characters other than the victims.

Justification.   Reviews of the effects research conclude that justification of violent acts leads to higher aggression. For example, Bryan and Schwartz observed that "aggressive behavior in the service of morally commendable ends appears condoned. Apparently, the assumption is made that moral goals temper immoral actions.... Thus, both the imitation and interpersonal attraction of the transgressing model may be determined more by outcomes than by moral principles."

Several experiments offer support for these arguments. First, Berkowitz and Rawlings (1963) found that justification of filmed aggression lowers viewers' inhibitions to aggress in real life.

Justification is keyed to motives. Brown and Tedeschi (1976) found that offensive violence was regarded as more violent even when the actions themselves were not as violent. For example, a verbal threat that is made offensively is perceived as more violent than a punch that is delivered defensively.

The one motive that has been found to lead to the strongest disinhibition is vengeance. For example, Berkowitz and Alioto introduced a film of a sporting event (boxing and football) by saying that the participants were acting either as professionals wanting to win or as motivated by vengeance and wanting to hurt the other. They found that the vengeance film led to more shocks and longer duration of shocks in a subsequent test of participants. When violence was portrayed as vengeance, disinhibition was stronger than when violence was portrayed as self-defense or as a means of achieving altruistic goals.

Young children have difficulty understanding motives. For example, Collins (1973) ran an experiment on children aged 8 to 15 to see if a time lag from portrayal of motivation to portrayal of aggression changed participants' behaviors or interpretations. Participants were shown either a 30-minute film in which federal agents confronted some criminals or a control film of a travelogue. In the treatment film, the criminals hit and shot the federal agents, displaying negative motivation (desire to escape justice) and negative consequences (a criminal fell to his death while trying to escape). Some participants saw the sequence uninterrupted; others saw the motivation, followed by a 4-minute interruption of commercials, then the aggression. Both 18 days before the experiment and then again right after the viewing, participants were asked their responses to a wide range of hypothetical interpersonal conflict situations. There was a difference by age. Third graders displayed more aggressive choices on the postviewing measure when they had experienced the separation condition; sixth and 10th graders did not exhibit this effect. The author concluded that among younger children, temporal separation of story elements obscures the message that aggression was negatively motivated and punished....

Realism.   When viewers believe that the aggression is portrayed in a realistic manner, they are more likely to try it in real life.

Production techniques.   Certain production techniques can capture and hold attention, potentially leading to differences in the way the action is perceived. Attention is increased when graphic and explicit acts are used to increase the dramatic nature of the narrative, to increase positive dispositions toward the characters using violence, and to increase levels of arousal, which is more likely to result in aggressive behavior....

3. Exposure to violence in the media can lead to fear effects.

The best available review is by Cantor (1994), who defines fear effect as an immediate physiological effect of arousal, along with an emotional reaction of anxiety and distress.

4. An immediate fear effect is influenced by a set of key factors about viewers and the portrayals.

4.1 Viewer Factors

Identification with the target.   The degree of identification with the target is associated with a fear effect. For example, characters who are attractive, who are heroic, or who are perceived as similar to the viewer evoke viewer empathy. When a character with whom viewers empathize is then the target of violence, viewers experience an increased feeling of fear.

The identification with characters can lead to an enjoyment effect. For example, Tannenbaum and Gaer (1965) found that participants who identified more with the hero felt more stress and benefited more from a happy ending in which their stress was reduced. However, a sad or indeterminate ending increased participants' stress.

Prior real-life experience.   Prior experience with fearful events in real life leads viewers, especially children, to identify more strongly with the characters and events and thereby to involve them more emotionally.

Belief that the depicted violent action could happen to the viewer.   When viewers think there is a good chance that the violence they see could happen to them in real life, they are more likely to experience an immediate fear effect.

Motivations for exposure.   People expose themselves to media violence for many different reasons. Certain reasons for exposure can reduce a fear effect. If people's motivation to view violence is entertainment, they can employ a discounting procedure to lessen the effects of fear.

Level of arousal.   Higher levels of arousal lead to higher feelings of fear.

Ability to use coping strategies.   When people are able to remind themselves that the violence in the media cannot hurt them, they are less likely to experience a fear effect.

Developmental differences.   Children at lower levels of cognitive development are unable to follow plot lines well, so they are more influenced by individual violent episodes, which seem to appear randomly and without motivation.

Ability to perceive the reality of the portrayals.   Children are less able than older viewers to understand the fantasy nature of certain violent portrayals.

4.2 Portrayal Factors

Type of stimulus.   Cantor (1994) says that the fright effect is triggered by three categories of stimuli that usually are found in combination with many portrayals of violence in the media. First is the category of dangers and injuries, stimuli that depict events that threaten great harm. Included in this category are natural disasters, attacks by vicious animals, large-scale accidents, and violent encounters at levels ranging from interpersonal to intergalactic. Second is the category of distortions of natural forms. This category includes familiar organisms that are shown as deformed or unnatural through mutilation, accidents of birth, or conditioning. And third is the category of experience of endangerment and fear by others. This type of stimulus evokes empathy for particular characters, and the viewer then feels the fear that the characters in the narrative are portraying.

Unjustified violence.   When violence is portrayed as unjustified, viewers become more fearful.

Graphicness.   Higher levels of explicitness and graphicness increase viewer fear.

Rewards.   When violence goes unpunished, viewers become more fearful.

Realism.   Live-action violence provokes more intense fear than cartoon violence does. For example, Lazarus et al. found that showing gory accidents to adults aroused them physiologically less when the participants were told that the accidents were fake. This effect has also been found with children. In addition, fear is enhanced when elements in a portrayal resemble characteristics in a person's own life.

5. Exposure to violence in the media can lead to desensitization.

In the short term, viewers of repeated violence can show a lack of arousal and emotional response through habituation to the stimuli.

6. An immediate desensitization effect is influenced by a set of key factors about viewers and the portrayals.

Children and adults can become desensitized to violence upon multiple exposures through temporary habituation. But the habituation appears to be relatively short-term.

6.1 Viewer Factors
People who are exposed to larger amounts of television violence are usually found to be more susceptible to immediate desensitization.

6.2 Portrayal Factors
There appear to be two contextual variables that increase the likelihood of a desensitization effect: graphicness and humor.

Graphicness.   Graphicness of violence can lead to immediate desensitization. In experiments in which participants are exposed to graphic violence, initially they have strong physiological responses, but these responses steadily decline during the exposure. This effect has also been shown with children, especially among the heaviest viewers of TV violence.

Humor.   Humor contributes to the desensitization effect.

Long-Term Effects of Violent Content

Long-term effects of exposure to media violence are more difficult to measure than are immediate effects. The primary reason is that long-term effects occur so gradually that by the time an effect is clearly indicated, it is very difficult to trace that effect back to media exposures. It is not possible to argue that any single exposure triggers the effect. Instead, we must argue that the long-term pattern of exposure leads to the effect. A good analogy is the way in which an orthodontist straightens teeth. Orthodontists do not produce an immediate effect by yanking teeth into line in one appointment. Instead, they apply braces that exert very little pressure, but that weak pressure is constant. A person who begins wearing braces might experience sore gums initially, but even then there is no observable change to the alignment of the teeth. This change in alignment cannot be observed even after a week or a month. Only after many months is the change observable.

It is exceedingly difficult for social scientists to make a strong case that the media are responsible for long-term effects. The public, policymakers, and especially critics of social science research want to be persuaded that there is a causal connection. But with a matter of this complexity that requires the long-term evolution of often conflicting influences in the naturalistic environment of viewers' everyday lives, the case for causation cannot be made in any manner stronger than a tentative probabilistic one. Even then, a critic could point to a "third variable" as a potential alternative explanation.

7. Long-term exposure to media violence is related to aggression in a person's life.

Evidence suggests that this effect is causative and cumulative (Eron, 1982). This effect is also reciprocal: Exposure to violence leads to increased aggression, and people with higher levels of aggression usually seek out higher levels of exposure to aggression.

Huesmann, Eron, Guerra, and Crawshaw (1994) conclude from their longitudinal research that viewing violence as a child has a causal effect on patterns of higher aggressive behavior in adults. This finding has appeared in studies in the United States, Australia, Finland, Israel, Poland, the Netherlands, and South Africa. While recognizing that exposure to violence on TV is not the only cause of aggression in viewers, Huesmann et al. conclude that the research suggests that the effect of viewing television violence on aggression "is relatively independent of other likely influences and of a magnitude great enough to account for socially important differences."

The long-term disinhibition effect is influenced by "a variety of environmental, cultural, familial, and cognitive" factors. A major influence on this effect is the degree to which viewers identify with characters who behave violently. For example, Eron found that the learning effect is enhanced when children identify closely with aggressive TV characters. He argued that aggression is a learned behavior, that the continued viewing of television violence is a very likely cause of aggressive behavior, and that this is a long-lasting effect on children.

Once children reach adolescence, their behavioral dispositions and inhibitory controls have become crystallized to the extent that their aggressive habits are very difficult to change, and achievement have been found to be related to this effect. Huesmann et al. concluded that low IQ makes the learning of aggressive responses more likely at an early age, and this aggressive behavior makes continued intellectual development more difficult into adulthood.

Evidence also suggests that the effect is contingent on the type of family life. In Japan, for example, Kashiwagi and Munakata (1985) found no correlation between exposure to TV violence and aggressiveness of viewers in real life for children in general. But an effect was observed among young children living in families in which the parents did not get along well.

8. Media violence is related to subsequent violence in society.

When television is introduced into a country, the violence and crime rates in that country, especially crimes of theft, increase. Within a country, the amount of exposure to violence that a demographic group typically experiences in the media is related to the crime rate in neighborhoods where those demographic groups are concentrated. Finally, some evidence suggests that when a high-profile violent act is depicted in the news or in fictional programming, the incidents of criminal aggression increase subsequent to that coverage.

All these findings are subject to the criticism that the researchers have only demonstrated co-occurrence of media violence and real-life aggression. Researchers are asked to identify possible "third variables" that might be alternative explanations for the apparent relationship, and then to show that the relationship exists even after the effects of these third variables are controlled. Although researchers have been testing control variables, critics are still concerned that one or more important variables that have yet to be controlled may account for a possible alternative explanation of the effect.

9. People exposed to many violent portrayals over a long time will come to exaggerate their chances of being victimized.

This generalized fear effect has a great deal of empirical support in the survey literature. But this relationship is generally weak in magnitude, and it is sensitive to third variables in the form of controls and contingencies. The magnitude of the correlation coefficients (r) is usually low, typically in the range of .10 to .30, which means that exposure is able to explain only less than 10% of the variation in the responses of cultivation indicators....

The magnitude of the cultivation effect is relatively weak even by social science standards. Cultivation theorists have defended their findings by saying that even though the effect is small, it is persistent....

This cultivation effect is also remarkably robust. In the relatively large literature on cultivation, almost all the coefficients fall within a consistently narrow band. Not only is this effect remarkable in its consistency, but this consistency becomes truly startling when one realizes the wide variety of measures (of both television exposure and cultivation indicators) that are used in the computations of these coefficients.

10. People exposed to many violent portrayals over a long time will come to be more accepting of violence.

This effect is the gradual desensitizing of viewers to the plight of victims, as well as to violence in general. After repeated exposure to media violence over a long period of time, viewers lose a sense of sympathy with the victims of violence. Viewers also learn that violence is a "normal" part of society, that violence can be used successfully, and that violence is frequently rewarded.

The probability of this long-term effect is increased when people are continually exposed to graphic portrayals of violence. For example, Linz, Donnerstein, and Penrod (1988a) exposed male participants to five slasher movies during a 2-week period. After each film, the male participants exhibited decreasing perceptions that the films were violent or that they were degrading to women.

Conclusion

After more than five decades of research on the effects of exposure to media violence, we can be certain that there are both immediate and long-term effects. The strongest supported immediate effect is the following: Exposure to violent portrayals in the media increases subsequent viewer aggression. We also know that there are other positive and negative immediate effects, such as fear and desensitization. As for long-term effects, we can conclude that exposure to violence in the media is linked with long-term negative effects of trait aggression, fearful worldview, and desensitization to violence. The effects process is highly complex and is influenced by many factors about the viewers, situational cues, and contextual characteristics of the violent portrayals.

Violence Viewing and Science

Examining the Research

For the moment, it is prudent not to question the forces that gave rise to the violence effects literature and have sustained it for five decades nor to tease out the unarticulated assumptions enmeshed in it. Let us begin by taking this extensive literature entirely on its own terms. What will become clear is that although the majority of the published studies on the topic do report antisocial findings, the average extent of the findings is slight—often so much so that the findings are open to several interpretations....

Those who pore over the violence effects literature agree that the case against televised fantasy viciousness is most broadly and clearly made in the large number of laboratory studies, such as those done by Bandura. Overall, these studies offer support for the imitative hypothesis—that younger viewers will exhibit a tendency to act out the aggression seen on the screen. In this group of studies, many find the issue reduced to a pristine clarity, parsed of all needless complexity and obscurity, and answered with sufficient experimental evidence. What is found in this literature can be rightfully generalized to the real world, some believe, to spark a host of inferences and even policies. However, the laboratory is not the real world, and may be so unreal as to discredit the results.

The unnaturalness of laboratory studies is frequently commented on by those who have reservations regarding this research (Buckingham, 1993, p. 11; Gunter & McAteer, 1990, p. 13; Noble, 1975, p. 125), but the extent of the artificiality is rarely defined, leaving those who are unfamiliar with these settings or the nature of these experiments with little sense of what is meant by "unnatural."...

[In a behavioral laboratory setting] in a room with other unmet children, the child may be unexpectedly frustrated or angered by the experimenters—shown toys but not allowed to touch them, perhaps, or spoken to brusquely. The child is then instructed to look at a video monitor. It would be highly unlikely for the young subject to sense that this experience in any way resembled television viewing as done at home.... Most signally, at home television viewing is an entirely voluntary activity: The child is in front of the set because the child has elected to do so and in most instances has elected the content, and he or she will elect other content if the current material does not satisfy. In the behavioral laboratory, the child is compelled to watch and, worse, compelled to watch material not of the child's choosing and probably not of the child's liking. The essential element of the domestic television-viewing experience, that of pleasure, has been methodically stripped away.

Furthermore, what the child views in a typical laboratory experiment will bear little resemblance to what the child views at home. The footage will comprise only a segment of a program and will feature only aggressive actions. The intermittent relief of commercials or changed channels is missing, as are television stories' routine endings bringing dramatic closure in which everything is set right, with the correct values ascendant.

The child then may be led to another room that resembles the one in the video segment and encouraged to play while being observed. This is the room that, in Bandura et al.'s (1963) famous experiment, contained the Bobo doll identical to the one shown on the screen. Is it any wonder that uneasy children, jockeying for notice and position in a newly convened peer group, having seen a videotaped adult strike the doll without repercussions, and being tacitly encouraged by hovering experimenters who do not seem to disapprove of such action, would also hit the doll? As Noble (1975) wryly asked, "What else can one do to a self-righting bobo doll except hit it?" (p. 133). There are typically only a limited number of options, all behavioral, for the young subjects. Certainly, no researcher is asking them about the meanings they may have taken from the screened violence.

In summary, laboratory experiments on violence viewing are concocted schemes that violate all the essential stipulations of actual viewing in the real world (Cook, Kendzierski, & Thomas, 1983, p. 180) and in doing so have nothing to teach about the television experience (although they may say much about the experimenters). Viewing in the laboratory setting is involuntary, public, choiceless, intense, uncomfortable, and single-minded, whereas actual viewing is voluntary, private, selective, nonchalant, comfortable, and in the context of competing activities. Laboratory research has taken the viewing experience and turned it inside out so that the viewer is no longer in charge. In this manner, experimenters have made a mockery out of the everyday act of television viewing. Distorted to this extent, laboratory viewing can be said to simulate household viewing only if one is determined to believe so. . . .

The inadequacies of laboratory research on television violence effects are apparent in the small body of research on the matter of desensitization or, as Slaby (1994) called it, "the bystander effect." The few attempts to replicate the finding of the four Drabman and Thomas experiments (Drabman & Thomas 1974a, 1974b, 1976; Thomas & Drabman, 1975)—that children exposed to violent footage would take longer to call for the intercession of an adult supervisor —have produced inconsistent results. Horton and Santogrossi (1978) failed to replicate in that the scores for the control group did not differ from the scores for the experimental groups. In addition, Woodfield (1988) did not find statistically significant differences between children exposed to violent content and children exposed to nonviolent content. . . .

A third attempt to replicate by Molitor and Hirsch (1994) did duplicate the original findings, apparently showing that children are more likely to tolerate aggression in others if they are first shown violent footage. An examination of their results, however, does give rise to questions about the rigor of the research. This experiment was set up with the active collaboration of the original researchers and may be less of an attempt to relicate (or not) than an attempt to vindicate. Forty-two Catholic school fourth- and fifth-grade children were assigned to two treatment groups (there was no control group). As for all laboratory experiments, the viewing conditions were so thoroughly alien that results may have been induced by subtle clues from the adult laboratory personnel, especially for obedient children from a parochial school setting. Children shown violent content (a segment from *Karate Kid*) waited longer on average before requesting adult intervention than did children shown nonviolent content (footage from the 1984 Olympic games). Again, this finding could be interpreted as evidence of catharsis: The violent content might have lowered levels of arousal and induced a momentary lassitude. The findings could also have resulted from a sense of ennui: Postexperiment interviews revealed that all the children shown *Karate Kid* had seen the movie before, some as many as 10 times (p. 201). By comparison, the Olympic contests might have seemed more exciting and stimulated swifter reactions to the videotaped misbehavior. The first author was one of the laboratory experimenters; therefore, the specter of expectancy bias cannot be dismissed.

Even if desensitization were to exist as a replicable laboratory finding, the pressing question is whether or not the effect generalizes to the real world. Are there any data in support of the notion that exposure to television violence makes people callous to hostility in everyday life? The evidence on this is scarce and in the negative. Studying many British youngsters, Belson (1978) could find no correlation between levels of television violence viewing and callousness to real violence or inconsiderateness to others (pp. 471–475, 511–516). Research by Hagell and Newburn (1994) can answer the question of whether some youngsters who view heightened hours of television become "desensitized" to violence and embark on criminal lives; unexpectedly, teenage criminals view on average less television, and less violent content, than their law-abiding peers.

Reviewers of the small desensitization literature conclude there is no empirical evidence that anything like the bystander effect actually exists in real life (Gauntlett, 1995, p. 39; Van der Voort, 1986, p. 327; Zillmann, 1991, p. 124). Even George Comstock (1989), normally sympathetic to the violence effects literature, concedes about desensitization studies that "what the research does not demonstrate is any likelihood that media portrayals would affect the response to injury, suffering, or violent death experienced firsthand" (p. 275).

I now turn from the contrivances of laboratory research to the more promising methodology of field experiments, in which typically children in circumstances familiar to them are rated on aggressiveness through the observation of their behavior, exposed to either violent or nonviolent footage, and then unobtrusively rated again. Although this literature holds out the hope of conclusive findings in natural settings, the actual results display a disquietingly wide range of outcomes. Some of the data gathered indicate, instead of an elevation in aggressive behaviors, a diminishment in aggressive behaviors following several weeks of high-violence viewing. Feshbach and Singer (1971) were able to control the viewing diets of approximately 400 boys in three private boarding schools and four homes for wayward boys. For 6 weeks, half the boys were randomly assigned to a viewing menu high in violent content, whereas the other half made their selections from nonaggressive shows. Aggression levels were determined by trained observers in the weeks before and after the controlled viewing period. No behavioral differences were reported for the adolescents in the private schools, but among the poorer, semidelinquent youths, those who had been watching the more violent shows were calmer than their peers on the blander viewing diet. The authors concluded that "exposure to aggressive content on television seems to reduce or control the expression of aggression in aggressive boys from relatively low socioeconomic backgrounds" (p. 145).

Although Wood et al. (1991) report that the eight field experiments they reviewed did, overall, demonstrate an imitative effect from watching televised violence, other reviewers of this literature do not concur (Cumberbatch & Howitt, 1989, p. 41; Freedman, 1988, p. 151). McGuire (1986) comments dismissively on "effects that range from the statistically trivial to practically insubstantial" (p. 213). Most decisively, Gadow and Sprafkin (1989), themselves contributors to the field experiment research, concluded their thorough review of the 20 studies they located by stating that "the findings from the field experiments offer little support for the media aggression hypothesis" (p. 404).

In the aftermath of the thoroughgoing artificiality of the laboratory studies, and the equivocation of the field experiment results, the burden of proof must fall on the third methodology, that of correlational studies. In the search for statistical correlations (or not) between violence viewing and aggressive or criminal behavior, this literature contains several studies impressive for their naturalness and their size. Not all these studies uncover a parallel between, on the one hand, increased levels of violence viewing and, on the other hand, increased rates of misbehavior, by whatever measure. For example, for a sample of 2,000 11- to 16-year-olds, Lynn, Hampson, and Agahi (1989) found no correlation between levels of violence viewing and levels of aggression. Nevertheless, many studies do report a positive correlation. It should be noted that the magnitude of this co-occurrence is usually quite small, typically producing a low correlation coefficient of 10 to 20 (Freedman, 1988, p. 153). Using these correlations (small as they are), the question becomes one of the direction(s) of possible causality. Does violence viewing lead to subsequent aggression as is commonly assumed? Could more aggressive children prefer violent content, perhaps as a vicarious outlet for their hostility? . . . Could any of a host of other factors give rise to both elevated variables?

Following his substantial correlational study of 1,500 London adolescents, Belson (1978) highlighted one of his findings—that boys with high levels of exposure to television violence commit 49% more acts of serious violence than do those who view less—and on this basis issued a call for a reduction in video carnage (p. 526). Closer examination of his data (pp. 380–382), however, reveals that the relationship between the two variables is far more irregular than he suggests in his text. Low viewers of television violence are more aggressive than moderate viewers, whereas very high violence viewers are less aggressive than those in the moderate to high range. Moreover, "acts of serious violence" constituted only one of Belson's four measures of real-life aggression; the other three were "total number of acts of violence," "total number of acts of violence weighted by degree of severity of the act," and "total number of violent acts excluding minor ones." Findings for these three variables cannot be said to substantiate Belson's conclusion. That is, for these measures, the linking of violence viewing to subsequent aggression was negated by reverse correlations —that aggressive youngsters sought out violent content (pp. 389–392). Three of his measures refuted his argument, but Belson chose to emphasize a fourth, itself a demonstrably inconsistent measure. . . .

For the total television effects literature, whatever the methodology, the reviews . . . by Andison (1977), Hearold (1986), and Paik and Comstock (1994) are not the only ones that have been compiled. Other overviews reach very different summary judgments about this body of studies in its entirety. A review published contemporaneously with that of Andison considered the same research projects and derived a different conclusion (Kaplan & Singer, 1976). Kaplan and Singer examined whether the extant literature could support an activation view (that watching televised fantasy violence leads to aggression), a catharsis view (that such viewing leads to a decrease in aggression), or a null view, and they determined that the null position was the most judicious. They wrote, "Our review of the literature strongly suggests that the activating effects of television fantasy violence are marginal at best. The scientific data do not consistently link violent television fantasy programming to violent behavior" (p. 62).

In the same volume in which Susan Hearold's (1986) meta-analysis of violence studies appeared, there was also published a literature review by William McGuire (1986). In contrast to Hearold, it was McGuire's judgment that the evidence of untoward effects from violence viewing was not compelling. Throughout the 1980s, an assured critique of the violence effects literature [was] issued from Jonathan Freedman (1984, 1986, 1988). Freedman cautiously examined the major studies within each of the methodological categories. . . . Regarding correlational studies, he noted that "not one study produced strong consistent results, and most produced a substantial number of negative findings" (1988, p. 158). Freedman's general conclusion is that "considering all of the research —laboratory, field experiments, and correlational studies—the evidence does not support the idea that viewing television violence causes aggression" (1988, p. 158).

Freedman's dismissal of the violence effects literature is echoed in other literature reviews from British scholars, who may enjoy an objective distance on this largely American research agenda. Cumberbatch and Howitt (1989) discussed the shortcomings of most of the major studies and stated that the research data "are insufficiently robust to allow a firm conclusion about television violence as studied" (p. 51). David Gauntlett (1995) . . . analyzed at length most of the consequential studies. He believes that "the work of effects researchers is done" (p. 1). "The search for direct 'effects' of television on behavior is over: Every effort has been made, and they simply cannot be found" (p. 120). Ian Vine (1997) concurs: "Turning now to the systemic evidence from hundreds of published studies of the relationship between viewing violence and subsequent problematic behaviors, the most certain conclusion is that there is *no* genuine consensus of findings" (p. 138)....

Discourse Within Discourse

Opened up for inspection, the sizable violence effects literature turns out to be an uneven discourse—inconsistent, flawed, pocked. This literature proves nothing conclusively, or equivalently, this literature proves everything in that support for any position can be drawn from its corpus. The upshot is that, no matter what some reformers affirm, the campaign against television violence is bereft of any strong, consensual scientific core. Flaws extend through to the very premises of the literature—flaws so total that they may crowd out alternative viewpoints and produce in some a mind-numbed acquiescence. Specifically, the literature's two main subjects—television and the viewer—are assumed to be what they are not.

Viewers are conceived of as feckless and vacuous, like jellyfish in video tides. Viewers have no intentions, no discretion, and no powers of interpretation. Into their minds can be stuffed all matter of content. Most often, the viewer postulated in the effects literature is young, epitomizing immaturity and malleability. This literature, wrote Carmen Luke (1990), "had constructed a set of scientifically validated truths about the child viewer as a behavioral response mechanism, as passive and devoid of cognitive abilities. The possibility that viewers bring anything other than demographic variables to the screen was conceptually excluded" (p. 281). Although there is ample evidence that the young are highly active, selective, and discriminating viewers (Buckingham, 1993; Clifford, Gunter, & McAleer, 1995; Durkin, 1985; Gunter & McAteer, 1990; Hawkins & Pingree, 1986; Hodge & Tripp, 1986; Noble, 1975), this is never the version in the violence effects literature.

Television, on the other hand, is seen as powerful, coercive, and sinister. The medium is not a servant but a tyrant. It rules rather than pleases. It is omnipotent; it cannot be regulated, switched, modulated, interpreted, belittled, welcomed, or ignored. All the things that television is in the real world it is not within the violence effects literature.

The relationship between television content and viewers, as implied in this research, is one way only, as television pounds its insidious message into a hapless audience; there is no conception of a return flow of information by which viewers via ratings indicate preferences for certain content rather than other content. The only result allowable from the viewing experience is that of direct and noxious effects. Other possibilities—of pleasures, relaxation, reinterpretations, therapy, and so on—are not to be considered. The television viewing experience, twisted beyond recognition, is conceived of in pathological terms; in fact, a large amount of the research throughout the past decades has been funded by national mental health budgets.

All these preconceptions apply before a bit of research is actually conducted. The surprising result is not that there have been worrisome findings reported but that, given these presuppositions, the negative findings were not much grander still. . . .

The war on television violence, the larger discourse, has united many allies with otherwise weak ties—prominent authorities and grassroots organizations, liberals and conservatives, and the religious and the secular. We must ask why they put aside their differences, lift their voices together, and join in this particular cause. This implausible alliance constitutes a force field that waxes and wanes throughout the decades, losing strength at one point and gaining it at another; it would seem to have a rhythm all its own. What can account for the regular reoccurrence of this public discourse denouncing television violence?

POSTSCRIPT

Is Television Harmful for Children?

Much of what we know about the effects of television comes from the study of children enjoying traditional television, but this knowledge is being challenged by the impact of emerging telecommunications technology. The Internet, cable television programming, video games, and VCRs have changed the face of television within the home. Indeed, VCRs have greatly increased the control that parents have over the material to which children are exposed at young ages and have greatly increased the diversity of content that children can be exposed to as they get older. The Internet, a 500-channel world, increasing international programming ventures, and regulatory changes will alter the way children interact with electronic media. What influence that will have is very hard to predict.

One conclusion is inescapable. There is now much more diversity of media content available, and there are many more choices for parents and children. One of the clearest findings of research on the impact of violence on child aggression is that parents, through their behavior and their positive and negative comments, can have a major influence on whether or not children behave aggressively subsequent to exposure. With choices come hard decisions for parents. The promise of television and other media can now be better fulfilled, with more choices than ever before. Alternatively, a diet of violence and mindlessness is easily found.

Although this issue concerns children, there are important developmental and social differences due to age. Young children, particularly preschoolers, are most likely to be controlled by their parents, are most likely to have difficulty understanding some of the narratives and conventions of media fare, and are arguably the most vulnerable to learning from the messages of the media to which they are exposed. The "tween" years are a transition to more adult programs and themes and are a time of great transition socially. Poised between the worlds of adulthood and childhood, the tween partakes of both, sometimes with difficult consequences. Tweens are not even considered by the media to be part of the "child" audience. Their viewing patterns are much more like those of adults, and like adults they are presumed to be cognitively able to protect themselves from the effects of violence or even advertising. So they proudly proclaim that the media have no effect on them.

The National Television Violence Study, 3 vols. (Sage Publications, 1996–1998), conducted by a consortium of professors from several universities, offers a commentary on the state of violence on American television for viewers, policymakers, industry leaders, and scholars. Robert Liebert and Joyce Sprafkin's *The Early Window: Effects of Television on Children and Youth,* 3rd ed. (Pergamon Press, 1988) is an excellent introduction to the history and issues of media effects. Judith Van Evra offers a view of existing research in *Television and Child Development,* 2d ed. (Lawrence Erlbaum, 1998). School violence has revived the debate on media violence and children, according to Paige Albiniak in "Media: Littleton's Latest Suspect," *Broadcasting & Cable* (May 3, 1999). Not only television but video games come under attack. Lieutenant Colonel Dave Grossman, a former Army ranger and paratrooper, writes about video games that teach children to kill by using the same warfare tactics used to train the military, in the *Saturday Evening Post* (July/August and September/October 1999). Many articles were written after the Columbine tragedy that implicated violent video games in the violence of U.S. society.

ISSUE 3

Is Emphasis on Body Image in the Media Harmful to Females Only?

YES: Mary C. Martin and James W. Gentry, from "Stuck in the Model Trap: The Effects of Beautiful Models in Ads on Female Pre-Adolescents and Adolescents," *Journal of Advertising* (Summer 1997)

NO: Michelle Cottle, from "Turning Boys into Girls," *The Washington Monthly* (May 1998)

ISSUE SUMMARY

YES: Marketing professors Mary C. Martin and James W. Gentry address the literature dealing with advertising images and the formation of body identity for preadolescent and adolescent females. They report a study to explore how social comparison theory influences young women.

NO: *Washington Monthly* editor Michelle Cottle takes the perspective that females are not the only ones influenced by media image. She cites polls and magazine advertising that indicate that males are exposed to images of idealized body type as well, and she argues that these images also have an impact on the male psyche.

There is plenty of evidence to support the idea that young girls are influenced by the body images of models and actresses they see in the media. In her book *The Beauty Myth* (Anchor Books, 1992), Naomi Wolf writes that the typical model or actress is significantly below what the medical establishment considers a "healthy" body weight. The desire to look like a model or actress has contributed to what could be termed an outbreak in eating disorders among females. Wolf warns that 1 out of 10 college women develop an eating disorder while in college, but the desire to be thin often starts as early as age eight for many girls.

Little attention has been given to the self-images of boys, while the unhealthy aspects of eating disorders and idealized body image has been primarily attributed to girls. In the following selections the authors help us to understand this phenomenon on an even broader scale.

Mary C. Martin and James W. Gentry take the position that idealized body image is a female problem, and they attempt to study whether or not social comparison theory (the idea that females compare their own physical attractiveness with models) influences self-esteem. Their studies of fourth- and sixth-graders help to illuminate differential cognitive levels and the way images influence self-perceptions.

Michelle Cottle adds an interesting dimension to the problem of images and idealized body type. She asserts that men's magazines have also taken the approach to making males feel inadequate through images and stories that work against male vanity. The images and stories she describes raise questions about the content of magazines and the way pictures and stories affect us psychologically.

These issues will undoubtedly spark lively discussions about whether or not images and stories actually do shape the way we think about ourselves in relation to idealized images. The psychological effects of media are difficult to assess, even though the presence of images is pervasive, but it is hard to ignore their potential power. The history of media effects research has much to offer in the way we think about the following selections.

Mary C. Martin and James W. Gentry  **YES**

Stuck in the Model Trap

Agrowing concern in our society is the plight of female pre-adolescents and adolescents as they grow up facing many obstacles, including receiving less attention than boys in the classroom, unrealistic expectations of what they can and cannot do, decreasing self-esteem, and being judged by their physical appearance. In particular, girls are generally preoccupied with attempting to become beautiful. As Perry suggests, "Today's specifications call for blonde and thin—no easy task, since most girls get bigger during adolescence. Many become anorexics or bulimics; a few rich ones get liposuction. We make their focus pleasing other people and physical beauty." Further, studies show that self-esteem drops to a much greater extent for female than male pre-adolescents and adolescents, with self-perceptions of physical attractiveness contributing to the drop.

Another growing concern in our society is the role of advertising in contributing to those obstacles. For example, advertising has been accused of unintentionally imposing a "sense of inadequacy" on women's self-concepts. Studies suggest that advertising and the mass media may play a part in creating and reinforcing a preoccupation with physical attractiveness and influence consumer perceptions of what constitutes an acceptable level of physical attractiveness. Further, studies have found that female college students, adolescents, and pre-adolescents compare their physical attractiveness with that of models in ads and that female pre-adolescents and adolescents have desires to be models. An aspiring young model, for example, describes "the model trap":

> Deep down inside, I still want to be a supermodel... As long as they're there, screaming at me from the television, glaring at me from magazines, I'm stuck in the model trap. Hate them first. Then grow to like them. Love them. Emulate them. Die to be them. All the while praying this cycle will come to an end.

Clearly, such findings raise concern about advertising ethics. Jean Kilbourne, for example, addresses how female bodies are depicted in advertising imagery and the potential effects on women's physical and mental health in her videos *Still Killing Us Softly* and *Slim Hopes*. The use of highly attractive models in ads as an "ethical issue" received little or no attention in published research from 1987 to 1993, but the ethics of that practice have begun to be questioned by consumers and advertisers. For example, a consumer movement against advertising has arisen in the United States. The organization Boycott Anorexic Marketing (BAM) is attempting to get consumers to boycott products sold by companies that use extremely thin models in their ads. Such criticisms of advertising are "much too serious to dismiss cavalierly."

Using social comparison theory as a framework, we propose that female pre-adolescents and adolescents compare their physical attractiveness with that of advertising models. As a result, their self-perceptions and self-esteem may be affected. In response to the criticisms, we conducted a study to assess those unintended consequences of advertising. However, unlike previous empirical studies of those effects, ours incorporated the role of a motive for comparison —self-evaluation, self-improvement, or self-enhancement—which may help to explain the inconsistent findings in the advertising/marketing and psychology literature. Specifically, our premise was that changes in self-perceptions and/or self-esteem may be influenced by the type of motive operating at the time of comparison.

Physical Attractiveness and Self-Esteem in Children and Adolescents

Cultural norms in the United States dictate the importance of being physically attractive, especially of being thin. The emphasis on being physically attractive begins in infancy and continues throughout childhood and adolescence. How physically attractive a child or adolescent perceives him/herself to be heavily influences his/her self-esteem, particularly beginning in fifth grade. However, the effect of self-perceptions of physical attractiveness on self-esteem differs between girls and boys. For example, Harter, in a cross-sectional study of third through eleventh graders, found that self-perceptions of physical attractiveness and levels of global self-esteem appeared to decline systematically over time in girls but not for boys. Other researchers have documented such decreases throughout adolescence for girls. Boys' self-esteem, in contrast, tends to increase from early through late adolescence.

The nature of physical attractiveness differs for male and female children and adolescents as well. Girls tend to view their bodies as "objects," and their physical beauty determines how they and others judge their overall value. Boys tend to view their bodies as "process," and power and function are more important criteria for evaluating their physical self. For example, Lerner, Orlos, and Knapp found that female adolescents' self-concepts derived primarily from body attractiveness whereas male adolescents' self-concepts were related more strongly to perceptions of physical instrumental effectiveness. The difference in body orientation results in girls paying attention to individual body parts and boys having a holistic body perspective. Because the ideal of attractiveness for girls is more culturally salient, girls have a greater likelihood of being negatively affected by the feminine ideal than boys have of being negatively affected by the masculine ideal.

Advertising and Social Comparison

Television commercials and magazine advertisements that contribute to the "body-as-object" focus for female pre-adolescents and adolescents, using difficult-to-attain standards of physical attractiveness to market products, are pervasive. For example, in an analysis of *Seventeen,* a magazine with "the potential to influence a substantial proportion of the adolescent female population," Guillen and Barr found that models' body shapes were less curvaceous than those in magazines for adult women and that the hip/waist ratio decreased from 1970 to 1990, meaning that models' bodies had become thinner over time. In addition, nearly half of the space of the most popular magazines for adolescent girls is devoted to advertisements.

Social comparison theory holds that people have a drive to evaluate their opinions and abilities, which can be satisfied by "social" comparisons with other people. With that theory as a framework, recent studies have found that female college students and female pre-adolescents and adolescents do compare their physical attractiveness with that of models in ads. In turn, those comparisons may result in changes in self-perceptions of physical attractiveness or self-perceptions of body image. Given the importance of self-perceptions of physical attractiveness in influencing female self-esteem, the comparisons may result in changes in self-esteem as well....

Using social comparison theory as a basis, Richins found no support for the hypothesis that exposure to advertising with highly attractive models would temporarily lower female college students' self-perceptions of physical attractiveness. "By late adolescence, however, the sight of extremely attractive models is 'old news' and unlikely to provide new information that might influence self-perception." Martin and Kennedy assessed the effects of highly attractive models in ads on female pre-adolescents and adolescents but found no support for a lowering of self-perceptions. Relying on Festinger's original conception of the theory, those researchers did not account for motive, and appear to have assumed that the motive for comparison was self-evaluation (i.e., girls compare themselves with models in ads to evaluate their own level of physical attractiveness). However, more recent research has shown that social comparisons may occur for other reasons, suggesting that female pre-adolescents and adolescents may compare themselves to models in ads for any one (or a combination) of three motives: self-evaluation, self-improvement, or self-enhancement. For example, Martin and Kennedy found that self-evaluation and self-improvement are common motives when female pre-adolescents and adolescents compare themselves with models in ads. Self-enhancement, in contrast, is not common and does not seem to occur naturally. Similarly, in a series of pretests reported by Martin, self-evaluation and self-improvement were found to be common motives in college students, but self-enhancement was not. Gentry, Martin, and Kennedy, however, found stronger support for self-enhancement in a study using in-depth interviews of first and fifth graders. As girls mature, their motives for comparison apparently vary.

The incorporation of motive may help to clarify the inconsistent findings in the literature. Our subsequent discussion explores possible differential effects of comparisons with advertising models on female pre-adolescents' and adolescents' self-perceptions and self-esteem, depending on whether self-evaluation, self-enhancement, or self-improvement is the primary motive at the time of comparison. We do not examine what motives are occurring naturally, but rather how advertising affects girls when they have a particular motive. Our overriding research question is whether motives make a difference in terms of self-perceptions and self-esteem. Finding differences between motives would clearly encourage consumer educators to stress one motive for social comparison over another. Our hypotheses specify the direction of change for each motive, thus implying response differences between subjects who have a particular comparison motive and subjects in a control group. Finding differences between motives would answer our research question even though differences between a motive group and the control group may not be significant.

Self-Evaluation as a Motive for Comparison

As the motive for comparison, Festinger originally proposed self-evaluation, the judgment of value, worth, or appropriateness of one's abilities, opinions, and personal traits. Information obtained from social comparison is not used for self-evaluation until the age of seven or eight, even though social comparison has been found to occur in children of preschool age. In the context of advertising, given that advertising models represent an ideal image of beauty, we expect comparison to be generally upward. That is, female pre-adolescents and adolescents will generally consider advertising models to be superior in terms of physical attractiveness. Therefore, if self-evaluation is the primary motive at the time of comparison (a girl is attempting to judge the value or worth of her own physical attractiveness or body image against that of advertising models), comparisons are likely to result in lowered self-perceptions and lowered self-esteem....

Method...

Subjects

Female pre-adolescents and adolescents in grades four (n = 82; mean age = 9.8 years), six (n = 103; mean age = 11.9 years), and eight (n = 83; mean age = 13.8 years) from a public school system in the Midwest participated in the study (total sample size 268). The public school system is in a county where 98% of the population is white and the median family income is $31,144. Although the sample is not representative of all pre-adolescent and adolescent girls in the United States, it does represent a segment of girls most susceptible to problems linked to physical attractiveness such as eating disorders. As an incentive to participate, the subjects took part in a drawing for two prizes of $50 each. In addition, a $500 donation was made to the public school system.

Fourth, sixth, and eighth graders were chosen for the study because research suggests that the period between the fourth and eighth grades is important in girls' development of positive perceptions of the self. It is a period when female bodies are changing drastically and adult definitions of "beauty" are becoming relevant social norms. We suggest that a girl's transition in this time period is more of a discontinuity than a linear transformation because of the conflicting biological and social processes. For example, Martin and Kennedy found, in an experiment with fourth, eighth, and twelfth grade girls, that self-perceptions of physical attractiveness decreased as the subjects got older. Fourth graders' self-perceptions were significantly higher than those of eighth graders, but eighth graders' self-perceptions were not significantly different from those of twelfth graders. Other evidence suggests that self-perceptions of physical attractiveness start to become particularly important during fifth grade. For example, Krantz, Friedberg, and Andrews found a very high correlation between self-perceived attractiveness and self-esteem in fifth graders.... The strength of the relationship in fifth graders more than tripled the variance accounted for at the third-grade level.

Classroom teachers administered the questionnaires to the subjects at the schools during an hour of class time. To separate the measurement of covariates from the manipulation, two separate booklets were used. The first booklet contained the covariate measures. After subjects completed that booklet, they handed it in and were given a second booklet with a set of ads and dependent variable measures. The assignment to treatments was randomized by giving each classroom a random assortment of the five types of questionnaires with ads. Teachers administered the questionnaires to minimize any source effects caused by having an unfamiliar authority figure collect the data. To facilitate understanding, the teachers administered the questionnaires orally by reading each question aloud and allowing appropriate time for the subjects to mark their responses.

Advertising Stimuli

Full-color ads were created by cutting and pasting stimuli from magazine ads in *Seventeen, Sassy, Teen,* and *YM.* Those magazines were chosen because they are the top four teen magazines in the United States and because they maintain consistency with respect to type of beauty. The stimuli were cut from original ads in a way that eliminated information about the sources. The ads created were for commonly advertised but fictional brand name adornment products: Satin Colors lipstick, Generation Gap jeans, and Hair in Harmony hair care products. The ads appeared to be professionally prepared, were kept very simple, and were realistic as they included partial- and full-body photos of models extracted from actual hair care, jeans, and lipstick ads.

To ensure that the subjects perceived the models in the ads as highly attractive, means of two items that measured the models' perceived attractiveness were calculated for each of the three ads. On 7-point semantic differential scales, subjects were asked to rate the model in the ad from "very overweight and out of shape, fat" to "very fit and in shape, thin" and "very unattractive, ugly" to "very attractive, beautiful" prior to measurement of the dependent variables. The range of mean responses to those items was 5.1 to 6.4, far above the midpoint value of four. Hence, the subjects perceived the models as highly attractive.

Manipulation of Motives

Motives were manipulated through instructions given prior to exposure to a set of ads, advertising headlines and copy, and a listing exercise. The manipulations were based on the following operational definitions of each motive.

1. Self-evaluation—a girl's explicit comparison of her physical attractiveness with that of models in ads to determine whether she is as pretty as or prettier than the models on specific dimensions such as hair, eyes, and body.
2. Self-improvement—a girl's explicit comparison of her physical attractiveness with that of models in ads to seek ways of improving her own attractiveness on specific dimensions such as hairstyle and makeup.
3. Self-enhancement 1—a girl's explicit comparison of her physical attractiveness with that of models in ads in an attempt to enhance her self-esteem by finding ways in which she is prettier than the model on specific dimensions (inducement of a downward comparison).
4. Self-enhancement 2—a girl's discounting of the beauty of models in ads and, in turn, the avoidance of an explicit comparison of her own physical attractiveness with that of the models in an attempt to protect/ maintain her self-esteem.

Prior to exposure to a set of ads, the subjects were given instructions in which they were shown a drawing of "Amy looking at an advertisement in a magazine" and were told a story about Amy comparing herself with a model in an ad for a particular motive. Then the subjects were asked to look at the ads on the following pages and view the ads as Amy had viewed them.

As consistency in ad design across experimental groups was essential, the headline and copy were the only components manipulated in the four sets of ads designed to induce particular motives. Minor deviations from the ad design were necessary for the control group because their ads did not include a model. The instructions, headlines, and copy were developed from "stories" written by female adolescents in projective tests in previous studies....

The subjects also completed a listing exercise after viewing each ad. They looked at each ad and listed specific ways in which the manipulated motive may have occurred. For example, in the self-improvement condition, subjects were asked to look at the model and "list ideas you get on how to improve your looks." The intent of the study was not to measure naturally occurring motives for social comparison, but rather to investigate how the use of various motives changes cognitive and affective reactions to stimuli showing physically attractive models.

If a subject successfully completed the listing exercises, the manipulation was considered successful. One author analyzed the responses to each listing exercise, coding for the subject's success or failure in completing it. Criteria for a successful response were specific references to aspects of physical attractiveness that were compared in the ad and no indication that another motive was present. For example, for a successful manipulation of self-improvement, one respondent listed the following ideas she got from looking at the model in the ad: "Use the product. Get a perm. Wear lots of make-up and have as pretty of a face as she does."

A response failed if it indicated that no motive or another motive was present. The failed responses were discarded, resulting in seven subjects being dropped (three subjects from the self-evaluation condition, one subject from the self-improvement condition, and three subjects from the self-enhancement 2 condition). For example, one subject in the self-evaluation condition was dropped because, when asked to list "ways in which your hair, face, and body look compared to the model's hair, face, and body," she wrote, "She looks different because I am a different person. I don't really compare to her." One subject in the self-improvement condition was dropped because, when asked to "list the ideas you get from the model on how you could improve the way you look," she wrote, "I could never look like her and will not try. I know that she has to be willing to work to look like she does. I don't worry about the way I look, it's just not at all that important to me." ...

Discussion

In general, our results suggest that motives do play an important role in the study context as we found differential effects for changes in self-perceptions of physical attractiveness, self-perceptions of body image, and self-esteem. Consistent with predictions of social comparison theory, female pre-adolescents' and adolescents' self-perceptions and self-esteem can be detrimentally affected, particularly when self-evaluation occurs: self-perceptions of physical attractiveness were lowered in all subjects.... In sixth graders, self-perceptions of body image were lowered (i.e., body was perceived as larger) in subjects who self-evaluated....

On a positive note, the inclusion of motives shows that detrimental effects do not always occur. That is, positive temporary effects occur when either self-improvement or self-enhancement is the motive for comparison: self-perceptions of physical attractiveness were raised in subjects who self-improved or self-enhanced through downward comparisons.... Self-perceptions and self-esteem were unaffected in most cases in subjects who self-enhanced by discounting the beauty of models.... The only exception occurred when sixth graders' self-perceptions of body image were raised (i.e., body was perceived as skinnier)....

Social comparison theory, as it currently stands, cannot explain all of our results. In particular, how the processes may change over the course of one's lifetime is not articulated theoretically or empirically. A closer examination of the results and some speculation may help to explain the inconsistent and contradictory support for the hypotheses. Though no statistically significant differences were detected, the findings for the fourth graders are interesting and offer some food for thought. Their self-evaluations produced the lowest self-perceptions of physical attractiveness and the highest (i.e., most skinny) self-perceptions of body image in comparison with the other motives. Perhaps in childhood girls (like boys) desire to grow up and "get bigger." Hence, if the fourth graders in our study desired to "get bigger," a skinnier body image would actually represent a "lowering" of self-perceptions. In that case, low self-perceptions of physical attractiveness and skinny self-perceptions of body image after self-evaluation would be consistent, supporting the notion that self-evaluation through comparisons with models in ads has detrimental effects on female pre-adolescents and adolescents.

In comparison with the fourth graders, the sixth graders produced somewhat different results. Sixth graders' self-evaluations produced the lowest self-perceptions of physical attractiveness and the lowest (i.e., the least skinny) self-perceptions of body image in comparison with the other motives. For sixth graders, unlike fourth graders, the direction of changes in self-perceptions of physical attractiveness and body image were consistent. Perhaps a transition occurs between the fourth and sixth grade, from "bigger is better" to "skinnier is better."

In self-esteem, only fourth graders were affected after self-enhancement. Self-esteem was raised in fourth graders who self-enhanced through downward comparisons.... However, self-esteem was lowered in fourth graders who self-enhanced by discounting the beauty of the models.... Martin and Kennedy found that fourth graders aspire to be models more than older adolescents, and perhaps fourth graders are discounting their own future when they discount the beauty of models. Further, fourth graders may be young enough not to realize that not all will grow up to be as beautiful as advertising models. The lack of effects of self-enhancement on sixth and eighth graders' self-esteem may be due to their reluctance to accept that they can look better than advertising models ... or that they can discount the beauty of models....

Implications and Directions for Future Research

Our results have implications for advertisers and educators. Educators can use the framework of social comparison theory to instruct children and adolescents about how (i.e., which motives to use) and when (i.e., in what circumstances and with whom) to use others for comparison. With respect to advertising models, children and adolescents may be able to use the processes of self-improvement and self-enhancement to their advantage, as both led to temporary increases in self-perceptions (in comparison with the control group or girls in another manipulated condition). As Martin and Kennedy found, however, self-enhancement is not a naturally occurring motive when female pre-adolescents and adolescents compare themselves with models in ads. Hence, the involvement of educators would be crucial. Not only would emphasis on self-enhancement be advantageous in terms of self-perceptions, but advertisers could benefit as well, as research suggests that making consumers feel physically attractive encourages sales of cosmetic and other adornment products. That possibility is encouraging, but must be viewed with caution until further research has been conducted. Our results suggest that the relationships between motives and self-perceptions and self-esteem are not straightforward and that there are particular times in childhood and adolescence when efforts to instruct young people in how to view ads may be most appropriate. Simply beginning education at a very early age is not the answer. For example, self-enhancement by discounting the beauty of models essentially did not work for fourth graders, as it caused their self-esteem to decrease. Discounting the beauty of models appears to have led fourth graders to discount their own futures in terms of physical attractiveness. In addition, if fourth graders believe "bigger is better," they may not have enough intellectual maturity to realize that "bigger is better" conflicts with the beauty and slenderness of advertising models.

Sixth and eighth graders, in contrast, may be reluctant to accept the notion of discounting models' beauty, hence the lack of effect on their self-esteem. That reluctance might be due partly to their having developed a more sophisticated level of advertising skepticism, as "adolescents have the confidence to rely on their own judgment and the discernment necessary to separate advertising truth from advertising hype." Boush and his coauthors found that self-esteem is related directly to mistrust of advertiser motives and disbelief of advertising claims. Hence, education before sixth grade may be critical to get female pre-adolescents and adolescents to accept the notion of discounting the beauty of advertising models.

The period between the fourth and eighth grades appears to be a critical one on which future research would be beneficial to assess further what role each of the motives has and for what ages. Other issues also warrant attention. For example, in our study, the models in the ads were in their late teens or early adulthood. Future research might address the effects of younger models, as well as more ordinary-looking models, in ads. Another need is to assess whether the type of physical attractiveness is important.... Further, future research should incorporate the role of "esteem relevance" and "perceived control" to determine whether and to what extent those variables account for natural tendencies to have one motive rather than another. In addition, differential levels of esteem relevance and perceived control may lead to different types and levels of responses. For example, cognitive responses (e.g., self-perceptions) may differ from affective responses (e.g., self-esteem) after comparisons with models in ads, which may help to explain the inconsistent results found here and in similar studies.

Finally, some researchers have acknowledged that the minimal effects or lack of effects found in studies assessing temporary changes in self-perceptions or self-esteem may differ from what may be found in the long term. Thornton and Moore concluded that "with long-term comparisons such as this, particularly with the pervasive presence of idealized media images in our culture and the continued, and perhaps increasing, emphasis placed on physical appearance, there exists the potential for bringing about more significant and lasting changes in the self-concept." The motive of self-improvement, however, represents a unique situation in that temporary changes may differ from the long-term changes. When one commonly compares oneself to advertising models for self-improvement, one may eventually realize that the ideal is not as attainable as originally believed. . . .

Given the criticisms of advertising based on its cultural and social consequences, a better understanding of the role of comparison motives and the other issues mentioned here is needed. Such understanding may lead to a unified effort by educators to help prevent detrimental effects on female preadolescents and adolescents. However, a unified effort by educators may not be enough, and a call for legislation to control the use of models in advertising may arise in response to consumer movements such as Boycott Anorexic Marketing (BAM). Advertising researchers must respond with studies to determine more clearly the unintended consequences of advertising.

Michelle Cottle

 **NO**

Turning Boys into Girls

I love *Men's Health* Magazine. There. I'm out of the closet, and I'm not ashamed. Sure, I know what some of you are thinking: What self-respecting '90s woman could embrace a publication that runs such enlightened articles as "Turn Your Good Girl Bad" and "How to Wake Up Next to a One-Night Stand"? Or maybe you'll smile and wink knowingly: What red-blooded hetero chick *wouldn't* love all those glossy photo spreads of buff young beefcake in various states of undress, rippled abs and glutes flexed so tightly you could bounce a check on them? Either way you've got the wrong idea. My affection for *Men's Health* is driven by pure gender politics—by the realization that this magazine, and a handful of others like it, are leveling the playing field in a way that *Ms.* can only dream of. With page after page of bulging biceps and Gillette jaws, robust hairlines and silken skin, *Men's Health* is peddling a standard of male beauty as unforgiving and unrealistic as the female version sold by those dewy-eyed pre-teen waifs draped across the covers of *Glamour* and *Elle*. And with a variety of helpful features on "Foods That Fight Fat," "Banish Your Potbelly," and "Save Your Hair (Before it's Too Late)," *Men's Health* is well on its way to making the male species as insane, insecure, and irrational about physical appearance as any *Cosmo* girl.

Don't you see, ladies? We've been going about this equality business all wrong. Instead of battling to get society fixated on something besides our breast size, we should have been fighting spandex with spandex. Bra burning was a nice gesture, but the greater justice is in convincing our male counterparts that the key to their happiness lies in a pair of made-for-him Super Shaper Briefs with the optional "fly front endowment pad" (as advertised in *Men's Journal,* $29.95 plus shipping and handling). Make the men as neurotic about the circumference of their waists and the whiteness of their smiles as the women, and at least the burden of vanity and self-loathing will be shared by all.

This is precisely what lads' mags like *Men's Health* are accomplishing. The rugged John-Wayne days when men scrubbed their faces with deodorant soap and viewed gray hair and wrinkles as a badge of honor are fading. Last year, international market analyst Euromonitor placed the U.S. men's toiletries market —hair color, skin moisturizer, tooth whiteners, etc.—at $3.5 billion. According to a survey conducted by DYG researchers for *Men's Health* in November 1996, approximately 20 percent of American men get manicures or pedicures, 18 percent use skin treatments such as masks or mud packs, and 10 percent enjoy professional facials. That same month, *Psychology Today* reported that a poll by Roper Starch Worldwide showed that "6 percent of men nationwide actually use such traditionally female products as bronzers and foundation to create the illusion of a youthful appearance."

What men are putting *on* their bodies, however, is nothing compared to what they're doing *to* their bodies: While in the 1980s only an estimated one in 10 plastic surgery patients were men, as of 1996, that ratio had shrunk to one in five. The American Academy of Cosmetic Surgery estimates that nationwide more than 690,000 men had cosmetic procedures performed in '96, the most recent year for which figures are available. And we're not just talking "hair restoration" here, though such procedures do command the lion's share of the male market. We're also seeing an increasing number of men shelling out mucho dinero for face peels, liposuction, collagen injections, eyelid lifts, chin tucks, and, of course, the real man's answer to breast implants: penile enlargements (now available to increase both length and diameter).

Granted, *Men's Health* and its journalistic cousins (*Men's Journal, Details, GQ,* etc.) cannot take all the credit for this breakthrough in gender parity. The fashion and glamour industries have perfected the art of creating consumer "needs," and with the women's market pretty much saturated, men have become the obvious target for the purveyors of everything from lip balm to lycra. Meanwhile, advances in medical science have made cosmetic surgery a quicker, cleaner option for busy executives (just as the tight fiscal leash of managed care is driving more and more doctors toward this cash-based specialty). Don't have several weeks to recover from a full-blown facelift? No problem. For a few hundred bucks you can get a micro-dermabrasion face peel on your lunch hour.

Then there are the underlying social factors. With women growing ever more financially independent, aspiring suitors are discovering that they must bring more to the table than a well-endowed wallet if they expect to win (and keep) the fair maiden. Nor should we overlook the increased market power of the gay population—in general a more image-conscious lot than straight guys. But perhaps most significant is the ongoing, ungraceful descent into middle age by legions of narcissistic baby boomers. Gone are the days when the elder statesmen of this demographic bulge could see themselves in the relatively youthful faces of those insipid yuppies on "Thirtysomething." Increasingly, boomers are finding they have more in common with the *parents* of today's TV, movie, and sports stars. Everywhere they turn some upstart Gen Xer is flaunting his youthful vitality, threatening boomer dominance on both the social and professional fronts. (Don't think even Hollywood didn't shudder when the Oscar for best original screenplay this year went to a couple of guys barely old enough to shave.) With whippersnappers looking to steal everything from their jobs to their women, post-pubescent men have at long last discovered the terror of losing their springtime radiance.

Whatever combo of factors is feeding the frenzy of male vanity, magazines such as *Men's Health* provide the ideal meeting place for men's insecurities and marketers' greed. Like its more established female counterparts, *Men's Health* is an affordable, efficient delivery vehicle for the message that physical imperfection, age, and an underdeveloped fashion sense are potentially crippling disabilities. And as with women's mags, this cycle of insanity is self-perpetuating: The more men obsess about growing old or unattractive, the more marketers will exploit and expand that fear; the more marketers bombard men with messages about the need to be beautiful, the more they will obsess. Younger and younger men will be sucked into the vortex of self-doubt. Since 1990, *Men's Health* has seen its paid circulation rise from 250,000 to more than 1.5 million; the magazine estimates that half of its 5.3 million readers are under age 35 and 46 percent are married. And while most major magazines have suffered sluggish growth or even a decline in circulation in recent years, during the first half of 1997, *Men's Health* saw its paid circulation increase 14 percent over its '96 figures. (Likewise, its smaller, more outdoorsy relative, Wenner Media's *Men's Journal*, enjoyed an even bigger jump of 26.5 percent.) At this rate, one day soon, that farcical TV commercial featuring men hanging out in bars, whining about having inherited their mothers' thighs will be a reality. Now *that's* progress.

Vanity, Thy Name Is Man

Everyone wants to be considered attractive and desirable. And most of us are aware that, no matter how guilty and shallow we feel about it, there are certain broad cultural norms that define attractive. Not surprisingly, both men's and women's magazines have argued that, far from playing on human insecurities, they are merely helping readers be all that they can be—a kind of training camp for the image impaired. In recent years, such publications have embraced the tenets of "evolutionary biology," which argue that, no matter how often we're told that beauty is only skin deep, men and women are hard-wired to prefer the Jack Kennedys and Sharon Stones to the Rodney Dangerfields and Janet Renos. Continuation of the species demands that specimens with shiny coats, bright eyes, even features, and other visible signs of ruddy good health and fertility automatically kick-start our most basic instinct. Of course, the glamour mags' editors have yet to explain why, in evolutionary terms, we would ever desire adult women to stand 5'10" and weigh 100 pounds. Stories abound of women starving themselves to the point that their bodies shut down and they stop menstruating—hardly conducive to reproduction—yet Kate Moss remains the dish du jour and millions of Moss wannabes still struggle to subsist on a diet of Dexatrim and Perrier.

   Similarly, despite its title, *Men's Health* is hawking far more than general fitness or a healthful lifestyle. For every half page of advice on how to cut your stress level, there are a dozen pages on how to build your biceps. For every update on the dangers of cholesterol, there are multiple warnings on the horrors of flabby abs. Now, without question, gorging on Cheetos and Budweiser while your rump takes root on the sofa is no way to treat your body if you plan on living past 50. But chugging protein drinks, agonizing over fat grams, and counting the minutes until your next Stairmaster session is equally unbalanced.

The line between taking pride in one's physical appearance and being obsessed by it is a fine one—and one that disappeared for many women long ago.

Now with lads' mags taking men in that direction as well, in many cases it's almost impossible to tell whether you're reading a copy of *Men's Health* or of *Mademoiselle:* "April 8. To commemorate Buddha's birthday, hit a Japanese restaurant. Stick to low-fat selections. Choose foods described as *yakimono,* which means "grilled," advised the monthly "to do list" in the April *Men's Health*. (Why readers should go Japanese in honor of the most famous religious leader in *India's* history remains unclear.) The January/February list was equally thought provoking: "January 28. It's Chinese New Year, so make a resolution to custom-order your next takeout. Ask that they substitute wonton soup broth for oil. Try the soba noodles instead of plain noodles. They're richer in nutrients and contain much less fat." The issue also featured a "Total Body Workout Poster" and one of those handy little "substitution" charts (loathed by women everywhere), showing men how to slash their calorie intake by making a few minor dietary substitutions: mustard for mayo, popcorn for peanuts, seltzer water for soda, pretzels for potato chips....

As in women's magazines, fast results with minimum inconvenience is a central theme. Among *Men's Health's* March highlights were a guide to "Bigger Biceps in 2 Weeks," and "20 Fast Fixes" for a bad diet; April offered "A Better Body in Half the Time," along with a colorful four-page spread on "50 Snacks That Won't Make You Fat." And you can forget carrot sticks—this think-thin eating guide celebrated the wonders of Reduced Fat Cheez-its, Munch 'Ems, Fiddle Faddle, Oreos, Teddy Grahams, Milky Ways, Bugles, Starburst Fruit Twists, and Klondike's Fat Free Big Bear Ice Cream Sandwiches. Better nutrition is not the primary issue. A better butt is. To this end, also found in the pages of *Men's Health* is the occasional, tasteful ad for liposuction—just in case nature doesn't cooperate.

But a blueprint to rock-hard buns is only part of what makes *Men's Health* the preeminent "men's lifestyle" magazine. Nice teeth, nice skin, nice hair, and a red-hot wardrobe are now required to round out the ultimate alpha male package, and *Men's Health* is there to help on all fronts. In recent months it has run articles on how to select, among other items, the perfect necktie and belt, the hippest wallet, the chicest running gear, the best "hair-thickening" shampoo, and the cutest golfing apparel. It has also offered advice on how to retard baldness, how to keep your footwear looking sharp, how to achieve different "looks" with a patterned blazer, even how to keep your lips from chapping at the dentist's office: "[B]efore you start all that 'rinse and spit' business, apply some moisturizer to your face and some lip balm to your lips. Your face and lips won't have that stretched-out dry feeling... Plus, you'll look positively radiant!"

While a desire to look good for their hygienists may be enough to spur some men to heed the magazine's advice (and keep 'em coming back for more), fear and insecurity about the alternatives are generally more effective motivators. For those who don't get with the *Men's Health* program, there must be the threat of ridicule. By far the least subtle example of this is the free subscriptions for "guys who need our help" periodically announced in the front section of the magazine. April's dubious honoree was actor Christopher Walken:

> Chris, we love the way you've perfected that psycho persona. But now you're taking your role in "Things to Do in Denver When You're Dead" way too seriously with that ghostly pale face, the "where's the funeral?" black clothes, and a haircut that looks like the work of a hasty undertaker.... Dab on a little Murad Murasun Self-Tanner ($21)... For those creases in your face, try Ortho Dermatologicals' Renova, a prescription anti-wrinkle cream that contains tretinoin, a form of vitamin A. Then, find a barber.

Or how about the March "winner," basketball coach Bobby Knight: "Bob, your trademark red sweater is just a billboard for your potbelly. A darker solid color would make you look slimmer. Also, see 'The Tale of Two Bellies' in our February 1998 issue, and try to drop a few pounds. Then the next time you throw a sideline tantrum, at least people won't say, 'look at the crazy *fat* man.' "

Just as intense as the obsession with appearance that men's (and women's) magazines breed are the sexual neuroses they feed. And if one of the ostensible goals of women's mags is to help women drive men wild, what is the obvious corollary objective for men's magazines? To get guys laid—well and often. As if men needed any encouragement to fixate on the subject, *Men's Health* is chock full of helpful "how-tos" such as, "Have Great Sex Every Day Until You Die" and "What I Learned From My Sex Coach," as well as more cursory explorations of why men with larger testicles have more sex ("Why Big Boys Don't Cry"), how to maintain orgasm intensity as you age ("Be one of the geysers"), and how to achieve stronger erections by eating certain foods ("Bean counters make better lovers"). And for those having trouble even getting to the starting line, last month's issue offered readers a chance to "Win free love lessons."

The High Price of Perfection

Having elevated men's physical and sexual insecurities to the level of grand paranoia, lads' mags can then get down to what really matters: moving merchandise. On the cover of *Men's Health* each month, in small type just above the magazine's title, appears the phrase "Tons of useful stuff." Thumbing through an issue or two, however, one quickly realizes that a more accurate description would read: "Tons of expensive stuff." They're all there: Ralph Lauren, Tommy Hilfiger, Paul Mitchell, Calvin Klein, Clinique, Armani, Versace, Burberrys, Nautica, Nike, Omega, Rogaine, The Better Sex Video Series.... The magazine even has those annoying little perfume strips guaranteed to make your nose run and to alienate everyone within a five-mile radius of you.

Masters of psychology, marketers wheel out their sexiest pitches and hottest male models to tempt/intimidate the readership of *Men's Health*. Not since the last casting call for "Baywatch" has a more impressive display of firm, tanned, young flesh appeared in one spot. And just like in women's magazines, the articles themselves are designed to sell stuff. All those helpful tips on choosing blazers, ties, and belts come complete with info on the who, where, and how much. The strategy is brilliant: Make men understand exactly how far short of the ideal they fall, and they too become vulnerable to the lure of high-priced underwear, cologne, running shoes, workout gear, hair dye, hair strengthener, skin softener, body-fat monitors, suits, boots, energy bars, and sex aids. As Mark Jannot, the grooming and health editor for *Men's Journal,* told "Today" show host Matt Lauer in January, "This is a huge, booming market. I mean, the marketers have found a group of people that are ripe for the picking. Men are finally learning that aging is a disease." Considering how effectively *Men's Health* fosters this belief, it's hardly surprising that the magazine has seen its ad pages grow 510 percent since 1991 and has made it onto *Adweek's* 10 Hottest Magazines list three of the last five years.

To make all this "girly" image obsession palatable to their audience, lads' mags employ all their creative energies to transform appearance issues into "a guy thing." *Men's Health* tries to cultivate a joking, macho tone throughout ("Eat Like Brando and Look Like Rambo" or "Is my tallywhacker shrinking?") and tosses in a handful of Y-chromosome teasers such as "How to Stay Out of Jail," "How to Clean Your Whole Apartment in One Hour or Less," and my personal favorite, "Let's Play Squash," an illustrated guide to identifying the bug-splat patterns on your windshield. Instead of a regular advice columnist, which would smack too much of chicks' magazines, *Men's Health* recently introduced "Jimmy the Bartender," a monthly column on "women, sex, and other stuff that screws up men's lives."

It appears that, no matter how much clarifying lotion and hair gel you're trying to sell them, men must never suspect that you think they share women's insecurities. If you want a man to buy wrinkle cream, marketers have learned, you better pitch it as part of a comfortingly macho shaving regimen. Aramis, for example, assures men that its popular Lift Off! Moisture Formula with alpha hydroxy will help cut their shave time by one-third. "The biggest challenge for products started for women is how to transfer them to men," explained George Schaeffer, the president of OPI cosmetics, in the November issue of *Soap-Cosmetics-Chemical Specialties.* Schaeffer's Los Angeles-based company is the maker of Matte Nail Envy, and unobtrusive nail polish that's proved a hit with men. And for the more adventuresome shopper, last year Hard Candy cosmetics introduced a line of men's nail enamel, called Candy Man, that targets guys with such studly colors as Gigolo (metallic black) and Testosterone (gunmetal silver).

On a larger scale, positioning a makeover or trip to the liposuction clinic as a smart career move seems to help men rationalize their image obsession. "Whatever a man's cosmetic shortcoming, it's apt to be a career liability," noted Alan Farnham in a September 1996 issue of *Fortune.* "The business world is prejudiced against the ugly." Or how about *Forbes'* sad attempt to differentiate between male and female vanity in its Dec. 1 piece on cosmetic surgery: "Plastic surgery is more of a cosmetic thing for women. They have a thing about aging. For men it's an investment that pays a pretty good dividend." Whatever you say, guys.

The irony is rich and bittersweet. Gender equity is at last headed our way —not in the form of women being less obsessed with looking like Calvin Klein models, but of men becoming hysterical over the first signs of crows feet. Gradually, guys are no longer pumping up and primping simply to get babes, but because they feel it's something everyone expects them to do. Women, after all, do not spend $400 on Dolce & Gabbana sandals to impress their boyfriends, most of whom don't know Dolce & Gabbana from Beavis & Butthead (yet). They buy them to impress other women—and because that's what society says they should want to do. Most guys haven't yet achieved this level of insanity, but with grown men catcalling the skin tone and wardrobe of other grown men (Christopher Walken, Bobby Knight) for a readership of still more grown men, can the gender's complete surrender to the vanity industry be far behind?

The ad for *Men's Health* web site says it all: "Don't click here unless you want to look a decade younger... lose that beer belly... be a better lover... and more! Men's Health Online: The Internet site For Regular Guys." Of course, between the magazine's covers there's not a "regular guy" to be found, save for the occasional snapshot of one of the publication's writers or editors—usually taken from a respectable distance. The moist young bucks in the Gap jeans ads and the electric-eyed Armani models have exactly as much in common with the average American man as Tyra Banks does with the average American woman. Which would be fine, if everyone seemed to understand this distinction. Until they do, however, I guess my consolation will have to be the image of thousands of once-proud men, having long scorned women's insecurities, lining up for their laser peels and trying to squeeze their middle-aged asses into a snug set of Super Shaper Briefs—with the optional fly front endowment pad, naturally.

POSTSCRIPT

Is Emphasis on Body Image in the Media Harmful to Females Only?

The selections by Martin and Gentry and by Cottle contain negative criticism about advertising, but they also suggest that age affects how susceptible people are to different aspects of advertising images. While one selection focuses on girls at a time in their lives when their bodies are changing, the second selection indicates that adult males, too, can be highly influenced by the images they see and by what seems to be a preoccupation with youth.

These selections also raise questions about the magazine industry and the hypersegmentation by market. If people's tastes and choices of media are being met by a wider variety of specialized publications (or even lifestyle TV channels, such as ESPN or Lifetime), perhaps there is a shift in the idea of a "mass audience." This concept has traditionally meant that the audience was characterized by homogeneity. Perhaps now the audience is less characterized by a sameness, but the content of the media may suggest a "homogenized" ideal for the different groups that make up the audience.

Standards of beauty and success are culturally defined. It is often interesting to pick up magazines or newspapers from other countries or ethnic groups and examine the images in ads to see if specific cultural differences are apparent.

There are many excellent references on the topics raised by this issue. John Tebbel and Mary Ellen Zuckerman have produced a history of magazines entitled *The Magazine in America, 1741–1990* (Oxford University Press, 1991). Books like Naomi Wolf's *The Beauty Myth* (Anchor Books, 1992) and Julia T. Wood's *Gendered Lives: Communication, Gender, and Culture* (Wadsworth, 1994) are particularly insightful regarding the images of women and minorities.

Some videotapes are also available for extended discussion, such as Jeanne Kilbourne's *Still Killing Us Softly* and *Slim Hopes* (Media Education Foundation).

ISSUE 4

Are Newspapers Insensitive to Minorities?

YES: Ruth Shalit, from "Race in the Newsroom," *The New Republic* (October 2, 1995)

NO: Leonard Downie, Jr. and Donald Graham, from "Race in the Newsroom: An Exchange," *The New Republic* (October 16, 1995)

ISSUE SUMMARY

YES: Ruth Shalit, a reporter for *The New Republic,* argues that inaccurate coverage of minority news and the treatment of minority news staff at some places are a form of racism. She focuses on the *Washington Post* as an extreme example of this activity.

NO: Executive editor Leonard Downie, Jr., and publisher Donald Graham of the *Washington Post* respond to Shalit's charges. They argue that their newspaper has achieved a higher standard of minority reporting and employment than Shalit claims.

As you will see by the following selections, minority representation in employment and the type of coverage a major newspaper provides for its readers present a controversial and problematic issue. Ruth Shalit makes several claims that seem to reflect poorly on the management of the *Washington Post,* but Leonard Downie, Jr., and Donald Graham's response shows that there are clashing views on the realities of minority representation within an organization. Similarly, because the *Washington Post* serves a community largely populated by minorities, one might expect to see some sensitivity reflected in its local news reporting. Shalit's original report elicited a response from Downie and Graham that points to the different realities presented by the conflict.

This subject is an important one because it asks us to consider the effectiveness of affirmative action, including what the term *diversity* means and how it might best be realized. As you read the selections, ask yourself whether the authors are demonstrating a bias or whether the "facts" speak for themselves. How does one know when an action is taken in bad faith or when a well-intentioned action has unintended negative consequences for someone?

The topics raised in this issue are relevant to almost any large organization that is attempting to reflect the interests of minority groups that more accurately represent the demographics of a community or of the nation. Media organizations have been highly criticized over the years for not responding to the needs of minorities, and the actions they have taken have provided high-profile examples of leadership in some cases and insensitivity in others. Because so many of these cases are presented to the public by other forms of media (in this case, the liberal *Washington Post* newspaper, critiqued by a reporter from the conservative *New Republic* magazine), some ideological posturing may also be present. Should these types of critiques also be treated objectively and without bias, or is it possible to maintain such a position under such circumstances?

You will probably find many aspects of organizational and social issues to explore as you read these selections. You may wish to explore other case studies in media ownership and the images with regard to different social groups. While some of the specific cases reflect changing demographics, an emphasis on different forms of media, or regulatory measures that have affected minority ownership and/or representation, all present constant struggles in the media landscape.

Ruth Shalit

 **YES**

Race in the Newsroom

If any organization could justify racial preferences as restitution for past sins, it would be *The Washington Post*. As the monopoly daily in a majority-black city, the paper had compelling reason to diversify what had been an overwhelmingly white newsroom. Twenty-five years ago, the *Post*—like most newspapers—was a largely white, middle-class bastion. There were no black assignment editors, no black foreign correspondents, no black reporters on the National staff: And its paternalism toward the black community was legendary. In 1950, for example, Publisher Philip Graham famously agreed to suppress news of a race riot in exchange for a promise by authorities to integrate the city's swimming pools.

In 1972, a contingent of black reporters, including the pathbreaking journalists Herbert Denton and Leon Dash, filed a complaint with the EEOC [Equal Employment Opportunity Commission] alleging they were victims of a racially discriminatory glass ceiling. Under an informal agreement, the paper grudgingly stepped up minority hiring, installing a black reporter on its National desk and bringing aboard several black sportswriters. If the *Post* was at first reluctant in its embrace of diversity, it soon got with the program. In the mid-'80s, the paper redoubled its affirmative action efforts following the publication of several internal reports lamenting the slow pace of integration. By 1986, the *Post* had hired its first full-time minority recruiter and set new, more aggressive affirmative action goals: one out of every four hires had to be a minority, and one out of every two a woman.

Over the years, these diversity efforts have been propelled by a peculiar series of racial psychodramas. On September 28, 1980, the paper ran the now-notorious story of "Jimmy," an 8-year-old heroin addict. Although written by a 26-year-old black reporter, Janet Cooke, the piece dripped with racial innuendo. Heroin, Jimmy supposedly told Cooke, "be real different from herb. That's baby s—. Don't nobody here hardly ever smoke no herb. You can't hardly get none right now anyway." The accompanying drawing featured a dazed-looking young man, his scrawny arm gripped by a giant fist as a needle is inserted. Black readers, including Mayor Marion Barry, immediately denounced the Pulitzer Prize–winning story as racist and preposterous; but the *Post* defended it almost to the end. When it was exposed as a hoax, the paper was mortified.

Then there was the infamous magazine incident. In 1986, the *Post* endured a prolonged black boycott after the debut issue of its Sunday magazine featured a cover story about a black murder suspect, along with a column by Richard Cohen about white jewelry-store owners who, fearing robbery, refused to buzz young black men into their stores. Hundreds of black protesters, led by talk-show host Cathy Hughes, dumped thousands of copies of the magazine, some in flames, on the steps of the *Post*'s building on 15th Street. They repeated the ceremony every Sunday for thirteen weeks, stopping only after *Post* Publisher Donald Graham apologized and agreed to a series of appearances on Hughes's talk show.

The Cooke and magazine incidents, says Managing Editor Robert Kaiser, were "the product of a different newspaper." And, indeed, there's no question that the *Post* has, over the years, benefited greatly from its enhanced racial and sexual representativeness. "When all of our staff came from the same background, we missed what was going on," says Downie, who argues persuasively that a diverse staff is necessary to covering a diverse community.

Yet it is also true that, after a decade of determined diversity hiring, something at newspapers in general, and the *Post* in particular, has gone wrong. According to advocacy groups such as the National Association of Black Journalists (NABJ), a rising tide of racial prejudice is washing over America's newsrooms. In *Muted Voices,* the NABJ's 1994 Print Task Force report, the authors write that their findings are "indicative of despair.... Black journalists are strangling with their pain." Much of this pain, however, seems to be caused less by old-fashioned bigotry than by a sort of post-affirmative action racism. "[T]he idea that an African-American has been hired because of a political agenda of management or external pressure [is] still alive," the report laments.

To hear *Muted Voices* tell it, black reporters and their (mostly white) bosses are living in different worlds. While two-thirds of black journalists surveyed by NABJ said newsroom managers are not committed to retaining and promoting blacks, 94 percent of managers say they are. Ninety-two percent of the managers say promotion standards are the same for blacks and whites; 59 percent of black journalists say they think blacks have to meet *higher* standards.

At the *Post,* tensions are running particularly high. "A great deal of babbling goes on here about diversity," says National reporter John Goshko. "Nobody is happy. Many of the older white males feel that they are being discriminated against. Many minorities, particularly blacks, feel discriminated against. Each side will give you chapter and verse." White reporters, especially white middle-aged males, have become increasingly hostile to racial preferences. "We used to say: 'Let's go out and get the best guy in the world,'" says columnist Richard Harwood, the *Post*'s former deputy managing editor. " 'Let's get the best, without regard to anything else.' If there is, over time, a policy of giving considerable preference on the basis of color, your standards change. And I think that's the problem we're facing."

Not surprisingly, the *Post*'s minority journalists see things quite differently. Far from coddling them, they say, the *Post* has ensured that for reporters of color the path of upward mobility is treacherous. Like Alice and the Red Queen, they must run twice as hard merely to stay in place. "You see a glass ceiling slowly turning into lead," says Metro reporter Ruben Castaneda. "You realize there's no future." "Everyone in management has good intentions," says Gary Lee, a black reporter on the *Post*'s National staff. "But there's an entrenched newsroom culture that doesn't change." Even the Asian Americans are grumpy and radicalized. "Some [Asian reporters] think it's not a very welcoming atmosphere," says Metro reporter Spencer Hsu. "There are issues of mentoring and racial typing that can have a significant impact on our careers."

"It is a paradox," muses Assistant Managing Editor David Ignatius, "that this liberal institution that professes to care deeply about the community has a bad reputation in the African American community and has had some very unhappy African American staffers." In the past five years alone, fifteen black reporters have quit the paper. Some of the departed have written biting accounts of their time at the *Post*. In her 1993 memoir, *Volunteer Slavery*, former *Post* reporter Jill Nelson argues that racial insensitivity at the paper shattered her self-esteem and stymied her career....

❧

These portrayals of the *Post* as a hotbed of racial iniquity have devastated the paper's top executives—Executive Editor Downie, Managing Editor Kaiser and Deputy Managing Editor Michael Getler. Children of the '60s all, they feel impelled to diversify not only because of legal and political pressures but because of personal inclination and social conscience. "There is a moral dimension to this," says Kaiser. "We've learned a lot, we white guys, in the last twenty or twenty-five years or so." ...

In 1993, the *Post* commissioned an internal task force on newsroom life, headed by Getler, then the paper's assistant managing editor for Foreign News. For five months, Getler roamed the newsroom, trying to find out why, as one reporter he spoke to put it, "Very few people appear to be happy, most seem afraid." At the end of his labors he issued a ninety-page study, henceforth referred to as the Getler report.

The report, Getler wrote in the introduction, was "a growl from the belly of the *Post.*" What people growled about mostly was race. Black staffers accused the *Post* of harboring a bias against them:

> Racial and ethnic minority staffers say the *Post* is not doing what it can, and should, by them.... Many African-Americans complained that, to be given good stories or challenging beats, they must work harder than whites at the same experience level....

At the same time, white staffers said they felt threatened by the *Post*'s rigid hiring targets. "One editor offered a common reaction," wrote Getler. " 'When you start to push for more black editors and more women, and maybe a few gays, the middle-aged straight white male is the last one you're going to worry about.' "

Getler and the other members of the *Post*'s diversity task force concluded the report by calling for the appointment of a deputy managing editor to oversee diversity issues. "Our group feels strongly," Getler wrote, "that the new person must be the third-ranking editor in the newsroom, with authority from the executive editor and the managing editor to make things happen." The job went to Getler. "I was surprised," he says modestly.

A friendly, approachable man who spent many years as a reporter and editor before becoming the *Post*'s diversity czar, Getler now spends his days patrolling the newsroom, blasting stereotypes and preaching inclusion. "There is racism, whether it's conscious or unconscious," he explains. "Most people say, 'Me? I'm not a racist. I'm a nice guy.' But you can have attitudes that you're not even aware of." Getler has set about remedying those attitudes. "The *Post*," he says, "is a very candid place. It's not defensive about itself. It's a place where you can say anything you want.... It's a place that lays open its warts in order to fix them." . . .

Kevin Merida, a lanky and dashing black reporter with a soft voice and easygoing manner, laughs out loud at the suggestion that minority journalists are being hired and promoted ahead of schedule. "The biggest myth in journalism," he calls it. To the contrary, he says, the newspaper business brutally limits the aspirations of African Americans. "A little light is always going on in your head," he says. "There's a general sense of feeling, somehow, that your value, your worth, is not completely taken into account." He says, "There's a sense that you're not valued as you would like to be valued."

Merida's consternation is puzzling to white reporters. The *Post*'s National staff is tiny, the waiting list, endless. But Merida didn't have to slug it out at the bottom in Metro with everybody else. After being lured away from *The Dallas Morning News,* where he was an assistant managing editor, he was immediately dispatched to the National desk. He's got what would seem a plum job, covering Congress and the '96 campaign. Moreover, he has the latitude and standing to pursue stories of special interest to him. "I'm a black man," he says. "The black experience is part of who I am. And I try to incorporate that in my coverage." Merida cites three recent examples: a sympathetic profile of embattled senator Carol Moseley-Braun; a story criticizing the art in the Capitol as colonialist and lacking in racial diversity; and a story about how the Senate had condemned Khalid Muhammad for his statements about Jews, yet seemed to be holding Senator Ernest Hollings, who disparaged "African potentates," to a different standard.

Merida's insecurity about his position in the newsroom may, more than anything else, be a function of the tokenist assumption—the suspicion that he got his job because he was black. At *The Dallas Morning News,* Merida advanced from reporter to AME [Assistant Managing Editor] in one fell swoop, a precipitous promotion that has dogged him all the way to Washington. "Have you ever heard of that happening in the entire history of the news business?" asks one white *Post* reporter. "There's supposed to be a very clear path. It's like being a private, and suddenly you're a general." It's the classic plight of the affirmative-action baby, whose genuine accomplishments are tainted by a preferential system beyond his control.

∼✦∼

The *Post's* diversity goals have spawned a burgeoning bureaucracy administered by Jeanne Fox-Alston, director of hiring and recruiting. In 1986, she was plucked off the *Post's* graphics desk and instructed to revamp the paper's personnel office so that, in her words, it "focused more on women and minorities." These days, one of her tasks is to winnow out white males, some of whom she regards as having an overly developed sense of entitlement. "Some of them have had some really good stories," she says. Fox-Alston is a small, reedy woman in her early 40s, with a gray topknot and the tight, pursed mouth you see on the assistant principal. "They've put their years in. Maybe they've even won awards. And they see people being hired who perhaps don't have as much experience as they do. Why?" Mockingly, Fox-Alston's voice keens into the upper register. " 'It must be because I'm a white male,' " she whines. "Well, there's more to it than that." Fox-Alston elaborates. "There's one guy from a New Orleans paper who's been trying to get hired here for quite a while. And he wrote the deputy managing editor a letter, saying, 'Friends at the *Post* tell me the only reason I haven't been hired is because I'm a white man.' Now, in talking to the deputy managing editor about this particular candidate, I said, 'Well, it's true that on his résumé he has some good experience and stuff like that. But you know, he's terribly annoying, and he's not as good as he thinks.' " Fox-Alston leans back in satisfaction. "He didn't get hired." ...

∼✦∼

... [D]iversity training may not be sufficient to stem the current white backlash against affirmative action, which sometimes bubbles over into pure racial animosity. In my discussions with white reporters and editors, I was surprised to hear many of them question, in the coarsest terms, the ability of their minority colleagues. "She can't write a lick," for example, or "He's dumb as a post." Or worse: "When she files, you literally don't understand what she's saying. And you have to go back to her again and again and ask: What are you trying to say?"

The ugliness of these sentiments suggests that covert racism may be simply inflamed by the push for diversity. But at the *Post,* the explosive interaction of aggressive hiring with instinctive white anxiety has given such feelings a pretext. Even President Clinton acknowledges that federal law requires that minorities be hired from the relevant pool of qualified applicants, not in proportion to their population in society at large. In other words, the *Post's* goal—to reproduce in its building the precise ethnic makeup of its community—is not only irrational but arguably illegal. "The concept of diversity begins with the idea that a newspaper's staff and coverage should reflect the racial, gender and ethnic makeup of its market," concludes the Getler report. But to comply with the Supreme Court's standards, the *Post* should instead be tailoring its goals to the pool of qualified aspiring journalists. According to *The Chronicle of Higher Education,* blacks and Hispanics compose 10.6 percent of the available pool of college graduates; within that group, the pool of students expressing an interest in communications is a mere 13 percent. Even without making allowances for the *Post*'s attempt to skim off the best people from the best schools, the attempt to mirror the 32.3 percent of blacks and Hispanics in metropolitan Washington itself seems flamboyantly unrealistic.

In 1994, the paper made thirty-eight new hires. Of those thirty-eight, ten were members of minority groups. "Our goal for about the past eight years has been that at least a quarter of our hires be people of color," says Fox-Alston. In pursuing this goal in spite of a minuscule pool, the *Post* has committed itself to a course of quite extraordinary affirmative action; and so the complaints about compromising standards, while undoubtedly overstated by aggrieved white reporters, are corroborated by the stark numerical reality....

Many reporters, meanwhile, resent being viewed as walking monuments to the paper's virtue. "I worked the night police," says Carlos Sanchez, who left the paper in 1994 and is now working at *The Fort Worth Star-Telegram.* "I had nothing to do with the Hispanic community unless they were killed. One evening I show up for work. And [Metro Editor] Milton Coleman is there, conveying his apologies for not informing me prior to that evening that I needed to attend a formal dinner with him. I wasn't dressed for dinner. I was extremely uncomfortable.... But I went." To Sanchez's chagrin, the dinner turned out to be a love-in with local Hispanic community leaders at a Salvadoran restaurant. "I found myself kinda being showcased," he says. "That bothered me."

... Consider the case of Leon Dash—a driven, brilliant journalist who has long concentrated his reporting on the least attractive features of black Washington. In 1986, his exceptional *Post* series on the teenage pregnancy epidemic among inner-city black youths punctured the conventional liberal wisdom that the crisis of black teenage parents was simply one of ignorance about birth control. Dash was one of the first reporters to note that for underclass pubescent girls, "a child was a tangible achievement in otherwise dreary and empty lives."

In October of 1994, the *Post* devoted eight days to Dash's "Rosa Lee" series, which probed the intertwined pathologies of a three-generational family of black, welfare-dependent petty criminals. The riveting series examined the intractability of underclass poverty, crime and drug use across generations. It won Dash a Pulitzer. Many black *Post* reporters, however, read the series with dismay. "I didn't like the Rosa Lee stories," says Kevin Merida. "We spend too much time in journalism chronicling failure and despair. Is this what we have to do to win a prize? Write about black pathology? I just don't know what good a series like that does."

Black reporters' complaints about the series prompted an anguished round of brown-bag lunches and assemblies, in which top *Post* editors defended themselves against the charge of conspiring to besmirch the black community. Downie issued a flurry of penitent memos, promising to redouble his efforts to publish "solutions stories." Dash, meanwhile, has been made a newsroom pariah. "Since the series came out, black people at the *Post* have shunned me," he says. "They are still shunning me." Dash says the brown-bag lunches were unpleasant experiences for him. "People kept asking me, why didn't I focus on Rhodes scholars and college graduates? Why didn't I focus on people who have overcome these situations? Well, because those people aren't part of the generation that is trapped in this permanent underclass."

Unfortunately, reporters like Leon Dash may be a dying breed, given the climate of victimism and aggrievement that prevails in today's newsrooms. For a glimpse of the paper of the future, consider the fifty-eight-page instruction book on "Content Audits," published by the American Society of Newspaper Editors. The brochure instructs editors to map their coverage out on a grid and compute "total number items," "total minority items," "percent minority"; and to rate stories "P" for positive ("Shows minorities smiling [unless text contradicts smile], achieving, in respected role, etc."), "N for Negative" ("the old arrest shot or other negative roles") or just "Neutral." ("Daily life. Not bad or good.") To "reap the rewards of the audit," papers are urged to "develop a pool of senior-level minority editors who can sit in on news editorial meetings and flag insensitive stories or narrowly focused pictures."

At the *Post*, the commandment to avoid offense at all costs dovetails conveniently with a long history of timorousness about racial matters. Over the years, for example, the paper has taken many hits for its tortured coverage of Mayor Marion Barry. Though the *Post* pleaded Barry's case in three glowing editorial endorsements—in '78, '82 and '86—Barry continues to pillory the paper as part of a white conspiracy to harass him. Then, of course, there's the '86 magazine boycott, the impact of which should not be underestimated. "I've come across a number of stories in my career where that incident was mentioned," says one *Post* reporter. " 'Change this, tone this down, do this, do that.' There is a feeling that if we say anything more complex than 'The sun rises in the East,' we step in shit."

In a memo circulated in December to the paper's editors, Joann Byrd, the *Post*'s ombudsman, elaborated on this theme. "The distance between the paper and many in the black community is an enormous and difficult challenge for the *Post*," she wrote. "It is the prism through which a huge segment of the population sees all the paper's reporting—and judges it to be indifferent or racist." Byrd's concerns were reflected in the Getler report, which concluded that one of the best ways to ensure responsible minority coverage was "to have minority editors to help steer us in a positive direction in our coverage of issues involving minorities." ...

⁕⟨⊙⟩⁕

After encountering the racial strife at *The Washington Post*, it's tempting to despair that major American institutions will ever achieve both racial integration and racial harmony. If the *Post*, which tries so hard and means so well, is failing so dramatically to achieve its goals, what hope is there for the rest of us?

"When racial things come up in this newsroom, we should talk about them," says Len Downie. "We should not run away from them. We ought to talk about them." In fact, the more everyone talks, the worse everyone feels. "It's a truism in this world of diversity training that things get worse before they get better," says David Ignatius hopefully. "And maybe that's what we're seeing. When people are talking about issues that are really painful, you're not going to hear violins start playing."

By focusing obsessively on the ideals and the instruments of diversity, by exhorting its staff to reflect endlessly on their own resentments, the *Post* is ensuring that the resentments will never be transcended.

Leonard Downie, Jr.
and Donald Graham

 **NO**

Race in the Newsroom:
An Exchange

Leonard Downie Jr., Executive Editor

To the editors:

In her polemic against diversity at *The Washington Post,* Ruth Shalit purports to be concerned that our efforts to diversify our newsroom staff may compromise our journalistic standards. In fact, Shalit's article demonstrates a shameful absence of journalistic standards on the part of *The New Republic* and Shalit herself.

She uses the maddening technique of big-lie propaganda to misrepresent how we work in our newsroom and how we cover the news. Fact, falsehood, rumor and quotes wrested out of context are laced together with the author's ideological preconceptions. This presents a misleadingly distorted, single-dimensional view of our complex, competitive, free-wheeling, outspoken newsroom.

Shalit herself signals her own controlling bias when she asserts that "if editors refuse to adjust their traditional hiring standards, they will end up with a nearly all-white staff"—presumably more like that of the magazine for which she works. Her assertion is as unfounded as it is ugly. We have not adjusted standards in any way in our hiring of dozens of talented journalists of color who do distinguished work, and we know we will continue to attract many more of their caliber. Shalit's racial McCarthyism will not deter our efforts to diversify the staff of *The Washington Post* so we can report intelligently on an increasingly diverse community and nation.

The Washington Post has no "goal to reproduce in its building the precise ethnic makeup of its community." Shalit repeatedly uses this straw man to feed the idea that our hiring is being dictated by the numbers, forcing a compromising of standards.

Our stated goal for many years has been to try to have our new hires be 50 percent women and 25 percent minorities, consistent with filling every vacancy with the best-qualified person possible. This has never meant turning away any journalist because he was a white man nor lowering our standards to hire any woman or minority journalist. Our nationally recognized newsroom recruiter, Jeanne Fox-Alston, who was portrayed in a particularly cruel, false light by Shalit, has definitely not been "winnowing out white males," as can be seen from our publicly available newsroom statistics. In the nine years since establishing this goal, we have hired ninety-eight minority staff members in our newsroom, forty-five of them women; at the same time, we have hired 232 whites, 109 of them women.

We emphatically have not "been forced to hire inappropriate people, reporters who lack the skills to do daily newspaper work competently." Many new hires are risky at a newspaper as demanding as *The Washington Post*; the eventual wash-out rate has been no different for minority hires than for whites.

Shalit displays an amateurish inability to get her facts straight. Revealingly, many of these errors could have been corrected if—during her extensive interviews with senior editors of the *Post*—she had asked us or anyone with first-hand knowledge about various unfounded rumors she passed off as facts. Shalit also omitted from her article a large number of interviews with reporters and editors here that conflicted with her point of view. And she juxtaposed quotes from other interviews with statements of her own that were quite different from the questions she asked to obtain the quotes.

Some of her most egregious errors are maliciously hurtful to fine people such as Milton Coleman, who has been our Assistant Managing Editor [AME] in charge of Metropolitan News for nearly ten years. Shalit asserts that Ben Bradlee and I had "settled on Kevin Klose" for this job in 1986 (Shalit misdescribes Klose, who was then our Chicago correspondent, as an editor on the National staff). Shalit says Don Graham, the publisher of the *Post*, then intervened to force Ben and me to select Coleman instead. This account is pure fiction. Kevin Klose was never our choice for the job, and the purported conversation with Don Graham that she describes never took place. In fact, in the eleven years since I became managing editor in 1984, Don Graham has never dictated a single newsroom personnel decision (or news coverage decision, for that matter). Ben Bradlee and I selected Milton Coleman ourselves, and remain proud that we did so.

Shalit also slurs Eugene Robinson, our Foreign editor, by suggesting that he was our second choice for the job and implying that we sought him for the position primarily because of his race. She asserts that the Foreign editorship was first offered to our former Cairo correspondent, Caryle Murphy. This is false. No one here ever discussed the job of Foreign editor with Murphy. Gene Robinson—a former city editor here and a distinguished foreign correspondent in Latin America and in London—quickly emerged as the best-prepared person for the job, regardless of race. He was the only person to whom the job was offered.

Shalit has considerable sport at the expense of Doug Farah, our Central American correspondent. She invents from whole cloth a purported meeting where senior editors were described by her as being surprised to discover that Farah was not an Hispanic. No such meeting ever occurred. Here the number of errors is quite breathtaking. Shalit says Farah was born in Bolivia; he was born in Massachusetts. She reports that his family is from Kansas, also incorrect. She claims that the idea of hiring him onto a Metro staff Hispanic-coverage task force was nixed because Farah himself was not Hispanic; in fact, he was hired as our full-time Central American correspondent (after spending several years there as our stringer) one year before the Hispanic task force was even created. She invents a "protracted battle" over whether or not to hire Farah: there was never any question that we would put Farah on the staff after his distinguished service as our stringer in Central America.

Shalit slurs National reporter Kevin Merida, suggesting that he was hired directly onto the National staff because he is black. She describes the National staff as "tiny," but it has nearly fifty reporters. She conjures up a long "waiting list" for membership on the staff; there is no such list. She writes that Merida was jumped ahead of this imaginary queue without being asked to "slug it out at the bottom in Metro"; in fact, we have hired a number of reporters directly from other newspapers onto our National staff. We had been talking to Kevin Merida about joining the National staff since the mid-1980s, while he built a fine reputation as a political reporter for *The Dallas Morning News,* where he covered the White House and national politics before becoming an assistant managing editor in Dallas.

Who is Ruth Shalit and what qualifies her to pass judgment on these fine journalists? The record shows that, in the relatively short time she has been on your staff, she has twice been caught committing plagiarism in the pages of *The New Republic* and that a number of her earlier articles have drawn critical letters complaining about numerous inaccuracies.

Shalit's cavalier disregard for facts is really quite astounding—as is *The New Republic's* willingness to print a story that contains so many errors. Among the many others are: Shalit claims that the National staff is reserving a race-relations reporting job for an African American, when the job was last held by Peter Perl, a white man. She claims applicants were rejected for a job writing about culture in Style because they were the "wrong color," but the only applicant for that position who was actually turned down after extensive interviews was black. She writes that the late Herb Denton joined an EEOC complaint filed by some *Post* reporters in 1972; Denton did not. She writes that there were no black reporters on our Foreign or National staffs "twenty-five years ago"; there were.

Shalit argues in her article that a preoccupation with racial sensitivity here has led us to abandon aggressive reporting on local problems and officials, particularly Washington's mayor, Marion Barry, as though it were some other newspaper that revealed Barry's drug use at a downtown hotel, or some other newspaper that showed how he was manipulating the city's campaign finance laws during the last mayoral election, or some other newspaper that detailed how Barry's Washington home was handsomely remodeled by friends and city contractors, or some other newspaper whose tough coverage (and reporters, many of them black) is currently being attacked at most of their public appearances by both the Mayor and Mrs. Barry.

In particular, Shalit chose to demonize Milton Coleman by accusing him of stopping, stalling or watering down local investigative reporting for racial reasons. This is a preposterous slur against one of our most courageous journalists and effective editors. I have been deeply involved in the editing of most investigative projects here during the time Milton Coleman has been AME for

Metropolitan News, and I have seen no evidence of racial attitudes involved in our joint decisions to send various projects back for more reporting and rewriting. We have demanding standards of accuracy, completeness, fairness, clarity and impact that stories must meet before they are published in *The Washington Post* (if only *The New Republic* had similar standards), and we have accordingly delayed or abandoned countless stories, regardless of subject, over the years.

Shalit falsely accuses us of adhering to a "commandment to avoid offense at all costs" in any coverage touching on race. Could she be referring to the same newspaper that published Leon Dash's distinguished series on Rosa Lee Cunningham, which both won the Pulitzer Prize and caused very strong emotional responses, both negative and positive, among our black and white readers? Aggressive accountability reporting in all areas is perhaps the single most important part of the mission of this newspaper.

We remain committed to increasing the diversity of our newsroom staff and to publishing the best possible newspaper we can every day. This is not always easy to do under the pressure of daily deadlines in a very competitive atmosphere, which can exacerbate the workplace tensions, racial and other kinds, found in most large offices these day. Reporting on and writing about this challenging situation in a thoughtful, well-informed fashion would be a real contribution to all of our understanding of the dynamics of diversity in American media. It is unfortunate, to say the least, that *The New Republic* and Ruth Shalit have instead made the water much muddier.

Donald Graham, Publisher

To the editors:

I am very sorry that so many *Washington Post* writers and editors do not meet Ruth Shalit's standards. They do meet mine.

Ms. Shalit makes a series of assertions backed up by a string of blind quotes, to the effect that affirmative action has led the *Post* to compromise its hiring standards and to pull its punches in news coverage. Her evidence is that some journalists in our newsroom are willing to grouse about the subject.

Since she works at *The New Republic,* the last practitioner of de facto segregation since Mississippi changed, Ms. Shalit has little or no experience in working with black colleagues. But she knows that newsroom second-guessing of any and all editors' decisions is as newsworthy as dog-bites-man. Ms. Shalit even prints a mean attack on our director of hiring and recruiting by people the *Post* has chosen not to hire.

Is the *Post's* minority staff lacking in talent? Ms. Shalit does not mention that the Pulitzer Prize has been awarded to two African American *Post* staffers in the last two years or that two others were finalists; does not mention the three Polk Awards, an ASNE award for writing, the Livingston award or the White House press photographers awards won by other *Post* minority staffers. Our journalists appear to meet the standards of those award panels. But not Ms. Shalit's.

I have spent a fair amount of time with Len Downie worrying about recent attempts to hire minority *Post* staffers by *The New York Times, The Wall Street*

Journal, The Dallas Morning News, Knight-Ridder ABC, *The New Yorker* and *Sports Illustrated,* among many others (not, of course, *The New Republic,* which I am told has never had a full-time black staffer). Our staffers seem to meet the standards of those publications. But not Ms. Shalit's.

I've watched *Post* editors hire reporters for a few years now. There are more truly outstanding reporters on the *Post* today, both sexes, all races, than there ever have been in the history of the paper. The *Post* does try hard to find minority reporters and editors. It tries to hire only excellent reporters, succeeds in many cases, and fails about as often with whites as with blacks, Hispanics and Asians.

Evaluations of individual reporters are necessarily subjective. But when it comes to news coverage, Ms. Shalit can be examined. She finds our coverage of Marion Barry since his release from prison "more uncritical than before." Really, Ms. Shalit? Did you see the ten to twelve editorials opposing his re-election? Did you see Colbert King's op-ed page columns, since the election? Did you see the *Post* editorials with headlines like "MAYOR BARRY'S RECKLESS THREATS," " 'WHAT CRISIS IN D.C.,' HE ASKS," "VICTORY FOR THE LAW OF THE STREETS" and "MELTDOWN"? Did you see the piece that launched the current grand jury investigation? Or the pieces from our city staff with headlines like "AUTHORITIES SEIZE FILES ON BARRY," "BARRY BRUSHES ASIDE QUESTIONS; MAYOR WALKS OUT WHEN ASKED ABOUT TIES TO BUSINESSMEN," "BARRY'S SECURITY COSTS ANGER D.C. COUNCIL," "RESIDENTS TRASH TRIP BY BARRY," "BARRY DENIES STEEP DISCOUNT ON HOTEL SUITE WAS ILLEGAL GIFT" and on and on.

Among honest people, evaluations of the same set of facts will differ. A reporter who claims to evaluate the *Post's* Barry coverage and leaves out all the articles I have mentioned is not an honest reporter.

I am mentioned in Ms. Shalit's piece only briefly: she alleges that I over-ruled Ben Bradlee and Len Downie to make Milton Coleman the Assistant Managing Editor for Metropolitan News. This is fantasy. I wasn't asked for my opinion and didn't give it. I would be proud if I had selected Milton Coleman, who has put together what I consider an outstanding Metro staff by (yes) particularly careful hiring. Ms. Shalit accuses Mr. Coleman of pulling his punches in coverage of black leaders, including Louis Farrakhan. The reason Ms. Shalit has heard Mr. Farrakhan's name is that he became nationally famous for threatening Milton Coleman's life over Coleman's coverage of the Jesse Jackson campaign of 1984. As I learned in 1984, Milton Coleman is one of the bravest people I've ever met. A choice between his standards and Ms. Shalit's would be my easiest call, any day of the week.

Ms. Shalit describes a place where blacks and whites watch each other closely, where race becomes an excuse for some and a flashpoint for others. Sounds like America in 1995. Except, of course, for *The New Republic.* (Motto: Looking for a qualified black since 1914.)

The Washington Post will go on trying to hire the best reporters we can, and will go on trying to identify and hire outstanding minority journalists. When Ms. Shalit alleges low standards, my answer is: J. A. Adande, Louis Aguilar, David Aldridge, John Anderson, Marie Arana-Ward, Juana Arias, Nora Boustany, Donna Britt, Dudley Brooks, Warren Brown, DeNeen Brown, Stephen

Buckley, Ruben Castaneda, Rajiv Chandrasekaran, Deirdre Childress, Kenneth Cooper, Leon Dash, Marcia Davis, Lynne Duke, Gabriel Escobar, Louis Estrada, Anthony Faiola, Michael Fletcher, John Fountain, Lisa Frazier, Mary Ann French, Patrice Gaines, Dorothy Gilliam, Robin Givhan, Malcolm Gladwell, Hamil Harris, Craig Herndon, Spencer Hsu, Desson Howe, Keith Jenkins, Jon Jeter, Colbert King, Athelia Knight, Gary Lee, Nathan McCall, Kevin Merida, Courtland Milloy, David Nakamura, Ellen Nakashima, Terry Neal, David Nicholson, Lan Nguyen, Lonnae O'Neal Parker, Peter Pae, Phillip Pan, Robert Pierre, Carol Porter, Rudy Pyatt, William Raspberry, Keith Richburg, Michelle Singletary, Marcia Slacum-Greene, Lena Sun, Pierre Thomas, Avis Thomas-Lester, Jacqueline Trescott, Eric Wee, Michael Wilbon, Daniel Williams, Juan Williams, Yolanda Woodlee and John Yang. I cite only reporters, columnists, photographers and artists because readers may judge their work for themselves. I am proud to have *The Washington Post* judged by their work.

POSTSCRIPT

Are Newspapers Insensitive to Minorities?

Media organizations have long been criticized for being resistant to change and for supporting the status quo. In the case of publishing houses for newspapers, magazines, or books, the specific parameters have been drawn to address each medium's need to reflect the community it serves. One might expect newspapers in locations that serve minorities to do a better job at representing minority interests, both in hiring and in the treatment of news, than publishers that serve broader constituencies. But how much change is enough?

Because the selections by Shalit and by Downie and Graham specifically deal with the efforts and practices of the *Washington Post,* some very specific actions are discussed. It might be interesting for you to consider how well your own community's media reflect the population they serve. What about your school newspaper, radio station, or arts organization? How well do they reflect the demographics of the community they serve?

There are many studies dealing with the topic of race and media. One of the best short essays on the subject is Michael Parenti's article "Cover Story: The Myth of a Liberal Media," *The Humanist* (January/February 1995). Also see James Fallows, *Breaking the News: How the Media Undermine American Democracy* (Pantheon Books, 1996). A recent book that takes a look at the organizational issues within business is Anthony Stith's *Breaking the Glass Ceiling: Racism and Sexism in Corporate America* (Warwick, 1998).

The Centre for Cultural and Media Studies

The Centre for Cultural and Media Studies (CCMS) is located at the University of Natal–Durban in South Africa. The Centre was established to develop strategies of cultural resistance through media and culture after the Soweto uprising of 1976. With the advent of democratic political processes in South Africa, the Centre now works in policy research and to develop support for communication projects.

http://www.und.ac.za/und/ccms/index.html

Freedom Forum

The Freedom Forum is a nonpartisan, international foundation dedicated to free press, free speech, and free spirit for all people. Its mission is to help the public and the news media understand one another better. The press watch area of this site is very intriguing.

http://www.freedomforum.org

Fairness and Accuracy in Reporting

Fairness and Accuracy in Reporting (FAIR) is a national media watch group that offers well-documented criticism of media bias and censorship. FAIR advocates for greater diversity in the press and scrutinizes media practices that marginalize public interest, minority, and dissenting viewpoints.

http://www.fair.org

Society of Professional Journalists

At this site you will find the Electronic Journalist, the online service for the Society of Professional Journalists. This site links you to articles on media ethics, accuracy in media, media leaders, and other media topics.

http://www.spj.org

Television News Archive, Vanderbilt University

Since August 5, 1968, the Television News Archive has systematically recorded, abstracted, and indexed national television newscasts. This database is the guide to the Vanderbilt University collection of network television news programs.

http://tvnews.vanderbilt.edu

PART 2

Media Ethics

*M*edia ethics concerns the delicate balance between society's interests and the interests of individuals, groups, and institutions such as the press and the government. Questions of ethics are, by definition, issues of right and wrong. But they are among the most difficult issues we face because they require decisions of us, even in the face of articulate and intelligent opposition. What is the appropriate balance between responsibility and liberty? Who should decide where the lines between right and wrong are to be drawn, and on what values should these decisions be made? Are all decisions relative to the individual case, or are there larger, overriding principles to which we should all pledge our allegiance? Most important, to whom should we entrust the power to make and implement ethical choices? In this section, the reader must grapple with the questions ethics ask of us and critically examine the purposes and actions of some of the most fundamental institutions we know.

- Should the Names of Rape Victims Be Reported?

- Should Tobacco Advertising Be Restricted?

- Is Advertising Ethical?

ISSUE 5

Should the Names of Rape Victims Be Reported?

YES: Michael Gartner, from "Naming the Victim," *Columbia Journalism Review* (July/August 1991)

NO: Katha Pollitt, from "Naming and Blaming: Media Goes Wilding in Palm Beach," *The Nation* (June 24, 1991)

ISSUE SUMMARY

YES: President of NBC News Michael Gartner justifies his decision to name the accuser in the William Kennedy Smith rape case, claiming that names add credibility to a story. He further argues that a policy of identifying accusers in rape cases will destroy many of society's wrongly held impressions and stereotypes about the crime of rape.

NO: Using examples from the William Kennedy Smith case, journalist and social critic Katha Pollitt identifies six reasons commonly cited by proponents of naming alleged rape victims and argues that not one of them justifies the decision to reveal victims' identities without their consent.

In 1991 a woman claimed she was raped at the Kennedy compound in Palm Beach, Florida, one night during the Easter weekend. After an investigation by the local police, William Kennedy Smith, nephew of Senator Edward M. Kennedy (D-Massachusetts), was charged with the assault. The subsequent trial later that same year resulted in an acquittal for Smith. The case received widespread media coverage, in part because it involved a Kennedy, and in part because the circumstances of the case tapped into the ongoing national debate over so-called acquaintance rape, or date rape. On the night of the incident, Smith and the woman met at an exclusive club, they spent some time drinking and partying, and the woman later drove Smith home and accepted his invitation to take a walk on the beach. According to the woman, the police, and the local prosecutor, what eventually took place that night was rape. Smith, his supporters, and the jury, however, saw it as consensual sex. In addition to raising the question of date rape, the case also provoked controversy because of how various news organizations handled the issue of whether or not to reveal the woman's identity.

Shielding the names and identities of victims of rape has long been a press tradition. But when the William Kennedy Smith story first broke, both the NBC television network and the *New York Times* reported the woman's name; furthermore, the *New York Times* ran a story that gave details on her personal background. These actions sparked controversy among the public and among journalists and media critics.

Who should control the decision to use the names of victims when the media reports rape cases? Should it be only the victims? Considering that the names of other crime victims are generally not withheld, does concealing identities in news coverage of rape perpetuate stereotypes about rape? What rights does the alleged rapist have? What, in short, are the legitimate privacy interests of those involved? How can those interests be balanced with the public interest and the press's responsibility to fully report a story?

These are difficult ethical questions for journalists. In making a decision, how does a journalist balance competing demands, such as the common good versus the rights of an individual, or absolute freedom of the press versus the right to privacy? Does one value predominate over another?

Michael Gartner, president of NBC News, decided to break with journalistic tradition and broadcast the name of the alleged victim of the incident at the Kennedy compound without her consent. In the following memo to his staff dated April 24, 1991, Gartner outlines his reasons for making the controversial decision. Some NBC affiliates complained, and even among his own staff the decision was not unanimously supported, but Gartner maintains that it is usually journalistically responsible to reveal the names of rape victims. Katha Pollitt, in opposition, argues that society's attitudes toward rape justify privacy for rape victims. Naming names is media exploitation, she asserts, and it does not serve a good purpose.

Michael Gartner  **YES**

Naming the Victim

This past April [1991]—following a woman's allegations that she had been raped by Senator Edward Kennedy's nephew William Kennedy Smith—NBC News broke ranks with a tradition honored by other mainstream news organizations by reporting the name of the alleged victim without her consent. The following day *The New York Times* published the woman's name, asserting that the NBC disclosure had already made her name public knowledge. These decisions set off a great deal of internal discussion at both organizations and in the press at large. In this memo to his staff, Michael Gartner, president of NBC News, justifies his decision.

To the staff:

Why did NBC News name the woman who says she was raped at the Kennedy compound in Florida over the Easter weekend? How was that decision made?

For years, the issue has been debated by journalists and feminists: should the names of rape victims or alleged rape victims be made public? Among journalists, there is no agreement; among feminists, there is no agreement.

At NBC, we debated the journalistic arguments.

Some background: I have been deeply interested in this subject for years, discussing it and debating it. Years ago, I concluded that journalistically it is usually right to name rape victims. Usually, but not always.

Here is my reasoning:

First, we are in the business of disseminating news, not suppressing it. Names and facts are news. They add credibility, they round out the story, they give the viewer or reader information he or she needs to understand issues, to make up his or her own mind about what's going on. So my prejudice is always toward telling the viewer all the germane facts that we know.

Second, producers and editors and news directors should make editorial decisions; editorial decisions should not be made in courtrooms, or legislatures, or briefing rooms—or by persons involved in the news. That is why I oppose military censorship, legislative mandate, and the general belief that we should only print the names of rape victims who volunteer their names. In no other category of news do we give the newsmaker the option of being named. Those are decisions that should be made in newsrooms—one way or another.

Third, by not naming rape victims we are part of a conspiracy of silence, and that silence is bad for viewers and readers. It reinforces the idea that somehow there is something shameful about being raped. Rape is a crime of violence, a horrible crime of violence. Rapists are horrible people; rape victims are not. One role of the press is to inform, and one way of informing is to destroy incorrect impressions and stereotypes.

Fourth, and finally, there is an issue of fairness. I heard no debate in our newsroom and heard of no debate in other newsrooms on whether we should name the suspect, William Smith. He has not been charged with anything. Yet we dragged his name and his reputation into this without thought, without regard to what might happen to him should he not be guilty—indeed, should he not even be charged. Rapists are vile human beings; but a suspect isn't necessarily a rapist. Were we fair? Probably, yes, because he was thrust into the news, rightly or wrongly. But so was Patricia Bowman, and we should treat her the same way journalistically. We are reporters; we don't take sides, we don't pass judgment.

Those are the points made in our internal debates. At NBC News, I first raised the issue when the woman was raped in Central Park. We had one story on Nightly News, and after that I told some colleagues that if that were to become a continuing national story we should debate the question of naming the woman. As it turned out, it did not become a continuing national story, and we did not have the debate at that time.

Two weeks ago, I began debating in my own mind the issue of the Florida case. I joined in the debate with some colleagues from outside NBC News last week. On Monday of this week, I raised the issue with three colleagues within NBC News. We discussed it at some length. Should we do this, and if we did it how should we frame it?

On Tuesday, the discussions continued. They were passionate and spirited, but not mean-spirited. By the end of the day, the debate probably encompassed 30 persons, men and women of all views. There was no unanimity; if a vote had been taken, it probably would have been not to print the name. But I decided, for the reasons listed here, to air the name. The fact that her identity was known to many in her community was another factor—but not a controlling one—in my decision.

There were those—including some involved in the preparation, production and presentation of the piece—who disagreed intellectually. But no one asked to be removed from the story, and everyone did a thorough job. The story was clear and fair and accurate; it was not sensational, and—for those who think it was done for the ratings or the like—it was not hyped or promoted. It was presented as just another very interesting story in a Nightly News broadcast that, that night, was full of especially compelling stories.

At 5:00 P.M., we did send an advisory to affiliates that we were naming the woman, for our Florida affiliates, especially, needed to be told in advance. In the time since, six of our 209 affiliates have complained to us about the decision; at least one, WBZ in Boston, bleeped out the woman's name and covered her picture. Several affiliates said we ran counter to their own policies, but just as we respect their views they respected ours and ran the story. Several other affiliates called to say they agreed with our decision. Most said nothing.

I am particularly proud of the process we went through in reaching our conclusion; in fact, the process was more important than the conclusion. There was vigorous and free debate about an issue of journalism; all sides were discussed. The story was shaped and reshaped as a result of that debate. When we ultimately decided to air the name, everyone involved at least understood the reasons, and everyone then did the usual first-rate work.

Our decision engendered a national debate. Much of the debate has been focused on the wrong issues, but much of it has been focused on the right issue: the crime of rape. The debate itself has raised the awareness of the horribleness of the crime, the innocence of victims, the vileness of rapists. That has been a beneficial side-effect.

Rape is rarely a national story. If another rape becomes a big story, we will have the same debate again. The position at NBC News is this: we will consider the naming of rape victims or alleged rape victims on a case-by-case basis.

NO ←

Katha Pollitt

Media Goes Wilding in Palm Beach

I drink, I swear, I flirt, I tell dirty jokes. I have also, at various times, watched pornographic videos, had premarital sex, hitchhiked, and sunbathed topless in violation of local ordinances. True, I don't have any speeding tickets, but I don't have a driver's license either. Perhaps I'm subconsciously afraid of my "drives"? There are other things, too, and if I should ever bring rape charges against a rich, famous, powerful politician's relative, *The New York Times* will probably tell you all about them—along with, perhaps, my name. Suitably adorned with anonymous quotes, these revelations will enable you, the public, to form your own opinion: Was I asking for trouble, or did I just make the whole thing up?

In April the media free-for-all surrounding the alleged rape of a Palm Beach woman by William Smith, Senator Ted Kennedy's nephew, took a vicious turn as the *Times*—following NBC, following the *Globe* (supermarket, not Boston, edition), following a British scandal sheet, following *another* British scandal sheet—went public with the woman's name, and a lot more: her traffic violations, her mediocre high school grades, her "little wild streak," her single motherhood, her mother's divorce and upwardly mobile remarriage. Pretty small potatoes, really; she sounds like half my high school classmates. But it did make a picture: bad girl, loose woman, floozy.

Or did it? In a meeting with more than 300 outraged staff members, national editor Soma Golden said that the *Times* could not be held responsible for "every weird mind that reads [the paper]." NBC News chief Michael Gartner was more direct: "Who she is, is material in this.... You try to give viewers as many facts as you can and let them make up their minds." Forget that almost none of these "facts" will be admissible in court, where a jury will nonetheless be expected to render a verdict.

In the ensuing furor, just about every advocate for rape victims has spoken out in favor of preserving the longstanding media custom of anonymity, and in large part the public seems to agree. But the media,[1] acting in its capacity as the guardian of public interest, has decided that naming the victim is an issue up for grabs. And so we are having one of these endless, muddled, two-sides-to-every-question debates that, by ignoring as many facts as possible and by weighing all arguments equally, gives us that warm American feeling that

From Katha Pollitt, "Naming and Blaming: Media Goes Wilding in Palm Beach," *The Nation* (June 24, 1991). Copyright © 1991 by Katha Pollitt. Reprinted by permission of the author.

91

truth must lie somewhere in the middle. Anna Quindlen, meet Alan Dershowitz. Thank you very much, but our time is just about up.

Sometimes, of course, the truth does lie somewhere in the middle. But not this time. There is no good reason to publish the names of rape complainants without their consent, and many compelling reasons not to. The arguments advanced in favor of publicity reveal fundamental misconceptions about both the nature of the media and the nature of rape.

Let's take a look at what proponents of naming are saying.

The media has a duty to report what it knows   Where have you been? The media keeps information secret all the time. Sometimes it does so on the ground of "taste," a waffle-word that means whatever an editorial board wants it to mean. Thus, we hear about (some of) the sexual high jinks of heterosexual celebrities but not about those of socially equivalent closet-dwellers, whose opposite-sex escorts are portrayed, with knowing untruthfulness, as genuine romantic interests. We are spared—or deprived of, depending on your point of view—the gruesome and salacious details of many murders. (Of all the New York dailies, only *Newsday* reported that notorious Wall Street wife-killer Joseph Pikul was wearing women's underwear when arrested. Not fit to print? I was *riveted*.) Sometimes it fudges the truth to protect third parties from embarrassment, which is why the obituaries would have us believe that eminent young bachelors are dying in large numbers only from pneumonia.

And of course sometimes it censors itself in "the national interest." The claim that the media constitutes a fourth estate, a permanent watchdog, if not outright adversary, of the government, has always been a self-serving myth. Watergate occurred almost twenty years ago and has functioned ever since as a kind of sentimental talisman. Like Charles Foster Kane's Rosebud sled. As we saw during the gulf war, the media can live, when it chooses, quite comfortably with government-imposed restrictions. Neither NBC nor *The New York Times,* so quick to supply their audiences with the inside scoop on the Palm Beach woman, felt any such urgency about Operation Desert Storm.

Anonymous charges are contrary to the American way   Anonymous charges are contrary to American *jurisprudence.* The Palm Beach woman has not made an anonymous accusation. Her name is known to the accused and his attorney, and if the case comes to trial, she will have to appear publicly in court, confront the defendant, give testimony and be cross-examined. But the media is not a court, as the many lawyers who have made this argument—most prominently Alan Dershowitz and Isabelle Pinzler of the American Civil Liberties Union's Women's Rights Project—ought to know.

The media itself argues in favor of anonymity when that serves its own purposes. Reporters go to jail rather than reveal their sources, even when secrecy means protecting a dangerous criminal, impeding the process of justice or denying a public figure the ability to confront his or her accusers. People wouldn't talk to reporters, the press claims, if their privacy couldn't be guaranteed—the same greater-social-good argument it finds unpersuasive when made about rape victims and their reluctance to talk, unprotected, to the police. The media's selective interest in concealment, moreover, undermines its vaunted mission on behalf of the public's right to know. Might not the identity of an anonymous informant (one of those "sources close to the White House" or "highly placed observers," for instance) help the public "make up its mind" about the reliability of the statements? I don't want to digress here into the complex issue of protecting sources, but there can be little question that the practice allows powerful people, in and out of government, to manipulate information for their own ends. Interestingly, the *Times* story on the Palm Beach woman concealed (thirteen times!) the names of those spreading malicious gossip about her, despite the *Times's* own custom of not using anonymous pejoratives. That custom was resuscitated in time for the paper's circumspect profile of William Smith, which did not detail the accusations against him of prior acquaintance rapes that have been published by *The National Enquirer* and the gossip columnist Taki, and which referred only vaguely to "rumors" of "a pattern of aggressiveness toward women in private." (These, the *Times* said, it could not confirm—unlike the accuser's "little wild streak.")

How *did* the *Times* manage to amass such a wealth of dirt about the Palm Beach woman so quickly? It's hard to picture the reporter, distinguished China hand Fox Butterfield, peeking into the window of her house to see what books were on the toddler's shelf. Could some of his information or some of his leads have come, directly or circuitously, from the detectives hired by the Kennedy family to investigate the woman and her friends—detectives who, let's not forget, have been the subject of complaints of witness intimidation? The *Times* denies it, but rumors persist. One could argue that, in this particular case, *how* the *Times* got the story was indeed part of the story—perhaps the most important part.

That anonymity is held to be essential to the public good in a wide variety of cases but is damned as a form of censorship in the Palm Beach case shows that what the media is concerned with is not the free flow of information *or* the public good. What is at stake is the media's status, power and ability to define and control information in accordance with the views of those who run the media.

Consider, for example, the case of men convicted of soliciting prostitutes. Except for the occasional athlete, such men receive virtual anonymity in the press. Remember the flap in 1979 when Manhattan D.A. Robert Morgenthau released a list of recently convicted johns and the *Daily News* and two local radio stations went public with it? Universal outrage! Never mind that solicitation is a crime, that convictions are a matter of public record, that the wives and girlfriends of these men might find knowledge of such arrests extremely useful or that society has a declared interest in deterring prostitution. Alan Dershowitz, who in his syndicated column has defended both the content of the *Times* profile and its use of the woman's name, vigorously supported privacy for johns, and in fact made some of the same arguments that he now dismisses. Reporting, he said, was vindictive, subjected ordinary people to the glaring light of publicity for a peccadillo, could destroy the johns' marriages and reputations, and stigmatized otherwise decent people. Dershowitz did not, however, think privacy for johns meant privacy for prostitutes: They, he argued, have no reputation to lose. Although solicitation is a two-person crime, Dershowitz thinks the participants have unequal rights to privacy. With rape, he treats the rapist and his victim as *equally* placed with regard to privacy, even though rape is a one-person crime.

But here the woman's identity was already widely known   Well, I didn't know it. I did, however, know the name of the Central Park jogger—like virtually every other journalist in the country, the entire readership of *The Amsterdam News* (50,000) and the listening audience of WLIB-radio (45,000). Anna Quindlen, in her courageous column dissenting from the *Times's* profile naming the Palm Beach woman, speculated that roughly equivalent large numbers of people knew the identity of the jogger as knew that of William Smith's alleged victim before NBC and the *Times* got into the act. Yet the media went to extraordinary lengths to protect the remaining shreds of the jogger's privacy— film clips were blipped, quotes censored.

What separates the jogger from the Palm Beach woman? You don't have to be the Rev. Al Sharpton to suspect that protecting the jogger's identity was more than a chivalrous gesture. Remember that she too was originally blamed for her assault: What was she doing in the park so late? Who did she think she was? It's all feminism's fault for deluding women into thinking that their safety could, or should, be everywhere guaranteed. But partly as a result of the severity of her injuries, the jogger quickly became the epitome of the innocent victim, the symbol, as Joan Didion pointed out in *The New York Review of Books,* for New York City itself (white, prosperous, plucky) endangered by the black underclass. A white Wellesley graduate with a Wall Street job attacked out of nowhere by a band of violent black strangers and, because of her comatose state, unable even to bring a rape complaint—this, to the media, is "real rape." The Palm Beach woman, on the other hand, is of working-class origins, a single mother, a frequenter of bars, who went voluntarily to her alleged attacker's house (as who, in our star-struck society, would not?). The jogger could have been the daughter of the men who kept her name out of the news. But William Smith could have been their son.

Rape is like other crimes and should be treated like other crimes. Isn't that what you feminists are always saying?   As the coverage of the Palm Beach case proves, rape isn't treated like other crimes. There is no other crime in which the character, behavior and past of the complainant are seen as central elements in determining whether a crime has occurred. There are lots of crimes that could not take place without carelessness, naïveté, ignorance or bad judgment on the part of the victims: mail fraud ("Make $100,000 at home in your spare time!"), confidence games and many violent crimes as well. But when my father was burglarized after forgetting to lock the cellar door, the police did not tell him he had been asking for it. And when an elderly lady (to cite Amy Pagnozzi's example in the *New York Post*) is defrauded of her life savings by a con artist, the con artist is just as much a thief as if he'd broken into his victim's safe-deposit box. "The complainant showed incredibly bad judgment, Your Honor," is not a legal defense.

Why is rape different? Because lots of people, too often including the ones in the jury box, think women really do want to be forced into sex, or by acting or dressing or drinking in a certain way, give up the right to say no, or are the sort of people (i.e., not nuns) who gave up the right to say no to one man by saying yes to another, or are by nature scheming, irrational and crazy. They also think men cannot be expected to control themselves, are entitled to take by force what they cannot get by persuasion and are led on by women who, because they are scheming, irrational and crazy, change their minds in mid-sex. My files bulge with stories that show how widespread these beliefs are: The Wisconsin judge who put a child molester on probation because he felt the 3-year-old female victim had acted provocatively; the Florida jury that exonerated a rapist because his victim was wearing disco attire; and so on.

In a bizarre column defending Ted Kennedy's role on the night in question, William Safire took aim at the Palm Beach woman, who was "apparently" not "taught that drinking all night and going to a man's house at 3:30 A.M. places one in what used to be called an occasion of sin." (All her mother's fault, as usual.) The other woman present in the Kennedy mansion that night, a waitress named Michelle Cassone, has made herself a mini-celebrity by telling any reporter who will pay for her time that she too believes that women who drink and date, including herself, are "fair game."

By shifting the debate to the question of merely naming victims, the media pre-empts a discussion of the way it reports all crimes with a real or imaginary sexual component. But as the *Times* profile shows, naming cannot be divorced from blaming. When the victim is young and attractive (and in the tabloids *all* female victims are attractive), the sexual element in the crime is always made its central feature—even when, as in the case of Marla Hanson, the model who was slashed by hired thugs and whose character was savaged in *New York*, there is no sexual element. I mean no belittlement of rape to suggest it was one of the lesser outrages visited on the Central Park jogger. She was also beaten so furiously she lost 80 percent of her blood and suffered permanent physical, neurological and cognitive damage. Yet, paradoxically, it was the rape that seized the imagination of the media, and that became the focus of the crime both for her defenders and for those who defended her attackers.

Naming rape victims will remove the stigma against rape Of all the arguments in favor of naming victims, this is the silliest, and the most insincere. Sure, NBC's Michael Gartner told *Newsweek*, the consequences will be "extraordinarily difficult for this generation, but it may perhaps help their daughters and granddaughters." How selfish of women to balk at offering themselves on the altar of little girls yet unborn! If Gartner wishes to make a better world for my descendants, he is amply well placed to get cracking. He could demand non-sensationalized reporting of sex crimes; he could hire more female reporters and producers; he could use NBC News to dispel false notions about rape—for example, the idea that "who the woman is, is material." Throughout the country there are dozens of speakouts against rape at which victims publicly tell of their experiences. Every year there are Take Back the Night marches in Manhattan. Where are the cameras and the reporters on these occasions? Adding misery to hundreds of thousands of women a year and—as just about every expert in the field believes—dramatically lowering the already abysmal incidence of rape reporting (one in ten) will not help my granddaughter; it will only make it more likely that her grandmother, her mother and she herself will be raped by men who have not been brought to justice.

This argument is, furthermore, based on a questionable assumption. Why would society blame rape victims less if it knew who they were? Perhaps its censure would simply be amplified. Instead of thinking, If ordinary, decent, conventional women get raped in large numbers it *can't* be their fault, people might well think, Goodness, there are a lot more women asking for it than we thought. After the invasion of Kuwait, in which scores of women were raped by Iraqi soldiers, there was no dispensation from the traditional harsh treatment of rape victims, some of whom, pregnant and in disgrace, had attempted suicide, gone into hiding or fled the country. One woman told *USA Today* that she wished she were dead. America is not Kuwait, but here, too, many believe that a woman can't be raped against her will and that damaged goods are damaged goods. (Curious how publicity is supposed to lessen the stigma against rape victims but only adds to the suffering of johns.)

One also has to wonder about the urgency with which Gartner and the other male proponents of the anti-stigma theory, with no history of public concern for women, declare themselves the best judge of women's interests and advocate a policy that they themselves will never have to bear the consequences of. Gartner cited, as did many others, the *Des Moines Register* profile of a named rape victim but neglected to mention that the victim, Nancy Ziegenmeyer, volunteered the use of her name, seven months after reporting the crime—in other words, after she had had a chance to come to terms with her experience and to inform her family and friends in a way she found suitable. (Ziegenmeyer, by the way, opposes involuntary naming.) Why is it that, where women are concerned, the difference between choice and coercion eludes so many? Rapists, too, persuade themselves that they know what women really want and need.

William Smith's name has been dragged through the mud. Why should his accuser be protected?   Actually, William Smith has been portrayed rather favorably in the media. No anonymous pejoratives for him: He is "one of the least spoiled and least arrogant of the young Kennedys" (*Time*); an "unlikely villain" (*Newsweek*); "a man of gentleness and humor," "the un-Kennedy," "a good listener" (*The New York Times*); from a "wounded," "tragic" family (*passim*). Certainly he has been subjected to a great deal of unpleasant media attention, and even if he is eventually found innocent, some people will always suspect that he is guilty. But no one forced the media to sensationalize the story; that was a conscious editorial decision, not an act of God. Instead of heaping slurs on the Palm Beach woman in order to even things up, the media should be asking itself why it did not adopt a more circumspect attitude toward the case from the outset.

The tit-for-tat view of rape reporting appeals to many people because of its apparent impartiality. Feminists of the pure equal-treatment school like it because it looks gender neutral (as if rape were a gender-neutral crime). And nonfeminist men like it because, while looking gender neutral, it would, in practice, advantage men. "Should the press be in the business of protecting certain groups but not others—," wrote *Washington Post* columnist Richard Cohen, "alleged victims (females), but not the accused (males)? My answer is no." Cohen, like Michael Gartner, presents himself as having women's best interests at heart: "If rape's indelible stigma is ever to fade, the press has to stop being complicitous in perpetuating the sexist aura that surrounds it." Thus, by some mysterious alchemy, the media, which is perhaps the single biggest promoter of the sexist aura surrounding crimes of violence against women, can redeem itself by jettisoning the only policy it has that eases, rather than augments, the victim's anguish.

Behind the tit-for-tat argument lies a particular vision of rape in which the odds are even that the alleged victim is really the victimizer—a seductress, blackmailer, hysteric, who is bringing a false charge. That was the early word on the Palm Beach woman, and it's hard not to conclude that publicizing her identity was punitive: She's caused all this trouble, is visiting yet more "tragedy" on America's royal family, and had better be telling the truth. In fact, the appeal of naming the victim seems to rest not in the hope that it "may perhaps" someday make rape reporting less painful but in the certainty that right now it makes such reporting *more* painful, thereby inhibiting false accusations. Although studies have repeatedly shown that fabricated rape charges are extremely rare, recent years have seen a number of cases: Tawana Brawley, for example, and Cathleen Crowell Webb, who recanted her testimony after finding Jesus and then hugged her newly freed, no-longer-alleged-assailant on the *Donahue* show. A year ago a Nebraska woman who admitted filing a false charge was ordered by a judge to purchase newspaper ads and radio spots apologizing to the man she had accused. (She was also sentenced to six months in jail.) It is not unknown for other criminal charges to be fabricated, but has anyone ever been forced into a public apology in those cases? The tenor of the equal-publicity argument is captured perfectly by the (female) letter writer to *Time* who suggested that newspapers publish both names and both photos too. Why not bring back trial by ordeal and make the two of them grasp bars of red-hot iron?

✦

Fundamentally, the arguments about naming rape victims center around two contested areas: acquaintance rape and privacy. While the women's movement has had some success in expanding the definition of rape to include sexual violation by persons known to the victim—as I write, *The New York Times* is running an excellent series on such rape, containing interviews with women named or anonymous by their choice (atonement?)—there is also a lot of backlash.

The all-male editorial board of the *New York Post,* which rather ostentatiously refused to print the Palm Beach woman's name, has actually proposed a change in the law to distinguish between "real rape" (what the jogger suffered) and acquaintance rape, confusedly described as a "sexual encounter, forced or not," that "has been preceded by a series of consensual activities." *Forced or not?*

At the other end of the literary social scale, there's Camille (No Means Yes) Paglia, academia's answer to Phyllis Schlafly, repackaging hoary myths about rape as a bold dissent from feminist orthodoxy and "political correctness." Indeed, an attack on the concept of acquaintance rape figures prominently in the many diatribes against current intellectual trends on campus. It's as though the notion of consensual sex were some incomprehensible French literary theory that threatened the very foundations of Western Civ. And, come to think of it, maybe it does.

Finally, there is the issue of privacy. Supporters of naming like to say that anonymity implies that rape is something to be ashamed of. But must this be its meaning? It says a great deal about the impoverishment of privacy as a value in our time that many intelligent people can find no justification for it but shame, guilt, cowardice and prudishness. As the tabloidization of the media proceeds apace, as the boundaries between the public and the personal waver and fade away, good citizenship has come to require of more and more people that they put themselves forward, regardless of the cost, as exhibit A in a national civics lesson. In this sense, rape victims are in the same position as homosexuals threatened with "outing" for the good of other gays, or witnesses forced to give painful and embarrassing testimony in televised courtrooms so that the couch potatoes at home can appreciate the beauty of the legal process.

But there are lots of reasons a rape victim might not want her name in the paper that have nothing to do with shame. She might not want her mother to know, or her children, or her children's evil little classmates, or obscene phone callers, or other rapists. Every person reading this article probably has his or her secrets, things that aren't necessarily shameful (or things that are) but are liable to misconstructions, false sympathy and stupid questions from the tactless and ignorant. Things that are just plain nobody's business unless you want them to be.

Instead of denying privacy to rape victims, we should take a good hard look at our national passion for thrusting unwanted publicity on people who are not accused of wrong-doing but find themselves willy-nilly in the news. ("How did it *feel* to watch your child being torn to pieces by wild animals?" "It felt terrible, Maury, terrible.") I've argued here that society's attitudes toward rape justify privacy for rape complainants, and that indeed those attitudes lurk behind the arguments for publicity. But something else lurks there as well: a desensitization to the lurid and prurient way in which the media exploits the sufferings of any ordinary person touched by a noteworthy crime or tragedy. Most of the people who have spoken out against anonymity are journalists, celebrity lawyers, media executives and politicos—people who put themselves forward in the press and on television as a matter of course and who are used to taking their knocks as the price of national attention. It must be hard for such people to sympathize with someone who doesn't want to play the media game —especially if it's in a "good cause."

I'm not at all sure there is a good cause here. Titillation, not education, seems the likely reason for the glare on the Palm Beach case. But even if I'm unduly cynical and the media sincerely wishes to conduct a teach-in on rape, the interests of the public can be served without humiliating the complainant.

Doctors educate one another with case histories in which patients are identified only by initials and in which other nonrelevant identifying details are changed. Lawyers file cases on behalf of Jane Doe and John Roe and expect the Supreme Court to "make up its mind" nonetheless.

If the media wants to educate the public about rape, it can do so without names. What the coverage of the Palm Beach case shows is that it needs to educate itself first.

Note

1. I use "media" in the singular (rather than the strictly grammatical plural) because I am talking about the communications industry as a social institution that, while hardly monolithic (as the debate over naming shows), transcends the different means—"media" plural—by which the news is conveyed.

POSTSCRIPT

Should the Names of Rape Victims Be Reported?

During the extensive televised coverage of the William Kennedy Smith trial, a dot was used to cover the woman's face. After the trial's conclusion, the woman herself went public and gave a handful of print and broadcast interviews.

With regard to rape and other sex crimes, the media must answer questions beyond whether or not to name the victims. Do common news practices, for example, yield biases that perpetuate myths and injustice? Helen Benedict, in *Virgin or Vamp: How the Press Covers Sex Crimes* (Oxford University Press, 1992), harshly critiques the manner in which newspapers have handled sex crimes.

Ethical guidelines require journalists to make specific choices as they balance freedom and responsibility in their day-to-day reporting. In making decisions, journalists are most often guided by the practices of the profession, their education, their on-the-job socialization, and the written codes of the organizations for which they work. Debates such as the one presented here are inevitable when traditional practices come under scrutiny.

The history of journalism has borne witness to many styles of approaching a story. In his book *Goodbye Gutenberg: The Newspaper Revolution of the 1980s* (Oxford University Press, 1980), Anthony Smith says, "Investigation has become the most highly praised and highly prized form of journalism, taking the place of opinion leadership, the historic purpose of the press." He suggests that the investigative reporter typically finds him- or herself in the position of both judge and jury—the authority to whom the public turns to get the whole story.

Ethical issues are not easily resolved: We should always struggle to discuss them, think about them, and let them guide our consciences. Only when we cease thinking about them is it too late to do anything about them.

There are many books on different styles of journalism, and the biographies of such people as Horace Greeley, William Randolph Hearst, Joseph Pulitzer, and even Rupert Murdoch show how each individual shaped a special time in journalism history. Other sources that describe journalistic themes and public reaction include Ben H. Bagdikian's *The Information Machines: Their Impact on Men and the Media* (Harper & Row, 1971); the Roper Organization's *Trends in Public Attitudes Toward Television and Other Media, 1969–1974* (Television Information Office, 1975); and John P. Robinson's *Daily News Habits of the American Public*, ANPA New Research Center Study No. 15 (September 22, 1978). Also, among the periodicals that cover journalistic styles and practices are *Columbia Journalism Review, Editor and Publisher,* and *American Society of Newspaper Editors (ASNE) Newsletter.*

Further readings on ethics and the media include Everette Dennis, Donald Gillmore, and Theodore Glasser, eds., *Media Freedom and Accountability* (Greenwood Press, 1989) and Bruce Swain, *Reporters' Ethics* (Iowa State University Press, 1978), which examine a number of issues that reporters must face. More recent books include *Ethical Issues in Journalism and the Media* edited by Andres Beasly and Ruth Chadwick (Routledge, Chapman & Hall, 1992) and *Good News: Social Ethics and the Press* by Clifford G. Christians, John P. Ferre, and Mark Fackler (Oxford University Press, 1993).

ISSUE 6

Should Tobacco Advertising Be Restricted?

YES: Joseph R. DiFranza et al., from "RJR Nabisco's Cartoon Camel Promotes Camel Cigarettes to Children," *Journal of the American Medical Association* (December 11, 1991)

NO: George J. Annas, from "Cowboys, Camels, and the First Amendment—The FDA's Restrictions on Tobacco Advertising," *The New England Journal of Medicine* (December 5, 1996)

ISSUE SUMMARY

YES: Doctor Joseph R. DiFranza and his colleagues report a national study that examines the possibility of children being tempted to smoke because of the tobacco industry's use of images that appeal to and are remembered by children. Because of the profound health risks, DiFranza et al. call for restrictions on tobacco ads.

NO: Attorney George J. Annas agrees that the tobacco industry has marketed products to children, but he maintains that efforts to restrict advertising are inappropriate, perhaps even illegal. He argues that some of the restrictions that have been placed on tobacco advertisements violate the First Amendment.

The marketing of tobacco products has been controversial for some time, but discussions have become more heated in recent years as the extent of the tobacco industry's knowledge of nicotine as an addictive drug and the long-term effects of smoking on a person's health has come into question. Court cases and public scrutiny of the tobacco industry have led to legal sanctions and restrictions on the marketing of tobacco products, most specifically with regard to tobacco ads that appeal to children. Although tobacco industry officials claim that they do not try to induce children to smoke, evidence indicates that advertising strategies do, indeed, target a potential audience of young people. Research shows that most long-term smokers begin smoking at the age of 12 or 13 and become hooked for life.

In the following selections, Joseph R. DiFranza and his colleagues raise ethical concerns about the effects of the tobacco industry's using appeals that may tempt children to start smoking, and they explain how advertising effectively reaches consumers. Arguing from a legal position, George J. Annas examines the Federal Drug Administration's current efforts to restrict advertising, particularly to the youth market. Citing several precedents regarding the restriction of advertising, he draws the conclusion that current governmental efforts to curb ads will remain ineffective and may violate the advertisers' First Amendment right to free speech.

This issue brings up several topics for discussion. One important question is whether or not children should be protected from activities and behaviors that may have long-term negative effects. Also, should advertisers exercise standards regarding the products they promote? Should the tobacco industry divulge all of their research regarding the hazards of smoking? Do ethical standards change when appeals are made to children as potential consumers?

Annas raises another important ethical dimension: How far can the First Amendment be used in defending free speech? Since the Bill of Rights was written—over 200 years ago—the type of "speech" that Americans engage in has changed dramatically. Does the right of free speech extend to advertising?

Advertising has traditionally been classified as "commercial" speech, which gives greater license to its use. Should commercial speech also be subject to a more stringent interpretation when the rights of children are involved? If so, should other products be given special consideration? At what point does censorship enter into the picture? Also, if tobacco advertising can be restricted, what about advertising for other potentially harmful products?

Issues involving tobacco advertising are timely and important. Many states have enacted laws to encourage counteradvertising to promote the health benefits of not smoking. In Britain, the figures of Joe Camel and the Marlboro Man have been banned from all advertising. A range of data suggests that antismoking campaigns have different levels of effects. In many ways, antismoking campaigns use many of the same tools and techniques to get the public's attention as do the advertisers of tobacco products. What can be learned from these campaigns about strategies for instituting long-term behavior change?

Joseph R. DiFranza et al.

 **YES**

RJR Nabisco's Cartoon Camel Promotes Camel Cigarettes to Children

With the number of US smokers declining by about 1 million each year, the tobacco industry's viability is critically dependent on its ability to recruit replacement smokers. Since children and teenagers constitute 90% of all new smokers, their importance to the industry is obvious. Many experts are convinced that the industry is actively promoting nicotine addiction among youth.

Spokespersons for the tobacco industry assert that they do not advertise to people under 21 years of age, the sole purpose of their advertising being to promote brand switching and brand loyalty among adult smokers. However, industry advertising expenditures cannot be economically justified on this basis alone. This study was therefore undertaken to determine the relative impact of tobacco advertising on children and adults.

There is abundant evidence that tobacco advertising influences children's images of smoking. In Britain, the proportion of children who gave "looks tough" as a reason for smoking declined after tough images were banned from cigarette advertisements. Children as young as the age of 6 years can reliably recall tobacco advertisements and match personality sketches with the brands using that imagery. In fact, cigarette advertising establishes such imagery among children who are cognitively too immature to understand the purpose of advertising. Subsequently, children who are most attuned to cigarette advertising have the most positive attitudes toward smoking, whether or not they already smoke. Children who are more aware of, or who approve of, cigarette advertisements are more likely to smoke, and those who do smoke buy the most heavily advertised brands.

Historically, one brand that children have not bought is Camel. In seven surveys, involving 3400 smokers in the seventh through 12th grades, conducted between 1976 and 1988 in Georgia, Louisiana, and Minnesota, Camel was given as the preferred brand by less than 0.5%. In 1986, Camels were most popular with smokers over the age of 65 years, of whom 4.4% chose Camels, and least popular among those 17 to 24 years of age, of whom only 2.7% preferred Camels.

From Joseph R. DiFranza, John W. Richards, Jr., Paul M. Paulman, Nancy Wolf-Gillespie, Christopher Fletcher, Robert D. Jaffe, and David Murray, "RJR Nabisco's Cartoon Camel Promotes Camel Cigarettes to Children," *Journal of the American Medical Association,* vol. 266, no. 22 (December 11, 1991), pp. 3149–3152. Copyright © 1991 by The American Medical Association. Reprinted by permission. References omitted.

In 1988, RJR Nabisco launched the "smooth character" advertising campaign, featuring Old Joe, a cartoon camel modeled after James Bond and Don Johnson of "Miami Vice." Many industry analysts believe that the goal of this campaign is to reposition Camel to compete with Philip Morris' Marlboro brand for the illegal children's market segment. To determine the relative impact of Camel's Old Joe cartoon advertising on children and adults, we used four standard marketing measures.

1. Recognition. We compared the proportions of teenagers and adults aged 21 years and over who recognize Camel's Old Joe cartoon character.
2. Recall. We compared the ability of teenagers and adults to recall from a masked Old Joe advertisement the type of product being advertised and the brand name.
3. Appeal. We compared how interesting and appealing a series of Old Joe cartoon character advertisements were to teenagers and adults.
4. Brand preference. We compared brand preferences of teenaged smokers prior to the Old Joe cartoon character campaign with those 3 years into the campaign to determine if the campaign had been more effective with children or with adults, and to determine if Camel had been repositioned as a children's brand.

Methods

Subjects

Since adolescent brand preferences may vary from one geographic location to another, we selected children from Georgia, Massachusetts, Nebraska, New Mexico, and Washington, representing five regions. One school in each state was selected based on its administration's willingness to participate. Schools with a smoking prevention program focused on tobacco advertising were excluded.

A target of 60 students in each grade, 9 through 12, from each school was set. In large schools, classes were selected to obtain a sample representative of all levels of academic ability. Students were told that the study concerned advertising and were invited to participate anonymously.

Since adult brand preferences are available from national surveys, adult subjects were recruited only at the Massachusetts site. All drivers, regardless of age, who were renewing their licenses at the Registry of Motor Vehicles on the days of the study during the 1990–1991 school year were asked to participate. Since licenses must be renewed in person, this is a heterogeneous population.

Materials

Seven Camel Old Joe cartoon character advertisements were obtained from popular magazines during the 3 years prior to the study. One ad was masked to hide all clues (except Old Joe) as to the product and brand being advertised.

The survey instrument collected demographic information and information on past and present use of tobacco, including brand preference. Children were considered to be smokers if they had smoked one or more cigarettes dur-ing the previous week. Previously validated questions were used to determine children's intentions regarding smoking in the next month and year and their attitudes toward the advertised social benefits of smoking.

Subjects rated the ads as "cool or stupid" and "interesting or boring." Subjects were asked if they thought Old Joe was "cool" and if they would like to be friends with him. Each positive response to these four questions was scored as a one, a negative response as a zero. The "appeal score" was the arithmetic sum of the responses to these four questions, with the lowest possible score per respondent being a zero and the highest a four.

Procedure

Subjects were first shown the masked ad and asked if they had seen the Old Joe character before. They were then asked to identify the product being adver-tised and the brand name of the product. Subjects who could not answer these questions were required to respond "Don't know" so they would not be able to write in the correct answer when the unmasked advertisements were shown. The subjects were then shown, one at a time, the six unmasked advertisements and asked to rate how the advertisements and the Old Joe cartoon character appealed to them. Subjects then completed the remainder of the survey instrument.

Adolescent brand preference data from this study were compared with the data obtained by seven surveys completed prior to the kickoff of Camel's Old Joe cartoon character campaign early in 1988.

Tests of significance were made using the Two-tailed Student's t Test for continuous data and the χ^2 and Fisher's Exact Test for discrete data. A P value of less than .05 was used to define statistical significance.

The study was conducted during the 1990–1991 school year.

Results

A total of 1060 students and 491 subjects from the Registry of Motor Vehicles were asked to participate. Usable surveys were obtained from 1055 students (99%) and 415 license renewal applicants (84.5%). Seventy drivers were under 21 years of age, leaving 345 adults aged 21 years or older. Students ranged in age from 12 to 19 years (mean, 15.99 years) and adults from 21 to 87 years (mean, 40.47 years). Females represented 51.0% of the students and 54.8% of the adults.

Children were much more likely than adults to recognize Camel's Old Joe cartoon character (97.7% vs 72.2%). It is not plausible that the children were simply saying they had seen Old Joe when they had not, since they also demonstrated a greater familiarity with the advertisement on the two objective measures.

When shown the masked advertisement, the children were much more successful than the adults in identifying the product being advertised (97.5% vs 67.0%) and the Camel brand name (93.6% vs 57.7%). Even when the analysis was limited to those subjects who were familiar with the Old Joe cartoon character, children were still more likely than adults to remember the product (98.6% vs 89.6%) and the Camel brand name (95.0% vs 79.1%). This confirms that Old Joe cartoon advertisements are more effective at communicating product and brand name information to children than to adults.

Because Massachusetts adults may not be representative of adults in the other four states where children were surveyed, the above analyses were repeated comparing only Massachusetts children and adults. In all cases the differences between adults and children were significant and of even greater magnitude, excluding the possibility that the above findings were due to a lighter level of advertising exposure in the Massachusetts area.

On all four measures, the children found the Camel cartoon advertisements more appealing than did the adults. Children were more likely to think the advertisements looked "cool" (58.0% vs 39.9%) or "interesting" (73.6% vs 55.1%). More of the children thought Old Joe was "cool" (43.0% vs 25.7%) and wanted to be friends with him (35.0% vs 14.4%).

The brand preference data revealed a dramatic reversal in the market segment pattern that existed prior to Camel's Old Joe cartoon character campaign. Camel was given as the preferred brand by 32.8% of children up to the age of 18 years who smoked, 23.1% of Massachusetts adult smokers aged 19 and 20 years, and 8.7% of those 21 years of age and over. The figures for the Massachusetts adults were significantly higher than the national market share for Camel, 4.4%, suggesting that Massachusetts adults may be more familiar with the Old Joe Camel campaign than adults in general. Camel cigarettes are now most popular with children and progressively less popular with older smokers.

About equal proportions of adults (28.2%) and children (29.0%) reported some current cigarette use, making it unlikely that this factor influenced any of the above findings. Although there were some statistically significant differences in the responses of children from different regions, these were not the focus of this study.

When compared with nonsmokers, children who were currently smoking gave higher approval ratings to the advertisements. Approving attitudes toward cigarette advertisements seem to precede actual smoking. Among the nonsmoking children, those who either were ambivalent about their future smoking intentions or expressed a definite intention to smoke were more approving of the advertisements than those children who intended not to smoke.

Children were more likely to smoke if they believed that smoking is pleasurable and that it makes a person more popular, all common themes in cigarette advertising. Among nonsmoking children, those who believed that smoking would make them more attractive were eight times more likely to express an intention to smoke in the next year.

Comment

Our data demonstrate that in just 3 years Camel's Old Joe cartoon character had an astounding influence on children's smoking behavior. The proportion of smokers under 18 years of age who choose Camels has risen from 0.5% to

32.8%. Given that children under 18 years account for 3.3% of all cigarette sales, and given a national market share of 4.4% for Camel, we compute that Camel's adult market share is actually 3.4%. Given a current average price of 153.3 cents per pack, the illegal sale of Camel cigarettes to children under 18 years of age is estimated to have risen from $6 million per year prior to the cartoon advertisements to $476 million per year now, accounting for one quarter of all Camel sales.

From both a legal and moral perspective, it is important to determine if the tobacco industry is actively promoting nicotine addiction among youngsters. However, from a public health perspective it is irrelevant whether the effects of tobacco advertising on children are intentional. If tobacco advertising is a proximate cause of disease, it must be addressed accordingly. In the following discussion we will examine the evidence produced by this study, the marketing practices of the tobacco industry as a whole as revealed in industry documents, and the marketing practices used by RJR Nabisco, in particular, to promote Camel cigarettes. The quotations cited below are from tobacco industry personnel and from documents obtained during litigation over Canada's ban of tobacco advertising.

Our data show that children are much more familiar with Camel's Old Joe cartoon character than are adults. This may be because children have more exposure to these advertisements, or because the advertisements are inherently more appealing to youngsters. The tobacco industry has long followed a policy of preferentially placing selected advertisements where children are most likely to see them. For example, print advertisements are placed in magazines "specifically designed to reach young people." Paid cigarette brand promotions appear in dozens of teen movies. Camels are featured in the Walt Disney movies *Who Framed Roger Rabbit?* and *Honey I Shrunk the Kids.*

The industry targets poster advertisements for "key youth locations/meeting places in the proximity of theaters, records [sic] stores, video arcades, etc." It is common to see Old Joe poster advertisements in malls, an obvious gathering spot for young teens. Billboards, T-shirts, baseball caps, posters, candy cigarettes, and the sponsorship of televised sporting events and entertainment events such as the Camel "Mud and Monster" series are all used to promote Camels. All are effective marketing techniques for reaching children.

The fact that children are much more attracted to the themes used in the Old Joe cartoon character advertisements may also explain why they are more familiar with them. The themes used in tobacco advertising that is targeted at children are the result of extensive research on children conducted by the tobacco industry to "learn everything there was to learn about how smoking begins." Their research identifies the major psychological vulnerabilities of children, which can then be exploited by advertising to foster and maintain nicotine addiction.

The marketing plan for "Export A" cigarettes describes their "psychological benefits"; "Export smokers will be perceived as . . . characterized by their self-confidence, strength of character and individuality which makes them popular and admired by their peers."

Consider a child's vulnerability to peer pressure. According to one industry study, "The goading and taunting that exists at the age of 11 or 12 to get nonsmokers to start smoking is virtually gone from the peer group circles by 16 or 17." If peer influence is virtually gone by the age of 16 years, who is the intended target group for RJR-MacDonald's Tempo brand, described as individuals who are "[e]xtremely influenced by their peer group"? (RJR-MacDonald is a wholly owned subsidiary of RJR Nabisco.) The recommended strategy for promoting this brand is the "[m]ajor usage of imagery which portrays the positive social appeal of peer group acceptance." In one Camel advertisement, a cowboy (a Marlboro smoker?) is being denied admission to a party because "only smooth characters [ie, Camel smokers] need apply". It appears that Camel advertisements are also targeted at individuals who are influenced by their peer group.

Children use tobacco, quite simply, because they believe the benefits outweigh the risks. To the insecure child, the benefits are the "psychological benefits" promised in tobacco advertisements: confidence, an improved image, and popularity. Children who believe that smoking will make them more popular or more attractive are up to 4.7 times more likely to smoke.

Previous research makes it clear that children derive some of their positive images of smoking from advertising. Children who are aware of tobacco advertising, and those who approve of it, are also more likely to be smokers. Children's favorable attitudes toward smoking and advertising precede actual tobacco use and correlate with the child's intention to smoke, suggesting that the images children derive from advertising encourage them to smoke. Our data confirm these earlier findings. Among nonsmoking children, those who were more approving of the Old Joe advertisements were more likely either to be ambivalent about their smoking intentions or to express a definite intention to smoke. Nonsmoking children who believed that smoking would make them more popular were eight times more likely to express an intention to smoke in the future.

Since a child's intention to smoke is considered to be a good predictor of future smoking behavior, it seems reasonable to conclude that a belief in the psychological benefits of smoking, derived from advertising, precedes, and contributes to, the adoption of smoking.

There are other lines of evidence indicating that tobacco advertising increases the number of children who use tobacco. In countries where advertising has been totally banned or severely restricted, the percentage of young people who smoke has decreased more rapidly than in countries where tobacco promotion has been less restricted. After a 24-year decline in smokeless tobacco sales, an aggressive youth-oriented marketing campaign has been followed by what has been termed "an epidemic" of smokeless tobacco use among children, with the *average* age for new users being 10 years.

Many of the tobacco industry documents cited above provide abundant evidence that one purpose of tobacco advertising is to addict children to tobacco. In the words of one advertising consultant, "Where I worked we were trying very hard to influence kids who were 14 to start to smoke." Two marketing strategy documents for Export A also reveal that it is the youngest children they are after. "Whose behavior are we trying to affect?: new users." The goal is "[o]ptimizing product and user imagery of Export 'A' against young starter smokers." The average age for starter smokers is 13 years.

The industry also researches the best ways of keeping children from quitting once they are "hooked on smoking." The purpose of one tobacco industry study was to assess the feasibility of marketing low-tar brands to teens as an alternative to quitting. The study found that for boys, "[t]he single most commonly voiced reason for quitting among those who had done so . . . was sports." The tobacco industry's sponsorship of sporting events, such as the Camel Supercross motorcycle race, should be seen in relation to its need to discourage teenage boys from quitting. Similarly, its emphasis on slimness serves as a constant reinforcement of teenage girls' fears of gaining weight as a result of quitting.

Our study provides further evidence that tobacco advertising promotes and maintains nicotine addiction among children and adolescents. A total ban of tobacco advertising and promotions, as part of an effort to protect children from the dangers of tobacco, can be based on sound scientific reasoning.

NO ↩

George J. Annas

Cowboys, Camels, and the First Amendment

The Marlboro Man and Joe Camel have become public health enemies number one and two, and removing their familiar faces from the gaze of young people has become a goal of President Bill Clinton and his health care officials.[1] The strategy of limiting the exposure of children to tobacco advertisements is based on the fact that almost all regular smokers begin smoking in their teens. This approach is politically possible because most Americans believe that tobacco companies should be prohibited from targeting children in their advertising.

Shortly before the 1996 Democratic National Convention, the President announced that he had approved regulations drafted by the Food and Drug Administration (FDA) to restrict the advertising of tobacco products to children. At the convention, Vice-President Al Gore told the delegates, "Until I draw my last breath, I will pour my heart and soul into the cause of protecting our children from the dangers of smoking."[2] In a press conference at the White House immediately following the announcement, Health and Human Services Secretary Donna Shalala said, "This is the most important public health initiative in a generation. It ranks with everything from polio to penicillin. I mean, this is huge in terms of its impact."[3]

No one doubts that a substantial reduction in the number of teenage smokers would mean a substantial reduction in the number of adult smokers when these teenagers grow up, and this reduction would have a major effect on health and longevity. Since almost 50 million Americans smoke, the result of reducing the number of young smokers substantially would indeed be "huge in terms of its impact." The real question is not whether the goal is appropriate but whether the means proposed to reach it are likely to be effective. In this regard, the FDA regulations may be unsuccessful for either of two related reasons: the implementation of the regulations may not reduce the number of teenagers who start smoking, or some of the regulations may be found to violate the First Amendment.

From George J. Annas, "Cowboys, Camels, and the First Amendment—The FDA's Restrictions on Tobacco Advertising," *The New England Journal of Medicine,* vol. 335, no. 23 (December 5, 1996).

The Regulations

The FDA's new regulations are designed to reduce the demand for tobacco products among teenagers, which is consistent with the goal of the Healthy People 2000 program to reduce by half (to 15 percent) the proportion of children who use tobacco products.[1,4] The FDA has somewhat modified the time line: the goal of its regulations is to cut underage smoking by half in seven years. Although the FDA has never before asserted jurisdiction over cigarettes or smokeless tobacco, the agency bases its claim to jurisdiction over these two types of products on its authority to regulate medical devices, defining cigarettes as a "drug-delivery device." Of course, this means that the FDA also defines nicotine as a drug. The regulations apply to sellers, distributors, and manufacturers of tobacco products. Sellers may not sell cigarettes or smokeless tobacco to anyone under the age of 18 years and must verify the age of purchasers under 26 by checking a form of identification bearing a photograph, in a "direct, face-to-face exchange." Exceptions are sales through mail orders and vending machines located in facilities that persons under the age of 18 years are not permitted to enter at any time. The distribution of free samples is also outlawed, as is the sale of cigarettes in packs of fewer than 20 (so-called kiddie packs). All cigarettes and smokeless tobacco products must bear the following statement: "Nicotine delivery devices for persons 18 or older."[1]

The most controversial portions of the regulations deal with advertising. One section outlaws all outdoor advertising within 1000 feet of public playgrounds and elementary and secondary schools. Advertising is restricted to "black text on a white background."[1] This restriction applies to all billboards but not to "adult publications." Such publications are defined by the regulations as "any newspaper, magazine, periodical or other publication... whose readers younger than 18 years of age constitute 15 percent or less of the total readership as measured by competent and reliable survey evidence; and that is read by fewer than 2 million persons younger than 18 years of age."[1] Tobacco manufacturers and distributors are prohibited from marketing any item (other than cigarettes or smokeless tobacco) that bears a brand name used for cigarettes or smokeless tobacco and are prohibited from offering any gift to a person purchasing cigarettes or smokeless tobacco products.[1] Finally, "no manufacturer, distributor, or retailer may sponsor or cause to be sponsored any athletic, musical, artistic, or other social or cultural event, or any entry or team in any event, [under] the brand name [of a tobacco product] (alone or in conjunction with any other words)."[1] Such events, may, however, be sponsored under the name of the corporation that manufactures the tobacco product, provided that the corporate name existed before 1995 and does not include a brand name.

The Legal Challenge

Tobacco companies have already filed suit to enjoin enforcement of the regulations. According to FDA Commissioner David Kessler, the FDA decided to assert its jurisdiction over cigarettes when the scientific community determined that the nicotine in tobacco products is addictive, and when the FDA concluded that the tobacco companies were probably manipulating the levels of nicotine to maintain their market of addicted users.[5] Under the legislation that gives the FDA its authority, a drug is any product "intended to affect the structure or any function of the body." The FDA contends that cigarettes and smokeless tobacco can be properly viewed as devices for delivering the drug nicotine, because they meet all three independent criteria for determining whether a product is a drug-delivery device: "a reasonable manufacturer would foresee that the product will be used for pharmacologic purposes [or] that consumers actually use it for such purposes [or] the manufacturer experts or designs the product to be used in such a manner."[5]

The primary argument of the tobacco companies is that Congress has consistently refused to give the FDA jurisdiction over tobacco products, and until now, the FDA itself has consistently said that it has no jurisdiction over such products. Moreover, the companies assert that if the FDA had jurisdiction over cigarettes as a drug or drug-delivery device, the FDA would have to ban them as not being "safe," which Congress has repeatedly refused to do or permit.

The second argument used by the tobacco companies, which is the focus of this article, is that the regulations violate the First Amendment of the U.S. Constitution by restricting the right to free speech in advertising. Congress could vote to give the FDA authority over tobacco but could not, of course, change the First Amendment.

The First Amendment and Advertising

The basic test used to determine whether the government can ban advertising is set out in the Supreme Court's 1980 opinion in *Central Hudson Gas & Electric Corporation v. Public Service Commission of New York.*[6] This case involved a regulation that prohibited electric utilities from advertising to promote the use of electricity. The court adopted a four-part test to determine whether this regulation was constitutional: (1) to be protected by the First Amendment, the advertising must concern a lawful activity and not be misleading, (2) for the ban to be valid, the state's interest in banning the advertising must be "substantial," (3) the ban must "directly advance" the state's interest, and (4) it must be no more extensive than necessary to further the state's interest.[6] In *Central Hudson,* the Supreme Court concluded that although the state had a substantial interest in energy conservation that was advanced by the ban on advertising, the ban nonetheless failed the fourth part of the test. The ban failed that part because it was overly broad, prohibiting the promotion of potentially energy-saving electric services, and there was no proof that a more limited restriction of advertising could not have achieved the same goal. The court suggested, as an example, that a narrower regulation could have required "that the advertisements include information about the relative efficiency and expense of the offered services."

In 1986, in *Posadas de Puerto Rico Associates v. Tourism Company of Puerto Rico,* the Supreme Court upheld a ban on advertisements for casino gambling in Puerto Rico.[7] The court held that this ban met the four parts of the test in

Central Hudson. Adding that the government could ban advertising for any activity that it could outlaw, the court said it would be "a strange constitutional doctrine which would concede to the legislature the authority to totally ban a product or activity, but deny to the legislature the authority to forbid the stimulation of demand for the product or activity through advertising."[7] The court gave a number of other examples of "vice" products or activities, including cigarettes, alcohol beverages, and prostitution, which struck many in the public health community as warranting restricted advertising. Of course, fashions change, and many states now promote and advertise gambling, in the form of lotteries and casinos, as good for the financial health of the government. Nonetheless, in the wake of the May 1996 decision in *44 Liquormart* v. *Rhode Island,*[8] the most recent and comprehensive case involving free speech in advertising, it is unlikely that *Posadas* will continue to be invoked. Moreover, the four-part test in *Central Hudson* will be more strictly applied in the future.

The *44 Liquormart* Case

In *44 Liquormart v. Rhode Island,* a liquor retailer challenged the Rhode Island laws that banned all advertisements of retail liquor prices, except at the place of sale, and prohibited the media from publishing any such advertisements, even in other states. 44 Liquormart had published an advertisement identifying various brands of liquor that included the word "wow" in large letters next to pictures of vodka and rum bottles. An enforcement action against the company resulted in a $400 fine. After paying the fine, 44 Liquormart appealed, seeking a declaratory judgment that the two statutes and the implementing regulations promulgated under them violated the First Amendment.

The U.S. District Court declared the ban on price advertising unconstitutional because it did not "directly advance" the state's interest in reducing alcohol consumption and was "more extensive than necessary to serve that interest."[9] The Court of Appeals reversed the decision, finding "inherent merit" in the state's argument that competitive price advertising would lower prices and that lower prices would induce more sales.[10] In reviewing these decisions, the Supreme Court unanimously found that the state laws violated the First Amendment, but no rationale for this opinion gained more than four votes. Justice John Paul Stevens (who wrote the principal opinion) began his discussion by quoting from an earlier case involving advertisements of prices for prescription drugs:

> Advertising, however tasteless and excessive it sometimes may seem, is nonetheless dissemination of information as to who is producing and selling what product, for what reason, and at what price. So long as we preserve a predominantly free enterprise economy, the allocation of our resources in large measure will be made through numerous private economic decisions. It is a matter of public interest that those decisions, in the aggregate, be intelligent and well informed. To this end, the free flow of commercial information is indispensable.[8]

Justice Stevens went on to note that "complete speech bans, unlike content-neutral restrictions on the time, place, or manner of expression... are particularly dangerous because they all but foreclose alternative means of disseminating certain information."[8] Bans unrelated to consumer protection, Stevens noted further, should be treated with special skepticism when they "seek to keep people in the dark for what the government perceives to be their own good." Stevens moved on to apply *Central Hudson's* four-point test. He concluded that "there is no question that Rhode Island's price advertising ban constitutes a blanket prohibition against truthful, nonmisleading speech about a lawful product." Stevens also agreed that the state has a substantial interest in "promoting temperance."

But can the state meet part three of the test, by showing that the ban is effective in advancing this interest? Four justices defined the third part of the test as requiring the state to "bear the burden of showing not merely that its regulation will advance its interest but also that it will do so 'to a material degree.' "[8] This requirement is necessary because of the "drastic nature" of the state's ban: "the wholesale suppression of truthful, nonmisleading information." Justice Stevens concluded that Rhode Island did not meet this requirement and could not do so without "any findings of fact" or other evidence. The common-sense notion that prohibitions against price advertising will lead to higher prices and thus lower consumption (an assumption made in *Central Hudson*) was found insufficient to support a finding that the restriction of advertising would "significantly reduce market-wide consumption."[8] "Speculation or conjecture" does not suffice.[9]

As for the fourth part of the test, Justice Stevens concluded that the ban also failed because Rhode Island did not show that alternative forms of regulation that do not limit speech, such as limiting per capita purchases or using educational campaigns that address the problem of excessive drinking, could not be equally or more effective in reducing consumption. All nine members of the Supreme Court agreed with this conclusion. Finally, Justice Stevens (again on behalf of four justices) argued that in *Posadas* the court had wrongly concluded that since the state could ban a product or activity, it could ban advertising about it. He argued that the First Amendment was much stronger than that decision implied, noting "We think it quite clear that banning speech may sometimes prove far more intrusive than banning conduct," and thus it is not true that "the power to prohibit an activity is necessarily 'greater' than the power to suppress speech about it.... The text of the First Amendment makes clear that the Constitution presumes that attempts to regulate speech are more dangerous than attempts to regulate conduct."[8] Stevens also rejected the idea that "vice" activities have less protection from the First Amendment than other commercial activities, noting that the distinction would be "difficult, if not impossible, to define."

Free Speech and the FDA Regulations

Selling cigarettes and smokeless tobacco to persons under the age of 18 is illegal is all states, so advertising to this age group is not protected by the First Amendment. Nor does outlawing vending machines that children have access to pose a problem with respect to the First Amendment. Because the FDA regulations are intended to apply only to children and do not foreclose alternative sources of information, it is impossible to predict with certainty how the Supreme Court will respond to a First Amendment challenge (assuming the court finds that the FDA has authority in this area). Nonetheless, the areas of primary concern can be identified.

Bans will be subject to a higher standard of review than restrictions. Forms of advertising that are banned include the distribution of products (other than cigarettes and smokeless tobacco) with the tobacco brand name or insignia on them, the placement of billboards within 1000 feet of playgrounds and elementary and secondary schools, and the use of brand names for sporting and cultural events. If the court adopts the strict version of the third part of the test in *Central Hudson*, the FDA will have to present evidence that these bans will reduce underage smoking to a material degree. Moreover, to meet the fourth part of the test, which the court unanimously found was not met in *44 Liquormart*, the FDA must also show that no other, less restrictive method, such as antismoking advertising or better enforcement of existing laws, would work as well. This will be difficult, especially since the FDA commissioner has already said he believes that antismoking advertising is effective in helping young people understand the risks of smoking and that, after the publication of its rules, the agency plans "to notify the major cigarette and smokeless-tobacco companies that it will begin discussing a requirement that they fund an education program in the mass media."[5] The court could decide that a nonspeech ban should have been tried first.

Restrictions on advertising may be easier to uphold, but even they are not obviously permissible. The tobacco companies spend $6 billion a year in advertising and promotion, about $700 million of which is spent on magazine advertisements.[11] The core antiadvertising regulation requires that advertisements on all billboards and in publications that do not qualify as adult publications be limited to black text on a white background.[1] This is a restriction (not a ban) and does not prohibit the inclusion of factual information (such as the price of liquor, which was at issue in *44 Liquormart*). The rationale for these rules is that images in bright colors, of which Joe Camel is the primary example, entice children to start smoking or continue to smoke. Since no objective information is being banned or restricted, the court may find that such a restriction need meet only a common-sense test.[12] If, however, the court takes a more sophisticated view of advertising—which is largely focused on image rather than text—it may well hold that the same rules apply and that therefore the burden of proof is on the FDA to demonstrate that such a restriction would reduce underage smoking to a material degree. No study has yet been able to show evidence of this effect. Consistent with the view that "pop art" should be protected at least as much as text is the view that advertising images are forms designed to elicit certain responses and as such are entitled to at least as much protection from the First Amendment as objective information.

Drastic restrictions on advertising may also be ineffective or even counterproductive. In Britain, for example, where both Joe Camel and the Marlboro

Man are outlawed and tobacco advertisers are prohibited from using anything that suggests health, fresh air, or beauty, creative advertisers have found other ways to promote tobacco products. Advertisements for Silk Cut cigarettes feature various images of silk being cut (e.g., scissors dancing a cancan in purple silk skirts and a rhinoceroses whose horn pierces a purple silk cap), and Marlboro advertisements portray bleak and forbidding western U.S. landscapes with the words, "Welcome to Marlboro Country." It has been suggested that by using such surreal images, tobacco advertisers may be appealing to fantasies of death and sexual violence that have a powerful (if unconscious) appeal to consumers.[13] Such imagery may actually have greater appeal for teenagers than Joe Camel. U.S. advertising agencies have already experimented with black-and-white, text-only advertisements. One agency proposed that the required phrase, "a nicotine-delivery device," can be used in conjunction with the phrase ".cyber cigarettes" on one line, under the phrase (in larger type) "pleasure.com" and a sideways smiling face, formed by a colon, a hyphen, and a closed parenthesis[:-)], to suggest that nicotine is a pleasure of the cyberspace age.[14]

The FDA knows it has a First Amendment problem here. In its comments accompanying the regulations, the agency argues that it is not required to "conclusively prove by rigorous empirical studies that advertising causes initial consumption of cigarettes and smokeless tobacco."[1] In fact, the FDA says it is impossible to prove this. Instead, the agency argues it need only demonstrate that there is "more than adequate evidence" that "tobacco advertising has an effect on young people's tobacco use behavior if it affects initiation, maintenance, or attempts at quitting."[1] The FDA's position follows from the conclusion of the Institute of Medicine:

> Portraying a deadly addiction as a healthful and sensual experience tugs against the nation's efforts to promote a tobacco-free norm and to discourage tobacco use by children and youths. This warrants legislation restricting the features of advertising and promotion that make tobacco use attractive to youths. The question is not, "Are advertising and promotion the causes of youth initiation?" but rather, "Does the preponderance of evidence suggest that features of advertising and promotion tend to encourage youths to smoke?" The answer is yes and this is a sufficient basis for action, even in the absence of a precise and definitive causal chain.[13]

The Surgeon General has reached a similar conclusion:

> Cigarette advertising uses images rather than information to portray the attractiveness and function of smoking. Human models and cartoon characters in cigarette advertising convey independence, healthfulness, adventure-seeking, and youthful activities—themes correlated with psychosocial factors that appeal to young people.[15]

The Supreme Court may make an exception for tobacco advertisements because of the clear health hazards and the use of restrictions instead of bans, but the extent of the restrictions will have to be justified. In this regard, the 15 percent young-readership rule for publications is difficult to justify as either not arbitrary or not more restrictive than necessary. The FDA admits, for example, that its rule would require the following magazines to use black-and-white, text-only advertisements: *Sports Illustrated* (18 percent of its readers are under the age of 18), *Car and Driver* (18 percent), *Motor Trend* (22 percent), *Road and Track* (21 percent), *Rolling Stone* (18 percent), *Vogue* (18 percent), *Mademoiselle* (20 percent), and *Glamour* (17 percent).[1] The FDA seems particularly offended by "a cardboard Joe Camel pop-out" holding concert tickets in the center of *Rolling Stone*.[5] (Some Americans might wish to censor the photograph of a naked Brooke Shields on the cover of the October 1996 issue as well, although that image is clearly protected by the First Amendment.) A 25 percent rule, for example, would exempt all these magazines.

The FDA justifies the 15 percent rule by arguing that young people between the ages of 5 and 17 years constitute approximately 15 percent of the U.S. population and that "if the percentage of young readers of a publication is greater than the percentage of young people in the general population, the publication can be viewed as having particular appeal to young readers."[1] A similar argument can, of course, be made with regard to sporting and cultural events—some of which may have very few young people in attendance.[15] On the other hand, the billboard restrictions seem to have a more solid justification.

Tobacco companies profit handsomely by selling products that cause serious health problems and contribute to the deaths of millions of Americans. There is also little doubt that nicotine is physically addictive and that it is in the interest of tobacco companies to get children addicted early, since very few people take up smoking after the age of 18 years. The FDA admits, however, that it cannot prove that cigarette advertising causes children to begin to smoke, and the agency has not tried alternative measures, such as strictly enforcing current laws that prohibit sales to minors and engaging in a broad-based educational campaign against smoking, to reduce the number of children who smoke. Until the FDA either proves that cigarette advertising causes children to start smoking or uses methods of discouraging smoking that stay clear of the First Amendment, bans and restrictions on advertising will raise enough problems with the First Amendment to ensure that they will be tied up in court for years. This does not mean, however, that no immediate legal actions can be taken against tobacco companies. In a future article, I will discuss current trends in litigation against these companies and assess the likely impact of antismoking lawsuits on the tobacco companies.

References

1. Food and Drug Administration, Department of Health and Human Services. Regulations restricting the sale and distribution of cigarettes and smokeless tobacco to protect children and adolescents. Fed Regist 1996;61 (168):44, 396–618.
2. Gore speech: "America is strong. Bill Clinton's leadership paying off." New York Times, August 29, 1996: B12.
3. Press Briefing by Secretary of HHS Donna Shalala, FDA Commissioner David Kessler, and Assistant Secretary Phil Lee. White House, Office of Press Secretary, August 23, 1996.
4. Trends in smoking initiation among adolescents and young adults—United States, 1980–1989. MMWR Morb Mortal Wkly Rep 1995;44:521–5.

5. Kessler DA, Witt AM, Barnett PS, et al. The Food and Drug Administration's regulation of tobacco products. N Engl J Med 1996; 335:988–94.
6. Central Hudson Gas & Electric Corp. v. Public Service Commission of New York, 447 U.S. 557 (1980).
7. Posadas du Puerto Rico Associates v. Tourism Company of Puerto Rico, 478 U.S. 328 (1986).
8. 44 Liquormart, Inc. v. Rhode Island, 116 S. Ct. 1495 (1996).
9. 44 Liquor Mart, Inc. v. Racine, 829 F. Supp. 543 (R.I. 1993).
10. 44 Liquor Mart, Inc. v. Rhode Island, 39 F. 3d 5 (1st Cir. 1994).
11. Committee on Preventing Nicotine Addiction in Children and Youths. Institute of Medicine. Growing up tobacco free: preventing nicotine addiction in children and youths. Washington, D.C.: National Academy Press, 1994:131.
12. Glantz L. Regulating tobacco advertising: the FDA regulations and the First Amendment. Am J Public Health (in press).
13. Parker-Pope T. Tough tobacco-ad rules light creative fires. Wall Street Journal. October 9, 1996:B1.
14. Brownlee L. How agency teams might cope with U.S. ad restraints. Wall Street Journal. October 9, 1996:B1.
15. Department of Health and Human Services. Preventing tobacco use among young people: a report of the Surgeon General. Washington, D.C.: Government Printing Office, 1994:195.

POSTSCRIPT

Should Tobacco Advertising Be Restricted?

There are several resources available with which to further examine this issue. The government report on the Hearing Before the Committee on Labor and Human Resources of the United States Senate, 101st Congress, Second Session, on the Tobacco Product Education and Health Protection Act of 1990 (Senate Hearing 101-707, available in most government repository libraries on microfiche) is one of the first fully documented sources on the tobacco industry's disclosure of addictive agents in cigarettes.

Simon Chapman has written a book on the techniques and marketing tools used for cigarette advertising entitled *Great Expectorations: Advertising and the Tobacco Industry* (Comedia Publishing Group, 1986). Bruce Maxwell and Michael Jacobson have examined appeals to certain target audiences in their book *Marketing Disease to Hispanics: The Selling of Alcohol, Tobacco, and Junk Foods* (Center for Science in the Public Interest, 1989).

There are a number of good, general references on advertising, including Roland Marchand's *Advertising the American Dream* (University of California Press, 1985) and Robert Goldman's *Reading Ads Socially* (Routledge, 1992).

Among books that are critical of the advertising industry in general, a recent text lends itself to the discussion of the potential for the regulation of the advertising industry: Matthew P. McAllister's *The Commercialization of American Culture: New Advertising, Control and Democracy* (Sage Publications, 1995).

ISSUE 7

Is Advertising Ethical?

YES: John E. Calfee, from "How Advertising Informs to Our Benefit," *Consumers' Research* (April 1998)

NO: Russ Baker, from "The Squeeze," *Columbia Journalism Review* (September/October 1997)

ISSUE SUMMARY

YES: John E. Calfee, a former U.S. Trade Commission economist, takes the position that advertising is very useful to people and that the information that advertising imparts helps consumers make better decisions. He maintains that the benefits of advertising far outweigh the negative criticisms.

NO: Author Russ Baker focuses on the way in which advertisers seek to control magazine content and, thus, go beyond persuasion and information into the realm of influencing the content of other media.

Professor Dallas Smythe first described commercial media as a system for delivering audiences to advertisers. This perception of the viewing public as a "market" for products as well as an audience for advertising—a main source of media revenue—reflects the economic orientation of the current media system in America. The unplanned side effects of advertising, however, concern many critics. For example, socialization into consumption, consumerism, materialism, and high expectations are one set of concerns. Many of these questions have often been asked: Is advertising deceptive? Does it create or perpetuate stereotypes? Does it create conformity? Does it create insecurity in order to sell goods? Does it cause people to buy things that they do not really need?

John E. Calfee addresses some of these questions in the following selection, but he focuses on how the information in ads benefits consumers. He takes the position that advertising is in the public interest and that even controversies about ads may be beneficial because they can result in competitive pricing for consumers. Citing some specific cases, he claims that individuals can learn about important issues (such as health) through ads. He even considers what he calls "less bad" ads, which give consumers important negative information that can be useful to their well-being.

In the second selection, Russ Baker provides many different examples to show that the advertising industry has become too large and too powerful. He maintains that by giving corporations too much say in magazine and newspaper copy, advertisers may ultimately distort free press and free inquiry. When publishers bow to corporate control over material that is not advertising, they may lose focus and become mere extensions of advertisers.

These two selections raise concerns about the ethical nature of ads. Calfee focuses only on the good that advertising does, while Baker addresses the ethical nature of the control that corporations and advertising have in influencing media content. Both authors examine important concepts of fairness, honesty, and integrity in the world of advertising.

John E. Calfee

YES

How Advertising Informs to Our Benefit

Agreat truth about advertising is that it is a tool for communicating information and shaping markets. It is one of the forces that compel sellers to cater to the desires of consumers. Almost everyone knows this because consumers use advertising every day, and they miss advertising when they cannot get it. This fact does not keep politicians and opinion leaders from routinely dismissing the value of advertising. But the truth is that people find advertising very useful indeed.

Of course, advertising primarily seeks to persuade and everyone knows this, too. The typical ad tries to induce a consumer to do one particular thing —usually, buy a product—instead of a thousand other things. There is nothing obscure about this purpose or what it means for buyers. Decades of data and centuries of intuition reveal that all consumers everywhere are deeply suspicious of what advertisers say and why they say it. This skepticism is in fact the driving force that makes advertising so effective. The persuasive purpose of advertising and the skepticism with which it is met are two sides of a single process. Persuasion and skepticism work in tandem so advertising can do its job in competitive markets. Hence, ads represent the seller's self interest, consumers know this, and sellers know that consumers know it.

By understanding this process more fully, we can sort out much of the popular confusion surrounding advertising and how it benefits consumers.

How useful is advertising? Just how useful is the connection between advertising and information? At first blush, the process sounds rather limited. Volvo ads tell consumers that Volvos have side-impact air bags, people learn a little about the importance of air bags, and Volvo sells a few more cars. This seems to help hardly anyone except Volvo and its customers.

But advertising does much more. It routinely provides immense amounts of information that benefits primarily parties other than the advertiser. This may sound odd, but it is a logical result of market forces and the nature of information itself.

The ability to use information to sell products is an incentive to create new information through research. Whether the topic is nutrition, safety, or more mundane matters like how to measure amplifier power, the necessity of achieving credibility with consumers and critics requires much of this research to be placed in the public domain, and that it rest upon some academic credentials. That kind of research typically produces results that apply to more than just the brands sold by the firm sponsoring the research. The lack of property rights to such "pure" information ensures that this extra information is available at no charge. Both consumers and competitors may borrow the new information for their own purposes.

Advertising also elicits additional information from other sources. Claims that are striking, original, forceful or even merely obnoxious will generate news stories about the claims, the controversies they cause, the reactions of competitors (A price war? A splurge of comparison ads?), the reactions of consumers and the remarks of governments and independent authorities.

Probably the most concrete, pervasive, and persistent example of competitive advertising that works for the public good is price advertising. Its effect is invariably to heighten competition and reduce prices, even the prices of firms that assiduously avoid mentioning prices in their own advertising.

There is another area where the public benefits of advertising are less obvious but equally important. The unremitting nature of consumer interest in health, and the eagerness of sellers to cater to consumer desires, guarantee that advertising related to health will provide a storehouse of telling observations on the ways in which the benefits of advertising extend beyond the interests of advertisers to include the interests of the public at large.

A cascade of information   Here is probably the best documented example of why advertising is necessary for consumer welfare. In the 1970s, public health experts described compelling evidence that people who eat more fiber are less likely to get cancer, especially cancer of the colon, which happens to be the second leading cause of deaths from cancer in the United States. By 1979, the U.S. Surgeon General was recommending that people eat more fiber in order to prevent cancer.

Consumers appeared to take little notice of these recommendations, however. The National Cancer Institute decided that more action was needed. NCI's cancer prevention division undertook to communicate the new information about fiber and cancer to the general public. Their goal was to change consumer diets and reduce the risk of cancer, but they had little hope of success given the tiny advertising budgets of federal agencies like NCI.

Their prospects unexpectedly brightened in 1984. NCI received a call from the Kellogg Corporation, whose All-Bran cereal held a commanding market share of the high-fiber segment. Kellogg proposed to use All-Bran advertising as a vehicle for NCI's public service messages. NCI thought that was an excellent idea. Soon, an agreement was reached in which NCI would review Kellogg's ads and labels for accuracy and value before Kellogg began running their fiber-cancer ads.

The new Kellogg All-Bran campaign opened in October 1984. A typical ad began with the headline, "At last some news about cancer you can live with." The ad continued: "The National Cancer Institute believes a high fiber, low fat diet may reduce your risk of some kinds of cancer. The National Cancer

Institute reports some very good health news. There is growing evidence that may link a high fiber, low fat diet to lower incidence of some kinds of cancer. That's why one of their strongest recommendations is to eat high-fiber foods. If you compare, you'll find Kellogg's All-Bran has nine grams of fiber per serving. No other cereal has more. So start your day with a bowl of Kellogg's All-Bran or mix it with your regular cereal."

The campaign quickly achieved two things. One was to create a regulatory crisis between two agencies. The Food and Drug Administration thought that if a food was advertised as a way to prevent cancer, it was being marketed as a drug. Then the FDA's regulations for drug labeling would kick in. The food would be reclassified as a drug and would be removed from the market until the seller either stopped making the health claims or put the product through the clinical testing necessary to obtain formal approval as a drug.

But food advertising is regulated by the Federal Trade Commission, not the FDA. The FTC thought Kellogg's ads were non-deceptive and were therefore perfectly legal. In fact, it thought the ads should be encouraged. The Director of the FTC's Bureau of Consumer Protection declared that "the [Kellogg] ad has presented important public health recommendations in an accurate, useful, and substantiated way. It informs the members of the public that there is a body of data suggesting certain relationships between cancer and diet that they may find important." The FTC won this political battle, and the ads continued.

The second instant effect of the All-Bran campaign was to unleash a flood of health claims. Vegetable oil manufacturers advertised that cholesterol was associated with coronary heart disease, and that vegetable oil does not contain cholesterol. Margarine ads did the same, and added that vitamin A is essential for good vision. Ads for calcium products (such as certain antacids) provided vivid demonstrations of the effects of osteoporosis (which weakens bones in old age), and recounted the advice of experts to increase dietary calcium as a way to prevent osteoporosis. Kellogg's competitors joined in citing the National Cancer Institute dietary recommendations.

Nor did things stop there. In the face of consumer demand for better and fuller information, health claims quickly evolved from a blunt tool to a surprisingly refined mechanism. Cereals were advertised as high in fiber and low in sugar or fat or sodium. Ads for an upscale brand of bread noted: "Well, most high-fiber bran cereals may be high in fiber, but often only one kind: insoluble. It's this kind of fiber that helps promote regularity. But there's also a kind of fiber known as soluble, which most high-fiber bran cereals have in very small amounts, if at all. Yet diets high in this kind of fiber may actually lower your serum cholesterol, a risk factor for some heart diseases." Cereal boxes became convenient sources for a summary of what made for a good diet.

Increased independent information   The ads also brought powerful secondary effects. These may have been even more useful than the information that actually appeared in the ads themselves.

One effect was an increase in media coverage of diet and health. *Consumer Reports*, a venerable and hugely influential magazine that carries no advertising, revamped its reports on cereals to emphasize fiber and other ingredients (rather than testing the foods to see how well they did at providing a complete diet for laboratory rats). The health-claims phenomenon generated its own press coverage, with articles like "What Has All-Bran Wrought?" and "The Fiber Furor." These stories recounted the ads and scientific information that prompted the ads; and articles on food and health proliferated. Anyone who lived through these years in the United States can probably remember the unending media attention to health claims and to diet and health generally.

Much of the information on diet and health was new. This was no coincidence. Firms were sponsoring research on their products in the hope of finding results that could provide a basis for persuasive advertising claims. Oat bran manufacturers, for example, funded research on the impact of soluble fiber on blood cholesterol. When the results came out "wrong," as they did in a 1990 study published with great fanfare in *The New England Journal of Medicine*, the headline in *Advertising Age* was "Oat Bran Popularity Hitting the Skids," and it did indeed tumble. The manufacturers kept at the research, however, and eventually the best research supported the efficacy of oat bran in reducing cholesterol (even to the satisfaction of the FDA). Thus did pure advertising claims spill over to benefit the information environment at large.

The shift to higher fiber cereals encompassed brands that had never undertaken the effort necessary to construct believable ads about fiber and disease. Two consumer researchers at the FDA reviewed these data and concluded they were "consistent with the successful educational impact of the Kellogg diet and health campaign: consumers seemed to be making an apparently thoughtful discrimination between high- and low-fiber cereals," and that the increased market shares for high-fiber non-advertised products represented "the clearest evidence of a successful consumer education campaign."

Perhaps most dramatic were the changes in consumer awareness of diet and health. An FTC analysis of government surveys showed that when consumers were asked about how they could prevent cancer through their diet, the percentage who mentioned fiber increased from 4% before the 1979 Surgeon General's report to 8.5% in 1984 (after the report but before the All-Bran campaign) to 32% in 1986 after a year and a half or so of health claims (the figure in 1988 was 28%). By far the greatest increases in awareness were among women (who do most of the grocery shopping) and the less educated: up from 0% for women without a high school education in 1984 to 31% for the same group in 1986. For women with incomes of less than $15,000, the increase was from 6% to 28%.

The health-claims advertising phenomenon achieved what years of effort by government agencies had failed to achieve. With its mastery of the art of brevity, its ability to command attention, and its use of television, brand advertising touched precisely the people the public health community was most desperate to reach. The health claims expanded consumer information along a broad front. The benefits clearly extended far beyond the interests of the relatively few manufacturers who made vigorous use of health claims in advertising.

A pervasive phenomenon Health claims for foods are only one example, however, of a pervasive phenomenon—the use of advertising to provide essential health information with benefits extending beyond the interests of the advertisers themselves.

Advertising for soap and detergents, for example, once improved private hygiene and therefore, public health (hygiene being one of the under-appreciated triumphs in twentieth century public health). Toothpaste advertising helped to do the same for teeth. When mass advertising for toothpaste and tooth powder began early in this century, tooth brushing was rare. It was common by the 1930s, after which toothpaste sales leveled off even though the advertising, of course, continued. When fluoride toothpastes became available, advertising generated interest in better teeth and professional dental care. Later, a "plaque reduction war" (which first involved mouthwashes, and later tooth-pastes) brought a new awareness of gum disease and how to prevent it. The financial gains to the toothpaste industry were surely dwarfed by the benefits to consumers in the form of fewer cavities and fewer lost teeth.

Health claims induced changes in foods, in non-foods such as toothpaste, in publications ranging from university health letters to mainstream newspapers and magazines, and of course, consumer knowledge of diet and health.

These rippling effects from health claims in ads demonstrated the most basic propositions in the economics of information. Useful information initially failed to reach people who needed it because information producers could not charge a price to cover the costs of creating and disseminating pure information. And this problem was alleviated by advertising, sometimes in a most vivid manner.

Other examples of spillover benefits from advertising are far more common than most people realize. Even the much-maligned promotion of expensive new drugs can bring profound health benefits to patients and families, far exceeding what is actually charged for the products themselves.

The market processes that produce these benefits bear all the classic features of competitive advertising. We are not analyzing public service announcements here, but old-fashioned profit-seeking brand advertising. Sellers focused on the information that favored their own products. They advertised it in ways that provided a close link with their own brand. It was a purely competitive enterprise, and the benefits to consumers arose from the imperatives of the competitive process.

One might see all this as simply an extended example of the economics of information and greed. And indeed it is, if by greed one means the effort to earn a profit by providing what people are willing to pay for, even if what they want most is information rather than a tangible product. The point is that there is overwhelming evidence that unregulated economic forces dictate that much useful information will be provided by brand advertising, and *only* by brand advertising.

Of course, there is much more to the story. There is the question of how competition does the good I have described without doing even more harm elsewhere. After all, firms want to tell people only what is good about their brands, and people often want to know what is wrong with the brands. It turns out that competition takes care of this problem, too.

Advertising and context   It is often said that most advertising does not contain very much information. In a way, this is true. Research on the contents of advertising typically finds just a few pieces of concrete information per ad. That's an average, of course. Some ads obviously contain a great deal of information. Still, a lot of ads are mainly images and pleasant talk, with little in the way of what most people would consider hard information. On the whole, information in advertising comes in tiny bits and pieces.

Cost is only one reason. To be sure, cramming more information into ads is expensive. But more to the point is the fact that advertising plays off the information available from outside sources. Hardly anything about advertising is more important than the interplay between what the ad contains and what surrounds it. Sometimes this interplay is a burden for the advertiser because it is beyond his control. But the interchange between advertising and environment is also an invaluable tool for sellers. Ads that work in collaboration with outside information can communicate far more than they ever could on their own.

The upshot is advertising's astonishing ability to communicate a great deal of information in a few words. Economy and vividness of expression almost always rely upon what is in the information environment. The famously concise "Think Small" and "Lemon" ads for the VW "Beetle" in the 1960s and 1970s were highly effective with buyers concerned about fuel economy, repair costs, and extravagant styling in American cars. This was a case where the less said, the better. The ads were more powerful when consumers were free to bring their own ideas about the issues to bear.

The same process is repeated over again for all sorts of products. Ads for computer modems once explained what they could be used for. Now a simple reference to the Internet is sufficient to conjure an elaborate mix of equipment and applications. These matters are better left vague so each potential customer can bring to the ad his own idea of what the Internet is really for.

Leaning on information from other sources is also a way to enhance credibility, without which advertising must fail. Much of the most important information in advertising—think of cholesterol and heart disease, antilock brakes and automobile safety—acquires its force from highly credible sources *other* than the advertiser. To build up this kind of credibility through material actually contained in ads would be cumbersome and inefficient. Far more effective, and far more economical, is the technique of making challenges, raising questions and otherwise making it perfectly clear to the audience that the seller invites comparisons and welcomes the tough questions. Hence the classic slogan, "If you can find a better whisky, buy it."

Finally, there is the most important point of all. Informational sparseness facilitates competition. It is easier to challenge a competitor through pungent slogans—"Where's the beef?", "Where's the big saving?"—than through a step-by-step recapitulation of what has gone on before. The bits-and-pieces approach makes for quick, unerring attacks and equally quick responses, all under the watchful eye of the consumer over whom the battle is being fought. This is an ideal recipe for competition.

It also brings the competitive market's fabled self-correcting forces into play. Sellers are less likely to stretch the truth, whether it involves prices or subtleties about safety and performance, when they know they may arouse a merciless response from injured competitors. That is one reason the FTC once worked to get comparative ads on television, and has sought for decades to dismantle government or voluntary bans on comparative ads.

'Less-bad' advertising   There is a troubling possibility, however. Is it not possible that in their selective and carefully calculated use of outside information, advertisers have the power to focus consumer attention exclusively on the positive, i.e., on what is good about the brand or even the entire product class? Won't automobile ads talk up style, comfort, and extra safety, while food ads do taste and convenience, cigarette ads do flavor and lifestyle, and airlines do comfort and frequency of departure, all the while leaving consumers to search through other sources to find all the things that are wrong with products?

In fact, this is not at all what happens. Here is why: Everything for sale has something wrong with it, if only the fact that you have to pay for it. Some products, of course, are notable for their faults. The most obvious examples involve tobacco and health, but there are also food and heart disease, drugs and side effects, vacations and bad weather, automobiles and accidents, airlines and delay, among others.

Products and their problems bring into play one of the most important ways in which the competitive market induces sellers to serve the interests of buyers. No matter what the product, there are usually a few brands that are "less bad" than the others. The natural impulse is to advertise that advantage —"less cholesterol," "less fat," "less dangerous," and so on. Such provocative claims tend to have an immediate impact. The targets often retaliate; maybe their brands are less bad in a different respect (less salt?). The ensuing struggle brings better information, more informed choices, and improved products.

Perhaps the most riveting episode of "less-bad" advertising ever seen occurred, amazingly enough, in the industry that most people assume is the master of avoiding saying anything bad about its product.

Less-bad cigarette ads   Cigarette advertising was once very different from what it is today. Cigarettes first became popular around the time of World War I, and they came to dominate the tobacco market in the 1920s. Steady and often dramatic sales increases continued into the 1950s, always with vigorous support from advertising. Tobacco advertising was duly celebrated as an outstanding example of the power and creativity of advertising. Yet amazingly, much of the advertising focused on what was wrong with smoking, rather than what people liked about smoking.

The very first ad for the very first mass-marketed American cigarette brand (Camel, the same brand recently under attack for its use of a cartoon character) said, "Camel Cigarettes will not sting the tongue and will not parch the throat." When Old Gold broke into the market in the mid-1920s, it did so with an ad campaign about coughs and throats and harsh cigarette smoke. It settled on the slogan, "Not a cough in a carload."

Competitors responded in kind. Soon, advertising left no doubt about what was wrong with smoking. Lucky Strike ads said, "No Throat Irritation—No Cough . . . we . . . removed . . . harmful corrosive acids," and later on, "Do you inhale? What's there to be afraid of? . . . famous purifying process removes certain impurities." Camel's famous tag line, "more doctors smoke Camels than any other brand," carried a punch precisely because many authorities thought smoking was unhealthy (cigarettes were called "coffin nails" back then), and smokers were eager for reassurance in the form of smoking by doctors themselves. This particular ad, which was based on surveys of physicians, ran in one form or another from 1933 to 1955. It achieved prominence partly because physicians practically never endorsed non-therapeutic products.

Things really got interesting in the early 1950s, when the first persuasive medical reports on smoking and lung cancer reached the public. These reports created a phenomenal stir among smokers and the public generally. People who do not understand how advertising works would probably assume that cigarette manufacturers used advertising to divert attention away from the cancer reports. In fact, they did the opposite.

Small brands could not resist the temptation to use advertising to scare smokers into switching brands. They inaugurated several spectacular years of "fear advertising" that sought to gain competitive advantage by exploiting smokers' new fear of cancer. Lorillard, the beleaguered seller of Old Gold, introduced Kent, a new filter brand supported by ad claims like these: "Sensitive smokers get real health protection with new Kent," "Do you love a good smoke but not what the smoke does to you?" and "Takes out more nicotine and tars than any other leading cigarette—*the difference in protection is priceless*," illustrated by television ads showing the black tar trapped by Kent's filters.

Other manufacturers came out with their own filter brands, and raised the stakes with claims like, "Nose, throat, and accessory organs not adversely affected by smoking Chesterfields. First such report ever published about any cigarette," "Takes the fear out of smoking," and "Stop worrying . . . Philip Morris and only Philip Morris is entirely free of irritation used [sic] in all other leading cigarettes."

These ads threatened to demolish the industry. Cigarette sales plummeted by 3% in 1953 and a remarkable 6% in 1954. Never again, not even in the face of the most impassioned anti-smoking publicity by the Surgeon General or the FDA, would cigarette consumption decline as rapidly as it did during these years of entirely market-driven anti-smoking ad claims by the cigarette industry itself.

Thus advertising traveled full circle. Devised to bolster brands, it denigrated the product so much that overall market demand actually declined. Everyone understood what was happening, but the fear ads continued because they helped the brands that used them. The new filter brands (all from smaller manufacturers) gained a foothold even as their ads amplified the medical reports on the dangers of smoking. It was only after the FTC stopped the fear ads in 1955 (on the grounds that the implied health claims had no proof) that sales resumed their customary annual increases.

Fear advertising has never quite left the tobacco market despite the regulatory straight jacket that governs cigarette advertising. In 1957, when leading cancer experts advised smokers to ingest less tar, the industry responded by cutting tar and citing tar content figures compiled by independent sources. A stunning "tar derby" reduced the tar and nicotine content of cigarettes by 40% in four years, a far more rapid decline than would be achieved by years of government urging in later decades. This episode, too, was halted by the FTC. In February 1960 the FTC engineered a "voluntary" ban on tar and nicotine claims.

Further episodes continue to this day. In 1993, for example, Liggett planned an advertising campaign to emphasize that its Chesterfield brand did not use the stems and less desirable parts of the tobacco plant. This continuing saga, extending through eight decades, is perhaps the best documented case of how "less-bad" advertising completely offsets any desires by sellers to accentuate the positive while ignoring the negative. *Consumer Reports* magazine's 1955 assessment of the new fear of smoking still rings true:

> " ... companies themselves are largely to blame. Long before the current medical attacks, the companies were building up suspicion in the consumer by the discredited 'health claims' in their ads. ... Such medicine-show claims may have given the smoker temporary confidence in one brand, but they also implied that cigarettes in general were distasteful, probably harmful, and certainly a 'problem.' When the scientists came along with their charges against cigarettes, the smoker was ready to accept them."

And that is how information works in competitive advertising.

Less-bad can be found wherever competitive advertising is allowed. I already described the health-claims-for-foods saga, which featured fat and cholesterol and the dangers of cancer and heart disease. Price advertising is another example. Prices are the most stubbornly negative product feature of all, because they represent the simple fact that the buyer must give up something else. There is no riper target for comparative advertising. When sellers advertise lower prices, competitors reduce their prices and advertise that, and soon a price war is in the works. This process so strongly favors consumers over the industry that one of the first things competitors do when they form a trade group is to propose an agreement to restrict or ban price advertising (if not ban all advertising). When that fails, they try to get advertising regulators to stop price ads, an attempt that unfortunately often succeeds.

Someone is always trying to scare customers into switching brands out of fear of the product itself. The usual effect is to impress upon consumers what they do not like about the product. In 1991, when Americans were worried about insurance companies going broke, a few insurance firms advertised that they were more solvent than their competitors. In May 1997, United Airlines began a new ad campaign that started out by reminding fliers of all the inconveniences that seem to crop up during air travel.

Health information is a fixture in "less-bad" advertising. Ads for sleeping aids sometimes focus on the issue of whether they are habit-forming. In March 1996, a medical journal reported that the pain reliever acetaminophen, the active ingredient in Tylenol, can cause liver damage in heavy drinkers. This fact immediately became the focus of ads for Advil, a competing product. A public debate ensued, conducted through advertising, talk shows, news reports and pronouncements from medical authorities. The result: consumers learned a lot more than they had known before about the fact that all drugs have side effects. The press noted that this dispute may have helped consumers, but it hurt the pain reliever industry. Similar examples abound.

We have, then, a general rule: sellers will use comparative advertising when permitted to do so, even if it means spreading bad information about a product instead of favorable information. The mechanism usually takes the form of less-bad claims. One can hardly imagine a strategy more likely to give consumers the upper hand in the give and take of the marketplace. Less-bad claims are a primary means by which advertising serves markets and consumers rather than sellers. They completely refute the naive idea that competitive advertising will emphasize only the sellers' virtues while obscuring their problems.

Russ Baker

 **NO**

The Squeeze

In an effort to avoid potential conflicts, it is required that Chrysler Corporation be alerted in advance of any and all editorial content that encompasses
sexual, political, social issues or any editorial that might be construed as
provocative or offensive. Each and every issue that carries Chrysler advertising requires a written summary outlining major theme/articles appearing in
upcoming issues. These summaries are to be forwarded to PentaCom prior
to closing in order to give Chrysler ample time to review and reschedule
if desired.... As acknowledgment of this letter we ask that you or a representative from the publication sign below and return to us no later than
February 15.

> — from a letter sent by Chrysler's ad agency, PentaCom, a division
> of BBDO North America, to at least fifty magazines

Is there any doubt that advertisers mumble and sometimes roar about reporting
that can hurt them? That the auto giants don't like pieces that, say, point to auto
safety problems? Or that Big Tobacco hates to see its glamorous, cheerful ads
juxtaposed with articles mentioning their best customers' grim way of death?
When advertisers disapprove of an editorial climate, they can—and sometimes
do—take a hike.

But for Chrysler to push beyond its parochial economic interests—by demanding summaries of upcoming articles while implicitly asking editors to
think twice about running "sexual, political, social issues"—crosses a sharply
defined line. "This is new," says Milton Glaser, the *New York* magazine co-
founder and celebrated designer. "It will have a devastating effect on the idea
of a free press and of free inquiry."

Glaser is among those in the press who are vocally urging editors and
publishers to resist. "If Chrysler achieves this," he says, "there is no reason
to hope that other advertisers won't ask for the same privilege. You will have
thirty or forty advertisers checking through the pages. They will send notes to
publishers. I don't see how any good citizen doesn't rise to this occasion and
say this development is un-American and a threat to freedom."

Hyperbole? Maybe not. Just about any editor will tell you: the ad/edit
chemistry is changing for the worse. Corporations and their ad agencies have
clearly turned up the heat on editors and publishers, and some magazines are

capitulating, unwilling to risk even a single ad. This makes it tougher for those who do fight to maintain the ad-edit wall and put the interests of their readers first. Consider:

- A major advertiser recently approached all three newsweeklies—*Time, Newsweek,* and *U.S. News*—and told them it would be closely monitoring editorial content. So says a high newsweekly executive who was given the warning (but who would not name the advertiser). For the next quarter, the advertiser warned the magazines' publishing sides it would keep track of how the company's industry was portrayed in news columns. At the end of that period, the advertiser would select one—and only one—of the magazines and award all of its newsweekly advertising to it.

- An auto manufacturer—not Chrysler—decided recently to play art director at a major glossy, and the magazine played along. After the magazine scheduled a photo spread that would feature more bare skin than usual, it engaged in a back-and-forth negotiation with that advertiser over exactly how much skin would be shown. CJR's source says the feature had nothing to do with the advertiser's product.

- Kimberly-Clark makes Huggies diapers and advertises them in a number of magazines, including *Child, American Baby, Parenting, Parents, Baby Talk,* and *Sesame Street Parents.* Kimberly-Clark demands—in writing in its ad insertion orders—that these ads be placed only "adjacent to black and white happy baby editorial," which would definitely not include stories about, say Sudden Infant Death Syndrome or Down's syndrome. "Sometimes we have to create editorial that is satisfactory to them," a top editor says. That, of course, means something else is likely lost, and the mix of the magazine is altered.

- Former Cosmo Girl Helen Gurley Brown disclosed to *Newsday* that a Detroit auto company representative (the paper didn't say which company) asked for—and received—an advance copy of the table of contents for her bon voyage issue, then threatened to pull a whole series of ads unless the representative was permitted to see an article titled "How to Be Very Good in Bed." Result? "A senior editor and the client's ad agency pulled a few things from the piece," a dispirited Brown recalled, "but enough was left" to salvage the article.

Cosmo is hardly the only magazine that has bowed to the new winds. Kurt Andersen, the former *New York* magazine editor—whose 1996 firing by parent company, K-III was widely perceived to be a result of stories that angered associates of K-III's founder, Henry R. Kravis—nonetheless says that he always kept advertisers' sensibilities in mind when editing the magazine. "Because I worked closely and happily with the publisher at *New York,* I was aware who the big advertisers were," he says. "My antennae were turned on, and I read copy thinking, 'Is this going to cause Calvin Klein or Bergdorf big problems?'"

National Review put a reverse spin on the early-warning-for-advertisers discussion recently, as *The Washington Post* revealed, when its advertising director sent an advance copy of a piece about utilities deregulation to an energy supplier mentioned in the story, as a way of luring it into buying space.

And Chrysler is hardly the only company that is aggressive about its editorial environment. Manufacturers of packaged goods, from toothpaste to toilet paper, aggressively declare their love for plain-vanilla. Colgate-Palmolive, for example, won't allow ads in a "media context" containing "offensive" sexual content or material it deems "antisocial or in bad taste"—which it leaves undefined in its policy statement sent to magazines. In the statement, the company says that it "charges its advertising agencies and their media buying services with the responsibility of pre-screening any questionable media content or context."

Procter & Gamble, the second-largest advertising spender last year ($1.5 billion), has a reputation as being very touchy. Two publishing executives told Gloria Steinem, for her book *Moving Beyond Words*, that the company doesn't want its ads near anything about "gun control, abortion, the occult, cults, or the disparagement of religion." Even nonsensational and sober pieces dealing with sex and drugs are no-go.

Kmart and Revlon are among those that editors list as the most demanding. "IBM is a stickler—they don't like any kind of controversial articles," says Robyn Mathews, formerly of *Entertainment Weekly* and now *Time*'s chief of makeup. She negotiates with advertisers about placement, making sure that their products are not put near material that is directly critical. AT&T, Mathews says, is another company that prefers a soft climate. She says she often has to tell advertisers, "We're a *news* magazine. I try to get them to be realistic."

Still, the auto companies apparently lead the pack in complaining about content. And the automakers are so powerful—the Big Three pumped $3.6 billion into U.S. advertising last year—that most major magazines have sales offices in Detroit.

After *The New Yorker*, in its issue of June 12, 1995, ran a Talk of the Town piece that quoted some violent, misogynist rap and rock lyrics—along with illustrative four-letter words—opposite a Mercury ad, Ford Motor Company withdrew from the magazine, reportedly for six months. The author, Ken Auletta, learned about it only this year. "I actually admire *The New Yorker* for not telling me about it," he says. Yet afterwards, according to *The Wall Street Journal*, the magazine quietly adopted a system of warning about fifty companies on a "sensitive advertiser list" whenever potentially offensive articles are scheduled.

❦

It is the Chrysler case, though, that has made the drums beat, partly because of Chrysler's heft and partly because the revelation about the automaker's practice came neatly packaged with a crystalline example of just what that practice can do to a magazine.

In the advertising jungle Chrysler is an 800-pound gorilla—the nation's fourth-largest advertiser and fifth-largest magazine advertiser (it spent some $270 million at more than 100 magazines last year, behind General Motors, Philip Morris, Procter & Gamble, and Ford). Where it leads, other advertisers may be tempted to follow.

The automaker's letter was mailed to magazines in January 1996, but did not come to light until G. Bruce Knecht of *The Wall Street Journal* unearthed it this April in the aftermath of an incident at *Esquire*. The *Journal* reported that *Esquire* had planned a sixteen-page layout for a 20,000-word fiction piece by accomplished author David Leavitt. Already in page proofs and scheduled for the April '97 issue, it was to be one of the longest short stories *Esquire* had ever run, and it had a gay theme and some raw language. But publisher Valerie Salembier, the *Journal* reported, met with then editor-in-chief Edward Kosner and other editors and voiced her concerns: she would have to notify Chrysler about the story, and she expected that when she did so Chrysler would pull its ads. The automaker had bought four pages, the *Journal* noted—just enough to enable the troubled magazine to show its first year-to-year ad-page improvement since the previous September.

━◦◉◦━

Kosner then killed the piece, maintaining he had editorial reasons for doing so. Will Blythe, the magazine's literary editor, promptly quit. "I simply can't stomach the David Leavitt story being pulled," he said in his letter of resignation. "That act signals a terrible narrowing of the field available to strong, adventuresome, risk-taking work, fiction and nonfiction alike. I know that editorial and advertising staffs have battled—sometimes affably, other times savagely— for years to define and protect their respective turfs. But events of the last few weeks signal that the balance is out of whack now—that, in effect, we're taking marching orders (albeit, indirectly) from advertisers."

The Chrysler letter's public exposure is a rough reminder that sometimes the biggest problems are the most clichéd: as financial concerns become increasingly paramount it gets harder to assert editorial independence.

After the article about *Esquire* in the *Journal*, the American Society of Magazine Editors—the top cops of magazine standards, with 867 members from 370 magazines—issued a statement expressing "deep concern" over the trend to give "advertisers advance notice about upcoming stories." Some advertisers, ASME said, "may mistake an early warning as an open invitation to pressure the publisher to alter, or even kill, the article in question. We believe publishers should—and will—refuse to bow to such pressure. Furthermore, we believe editors should—and will—follow ASME's explicit principle of editorial independence, which at its core states: 'The chief editor of any magazine must have final authority over the editorial content, words, and pictures that appear in the publication.'"

On July 24, after meeting with the ASME board, the marketing committee of the Magazine Publishers of America—which has 200 member companies that print more than 800 magazines—gathered to discuss this issue, and agreed to work against prior review of story lists or summaries by advertisers. "The magazine industry is united in this," says ASME's president, Frank Lalli, managing editor of *Money*. "There is no debate within the industry."

How many magazines will reject Chrysler's new road map? Unclear. Lalli says he has not found any publisher or editor who signed and returned the Chrysler letter as demanded. "I've talked to a lot of publishers," he says, "and I don't know of any who will bow to it. The great weight of opinion among publishers and editors is that this is a road we can't go down."

Yet Mike Aberlich, Chrysler's manager of consumer media relations, claims that "Every single one has been signed." Aberlich says that in some cases, individual magazines agreed; in others a parent company signed for all its publications.

CJR did turn up several magazines, mostly in jam-packed demographic niches, whose executives concede they have no problem with the Chrysler letter. One is *Maxim*, a new book aimed at the young-men-with-bucks market put out by the British-based Dennis Publishing. "We're going to play ball," says *Maxim's* sales manager, Jamie Hooper. The startup, which launched earlier this year, signed and returned the Chrysler letter. "We're complying. We definitely have to."

At *P.O.V.*, a two-and-a-half-year-old magazine backed largely by Freedom Communications, Inc. (owners of *The Orange County Register*) and aimed at a similar audience, publisher Drew Massey says he remembers a Chrysler letter, can't remember signing it, but would have no problem providing advance notice. "We do provide PentaCom with a courtesy call, but we absolutely never change an article." Chrysler, alerted to *P.O.V.'s* August "Vice" issue, decided to stay in. Massey argues that the real issue is not about edgy magazines like *P.O.V.*, but about larger and tamer magazines that feel constrained by advertisers from being adventurous.

Hachette Filipacchi, French-owned publisher of twenty-nine U.S. titles, from *Elle* to *George*, offered Chrysler's plan for a safe editorial environment partial support. Says John Fennell, chief operating officer: "We did respond to the letter, saying we were aware of their concern about controversial material and that we would continue—as we have in the past—to monitor it very closely and to make sure that their advertising did not appear near controversial things. However, we refused to turn over or show or discuss the editorial direction of articles with them."

❧❧❧

It has long been a widely accepted practice in the magazine industry to provide "heads-up"—warnings to advertisers about copy that might embarrass them—say, to the friendly skies folks about a scheduled article on an Everglades plane crash, or to Johnnie Walker about a feature on the death of a hard-drinking rock star. In some instances, advertisers are simply moved as far as possible from the potentially disconcerting material. In others, they are offered a chance to opt out of the issue altogether, ideally to be rescheduled for a later edition.

In the 1980s, Japanese car makers got bent out of shape about news articles they saw as Japan-bashing, says *Business Week*'s editor-in-chief, Stephen B. Shepard, a past ASME president. Anything about closed markets or the trade imbalance might be seen as requiring a polite switch to the next issue.

Chrysler, some magazine people argue, is simply formalizing this long-standing advertiser policy of getting magazine executives to consider their special sensitivities while assembling each issue. But Chrysler's letter clearly went beyond that. PentaCom's president and c.e.o., David Martin, was surprisingly blunt when he explained to *The Wall Street Journal* the automaker's rationale: "Our whole contention is that when you are looking at a product that costs $22,000, you want the product to be surrounded by positive things. There's nothing positive about an article about child pornography."

Chrysler spokesman Aberlich insists the brouhaha is no big deal: "Of the thousands of magazine ads we've placed in a year, we've moved an ad out of one issue into the next issue about ten times a year. We haven't stopped dealing with any magazine." He compares placing an ad to buying a house: "You decide the neighborhood you want to be in." That interesting metaphor, owning valuable real estate, leads to other metaphors—advertisers as editorial NIMBYs (Not In My Back Yard) trying to keep out anybody or anything they don't want around.

As for the current contretemps, Aberlich says it's nothing new, that Chrysler has been requesting advance notice since 1993. "We sent an initial letter to magazines asking them to notify us of upcoming controversial stuff —graphic sex, graphic violence, glorification of drug use." But what about the updated and especially chilling language in the 1996 letter, the one asking to look over editors' shoulders at future articles, particularly *political, social* material and *editorial that might be construed as provocative*? Aberlich declines to discuss it, bristling, "We didn't give you that letter."

⁂

How did we get to the point where a sophisticated advertiser dared send such a letter? In these corporate-friendly times, the sweep and powers of advertisers are frenetically expanded everywhere. Formerly pure public television and public radio now run almost-ads. Schools bombard children with cereal commercials in return for the monitors on which the ads appear. Parks blossom with yogurt- and sneaker-sponsored events.

Meanwhile, a growing number of publications compete for ad dollars—not just against each other but against the rest of the media, including news media. Those ads are bought by ever-larger companies and placed by a shrinking number of merger-minded ad agencies.

Are magazines in a position where they cannot afford to alienate any advertiser? No, as a group, magazines have done very well lately, thank you. With only minor dips, ad pages and total advertising dollars have grown impressively for a number of years. General-interest magazines sold $5.3 billion worth of advertising in 1987. By 1996 that figure had more than doubled, to $11.2 billion.

Prosperity can enhance independence. The magazines least susceptible to advertiser pressures are often the most ad-laden books. Under its new editor-in-chief, David Granger, the anemic *Esquire* seems to be getting a lift, but *GQ* had supplanted it in circulation and in the serious-article business, earning many National Magazine Awards. This is in part because it first used advertiser-safe service pieces and celebrity profiles to build ad pages, then had more space to experiment and take risks.

Catherine Viscardi Johnston, senior vice president for group sales and marketing at *GQ*'s parent company, the financially flush Condé Nast, says that in her career as a publisher she rarely was asked to reschedule an ad—perhaps once a year. Meddling has not been a problem, she says: "Never was a page lost, or an account lost. Never, never did an advertiser try to have a story changed or eliminated."

At the other extreme, *Maxim*, which signed the Chrysler letter, does face grueling ad-buck competition. The number of new magazine startups in 1997 may well exceed 1,000, says Samir Husni, the University of Mississippi journalism professor who tracks launches. And *Maxim*'s demographic—21- to 24-year-old males—is jam-packed with titles.

This is not to say that prosperity and virtue go hand in hand. Witness Condé Nast's ad-fat *Architectural Digest*, where editor-in-chief Paige Rense freely admits that only advertisers are mentioned in picture captions. The range of standards among magazines is wide.

And that range can be confusing. "Some advertisers don't understand on a fundamental level the difference between magazines that have a serious set of rules and codes and serious ambitions, and those that don't," says Kurt Andersen. "The same guy at Chrysler is buying ads in *YM* and *The New Yorker*."

If it is up to editors to draw the line, they will have to buck the industry's impulse to draw them even deeper into their magazines' business issues. Hachette Filipacchi's U.S. president and c.e.o., David Pecker, is one who would lower the traditional ad-edit wall. "I actually know editors who met with advertisers and lived to tell about it," he said in a recent speech. Some editors at Hachette—and other news organizations—share in increased profits at their magazines. Thus, to offend an advertiser, it might be argued, would be like volunteering for a pay cut. So be it; intrepid editors must be prepared to take that.

•◀◎▶•

Ironically, in fretting over public sensibilities, advertisers may not be catering to their consumers at all. In a recent study of public opinion regarding television—which is even more dogged by content controversies than magazines—87 percent of respondents said it is appropriate for network programs to deal with sensitive issues and social problems. (The poll was done for ABC, NBC, and CBS by the Roper Starch Worldwide market research firm.) Asked who should "have the most to say about what people see and hear on television," 82 percent replied that it ought to be "individual viewers themselves, by deciding what they will and will not watch." Almost no one—just 9 percent—thought advertisers should be able to shape content by granting or withholding sponsorship. Even PentaCom admitted to the *Journal* that its own focus groups show that Chrysler owners are not bothered by Chrysler ads near controversial articles.

So what's eating these folks? Partially, it may be a cultural phenomenon. Ever since magazines began to attract mass audiences and subsidize subscription rates with advertising, many magazines have chased readers—just as networks chase viewers now—with ever more salacious fare. But corporate executives have often remained among the most conservative of Americans. Nowhere is this truer than in heartland locations like Chrysler's Detroit or Procter & Gamble's Cincinnati.

Ad executives say one factor in the mix is sponsors' fear of activist groups, which campaign against graphic or gay or other kinds of editorial material perceived as "anti-family." Boycotts like the current Southern Baptist campaign against Disney for "anti-family values" may be on the rise, precisely because advertisers do take them seriously. This, despite a lack of evidence that such boycotts do much damage. "Boycotts have no discernible impact on sales. Usually, the public's awareness is so quickly dissipated that it has no impact at all," says Elliot Mincberg, vice-president and general counsel of People For the American Way, a liberal organization that tracks the impact of pressure groups. Why, then, would advertisers bother setting guidelines that satisfy these groups at all? "They're trying to minimize their risk to *zero*," says an incredulous Will Blythe, *Esquire*'s former literary editor.

Yet not every advertiser pines for the bland old days. The hotter the product, it seems, the cooler the heads. The "vice" peddlers (booze & cigarettes), along with some apparel and consumer electronics products, actually like being surrounded by edgy editorial copy—unless their own product is zapped. Party *on*!

Even Chrysler's sensitivities appear to be selective. *Maxim*'s premier issue featured six women chatting provocatively about their sex lives, plus several photos of women in scanty come-hither attire, but Chrysler had no grievances.

❧

The real danger here is not censorship by advertisers. It is self-censorship by editors. On one level, self-censorship results in omissions, small and large, that delight big advertisers.

Cigarettes are a clear and familiar example. The tobacco companies' hefty advertising in many a magazine seems in inverse proportion to the publication's willingness to criticize it. Over at the American Cancer Society, media director Susan Islam says that women's magazines tend to cover some concerns adequately, but not lung cancer: "Many more women die of lung cancer, yet there have hardly been any articles on it."

To her credit, *Glamour*'s editor-in-chief, Ruth Whitney, is one who has run tobacco stories. She says that her magazine, which carries a lot of tobacco advertising, publishes the results of every major smoking study. But Whitney concedes they are mostly short pieces. "Part of the problem with cigarettes was—we did do features, but there's nobody in this country who doesn't know cigarettes kill." Still, everybody also knows that getting slimmer requires exercise and eating right, which has not prevented women's magazines from running that story in endless permutations. Tobacco is in the news, and magazines have the unique job of deepening and humanizing such stories.

Specific editorial omissions are easier to measure than how a magazine's world view is altered when advertisers' preferences and sensitivities seep into the editing. When editors act like publishers, and vice versa, the reader is out the door.

Can ASME, appreciated among editors for its intentions, fire up the troops? The organization has been effective on another front—against abuses of special advertising sections, when advertisements try to adapt the look and feel of editorial matter. ASME has distributed a set of guidelines about just what constitutes such abuse.

To enforce those guidelines, ASME executive director Marlene Kahan says the organization sends a couple of letters each month to violators. "Most magazines say they will comply," she reports. "If anybody is really egregiously violating the guidelines on a consistent basis, we'd probably sit down and have a meeting with them." ASME can ban a magazine from participating in the National Magazine Awards, but Kahan says the organization has not yet had to do that. In addition, ASME occasionally asks the organization that officially counts magazine ad pages, the Publishers Information Bureau, not to count advertising sections that break the rules as ad pages—a tactic that ASME president Lalli says tends to get publishers' attention.

Not everyone in the industry thinks ASME throws much of a shadow. "ASME can't bite the hand that feeds them," says John Masterton of *Media Industry Newsletter*, which covers the magazine business. During Robert Sam Anson's brief tenure as editor of *Los Angeles* magazine, the business side committed to a fifteen-page supplement, to be written by the editorial side and called "The Mercedes Golf Special." Mercedes didn't promise to take any ads, but it was hoped that the carmaker would think kindly of the magazine for future issues. The section would appear as editorial, listed as such in the table of contents. Anson warned the business side that, in his opinion, the section would contravene ASME guidelines, since it was in effect an ad masquerading as edit. A senior executive told him not to worry—that at the most they'd get a "slap on the wrist." The section did not run in the end, Anson says, because of "deadline production problems."

ে⊙৹

The Chrysler model, however—with its demand for early warnings, and its insistence on playing editor—is tougher for ASME to police. Special advertising sections are visible. Killed or altered articles are not. And unless it surfaces, as in the *Esquire* case, self-censorhip is invisible.

One well-known editor, who asks not to be identified, thinks the problem will eventually go away. "It's a self-regulating thing," he says. "At some point, the negative publicity to the advertisers will cause them to back off."

Of course, there is nothing particularly automatic about that. It takes an outspoken journalistic community to generate heat. And such attention could backfire. The *Journal*'s Knecht told the audience of public radio's *On the Media* that his reporting might actually have aggravated the problem: "One of the negative effects is that more advertisers who weren't aware of this system have gone to their advertising agencies and said, 'Hey, why not me too! This sounds like a pretty good deal!'"

Except, of course, that it really isn't. In the long run everybody involved is diminished when editors feel advertisers' breath on their necks. Hovering there, advertisers help create content that eventually bores the customers they seek. Then the editors of those magazines tend to join the ranks of the unemployed. That's just one of the many reasons that editors simply cannot bend to the new pressure. They have to draw the line—subtly or overtly, quietly or loudly, in meetings and in private, and in their own minds.

POSTSCRIPT

Is Advertising Ethical?

Since a number of media technologies have become vehicles for advertising (such as the Internet and even broadcast/cable infomercials), questions about the ethics of advertising have taken yet another turn. In some ways, the current presence of advertising raises questions that are very basic to the phenomenon of advertising. Do the ads we see register on our conscious or subconscious minds? Do ads really make us buy things or think of things in a certain way? Do we perceptually "screen" unwanted information?

In recent years some of the basic questions about ads have shifted because our "use patterns" of media have changed. Today a prime-time network television program has more ad time than ever before. Remote controls allow viewers to "zap" through commercials on tape or change channels when commercials appear. Ads in the form of company logos are displayed on clothing and other personal items, which have, in turn, emphasized brand affiliation and status.

Since the development of the advertising industry, the question of advertising ethics has periodically resurfaced. *The Journal of Advertising Ethics* is a good source to begin investigating what leaders in the industry themselves say about ethical practices, but articles are often tied to specific products or issues. There have been some defenses of the ad industry, such as Yale Brozen's *Advertising and Society* (New York University Press, 1974) and Theodore Levitt's article "The Morality(?) of Advertising," *Harvard Business Review* (July/August 1970).

Stuart Ewen and Elizabeth Ewen's *Channels of Desire: Mass Images and the Shaping of American Consciousness* (McGraw-Hill, 1982) offers the idea that advertising in Western society has had a major influence on public consciousness. Stuart Ewen's more recent book *PR! A Social History of Spin* (Basic Books, 1996) also investigates the origin, effect, and impact of the public relations industry in America.

Center for Media and Public Affairs

The site for the Center for Media and Public Affairs (CMPA) offers information about ongoing debates concerning media fairness and impact, with particular attention to political campaigns and political journalism.

http://www.cmpa.com

Megasources

This site was created for working journalists to find information via the Internet and contains links to a variety of experts and sources.

http://www.acs.ryerson.ca/~journal/megasources.html

Media Watchdog Organizations

This site provides links to media watchdog organizations. It focuses on the accuracy of the media and exposes the biases of mainstream media reporting.

http://www.newswatch.org/watchdog.htm

Poynter Online: Research Center

The Poynter Institute for Media Studies provides extensive links to information and resources on all aspects of media, including political journalism. This is a good general resource with an extensive list of references.

http://www.poynter.org/research/index.htm

PART 3

Media and Politics

*T*he presence of the media has changed the relationship between government, politics, and the press. Media has changed democratic practices such as voting and debating, and influences personal choice. How does the First Amendment protect the press? Is the press concerned more with protecting the public or gaining profits? What are the principles and practices of campaigns? How does the operation of the press influence campaigning? What part do the media play in the creation of negativity concerning politics? What is the responsibility of the politician and the public?

- Is the First Amendment Working?

- Is Negative Campaigning Bad for the American Political Process?

- Has Democracy Been Transformed by New Uses of Media?

ISSUE 8

Is the First Amendment Working?

YES: Kathleen H. Jamieson, from "For the Affirmative," *Political Communication* (1993)

NO: Thomas E. Patterson, from "For the Negative," *Political Communication* (1993)

ISSUE SUMMARY

YES: Kathleen H. Jamieson, dean of the Annenberg School of Communications at the University of Pennsylvania, argues that the First Amendment has protected print media from governmental censorship. In essence, the press has maintained this right by providing audiences with information that is deemed important even while it may seem harmful to those in power. She concludes that the press is able to keep a watchful eye on the government because of the First Amendment.

NO: Thomas E. Patterson, professor of political science and author, counters that the press has done a poor job of responding to the challenge of the First Amendment. He asserts that because the establishment press has been overly concerned with profit, it has squandered its rights and failed to provide the country with a vigorous marketplace of ideas. The press has the capacity to be influential in society, but is not living up to its obligations, concludes Patterson.

As the founding fathers of America determined in the Bill of Rights, one of the inalienable rights of the citizenry should be the freedom of the press. They intended for the media to have their voice protected by the government so that the public can have access to crucial information pertaining to society. In reality, while granting the media this freedom, it also places a lot of pressure on the press as an institution. As we develop new technologies and expand the reaches of the press, the freedoms of the First Amendment are constantly brought into question. What should be protected? What needs to be regulated? What is censorship? All of these questions, while hard to answer, are continuously debated among scholars, media critics, and media professionals. Many feel that the press has benefited from protection under the First Amendment, while others believe that the press has squandered this right.

Obviously, the press has changed drastically since the ratification of the First Amendment. As the press has changed, the meanings of this freedom have also changed. While the press is still protected to a certain degree, have other factors limited what it can and cannot say? Can it still act in a way that provides the necessary information to citizens so that individuals will be accountable and responsible? Has the press been able to maintain its independence from other institutions so that it can provide objective reporting to its audience? On the other hand, has the press simply become a commercial enterprise with the sole purpose of earning a profit without caring about its First Amendment obligations? This debate is taken up in the following selections, as two academics present their views on the role of today's media and their relationship with the First Amendment.

Kathleen H. Jamieson defends the press and maintains that the First Amendment is "alive and well." She contends that even as the media have grown into their present state, the government has protected them and allowed them to serve as a watchdog for the public. In citing several landmark cases, Jamieson explains that the press has continued to take advantage of its rights under the law while gaining support from public officials. The First Amendment works, she says, and it works in the way that the founding fathers would have expected.

Thomas E. Patterson asserts that the First Amendment is no longer even a consideration of the press as its members have become pawns of commercial interests. Further, since the press has new functions, it has not lived up to its obligations under the First Amendment. Patterson adds that the press has become deficient and no longer provides the public with an arena to discuss important issues of the day. The rights guaranteed under the First Amendment may still exist, but instead of informing the public, the press has added to its political alienation.

Kathleen H. Jamieson  **YES**

For the Affirmative

The First Amendment Is Alive and Well

In the First Amendment, the Founders posited one and only one salient characteristic for the press. It should be unfettered by the government. "Congress shall make no law," says the Amendment, "abridging the freedom of speech, or of the press." Within the clause that protects the press from governmental strictures is the phrase that explains the context for that precept. Freedom of the press is a guarantor of freedom of speech. This interpretation is bolstered by the fact that this amendment also ensures the right to peaceably assemble and the right to petition.

The reasons for envisioning a press free from governmental stricture were plain. Writing as Cato in 1720, Thomas Gordan argued that "all Ministers... who were Oppressors, or intended to be Oppressors, have been loudest in their complaints against Freedom of Speech, and the License of the Press; and always restrained, or endeavored to restrain, both" (Cato, Essay 15). Cato's ideas were "popular, quotable, [and] an esteemed source of political ideas in the colonial period" (Rossiter, 1953, p. 141). His concerns were shared by Alexander Hamilton who worried in the 84th Federalist about pretenses under which men would claim a power to regulate the press.

Echoed throughout the ratifying conventions of Virginia, Pennsylvania, and North Carolina was the concern, warranted in the British past of the colonists, that tyranny would ascend after muzzling free speech and its outlet, the press. "An aristocratic government cannot bear the liberty of the press," noted John Smilie in the Pennsylvania Ratifying Convention of 1787 (Jenson, 1976, pp. 439–441). North Carolina said it would not ratify the Constitution unless it was amended to ensure freedom of speech and of the press, which were seen there as reciprocals, one ensuring the other. "That the people have a right to freedom of speech, and of writing and publishing their sentiments [read the proposed amendment,] that the freedom of the press is one of the greatest bulwarks of liberty, and ought not to be violated" (Schwartz, 1980, p. 482).

From Kathleen H. Jamieson, "For the Affirmative," *Political Communication*, vol. 10, no. 1 (1993). Copyright © 1993 by Taylor & Francis, Inc. Reprinted by permission. References omitted.

The first amendment has lived up to the expectations the founders had for it precisely because the courts have protected the print press from governmental censorship and regulated the broadcast press in ways that ensure free and contested exchange of multiple points of view. At the same time, the founders would note with pleasure that the Courts continue to serve as a recourse for those who believe that either freedom of speech or of the press is being restrained in a way unsanctioned by the Constitution or community consensus.

Even when the state insisted that it has a self-interest in expression or suppression, the Court has protected the rights of newspapers to publish or to refuse to publish. The former was tested in *Miami Herald Publishing Co. v. Tornillo* (1974), which examined a Florida statute requiring that papers publish without cost the response of candidates criticized in their columns. In striking down that statute the court held that "any... compulsion to publish that which 'reason' tells them [newspapers] should not be published is unconstitutional" (*Miami Herald Publishing Co. v. Tornillo*, 418 U.S. 241, 1974).

In addition, government cannot, with few exceptions, stop the publication of material damaging to those in office or in power. An early test of this principle occurred in 1924 when Minnesota passed a gag law. In 1927, that law was enforced against the *Saturday Press,* a weekly that charged that the law enforcement agencies of Minneapolis were not enforcing the laws against gamblers, bootleggers, and racketeers. The paper had a specific racketeer in mind and in print. Under the gag law, the paper was convicted. In *Near v. Minnesota* (283 U.S. 697 [1931]), the Supreme Court reversed the decision on the grounds that the state was forbidden by the first amendment to censor the press.

More recently, when the Nixon administration tried to stop *The New York Times* and *The Washington Post* from publishing the Pentagon Papers, Justice Black wrote for the majority that

> the Government's power to censor the press was abolished so that the press would remain forever free to censure the Government. The press was protected so that it could bare the secrets of government and inform the people. Only a free and unrestrained press can effectively expose deception in government. And paramount among the responsibilities of a free press is the duty to prevent any part of the government from deceiving the people and sending them off to distant lands to die of foreign fevers and foreign shot and shell.

In other words, Black found that the two newspapers were doing "precisely that which the Founders hoped and trusted they would do" (*New York Times v. U.S.*, 403 U.S. 713, 717, 1971). This was the decision despite the administration's argument that publication would cause "the death of soldiers, the destruction of alliances, the greatly increased difficulty of negotiation with our enemies, [and] the inability of our diplomats to negotiate."

Under what circumstances might the court restrain the press? In 1989 in *Florida Star v. B. J. F.,* the court answered that if "a newspaper lawfully obtains truthful information about a matter of public significance then state officials may not constitutionally punish publication of the information, absent a need to further state interest of the highest order" (499 So. 2d, 883). There is, in the words of Justice White, writing in *Miami Herald v. Tornillo,* a "virtually insurmountable barrier between government and the print media" (418 U.S. 241, 1974).

Ironically, there is no such barrier between the government and the broadcast media. However, here too, the wishes of the Founders are being honored and the future they envisioned realized. Recall that freedom of speech and of the press are umbilically linked in the First Amendment. Whereas the barrier between government and the print press provides an agency for exposing what government would prefer be hidden, regulation of the broadcast media ensures that competing voices and a free range of speech can be heard.

The argument for what some have called the "marketplace of ideas" drew strength from the theorizing of two of the fathers of the revolution: Benjamin Franklin and Thomas Jefferson. In his 1731 *Apology for Printers,* Franklin noted that "both Sides ought equally to have the Advantage of being heard by the Publick," (Labaree, 1959, p. 260). In 1801, Jefferson's inaugural reflected his support for the concept: "If there be any among us who would wish to dissolve this union or to change its republican form, [he wrote,] let them stand undisturbed, as monuments of the safety with which error of opinion may be tolerated, where reason is left free to combat it." (LAX, 1985, p. 9) The protections of political speech that govern contemporary politics are a legacy of this view, and it is in the broadcast media that they find a forum.

The Communications Act of 1934 both created the Federal Communications Commission (FCC) and gave it the authority to regulate broadcasting in the public interest. Here as with the print press, censorship is proscribed (section 326). However, unlike print, in the broadcast medium those attacked "during discussion of a controversial issue of public importance [are given] a reasonable opportunity to respond over the licensee's facilities" (11 C.F.R. Sec. 13, 1920 [1990]). When one legally qualified candidate is permitted use of the station, others must be afforded equal opportunities. If one candidate is permitted to purchase time, then other candidates for the same office are entitled to purchase comparable time as well (312[a] [7] 1988). "It is the purpose of the First Amendment [wrote the Court in the famous *Red Lion* case] to preserve an uninhibited marketplace of ideas in which truth will ultimately prevail, rather than to countenance monopolization of that market, whether it be by the Government itself or a private licensee" (*Red Lion Broadcasting Co. v. Federal Communications Commission* 395, U.S., 390, 1969).

The success of that principle was evident when, in the Spring of 1954, Senator Joseph McCarthy was given a half hour of network time to respond to Edward R. Murrow and Fred W. Friendly's hour-long attack on him. McCarthy did more damage to himself in the response than his opponents had in the attack. It was on television that the country watched the "crushing experience for McCarthy" (McDonald, 1985, p. 55), the Army–McCarthy Hearings, the unraveling of the Nixon presidency, and the unfolding of the controversy over Iran-Contra.

The Supreme Court has held that the candidates have an affirmative right of access to the broadcast media. The ruling, handed down in July 1981, was the result of a challenge by the Carter campaign to network denial of the right to purchase 30 minutes of prime time in December 1979. Writing for the Court, Justice Warren Burger argued that "it is of particular importance that candidates have the opportunity to make their views known so that the electorate can intelligently evaluate the candidates' personal qualities and their positions on vital public issues before choosing among them on election day (*CBS Inc. v. FCC,* 453 U.S. 367, 1981).

The protections afforded broadcast political speech have broadened the latitude of discourse in ways that some find offensive. For example, J. B. Stoner (1972), a politician running for state office in Georgia, paid to air an ad that said in part that "the main reason why niggers want integration is because niggers want our white women." The National Association for the Advancement of Colored People (NAACP) protested and asked the FCC to ban further airing. The Commission refused on the grounds that only a clear and present danger of imminent violence would justify tampering with a political commercial. The ruling was justified by the guarantee of free speech even for claims that are abhorrent ("FCC Won't Back Racist Ad in South," *New York Times,* August 4, 1972, p. 37). Independent presidential candidate Barry Commoner was also not stopped in 1980 from airing an ad that contained [an expletive] barred from entertaining programming.... Also, in 1972, presidential candidate Ellen McCormick was permitted to air an ad showing aborted fetuses that would not have been permitted to air had it not been considered protected political speech.

The marketplace was contentious in the Winter of 1992 as well. In the New Hampshire primary, voters saw ads for a Western liberal named Kerrey; a Libertarian named Marroux; a Marxist named Fulani; an actor, Tom Laughlin, better known as Bille Jack; a renegade speechwriter journalist named Buchanan; a born-again Zen Buddhist named Brown; a pork-rind eating Texan named Bush; and a good-old-boy Arkansan named Clinton, among others. At one end of the dialogue, Marroux was calling for a federal government that provided only courts, an army, and a federal treasury, whereas, on the other, Kerrey was calling for a government that would provide everything it now does and in addition give us national health insurance.

This notion of an uninhibited marketplace has carried over into cable where, on any given day, a viewer can turn in to find Madeline Murray O'Hair praising the virtues of atheism on one channel, while on another, Jerry Falwell reminds us that the wages of sin are death. One can also hear Ed Herman arguing that the media are the dupes of capitalism while on the other, Mercedes is touted as more than a car. Cable News Network brings in 3 minutes of unedited news from up to 40 countries around the world each week, whereas, nightly C-SPAN carries the nightly news from Moscow. Also, if General Electric owns NBC, and AT&T ties a loose lace around MacNeil Lehrer, one is hard pressed to argue that corporate ties bind the Hell's Angels who appeared one afternoon on community access in Austin, Texas. In an environment in which, in 1988, C-SPAN provided over 1,000 hours of access to candidate discourse including speeches and press conferences by a Marxist, a Libertarian and a LaRouchite, the world does seem safe for the kind of free speech and free press envisioned by the founders.

Finally, the founders would take comfort in the fact that the courts have indicated a readiness to intervene when the government has failed to live up to First Amendment expectations. It was the Washington, D.C. District Court after all, that struck down the excesses of the FCC of the early 1970s.

After Nixon had delivered six televised speeches to the nation, five of them on Vietnam, CBS offered Democratic National Committee chair Lawrence O'Brien 25 minutes of response time. The Republican National Committee petitioned the FCC for equal time to respond to O'Brien. The FCC agreed with the Republicans. When the Democratic National Convention petitioned for reconsideration, the Commission denied reconsideration. On appeal, the Washington, D.C. Circuit Court sided with the Democrats' arguments (454 F.2d, 1973).

Restrictions on press coverage of what is called the War in the Gulf are often cited as evidence that the government has in fact managed to encroach on the freedom of the press. However, even here, despite the restrictions placed on movements of reporters and on release of information, ultimate responsibility for determining what should be published was left not with the government but with the news organizations. The Pentagon guidelines specify that criticism of the military operation will not constitute grounds on which reports will be scrutinized. The relevant portion of the guidelines read:

> In the event of hostilities, pool products will be subject to review before release to determine if they contain sensitive information about military plans, capabilities, operations, or vulnerabilities (see attached ground rules) that would jeopardize the outcome of an operation or the safety of U.S. or coalition forces. Material will be examined solely for its conformance to the attached ground rules, not for its potential to express criticism or cause embarrassment. The public affairs escort officer on scene will review pool reports, discuss ground rule problems with the reporter, and in the limited circumstances when no agreement can be reached with a reporter about disputed materials, immediately send the disputed materials to JIB [Joint Information Bureau] Dhahran for review by the JIB Director and the appropriate news media representative. If no agreement can be reached, the issue will be immediately forwarded to the Office of the Assistant Secretary of Defense (Public Affairs) [OASD(PA)] for review with the appropriate bureau chief. The ultimate decision on publication will be made by the originating reporter's news organization. (Department of Defense, January 14, 1991).

Defending the procedure, Pentagon spokesperson Pete Williams noted that of the 1,351 pool reports filed, five required Washington's review. Within hours of submission, four of the five were cleared for publication. The fifth, which focused on intelligence gathering methods, was modified by the reporter's editor at the request of the Department of Defense ("Let's Face It, This Was the Best War Coverage We've Ever Had," *Washington Post*, March 17, 1991, pp. D1–D4).

As important as the provision that the ultimate decision to publish rested with the news organization was the fact that those who were unhappy with the limited access the Pentagon provided to the battlefield had the option to take their grievances into court. In January 1991, *Harper's, The Nation,* Pacifica Radio News, the Guardian, the *Progressive, Mother Jones,* the *Village Voice,* and a number of writers and reporters did just that. Filed in the federal court in New York, their suit names as defendants the U.S. Department of Defense, Secretary of Defense Richard Cheney, Assistant Secretary of Defense for Public Affairs Pete Williams, Chairman of the Joint Chiefs of Staff Colin Powell, and President George Bush.

The war ended before the suit against George Bush and the Department of Defense was adjudicated. However, before the war's end, the judge hearing the case stated that the suit raised serious constitutional questions worthy of examination (*The Nation et al. v. The United States Department of Defense et al.,* 762 F. Supp. 1558 [S.D. N.Y. 1991] April 16, 1991, statement by Hon. Leonard B. Sand). Moreover, during the build-up to the war and during the war itself, the military's efforts to control coverage were revealed by reporters (Morgan & Lardner, 1991; Reporters Committee, 1991; Schanberg, 1991; Sciolini, 1991). In the aftermath of the war, it was the press unrestrained by the government that revealed what had happened, why, and with what effect (Morgan & Lardner, 1991; Schmitt, 1991; Wicker, 1991).

What the court did not have the opportunity to test was whether a broader right to access existed. Those who argue that it does must take into account the fact that the Constitution contains a number of provisions that suggest that the government has the right to withhold some forms of information from the public. Article 1, section 5 of the Constitution requires each of the houses of Congress to keep a journal "of its Proceedings, and from time to time publish the same, excepting such Parts as may in their judgment require Secrecy." Even the Freedom of Information Act makes an exception for national security information.

The civility of the print press might surprise the founders who, afterall, were accustomed to the slings and arrows of its far more partisan ancestors. They would, I think, be pleased to find that through the collective wisdom of Congress and the courts, the print press has been protected from governmental dictates about what to print and not to print, whereas the broadcast press has been regulated in ways designed to safeguard the marketplace of ideas.

Thomas E. Patterson  **NO**

For the Negative

Fourth Branch or Fourth Rate? The Press's Failure to Live Up to the Founders' Expectations

The founders were philosophical liberals. They believed in the Lockean ideal of negative government, which holds that government governs best by staying out of people's lives, thus giving individuals as much freedom as possible to determine their own pursuits. The First Amendment said no to government: "Congress shall make no law... abridging the freedom of speech, or of the press."

The First Amendment was a response to the autocratic rule of kings and mandarins. In the democratic constitutions that were written a century later, after the Industrial Revolution had produced unforeseen concentrations of private power, there were also provisions for positive government. It no longer made sense to believe that government was the sole threat to liberty or that government action invariably threatened freedom. Private power could be suffocating, and public power could be liberating. In some situations, greater freedom was possible only if government intervened to redress inequities, to establish the conditions that would help people to realize their human potential, or to impose public obligations on private organizations.

The First Amendment was also a reflection of the nature of the late 18th century press. In 1791 there were no mass media of communication. A large newspaper counted its circulation in the hundreds, not in the hundreds of thousands. Also, there was no journalism—there were no reporters and no news stories. The First Amendment was ratified to protect the expression of opinion, not the production of information. The printer and the pamphleteer were the press.

A century later, the press was a very different institution. Newspaper ownership had outpriced even the political parties, much less the average citizen. Social and technological change had made possible a national news system centering on the wire services and mass-circulation newspapers. Shortly after the turn of the century, Charles Horton Cooley (1909) wrote that the change was so substantial "as to constitute a new epoch in communication" (pp. 80–81). The 20th century would bring a further transformation in the form of the radio and

From Thomas E. Patterson, "For the Negative," *Political Communication*, vol. 10, no. 1 (1993). Copyright © 1993 by Taylor & Francis, Inc. Reprinted by permission. Notes and references omitted.

television networks and a pattern of chain ownership that would eventually embrace three fourths of the nation's dailies (Bagdikian, 1990).

Any realistic evaluation of whether the press has met the founders' expectations must be made in the context of the great changes that have taken place in the two centuries since the First Amendment was written. Even if the debate were narrowly confined to legal grounds, the standards of 1791 would not apply. The question of constitutional interpretation is not how the founders would settle today's disputes by yesterday's standards but what they had in mind by a particular provision. The founders' expectations, moreover, cannot be settled by mere reference to legal briefs. The critical question is one of sustained performance: What has the press done in its 200-year history to enhance free expression in America?

I will argue that the establishment press has done a poor job of responding to the challenge of the First Amendment. I will suggest that the establishment press has done remarkably little to enhance the First Amendment, that the establishment press has an overly self-centered conception of the First Amendment, and that the establishment press has squandered its precious First Amendment rights on a commercial binge that has lasted for more than a century and a half.

Whither the Intrepid Press?

The Pentagon Papers and the Watergate affair are towering achievements in the history of the First Amendment. For a few years in the early 1970s, the establishment press resisted attempts by government to quiet its voice and, in the process, greatly strengthened the nation's commitment to constitutionalism.

The Pentagon Papers and the Watergate affair, however, are lonely outposts in the history of the press and the First Amendment. During the entire 19th century, for example, there was no Supreme Court case that emerged from a titanic battle between the press and the national government over the limits of the First Amendment.

It was not until two cases in 1919 that the Supreme Court offered a judgment on the First Amendment. Neither case was provoked by an intrepid journalist who had challenged the powers that be. The defendants were draft protesters and anarchists who had been arrested and convicted for protesting America's involvement in World War I. In upholding their convictions under the Espionage Act of 1917, the Supreme Court rejected a literal interpretation of the First Amendment. The Court held in *Schenck*, 249 U.S. 47 (1919), that the "make no law" provision of the First Amendment did not apply to actions that posed "a clear and present danger" to the nation's security. The mainstream press had no apparent objection to this restriction on the First Amendment. Astonishingly, the press did not even protest the *Abrams* (250 U.S. 616, 1919) decision that narrowed free expression severely by saying that it could be prohibited whenever it promoted a "bad tendency."

Twelve years later, the establishment press, with some reluctance, backed Jay Near's case when it reached the Supreme Court. Mr. Near was the publisher of a Minneapolis weekly newspaper that regularly made scurrilous attacks on

Blacks, Jews, Catholics, and labor union leaders. His paper was closed down on authority of a state law that banned "malicious, scandalous, or defamatory" publications. Near appealed the shutdown, and the Supreme Court ruled in his favor, saying that the Minnesota law was "the essence of censorship" (*Near v. Minnesota*, 283 U.S. 697 [1931]). This was a landmark decision; it was the first time the Supreme Court had addressed the issue of prior restraints, and it protected press freedom from infringement by the states (the First Amendment applied originally to action by the federal government only). However, the mainstream Minnesota newspapers and much of the New York press hesitated in their support for Near. The Minneapolis *Star* was the only major newspaper in Minnesota to laud the Supreme Court's decision but said in an editorial: "The court's decision need not signalize the return of scandal sheets to Minnesota. There are laws enough to handle the situation if they are used and enforced with nerve and determination" (Friendly, 1981, p. 158).

Two decades later, during the early years of McCarthyism, the press was strangely silent as the junior senator from Wisconsin waged his vulgar war on free expression. Based on his study of news content during the McCarthy period, the newspaperman Edwin R. Bayley concluded the following:

> What is most surprising in the examination of newspaper performance in the McCarthy period is not that so much news of McCarthy was published in some papers, but how little was published in many others, especially in the first years. The timidity of the wire services, the fear of controversy on the part of publishers, and an apparent lack of understanding of the importance of the issue by many editors worked to deprive many readers of full information...The editing of McCarthy stories seemed singularly inept. Wire service stories containing important news were often overlooked, and choked-up overnight leads took the play; the few interpretive pieces by agency reporters were largely ignored by editors; headlines seemed to substantiate McCarthy's charges and even to exaggerate them. (pp. 218–219)

Press freedom received a major boost in *New York Times Co. v. Sullivan*, 376 U.S. 259 (1964), but the achievement cannot reasonably be credited to the press. The case began, not with the action of a journalist, but with a *Times* advertisement in which civil rights leaders accused Alabama officials of physically abusing black citizens during civil rights demonstrations. An Alabama state court found the *Times* guilty of libel for printing the advertisement, which compelled the newspaper to appeal the decision. The Supreme Court ruled that libel of a public official requires proof of actual malice, which was defined as a knowing or reckless disregard for the truth with intent to damage the official's reputation. This imposing standard of proof for libel is a monument to the Court's commitment to the civil rights movement rather than to the press itself.

The United States' involvement in the Persian Gulf War provides a recent example of the establishment press's less-than-zealous pursuit of First Amendment freedoms. The press was substantially restricted during the war. Military authorities severely limited journalists' travel and required reporters to have a military escort; allowed journalists to interview only selected soldiers and usually had a superior officer standing nearby as the interviews took place; and subjected all news reports to review by military censors. Journalists critical of the war were kept out of the media pool, which included a small number of journalists who were allowed to act as stand-ins for the full press corps. The American press only mildly protested the military's tight censorship. A suit by The Nation and other liberal publications that charged that the censorship policy imposed an unconstitutional prior restraint on freedom of the press was not joined by a single major news organization, print or television.

The establishment press, in summary, has avoided the forefront of the fight for free expression in the United States. Although a chief beneficiary of the gains from the struggle, the press has contributed surprisingly little to what has been won.

Whose Amendment Is It Anyway?

The writers of the Constitution were practitioners of the art of intentional ambiguity. They meant for their document to last for generations, which required that it espouse first principles and that it do so in the most general of terms (Levy, 1985, p. 348). The founders used expansive words, as illustrated by the "necessary and proper" clause (or, as it is called, the elastic clause) that was used in granting Congress the authority to make the laws that would carry out its enumerated powers. There is no reason to believe that the First Amendment was the exception to this constitutional approach. The First Amendment's prohibition on actions that would inhibit free expression was boldly stated. As Levy (1985) has noted, the founders "gave constitutional recognition to the principle of freedom of speech and press in unqualified and undefined terms" (p. 349).

This expansive notion of the First Amendment was expressed in the constitutional argument that Justice Oliver Wendell Holmes put forth in his opinions on the *Schenck* and *Abrams* cases. His opinion in *Abrams*, which Lerner (1943) described as "the greatest utterance on intellectual freedom by an American" (p. 306), argued that the First Amendment was intended to foster a "free trade in ideas" (p. 306) that can exist only when government allows for free expression and only when citizens have reasonable opportunities to have their opinions heard in the marketplace.

Holmes's argument was not a 20th-century facelift to a 1791 idea. Holmes was acknowledging that the great changes in the economy, society, and communication required a concept of press freedom that recognized the rights of leaders and audiences in addition to the rights of media owners and media professionals.

The principles that Holmes expounded were similar to those embodied in the Federal Communications Act of 1934. Broadcasters would be substantially free from governmental interference but would be obligated to give voice to opposing candidates for public office. Later, the fairness doctrine imposed a positive obligation on broadcasters to recognize the communication rights of their audience: They would be required to cover important issues of public concern and would have to air opposing positions on these issues. Broadcasters could take positions on public issues, but they could not use their privileged position as the holder of a scarce frequency to suppress the views of those with whom they disagreed.

Broadcasters rejected the notion that the First Amendment gave the listening public any right to hear ideas that the broadcasters did not want them to hear. The broadcast industry fought against the fairness doctrine from the beginning, and the issue finally reached the Supreme Court in the late 1960s. In *Red Lion Broadcasting Co. v. FCC*, 395 U.S. 367 (1969), the Supreme Court upheld the constitutionality of the fairness doctrine, applying much of the same reasoning that Holmes had used a half century earlier. The Court said: "It is the purpose of the First Amendment, to preserve an uninhibited marketplace of ideas in which truth will ultimately prevail, rather than to countenance monopolization of that market, whether it be by the Government itself or a private licensee" *Red Lion Broadcasting Co. v. FCC*, 395 U.S. The *Red Lion* decision articulated a trustee model of public communication in which the paramount interest is that of the public and not that of the news organization, which, in return for its privileged position, must serve the public's interest rather than its own.

Broadcasters argued that the *Red Lion* decision betrayed two centuries of tradition, an argument that was not factually true. State cases in the 19th century (the First Amendment did not apply to state authority until the early 1900s when it was selectively incorporated through the Fourteenth Amendment) were settled by the common law principle of the public benefits of that expression, not by the principle that press freedom entails no obligations on the part of its user (Gleason, 1990, p. 4). Furthermore, the idea that freedom of the press is the right of a small group of citizens only cannot be reconciled with the founders' philosophy. Rights were seen as inalienable—held by all and surrenderable by none. This view of the First Amendment was affirmed by the Supreme Court in *Associated Press* v. U.S., 326 U.S. 20 (1945):

> Surely a command that the government itself shall not impede the free flow of ideas does not afford non-governmental combinations a refuge if they impose restraints upon that constitutionally guaranteed freedom. Freedom to publish means freedom for all and not for some. (326 U.S. 20, 1945)

However, many journalists today apparently think that press freedom is their private preserve. U.S. journalists were asked in a recent survey whether they believed press freedom "is intended primarily to enable the news media to freely communicate the information and opinions they deem important [or whether it] is intended primarily to enable the many groups in society to freely express the values and beliefs they deem important." Only 24% of the respondents said press freedom exists primarily for the society's sake.

In claiming freedom of the press as an exclusive right, the media assume the power to decide who else will also enjoy the right and under what conditions their right will be recognized. The groups who are likely to be kept out are the unpopular ones, precisely those whose voices were meant to be protected through the First Amendment. However, even this concern is beside the point. The question of constitutional rights is not a question of noblesse oblige. Freedom of the press has very little meaning in a mass society unless interests have a right to have their views expressed through the mass media of communication (Barron, 1973). At present, they do not have that right: "From a marketplace of ideas perspective, the dominant trend is that media institutions have arisen to monopolize the marketplace, gradually forcing out the individual's voice" (Schwarzlose, 1989, 34).

Why do the American media have such a self-centered view of press freedom? Part of the answer is undoubtedly found in the American legal tradition, but I would submit that the answer rests also with the historical development of American journalism. The press, as I argued in the previous section, has gone through history without much testing and debate of its constitutional rights and responsibilities. The First Amendment and journalism did not grow up together; theirs is not a deeply nurtured relationship.

As a result, journalists' notions of press freedom are, in a word, immature. Journalists conveniently overlook the fact that they are themselves the instruments of a powerful institution. In all aspects—technology, markets, ownership patterns, and influence—the media bear little resemblance today to the press that the founders wanted to protect against—the awesome capacity to restrict the boundaries of public debate.

Journalists use their strength of feeling about press freedom as a substitute for reflective judgment. Just as the American Medical Association cries "socialized medicine" at the mention of universal health care, the media cry "press freedom" whenever balancing issues of the press are raised. A recent comparative study of journalists discovered that American journalists are far more likely than journalists elsewhere to believe that

- libel laws should be structured in a way that makes it very difficult for "public officials who have been seriously harmed by false and careless reporting to win libel suits;"
- "a news source who is promised confidentiality should not be able to sue for breach of promise if the journalist breaks the promise;"
- "journalists should not be required to reveal confidential sources if a court determines this information would provide important evidence in a trial;" and
- "private citizens who are falsely criticized by the press should not have a legal right of reply through the news organization that led the criticism."

The American press refuses to grant to others what it demands for itself. The *Miami Herald v. Tornillo* case, 418 U.S. 241 (1974), may have been a victory for the press's self-centered view of its rights, but it was a defeat for the principle that the aim of the First Amendment is society's right to hear what all sides in a political debate are saying. What is the right of reply, anyway, other than political leader's or citizen's form of press freedom? If the meaning of such ideas as the "right to know" and the "right of access" are vague and subject to dispute in practice, they are nonetheless a reasonable part of any modern interpretation of the First Amendment (Barron, 1973; Owen, 1975).

The American press is remarkably insular for an institution that demands openness from all other institutions. The 1947 Hutchins Commission's recommendations for enhancing the press's social responsibility role were viewed skeptically by the media and were never implemented. The press does not even have faith in its ability to police itself. The National News Council, which was formed in 1973, was opposed by some leading news organizations, including the *New York Times,* and was dissolved a decade after its creation. This "no one can tell us what to do" attitude is characteristic of the American press and is a sign of an insecure institution rather than of a mature one. Compare the American case with, for example, the Swedish press council that was established in 1916. It developed a strong code of ethics, has vigorously pursued complaints against the press, and in 1969 was reformed to include lay people as a third of its membership (Bertrand, 1985).

If it makes sense to call the American press the fourth branch of government, it also makes sense to ask why the press is the only branch that has not undergone a process of constitutional reformation during the nation's history. The presidency in its tribune role, the Congress in its delegation of regulatory powers, and the Supreme Court in its acceptance of a social policy role have adapted to the special requirements of modern society. The media's interpretation of its constitutional position is mired in 1791 when the press was the printer's shop.

Which Is Mightier, the Pen or the Dollar?

A key question to be asked of the First Amendment is not whether, after 200 years, the press is free to do whatever it wants but whether the press during its 200 years under the First Amendment has striven to promote a free and intelligent public discourse. What is the press's service record?

The formative influence on the American press has not been public service. It has been money. Unlike the 19th-century British press, which was intent on testing the boundaries of its political power, the American press in its first century willingly shed its political role for a commercial one. The first important newspapers of the American Republic had formed out of government subsidies and were loyal to their party sponsors. However, the drive for profits was a stronger incentive for newspaper owners than the power of the pen. The first of the penny newspapers, Benjamin Day's *New York Sun,* was built on gossip and the human interest story. The *Sun* also employed the country's first reporter, an Englishman who was assigned to the crime beat. If Hearst and Pulitzer a half century later were more politically minded than Day had been, their agendas were commercial enough to allow news boys to hawk as many as 40 editions a day of their newspapers on the streets of New York.

Commission of Freedom of the Press (1947) concluded that the press, t was driven so thoroughly by commercial values, was not meeting needs and was using "practices which the society condemns" (p. 8). nission concluded that the press was within its legal right to act in this fashion but that it was failing in the moral obligation that attends the granting of rights. William Earnest Hocking (1947) wrote:

> The important thing is that the press accept the public standard and try for it. The legal right will stand if the moral right is realized or tolerably approximated. There is a point at which the failure to realize the moral right will entail encroachment by the state upon the existing legal right. (p. 230)

In the nearly half century since the Commission issued its judgment, there have been some major improvements in news reporting, but the American press still prefers the story that shocks, titillates, and sells. European observers of the 1992 presidential campaign marveled at the attention that the American press gave to such issues as Gennifer Flowers and Murphy Brown.

The most significant change in the American press since the 1940s is the emergence of television as a major news source. By nearly every account (e.g., Entman, 1989; Patterson, 1980), television has cheapened the quality of public debate. In a recent study, Lyengar (1991) concluded that "rather than providing a 'marketplace of ideas,' television provides only a passing parade of specific events, a 'context of no context'" (p. 140). In a study of television election coverage, Patterson and McClure (1976) observed that

> instead of analyzing character and examining backgrounds, the networks simply parade faces ... They seldom discuss the candidates' personal fitness for office—their moral codes, personal habits and private behaviors, personal reactions to past political stresses, or leadership styles. Likewise the networks avoid intimate interviews that would provide viewers themselves with a chance to study closely presidential candidates. Instead, television news emphasizes superficial pictures of the candidates in action. (p. 31)

Television has also introduced a greater degree of negativism in news coverage, a result of the narrative quality of broadcast news and the traditional skepticism of the press. This tendency has contributed to the growing political alienation of the American public. Robinson (1976) observes that

> events are frequently conveyed by television news through an inferential structure that often injects a negativistic, contentious, or anti-institutional bias. These biases, frequently dramatized by film portrayals of violence and aggression, evoke images of American politics and social life which are inordinately sinister and despairing ... Unable or unwilling to reject the network reports, the inadvertent viewer may turn against the group most directly responsible for the conflict, against the social and political institutions involved, or against himself, feeling unable to deal with a political system "like this." (p. 430)

The press fails even to provide the country with a vigorous marketplace of ideas. To cut costs, most news organizations subscribe to one wire service only. It is hardly the case that the news business is a bad business. In recent decades, the profit margin of news organizations has been roughly twice that of other firms, though that may be changing (Bagdikian, 1990).

The daily news is pretty much the same in all leading news outlets: The same events, the same interpretations, and the same people—all within a relatively narrow range—constitute the output of the mainstream American press. In America, competition between news organizations takes place for customers rather than for ideas. The pattern is a longstanding one, not a recent one. Villard (1944) noted a half century ago that the "newspaper of striking individuality [had given way to a] desire to print everything offered by one's rivals" (p. 6). Suppression of speech, as Schwarzlose observes, can be caused by irresponsible media as well as by oppressive government or tyrannical majorities. Diversity, he notes, has been sacrificed for "manageable and marketable messages" (pp. 13, 24).

The established press has even worked hard to keep alternative voices out of the news system. One of the great shortcomings of the American system is the absence of a high-quality, high-profile public broadcast system such as the British BBC or the German ARD. Why doesn't the United States have such a broadcast system? A chief reason is that the commercial networks fought the formation of a strong public broadcasting system by every means available.

The United States is the only democracy in which nearly all media are commercially owned. Whatever their virtues, commercial media are concerned with making a profit and with heading off new forms of competition (Schwarzlose, 1989). Why did it take so long for FM radio stations and UHF television stations to make inroads in American communities? In great part, it was because the established AM radio stations and VHF television stations worked hard to keep them out. What about cable television? The technology for cable was in place years before cable became widely adopted. The broadcast networks lobbied hard to prevent and then slow down the use of cable.

Rights entail duties. The Supreme Court has said that freedom of the press is a preferred freedom. It ranks above other rights because it is an indispensable condition of a free society. The press, however, has not treated its freedom as a calling higher than its quest for the almighty dollar. It would be hard to conclude that the press has been an exemplary beacon of freedom. The press, to be sure, has made important contributions to the country's freedom. However, its contribution ranks below what could reasonably be asked of a foremost beneficiary of the First Amendment's benefits.

POSTSCRIPT

Is the First Amendment Working?

Under the auspices of the First Amendment, the press gains protection from government control and from prior restraint, or what can be called censorship. Over time, the press has evolved, and as this has occurred, many questions have arisen that have seemed to challenge the protections offered by the Constitution to the press. What is the proper balance between freedom and obligation? If the press polices the government, then who or what polices the press, particularly when the press is part of big business?

In *Political Communication* (vol. 10, no.1), Jack McLeod and Roderick P. Hart continue the discussion that was begun by Jamieson and Patterson. Further analysis of the role of the press and its protection under the First Amendment is presented in this symposium. C. N. Olien, P. J. Tichenor, and G. A. Donohue in *Journal of Communication* (Spring 1995) present the "guard-dog" role of the media in contrast to the traditional watchdog of the fourth estate, the submissive lapdog of the existing power structures, or the view of the media as neither a watchdog or lapdog but simply as an existing component of the current social system. The authors show evidence of the guard-dog approach through media coverage of different public issues.

Patterson charges that press behavior has weakened the American political process. In "Bad News, Period," *PS: Political Science and Politics* (March 1996), he discusses the emergence of "attack journalism" and its impact on both politicians and the general public. Patterson reveals the myth behind assertions of a liberal bias in the media and shows instead evidence of the media as simply negative. According to him, this negativity has increased in the last 20 years and has led to Americans' disillusionment with political leaders and institutions. Patterson argues that this disillusionment has rendered U.S. leaders ineffective. James M. Fallows, in *Breaking the News: How the Media Undermine American Democracy* (Pantheon Books, 1996), argues that the media's self-aggrandizement gets in the way of solving American's real problems. Americans are impatient with arrogant journalists, he says, who seem to care very little about their mistakes and who hide behind the protections offered by the First Amendment.

ISSUE 9

Is Negative Campaigning Bad for the American Political Process?

YES: Larry J. Sabato, Mark Stencel, and S. Robert Lichter, from *Peepshow: Media and Politics in an Age of Scandal* (Rowman & Littlefield, 2000)

NO: William G. Mayer, from "In Defense of Negative Campaigning," *Political Science Quarterly* (Fall 1996)

ISSUE SUMMARY

YES: Larry J. Sabato, professor of government, Mark Stencel, politics editor for Washingtonpost.com, and S. Robert Lichter, president of the Center for Media and Public Affairs, assert that the line dividing public life and private life is more blurred than ever. The authors state that this is creating an age of scandal. They conclude that this focus on politics-by-scandal results in disaffected voters, discouraged political candidates, and news devoid of analysis of policy issues and substantive debate.

NO: William G. Mayer, assistant professor of political science, defends negative campaigning as a necessity in political decision making. He argues that society must provide the public with the substantive information needed to make informed decisions at the polls and insists that this must occur during political campaigns. Therefore negative campaigns are needed so that citizens can make intelligent choices concerning their leaders.

$\mathbf{P}$robably nothing has so transformed the American political process as the emergence of television as a force in elections. Today many more people see candidates on television than hear them in person. Candidates appear on a variety of media formats—television and radio talk shows, late-night entertainment programs, morning news and information programs, online, and even MTV. Never before have candidates used the power of media to such a comprehensive extent to reach potential voters.

But clearly the public is fed up with political campaigns. Voter apathy is high, as is public disgust with candidates and with politics itself. Viable candidates choose not to run rather than to subject themselves and their families to the scrutiny of the press. Many point the finger of blame at a relentless negativism governing the coverage and the conduct of political campaigns that favor a horse-race mentality, leap at opportunities to "go negative," and gleefully break stories of private failures.

Larry J. Sabato, Mark Stencel, and S. Robert Lichter indict campaigning, indeed much of American politics, in their volume *Peepshow: Media and Politics in an Age of Scandal,* from which the following selection has been taken. Marvin Kalb, executive director of the Shorenstein Center on the Press, bills this volume as a serious study of how scandal coverage has corrupted political coverage and ultimately criticizes journalists, candidates, and voters for degrading politics. Sabato et al. argue that the voracious appetites for scandal exhibited by all three of these groups contribute to the success of attack journalism. Furthermore, by focusing so much attention on the lives of public servants, the press squanders what little chance it has to engage the electorate. This leads to a greater chance that citizens will elect people who should not be in public office.

What should be the rules for politicians and journalists in an era of media preoccupation with private lives and political scandal? Despite the incivility of present campaigns, do we want to return to an era in which private lives were never considered appropriate for public discussion? Does it matter if candidates have experimented with drugs, joined subversive organizations as college students, evaded war service, or had affairs? What changes would make political campaigns and their coverage more substantive?

Sabato et al. and William G. Mayer call for a definition of negativity. To Sabato et al., negative campaigns have harmful effects on the political process. Mayer counters that negative campaigning is beneficial to the public and allows people to distinguish between the candidates. Each author reviles misleading campaign rhetoric and calls for careful policing of false assertions. Sabato et al. and Mayer see a need for media to be more careful in the information they provide, but Mayer challenges the common perception that negativity is bad. Rather than a bland campaign where each candidate speaks in favor of broad generalities, let records and behaviors be revealed and debated, he says. The character issue is real, and there must be a way for people to judge the character of those they elect. Otherwise, the information needed to discriminate among candidates will never emerge. And, the political process will be further diminished.

Larry J. Sabato, Mark Stencel, and S. Robert Lichter

 **YES**

Peepshow: Media and Politics in an Age of Scandal

The Scene of the Crime

The line political reporters draw between private and public life is perhaps more blurry than ever before. With increasing regularity, that blurry line is the smudged chalk outline of an ambitious politician.

For both politicians and journalists, deciding when private matters are the public's business is almost always challenging. Competition from new and alternative news sources makes those decisions even more complicated. Mainstream news outlets—newspapers, magazines, broadcast and cable television—no longer serve as almost exclusive gatekeepers of information about those who hold or seek elected office. At the same time, evolving public standards and increasing competitive pressures for a shrinking news audience are changing the ways editors and producers determine when and how to delve into the private lives of political figures. These forces make some editorial decisions seem almost arbitrary....

The press attention focused on the thirteen-month investigation and impeachment of President Clinton has put the press on trial for both its excesses and its oversights. To some, the coverage of President Clinton's sexual relationship with a former low-level White House functionary was an alarming invasion of privacy, a political smear. To others, it was a criminal matter that prompted a long-overdue examination of a pattern of reckless behavior that endangered the moral and ethical standing of the presidency. At the state and local level, candidates now regularly answer probing media questions about adultery, substance abuse and other private behavior—queries that even presidential candidates once weren't expected to answer. Nonetheless, many stories about politicians' private lives still never make it into print or on the air, even after news about those with similar pasts and public responsibilities is reported.

Just what are the rules for politicians and journalists in the aftermath of Washington's biggest sex scandal? When are a public official's or candidate's private affairs fair game and when are they out of bounds? The public, the press and those they cover are divided....

From Larry J. Sabato, Mark Stencel, and S. Robert Lichter, *Peepshow: Media and Politics in an Age of Scandal* (Rowman & Littlefield Publishers, 2000). Copyright © 2000 by Rowman & Littlefield Publishers, Inc. Reprinted by permission. Notes omitted.

[A] Pew Center's poll... suggests that a candidate's personal life is not a major campaign issue for most Americans, even in presidential politics. In a September 1999 survey, strong majorities thought the press should almost always report stories about a presidential candidate's spousal abuse (71 percent), income tax evasion (65 percent), exaggerated military record (61 percent) and exaggerated academic record (61 percent). But there was significantly less interest in reports about a candidate's ongoing affairs (43 percent), sexuality (38 percent), past drinking (36 percent) or cocaine use (35 percent). Less than a quarter of those surveyed (23 percent) said the press should almost always report on a past affair or marijuana use. Less than a third said the press should routinely delve into other personal issues—psychiatric treatment, antidepressant use, even abortions.

Editorial judgment is not always, if ever, a perfect reflection of public opinion. News organizations have a journalistic obligation to try to inform all readers and viewers, even the sizable minority to whom a candidate's or elected official's personal morality is a decisive voting issue. In the Pew Center poll, for example, a significantly higher percentage of Republicans than Democrats said the press should cover many of the personal issues mentioned above, with the division as high as 27 percent on stories about ongoing affairs.

Scandal coverage also can have positive effects on the political process. Intense scrutiny by the press and political opponents can drive away scalawags, increase public accountability and foster realistic attitudes about the human fallibility of elected leaders. But the costs of today's politics-by-scandal outweigh any remedial effects. While public trust in politicians is near all-time lows, confidence in the media is no higher, and participants on both sides say the emphasis on scandal is reducing voter turnout, distracting from important policy debates and discouraging the best politicians and best journalists....

Precedent

The press is on trial with readers and viewers. The charge: Unnecessary violation of the privacy of politicians and their families. Mainstream American political journalism offers an indicting array of examples in recent years, including coverage of extramarital affairs, office romances, divorces, drug use, drinking, sexuality, illegitimate children and plain, unsubstantiated rumor. Individual cases can be made to justify almost any news story that fell into these categories. Collectively, however, the predominance of such so-called character questions is eroding the credibility of political journalists and turning American democracy into a sort of peepshow or soap opera. Public opinion surveys suggest that journalists have stepped over the line most—but not all—Americans would set for legitimate editorial inquiry. Whether reporters, editors and producers are in fact guilty of violating the standards of their own profession depends on whether there really are any standards in an age of multimedia competition among information sources....

The Verdict

Colin L. Powell was preparing to step before more than three dozen television cameras and deliver the news that had already seeped out: The popular retired Army general and first black chairman of the Joint Chiefs of Staff would sit out the 1996 campaign for the White House. Polls showed that Powell was the only Republican likely to best incumbent Democrat Bill Clinton on Election Day a year hence. But as NBC anchorman Tom Brokaw broke into the day's programming to present Powell's news conference, he said one reason for the general's decision was well known. "It is widely believed that his wife, Alma, had a major role in this decision," Brokaw said. "She has a long history of depression, and that no doubt would get a very vigorous examination by not only the general's political opponents but also by reporters."

In fact, the press had already explored the issue of Alma Powell's depression. Dick Polman and Steve Goldstein of the *Philadelphia Inquirer* first reported that she used medication to treat depression. The news was mentioned briefly in a long, front-page story about Powell's possible candidacy more than two weeks earlier. "A close family friend said the Powells consider her condition a minor situation but understand it has to be considered in a family decision of this magnitude," the *Inquirer* reported. *Newsweek* magazine confirmed the report a week later, giving Alma Powell's depression and "worries about the family's privacy" slightly more play than the *Inquirer* in a long article about Powell's campaign contemplation and a sidebar about his wife's role.

At Powell's news conference, however—after Brokaw had already cut away to analyze the ongoing event—the general contradicted the anchorman's introduction. Alma's depression was not a major factor in his decision to sit out the race, he said in answer to a reporter's question, "and we found no offense in what was written about it."

> My wife has depression. She's had it for many, many years, and we have told many, many people about it. It is not a family secret. It is very easily controlled with proper medication, just as my blood pressure is sometimes under control with proper medication.
>
> And you obviously don't want your whole family life out in the press, but when the story broke we confirmed it immediately, and I hope that people who read that story who think they might be suffering from depression make a beeline to the doctor, because it is something that can be dealt with very easily.

Increasing media scrutiny no doubt takes its toll on public figures and their families. The promise of higher pay in the private sector (without prying personal examinations by the press) is appealing. At the same time, the fear that intrusive reporters are driving "good people" out of politics is perhaps overstated, as it was in Colin Powell's case. Media scrutiny can also be a deterrent to scoundrels who might seek political office. In some ways, the consequences of intensive press focus on the private lives of politicians are as great on the press itself as they are on those in politics, at least as measured by public confidence in the credibility of reporters and reporters' confidence in themselves. But the focus of public debate about the issue of political privacy is almost always on the quality candidates who are driven from the process, and the mediocre political figures who are left behind.

Political commentary bemoaning significant numbers of congressional retirements in the 1990s contributed to the sense that the best political leaders are abandoning public service. In the three election cycles that ran from 1991 to 1996, twenty-nine members of the Senate retired, including a record thirteen members in 1996. That was more than the total number of Senate retirements in the previous six cycles. In the same three election cycles, 162 members of the House voluntarily relinquished their seats at the end of their terms. That included a record sixty-five House retirements in 1992, when a check-kiting scandal involving the House of Representatives bank endangered many incumbents' chances for reelection.

The situation was very different in 1998. Even in the midst of the Monica Lewinsky investigation and embarrassing revelations about the personal lives of several prominent Republican congressmen, just four senators and twenty-three members of the House gave up their seats. Both 1998 figures were well below the average number of congressional retirements since 1950. The dropoff in congressional departures suggests that the high number of retirements earlier in the 1990s might have had less to do with the burdens of service than with the political shifts that gave Republicans control of both chambers of Congress for the first time since 1955.

Congressional retirements have indeed depleted the ranks of House and Senate moderates, making the legislative branch a less civil and more partisan place to work. That increasing partisanship also makes Congress a firetrap for political scandal and intrigue. The way the media frames political debate contributes, too, particularly in pyrotechnic talk television and radio formats that give prominence to those who most disagree on an issue. The redistricting process after the 1990 census was another factor. The creation of many minority districts meant that those running for other seats were campaigning in far less ideologically diverse areas. The isolation of certain voting blocs after 1990, particularly of ethnic voters, meant many candidates did not need to appeal to a broad range of voters to win their races.

Some fret that this political climate is only favorable to partisan, blow-dried, sound-biting politicians. But any long-term observer or member of Congress will tell you that the body's current membership is, in general, far better informed, better educated, and in many ways better at communicating than in the past. The vast majority are bright and able, and achieve a fair amount, whether or not one agrees with the object of the members' efforts. This is one subject on which serious reporters, academics, and politicians are agreed. Fifty years ago, many good people served in Congress who could not be elected in the television age. Being good on TV, however, does not mean being a bad public servant. To the contrary, it means one has the communication skills to build support for a public agenda. This can be critical in a country with a growing population that cares much less about politics than in the past.

People who lament the passing of the so-called golden age of public service either have poor memories or weren't alive at all. If law enforcement had been as tough and as thorough in investigating public officials fifty years ago as it is today, and if Congress itself had policed its members then to the extent that it does now, it would have been a good year when a dozen members were not indicted. The degree of corruption in politics is no higher now than in decades past. Reforms passed after Watergate, especially financial disclosure requirements, ensure that the degree of corruption may in fact be far less than it once was. The sins of the past are simply forgotten, because reporters frequently failed to report them and law enforcement failed to pursue them.

The same is true in presidential politics, despite an even more intense media spotlight on nearly every corner of a White House candidate's life. While Bill Clinton may be deficient in his personal morality, he is also one of the smartest and most knowledgeable individuals ever to sit in the Oval Office. And despite the scrutiny that will inevitably follow Clinton's tumultuous two terms, the initial crop of major party contenders who set out to run for the White House in 1999 included a two-term incumbent vice president, a former vice president, a former senator, two former Cabinet secretaries, a current governor, a House committee chairman, three current senators and two former White House advisers.

The field of prospective presidents in 2000 offers more experience and more diversity of views and is arguably a better crop of candidates than in 1960, when the field included three future presidents, one of whom was an incumbent vice president, and one future vice president—all of whom served in the Senate. Further, the presidential debates of the 1960 campaign did not include any discussion of the New Frontier, the Great Society, or the dramatic gestures of international peace and détente on which the three future presidents running that year would base their legacies. Nostalgia should not blind our assessment of past political campaigns, heroes and villains.

All of this is not to minimize the impact of attack journalism on the electoral process. While ambition has provided a healthy antidote to the poison pens of some reporters, the "politics of personal destruction" inevitably takes its toll. A democracy is based on electing human representatives with human failings. But some qualified candidates will remain on the sidelines rather than submit themselves and their families to a grueling personal examination by the press and their opponents. Even candidates standing on top of the polls have stood aside.

Moreover, the level of scrutiny once applied only to candidates for the highest offices is being applied farther down the ballot. In Georgia, for example, Lieutenant Governor Pierre Howard dropped out of the 1998 Democratic gubernatorial contest, relinquishing his front-runner status fifteen months before the election because of the impact on his family. Howard's announcement came two months after the leading Republican in the race, Mike Bowers, confessed to a long-standing extramarital affair that cost him critical support among his party's conservative wing. At the August 1997 news conference announcing his decision, Howard denied he was bowing out of the race to prevent any Bowers-like revelation about himself. "There is nothing in my background that worried me and caused me to want to get out of the race," Howard told suspicious reporters. Almost two weeks later, Jim Wooten, editor of the *Atlanta Journal*'s editorial page, wrote that suspicions lingered nonetheless.

People looking for some dark reason that he withdrew are likely to find it to be nothing more than he stated: His family was not into it. Neither was he.

Since Howard's abrupt announcement, the state has been abuzz with speculation. The most plausible explanation, after 10 days of conversation with people in politics—an industry that rivals journalism in its inability to keep a secret—is that there are no secrets to keep.

And that is the level of scrutiny applied to a *former* gubernatorial candidate.

The public and the press are deeply divided on the importance and the impact of this kind of reporting. A 1998–1999 survey conducted by the Pew Research Center for the People and the Press for the Committee for Concerned Journalists clearly showed this divide. . . . About half of those in the news survey—49 percent of national media and 56 percent of local outlets—said news organizations' coverage of the personal and ethical aspects of public figures is intended to drive controversy. In contrast, almost three-quarters of the public —72 percent—said news organizations are more interested in the controversy than in reporting the news on such stories. The division is more dramatic when asked about journalists' roles as public watchdogs. Almost 90 percent in the media said criticism by news organizations keeps political leaders from "doing things that should not be done." Only a small majority of the public, 55 percent, agrees—down from 67 percent in a 1985 poll. At the same time, a growing number said press criticism was keeping political leaders "from doing their jobs"—39 percent in the 1998–1999 survey, up from 17 percent in the 1985 poll.

Many journalists contend that their readers and viewers are hypocritical on these questions. They point to increased circulation and TV ratings of scandal news to make their case. After all, almost 50 million Americans tuned in to see Barbara Walters's exclusive March 1999 television interview with Monica Lewinsky on ABC's *20/20*, despite numerous polls in the preceding months suggesting the public had had its fill of news about the former White House aide. While there may be a certain amount of truth to this argument, it misses one key point: Increases in readership and television viewing measured against usual audience size are relatively small shifts, since the overall growth in circulation and network TV audiences stagnated long ago. In other words, the increased audience for scandal coverage is by and large an increase among the relatively small subset of the population who are already news consumers, not the growing number of news "disconnecteds" who have already turned off or tuned out.

"Gotcha" journalism is not the driving force behind these diminishing news audiences. But news coverage driven by values contrary to the public's only contributes to the public's sense that the media does not share their interests. Journalists themselves are beginning to recognize this as a problem. In the aforementioned Pew poll, more than half of news professionals surveyed —57 percent nationally and 51 percent locally—agreed that "journalists have become out-of-touch with their audiences."

Personal scrutiny also ensures that journalists are quite literally "out of touch" with some of the figures they cover. One immediate consequence of political journalists' increased focus on the private lives of politicians is decreased access. In 1998, Idaho representative Helen Chenoweth challenged a news story in the *Spokane Spokesman-Review*, which reported that she had lied in denying an affair with a married business partner. (She was asked about it directly by a reporter during an interview in a previous campaign.) Later, when the *Spokesman-Review* sought to interview Chenoweth for other news stories and profiles, she said she was too busy. "I know my staff was just looking out for my best interests as far as my time," she said, dismissing a reporter's questions about her interview policy after a candidate debate late in the campaign.

The losers in Chenoweth's feud with the *Spokesman-Review* were not the publication's reporters but the representative's constituents who read the newspaper and depend on it to relay their questions and her answers. However, there was no public outcry about Chenoweth's refusal to answer the newspaper's questions. In fact, she was reelected to a third term with 55 percent of the vote. The *Spokesman-Review* was right to report the discrepancies between its reporter's notes and Chenoweth's claim that she had never lied about her relationship. Nonetheless, the public will not side with reporters who they think are only interested in asking questions that they have no interest in seeing answered. This puts reporters and editors in an impossible bind.

The mission of the popular press is not to be popular. And in blaming the press for the sins about which it reports, the public—and even some critics—may be shooting the messenger. But ignoring public attitudes about press behavior could have grave consequences for the media as well as the political process. In combination with court rulings and high jury awards against reporters and declining public support for First Amendment press rights, diminished public confidence in the media poses more than a business threat to journalism's future. It is a potential threat to the very idea of an unrestricted press that was key to the nation's founding, its survival, and its future. Meanwhile, readers and viewers may increasingly turn to alternative sources of information... for pseudonews that does not stand up to traditional journalistic standards of balance and accuracy. Reporters, editors and producers cannot be stubborn or cavalier about public attitudes. Ignoring these threats is as self-destructive as the reckless personal behavior of politicians that today's journalists so meticulously document.

So far, the threats to journalism's future and the tabloidization of political coverage are not causing news organizations to hemorrhage talent. As with elected office itself, ambition almost guarantees that there will be hungry, talented young reporters interested in covering politics and government. These high-profile beats are still prime assignments in most newsrooms. More generally, journalism still provides opportunities to watch history being made and to get to know those who make it.

Nonetheless, some prominent national journalists have left their daily beats to try to reform their profession and the process of political discourse. Some have become nonprofit crusaders for better media. For example, former *Washington Post* political reporter Paul Taylor joined former CBS News anchorman Walter Cronkite before the 1996 presidential race to mount their own campaign to convince the major television networks to give free airtime to candidates. Tom Rosenstiel, a former reporter for the *Los Angeles Times* and *Newsweek*, now serves as director of the Project for Excellence in Journalism and vice chairman of the Committee of Concerned Journalists, where he has led efforts to raise standards and organize support for sensible journalistic reforms.

Some news organizations have embraced a new kind of social responsibility journalism, championed by the Pew Center for Civic Journalism, a nonprofit initiative financed by the Pew Charitable Trusts. No longer willing merely to report the news, some journalists see it as their duty to improve American society. This kind of reporting—which often uses extensive polling, focus groups, voter interviews and public forums to define an editorial agenda—represents a well-intentioned desire by journalists to reconnect with their audience. However, it is also a manifestation of the same editorial idealism that has led to the press emphasis on "character questions." Ultimately, journalism that does not reflect its audience's interests will lose that audience. But it is risky to assume that journalists will be any more successful at representing their readers and viewers when reporting on issues of public concern than they have been when reporting on the private lives of elected officials. These well-meaning journalistic experiments, with their potential to reengage the public, deserve careful attention and close scrutiny.

At the same time, the interactive nature of Internet journalism is pushing some for-profit online news operations in the same direction as the new civic journalists. These online editorial experiments, involving such unconventional media forces as America Online (AOL) and Yahoo!, also have potential to change the direction of mainstream reporting—and are attracting innovative and reform-minded talent from the ranks of traditional journalism. Former ABC News political reporter and Pentagon spokeswoman Kathleen deLaski went to America Online in 1996 to try to develop a new kind of political communication. The idea of covering politics in the interactive medium that AOL offered was enticing "because I thought political journalism could be better when the consumer is choosing what he/she wants to learn," deLaski said. At the same time, the former broadcast reporter said working online was a welcome alternative to the direction of political news on television:

> I went to AOL because I felt I was not serving the viewing audience well when I was on the campaign trail as a TV reporter. I would pick the five sentences of description each day and two sound bites that I could cram into my one-minute and thirty-second spot for ABC News to sum up the candidate's day. The stories often began, "Dogged by the polls. . . ." If you watched one of my stories, you had no idea what the candidate stood for. You learned how his day went versus the other guy's day.

Editorial experimentation in the nonprofit and corporate worlds offers evidence that some thoughtful journalists recognize the problems in their profession and are devoting their careers to addressing them. News organizations must be careful not to drive journalism's "best and brightest" reformers from their ranks.

One unanticipated consequence of media overcoverage of politicians' personal lives is a desensitizing effect among readers and viewers. Eventually, the public will tune out coverage of stories about which it has little interest, no matter how big the headlines or how prominent the TV news reports, as public reaction to the Monica Lewinsky scandal demonstrated. Even private behavior of legitimate public concern can fade into a mix of sensational news, like the blur of celebrity headlines on the cover of a supermarket tabloid. Revelations that once doomed candidacies and careers (such as Republican Nelson Rockefeller's divorce or Democrat Gary Hart's liaisons) are shrugged off later, as was the case with Republican Bob Dole's affair before his first divorce and President Clinton's Oval Office escapades. To some, this effect shows growing maturity on the part of voters and the press. But it also suggests a dangerous opportunity for politicians to exploit the public's scandal fatigue and convince voters to overlook failings that should raise legitimate questions about their fitness to serve.

The public itself has little time or interest in modern politics. By focusing so much attention on the personal lives of public servants, the press squanders what little chance it has to engage the electorate, to remind voters about the connections between public policy and their own personal lives. Voters are willing to devote only so much time to the study of politics. If coverage of personal politics dominates the news, then the public learns less about the matters that ought to be foremost in their minds when they vote. The less informed voters are when they walk into their polling places, the greater the chance that they will elect people who should not be in public office. The election of a real political cad or scoundrel would be the most tragic and ironic consequence of a media process that is intended to protect the public from just such a decision....

The media elite often seems removed from the average news consumer who buys a daily newspaper or a weekly newsmagazine and watches the occasional news show. But those elites are far more closely tied to average citizens than they themselves believe or would want to admit. In the end, the news establishment depends on casual news readers and viewers to support their empires, many of which are already on shaky financial ground. That being true, news executives must be responsive to reasonable and thoughtful public opinion whenever it is manifested. (Many outside the news business are surprised to discover just how few letters or calls it can take to change a newspaper's policy about this or a TV station's approach to that.)

The obverse relationship deserves emphasis. Citizens have the responsibility to shake off the tendency to be mere spectators and passive news receptacles. In a democracy, whether we like it or not, whether it is the ideal or not, citizens themselves must set the rules and, even more critically, enforce those rules with their eyes, their ears, and their pocketbooks.

Public standards and news standards do not always correspond, and public opinion should not substitute for news judgment. But public accountability can be a force that helps guide editorial decision-makers through their most difficult questions about what is news and what is not.

NO ←

William G. Mayer

In Defense of Negative Campaigning

When televised presidential debates were first held in 1960, many commentators deplored them for their shallow, insubstantial nature. But when scholars write about those debates today, they almost invariably comment about how much better the Kennedy–Nixon encounters seem than any of the more recent presidential debates. Students to whom I have shown excerpts from these debates usually have the same reaction. Compared to the Great Confrontations of [today], the 1960 debates seem more civil, more intelligent, more substantive. Especially noticeable is what is missing from the 1960 debates: the nastiness, the evasions, the meaningless memorized one-liners designed only to be featured on the postdebate newscasts, the boos and applause from the studio audience.

Nostalgia is not in general a helpful tool in policy analysis. Claims about how wonderful things were back in some past golden age usually do severe violence to the facts of history. But it is difficult to avoid the conclusion that American election campaigns have become significantly worse over the last three decades.... [T]here has been a burst of activity—including study commissions, academic research, grassroots organizing, and legislative proposals, as well as the usual quota of lamentation and hand-wringing—all with the intention of figuring out why things have gotten so bad and what we can do to make them better.

This nascent reform movement has a number of specific targets and criticisms, but one of the most widely mentioned is negative campaigning. Whenever commentators compile a catalogue of the most heinous sins in current American politics, negative campaigning and attack advertising usually wind up near the top of the list. As a 1990 *New York Times* article noted, "Ever since the Willie Horton commercial that skewered Michael S. Dukakis's presidential campaign, politicians have been competing to express their outrage over the notion that negative campaigning and superficial news coverage have mired American politics in a swamp of trivia." ...

From William G. Mayer, "In Defense of Negative Campaigning," *Political Science Quarterly*, vol. 111, no. 3 (Fall 1996). Copyright © 1996 by The Academy of Political Science. Reprinted by permission of *Political Science Quarterly*. Notes omitted.

Many elected officials share the sense of outrage. As former Senator Howard Baker declared in 1985:

> There is one singular new development in American politics that violates fair play, and that is negative advertising, the paid commercial, usually on TV or radio, that is a smear attack on a decent person. Not only is the negative ad the sleaziest new element in politics, it may also be the most dangerous. The first victim is the person under attack. But the greater victim is the integrity and credibility of the political system itself.

To many observers, the problem is sufficiently serious to require laws and regulations that would discourage or penalize negative campaigning.... One frequently made proposal ... would require any candidate who uses radio or television commercials to attack another candidate to deliver the attack in person. Another suggestion is to allow television and radio stations to charge higher rates for negative commercials than for positive ones. Some critics have even argued that the United States should follow the example of Venezuela and bar candidates entirely from referring to their opponents by name or by picture in their ads.

Whether any of these proposals stands a reasonable chance of being enacted is unclear.... The more likely result, at least in the short run, is a concerted effort on the part of civics groups, journalists, and commentators to create a climate of opinion that would discourage or penalize negative campaigning and that would try to convince voters that the very act of negative campaigning casts the candidate who engages in it in a highly unfavorable light....

There is little doubt that contemporary American election campaigns do fall short of the standards commended in our civics books. But in the laudable desire to improve our campaigns, surprisingly little attention has been paid to the easy, almost reflexive assumption that negative campaigning is bad campaigning: negative speeches and advertising are always morally wrong and damaging to our political system. In part, perhaps, the problem is one of semantics. Negative campaigning certainly sounds bad: it's so, well, you know, negative. But if we move beyond the label, what really is so bad about negative campaigning?

The purpose of this article, as its title indicates, is to challenge the accepted wisdom about negative campaigning. Negative campaigning, in my view, is a necessary and legitimate part of any election; and our politics—and the growing movement to reform our election campaigns—will be a good deal better off when we finally start to acknowledge it.

The Value of Negative Campaigning

What exactly is negative campaigning? Most people who use the term seem to have in mind a definition such as the following: Negative campaigning is campaigning that attacks or is critical of an opposing candidate. Where positive campaigning dwells on the candidate's own strengths and merits, and talks about the beneficial policies he would adopt if elected, negative campaigning focuses on the weaknesses and faults of the opposition: the mistakes they have made, the flaws in their character or performance, the bad policies they would pursue. And the more one focuses on the reality and consequences of such practices, the more clear I think it becomes that negative campaigning is not the plain and unmitigated evil that it is frequently portrayed to be. To the contrary, negative campaigning provides voters with a lot of valuable information that they definitely need to have when deciding how to cast their ballots.

To begin with, any serious, substantive discussion of what a candidate intends to do after the election can only be conducted by talking about the flaws and shortcomings of current policies. If a candidate is arguing for a major change in government policy, his first responsibility is to show that current policies are in some way deficient. If the economy is already growing rapidly with low rates of inflation, if the "environmental crisis" has been greatly exaggerated, if present policies have largely eliminated the possibility that nuclear arms will actually be used, then everything the candidates are proposing in these areas is useless, even dangerous. The need for such proposals becomes clear only when a candidate puts them in the context of present problems—only, that is to say, when a candidate "goes negative." . . .

But the information and analysis embodied in negative campaigning are also valuable on their own terms, for they tell us something extremely relevant about the choices we are about to make. We need to find out about the candidates' strengths, it is true, but we also need to learn about their weaknesses: the abilities and virtues they don't have; the mistakes they have made; the problems they haven't dealt with; the issues they would prefer not to talk about; the bad or unrealistic policies they have proposed. If one candidate performed poorly in his last major public office, if another has no clear or viable plan for dealing with the economy, if a third is dishonest, the voters really do need to be informed about such matters. I need hardly add that no candidate is likely to provide a full and frank discussion of his own shortcomings. Such issues will only get a proper hearing if an opponent is allowed to talk about them by engaging in negative campaigning.

Finally, negative campaigning is valuable if for no other reason than its capacity to keep the candidates a bit more honest than they would be otherwise. One doesn't have to have a lot of respect for the truth and intelligence of current campaign practices in order to conclude that things would be a lot worse without negative campaigning. If candidates always knew that their opponents would never say anything critical about them, campaigns would quickly turn into a procession of lies, exaggerations, and unrealistic promises. Candidates could misstate their previous records, present glowing accounts of their abilities, make promises they knew they couldn't keep—all with the smug assurance that no one would challenge their assertions. Every campaign speech could begin with the words, "I think I can say without fear of contradiction. . . ."

The Need for Clarity

In presenting earlier versions of this article, I have frequently encountered [this] surprising reaction: that I have actually overstated and mischaracterized the opposition to negative campaigning. As one panel discussant put it,

"Nobody criticizes *all* negative campaigning. When people criticize negative campaigning, they're not worried about attacks that are true and deal with significant issues. What they're upset about is that so much of this attack advertising is misleading or nasty or about made-up issues that have no real relevance to governing. *That's* what the furor's all about."

To this argument, I would make two responses. First, I would urge anyone who thinks I am overstating the case to read through a substantial part of the writing that has built up recently around the question of negative campaigning. What you will find is that the vast majority of this work... does, indeed, indict all campaign activities that are aimed at criticizing one's opponents, regardless of the particular issues they deal with, without even investigating whether the attacks are true or not. Very occasionally, one will come across an author who notes, usually in passing, that perhaps not all negative campaigning is bad, that some of it may even serve a useful purpose. But only a very small percentage of the writing on negative campaigning includes this qualification; most writing on the topic criticizes *all* negative campaigning, without any attempt to draw distinctions about its truth, relevance, or civility....

If the problem really is with campaign ads that are misleading or irrelevant or nasty, why not just say so? Why not abandon the attack on negative campaigning and go after misleading campaigning or trivial campaigning instead?... As many studies of the policy development process have emphasized, the way a problem is defined has a major effect on the kinds of "solutions" that will be proposed to cope with it.

This has clearly been true of the current effort to improve the conduct of American election campaigns. By defining the problem as one of negative campaigning, critics have naturally been led to look for solutions that would make it more difficult for candidates to criticize their opponents. What all of these proposals have in common, not surprisingly, is that they are targeted at negative campaigning as a generic, undifferentiated category. They would apply, in other words, to all advertising that criticizes one's opponents; they do not even attempt to distinguish between truthful and misleading attacks, or between trivial and relevant issues. And thus, to the extent they are successful, they will not only eliminate scurrilous and unfair attacks, but also those that are true, relevant, responsible, and serious.

There is, in short, a need for much greater care and clarity in thinking and writing about negative campaigning.

The Character Issue

Given the likely consequences of an attempt to limit or discourage critical comments of any kind, many commentators might want to modify their definition of negative campaigning. Perhaps what they really mean is something more like this: "Critical comments about your opponents' policy proposals are acceptable. But critical comments about your opponents' character, ability, or personal behavior are wrong. That's what negative campaigning is."

This argument, of course, is simply one variant of another common theme in the recent public debate about election campaigns. Whenever a candidate's personal character or behavior are questioned by his opponents or by the media, a number of voices will be heard insisting that such matters have no legitimate place in our elections and that campaigns should stick "strictly to the issues." But this argument, too, is fundamentally mistaken. Its basic flaw is the failure to appreciate the fact that candidates for public office are not computer programs with lengthy sets of preestablished policy subroutines, but flesh-and-blood human beings.

Campaign promises are at best only a rough guide to the actual decisions that a public official will make when in office.... Whatever the cause, it is striking how many of the most important policy initiatives of the last thirty years were never discussed in the previous campaign, or were taken by presidents who had promised or implied that they would do otherwise. The issue positions assumed during a campaign, in other words, are short-lived and changeable; a better guide to what a candidate will do is often provided by his personality and character.

Once a public official does reach a decision, there is surely no guarantee that it will automatically be promulgated and executed with the full force of law.... They must... be good managers and political strategists, meet frequently with other elected officials, lead public opinion, persuade the recalcitrant, and attract and retain talented staff. And all of these are matters of ability, temperament, and character.

For both of those reasons, candidate character and behavior are entirely relevant issues, more important than many policy questions. Indeed, if you examine the records of the last few presidents, what strikes you is how their most serious failings—at least in the minds of the voters—were not brought on by their policy views, but by their character flaws: Nixon's dishonesty and vindictiveness, Carter's inability to work with other elected officials, Reagan's management style, Bush's general disinterest in domestic policy. Small wonder, then, that public opinion polls continually show that voters are highly concerned about the personal qualities of the people on the ballot.

After acknowledging this, however, the issues become somewhat murkier. Character matters, but what particular character traits would recommend or disqualify a candidate? Does sexual promiscuity make for a bad president? Does avoiding the draft? Many of the most important character traits, moreover, are remarkably difficult to assess. We not know something about how to determine if a candidate is promiscuous, but how do we "prove" that he is vindictive or paranoid or unintelligent? If a candidate loses his temper at a campaign stop, is this an isolated incident or a sign of a deep-seated mean streak? When a candidate cheats on his wife, is this a regrettable but common human failing, or a symptom of a larger personality disorder?

There are no simple answers to such questions; but particularly in elections for executive offices such as president, governor, or mayor, where character flaws can have such important repercussions, I think we are well advised to cast the net widely....

Furthermore, when difficult and border-line cases do arise as to whether a particular behavior or character trait is relevant to a candidate's performance in office, the bias should clearly be in favor of reporting and discussing the issue. If many voters believe that such matters are irrelevant, then presumably they can be trusted to ignore the issue when deciding how to cast their own ballots. But the final say should rest with the electorate, not with the reporters, political consultants, or fair campaign practice committees who might wish to screen such matters from public attention.

And if issues of character and behavior should be discussed, then they should be examined in both their positive and negative aspects. If candidates are free to portray themselves as leaders or deep thinkers or good managers or highly moral, then their opponents should be free to contest these claims. If Joseph Biden wanted to project an image as a passionate orator, fine. But the campaign manager for one of his leading opponents should then have been allowed to point out that some of Biden's passion and rhetoric were borrowed.

The Role of the Media

Another possible line of reply to the argument presented here is that I have left one important element out of the equation: the news media. If the purpose of negative campaigning is to expose the candidates' weaknesses and shortcomings, and to prevent lies and misrepresentations, then perhaps we can rely on television, newspapers, and magazines to help perform these functions....

But when it comes to the need for negative campaigning, the news media cannot substitute for the candidates. Yes, the media will often be negative—but about the wrong things and in the wrong ways. Two major characteristics of the American news media, amply verified in a long list of studies, make them ill suited to perform the functions that have traditionally been served by negative campaigning. In the first place, the media have a long-standing aversion to issues of any kind—positive or negative—or to detailed discussions of the candidates' previous performance and governing abilities. As one recent analysis of the media performance literature has noted:

> Countless studies of campaign journalism (both print and broadcast) have shown that the news invariably focuses on the campaign as a contest or race. News reports on the candidates' standing in public opinion polls, their advertising strategies, the size of the crowds at their appearances, their fund-raising efforts, and their electoral prospects far surpass coverage detailing their issue positions, ideology, prior experience, or decision-making style.

This same sort of disproportion can be found in negative articles about the campaign. If a candidate makes a major gaffe, if his poll ratings are slipping, if there is in-fighting among his advisers—all these will be reported promptly and in exhaustive detail. But do not expect such detailed examination of the shortcomings in a candidate's economic policies, his environmental record, or his plans for dealing with the Middle East. The media's past record suggests that they are unlikely to provide it. Studies of campaign advertising, by contrast, usually conclude that political commercials have far more substantive content than is generally appreciated. Moreover, according to a recent study by Darrell West, negative spots usually have more specific and issue-based appeals than positive commercials.

A second obstacle to the media's attempt to "police" an election campaign are the norms of objectivity and nonpartisanship that govern most major American news outlets. What exactly objectivity means, and whether the media always live up to that standard, are complex and difficult questions, but ones that need not concern us here.... [T]he media are generally averse to saying anything explicit about the issues that could be construed as judgmental, interpretive, or subjective. As Michael Robinson and Margaret Sheehan found in their study of news coverage during the 1980 election:

> As reluctant as the press is about saying anything explicit concerning the leadership qualities of the candidates, the press is markedly more reluctant to assess or evaluate issues.... [We found] an almost total refusal by [CBS and UPI] to go beyond straightforward description of the candidate's policy positions. During the last ten weeks of Campaign '80, CBS failed to draw a single clear inference or conclusion about a single issue position of a single candidate—UPI as well.

How do the media cover issues, then? The answer is that they report on what the candidates themselves are saying.... As a result, the only kinds of policing of the issues that the media will undertake on their own initiative are questions that can clearly and unambiguously be labeled as matters of fact. If a candidate makes a blatant factual error—by misquoting a report, or claiming that nuclear missiles can be called back after they are launched, or adding items to his resume that never actually occurred—the media will sometimes call him on it.... Even the recent profusion of ad watches, which represents a more self-consciously aggressive attempt to scrutinize the candidates, generally adheres to these same guidelines.

In most campaigns, however, the most significant issue controversies are not matters of fact, but questions that require a substantial amount of judgment and interpretation. Would George McGovern's proposed defense cuts have left America unprotected? Was Jimmy Carter avoiding the issues in 1976? Was Ronald Reagan a warmonger?... Did George Bush have any vision for America's future?... On these and similar controversies, the media's record is that they will publicize these issues only if a candidate's opponents have talked about them first....

But even if the news media were to adopt a new set of norms and were willing to police our election campaigns, it is doubtful that we would want to put this burden primarily on their shoulders. The right of any individual or group to criticize, to object, to dissent is one of the signal achievements of American democracy, enshrined in the First Amendment. To say that we should restrict or penalize negative campaigning is to say, in effect, that candidates should now largely abdicate that right and rest content with whatever the media decide to broadcast or publish. If candidates did agree to abide by such strictures, they would thus be renouncing many of the most important duties we have traditionally expected from our best leaders and political heroes: such tasks as articulating grievances; speaking on behalf of the ignored and the forgotten; taking an unappreciated problem, bringing it to public attention, and thereby compelling the system to take action.

On a more general level, it has become increasingly clear over the last thirty years to both liberals and conservatives that some of the most difficult challenges facing American democracy in the twenty-first century concern the enormous power vested in the mass media, an entity that is self-selected, demographically and ideologically unrepresentative, increasingly monopolistic, almost entirely unregulated, and not directly accountable to the voters. There are no easy solutions for this complicated set of issues; but the very fact that these questions are so difficult strongly commends the wisdom of one general maxim: we ought to be extremely leery about any proposal that wants to increase the power of the media by asking them to take on one more function that has traditionally been performed by the candidates or the political parties. If candidates abuse their power of negative campaigning, the voters retain the ultimate power of punishing them at the polls. But what real alternative do the voters have if our election campaigns are improperly policed by CBS News or *The New York Times?*

What Restrictions on Negative Campaigning Would Mean for American Politics

Of the proposals... for reducing or restricting negative campaigning, it is unclear how many would actually accomplish their intended goal....

But let us suppose, for a moment, that one or another of these proposals would be effective: it would significantly reduce the volume of negative campaigning and make it considerably more difficult for a candidate to attack or criticize his opponent. What impact would this have on the character of American politics?

The most obvious consequence, of course, is that it would deprive the electorate of a lot of valuable information, and thereby make it that much more difficult for the voters to make intelligent choices about the people they elect to public office. Like our political system generally, our electoral system is based on the belief that good decisions are more likely to result from a full, thorough, and unrestricted discussion of the issues. As the Supreme Court stated in one of the most important free speech cases of the twentieth century, there is

> a profound national commitment to the principle that debate on public issues should be uninhibited, robust, and wide-open, and *that it may well include vehement, caustic, and sometimes unpleasantly sharp attacks on government and public officials.*

Deprived of the important information conveyed in negative campaigning, the voters would be in the position of a blackjack player who must decide how to play his hand without getting to look at his hole card. He may, of course, stumble into the right decision, but the odds are surely better if he knows all the cards he has been dealt.

But beyond this general enfeebling of democracy, any limitation on negative campaigning is likely to have important systemic consequences for our politics. In congressional elections, restrictions on negative campaigning would almost certainly work to the advantage of incumbents, making them even more entrenched and difficult to unseat....

In the end, a challenger in a congressional election stands almost no chance of winning unless he "goes negative": unless, in other words, he can succeed in raising doubts about the incumbent's character, voting record, and attention to the district....

Any move to limit negative campaigning, in short, would just add one more weapon to the already formidable arsenal with which incumbents manage to entrench themselves in office....

And the more negative campaigning is discouraged or penalized, the more likely it becomes that all voters will ever learn about how the challenger performed in his previous position is the candidate's own highly colored version of that record. Thus, in a close election... where the campaign could make a difference in the final outcome, limits on negative campaigning would be distinctly to the advantage of the challenger.

It is no accident that when various commentators recommended a moratorium on negative campaigning during the last few weeks of the 1992 presidential race, Bill Clinton readily agreed to the idea and George Bush tried to resist it. Both major-party campaigns understood quite well that Bush's only chance for victory lay in a negative campaign against Clinton. To be sure, there is something a little sad about an incumbent president whose best argument as to why he should be reelected is to say, in effect, "Sure, I may not have been a very good president—but my opponent would be even worse." But the fact that this argument is sad does not mean that it may not be in some cases entirely valid.

The Search for Better Campaigns

To defend negative campaigning, of course, is not to deny that positive campaigning is also important. What our politics really needs is a mixture of the two. A candidate who is challenging an incumbent should be required to show the weaknesses and shortcomings of his opponent, and then to indicate how and why he would do better. An incumbent should defend his own record, and then (since that record is unlikely to be entirely without blemish) should be able to point out the ways in which the challenger would be deficient. The point is that both are valid ways of appealing to and informing the electorate—just as economic affairs and foreign policy are both relevant issues.

The effort to stamp out negative campaigning thus deals a double blow to any attempt to improve the quality of future American election campaigns. It seeks to deny the voters important information that is relevant to their decisions; but it also helps divert attention from the many serious problems that genuinely afflict our campaigns. Most of the practices that are condemned on the grounds of negative campaigning are actually objectionable for very different reasons. Sending a forged letter about one's opponent, as the Nixon people did in 1972, is wrong, not because it is negative campaigning, but because it's a lie. Demanding that your opponent take a drug test isn't objectionable because it's negative, but because the issue it raises is trivial. Calling your opponent "unChristian" is wrong because it is a misuse of religion. Accusing a congressional incumbent of taking too many junkets would be wrong if it takes such incidents out of context. (It may also be a real indication that the incumbent is neglecting his duties and abusing the perquisites of office.)

There is a simple test that can be applied to all of these issues. If you think that a particular campaign practice is wrong because it is an instance of negative campaigning, then it follows that the same behavior would be acceptable just as long as it was done in a positive manner. So, if negative campaigning is the real villain in all of these cases, sending a forged letter that attacks an opponent is wrong, but forging a letter that says positive things about one's own candidate is acceptable. Or: it's wrong to criticize your opponent for failing to take a drug test, but it's okay if you yourself take a drug test and then trumpet the results as proof of your spectacular fitness for office. It's wrong to call your opponent "unChristian," but acceptable to call yourself "the Christian candidate in this election."

Rather than trying to limit or discourage negative campaigning as a generic category, we ought to recognize that some negative campaigning is good and some negative campaigning is bad—and then think more carefully about the kinds of moral criteria that really should make a difference.... Probably the most significant problem with campaign advertising, positive and negative, is that so much of it is misleading, taking votes and actions out of context, or implying connections between events that may be completely unrelated. Many ads also deal with matters of highly questionable relevance that tell us little or nothing about either candidates' ideology or fitness for office. It also seems clear that many voters are troubled by the incivility of many negative ads, the tone of which is frequently harsh and mean-spirited. All of these are real and serious problems, eminently worthy of our best efforts to rectify them. But we will make little progress in this direction by a war against negative campaigning.

POSTSCRIPT

Is Negative Campaigning Bad for the American Political Process?

A 1996 Freedom Forum poll found that three-quarters of American voters believe that the press has a negative impact on U.S. presidential campaigns, detracts from a discussion of the issues, gives undue advantage to front-running candidates, is often confusing and unclear, and even discourages good people from running for president. Despite the criticism, these same voters rely heavily on journalists to provide the information needed to make informed voter decisions. They turn to journalists for information about the candidates, particularly their issue positions, and for information about how election outcomes will affect voters.

The implications of these arguments for judgments about negativity in political campaigns are important. It seems clear that people are unhappy with current political coverage. People want more information, and they want it tailored to their questions and their needs. Political Internet sites are perhaps one answer. They are proliferating; yet, even these suffer from the familiar problem of too much trivia and too little debate. It remains to be seen whether or not the advent of new technology will be able to fulfill its promise of creating a more positive dialogue between candidate and voter.

Lest a reader begin to feel too self-righteous about these issues, let us remember the complicity of the viewing public. Candidate debates attract small numbers of viewers; political scandal sells. Just as in television entertainment, what the public gets is influenced by what the public selects from the available options. Certainly with the advent of cable niche programming, the public can select much more informative and less scandal-oriented programming than ever before. Thus, the critique that implicates the press and the politician also implicates the viewer.

A number of books try to analyze the consequences of negativity. One book that has specifically tackled the history and problem of campaign advertising is *Going Negative: How Attack Ads Shrink and Polarize the Electorate,* by Stephen Ansolabehere and Shano Iyengar (Free Press, 1997). Examining the consequences for the voter are Joseph Capella and Kathleen Hall Jamieson in *Spiral of Cynicism* (Oxford University Press, 1997). See also, Justin Lewis, "Reproducing Political Hegemony in the U.S.," *Critical Studies in Mass Communication* (vol. 16, no. 3, 1999) and Victor Kamber, "Poison Politics," *California Journal* (vol. 28, no. 11, 1997). For a journalistic take on the issue, see Mike McCurry, "Getting Past the Spin," *The Washington Monthly* (July/August 1999).

ISSUE 10

Has Democracy Been Transformed by New Uses of Media?

YES: Dale Herbeck, from "Democratic Delusions: The Town Meeting in an Electronic Age," in David Slayden and Rita Kirk Whillock, eds., *Soundbite Culture: The Death of Discourse in a Wired World* (Sage Publications, 1999)

NO: Elizabeth Weise, from "Not Yet for the Net," *Media Studies Journal* (Winter 2000)

ISSUE SUMMARY

YES: Professor Dale Herbeck discusses the traditional model of the New England town meeting and how it has been used by television since 1992 to get the political candidate's campaign message to as many people as possible in an intimate setting. He states that this type of event has transformed a portion of direct democracy, and he discusses what happens in a mediated environment.

NO: Elizabeth Weise, a writer for *USA Today,* addresses the New England town meeting facilitated by the Internet. She cites a number of studies and issues that support her view that the Internet is not yet an appropriate venue for this type of democratic interaction, largely because key individuals have not yet learned how to use it effectively.

Since the televised Nixon–Kennedy debates, television has been criticized for contributing to a change in the democratic process, substituting image for substance on the part of the political candidates. It is only natural to consider how other emerging forms of technology might also contribute to new practices. In the case of the Internet, a great promise has been the possibility of a "direct democracy" in which individuals can access information on the Internet, and make their opinions known immediately through e-mail.

In the following selections, Dale Herbeck and Elizabeth Weise each examine how one form of democratic practice, the town meeting, has been adapted to both television and the Internet. As Herbeck demonstrates, television has not only radically changed the way political debates operate but also how opinion polls are made to appear to be representative of the public's position on any given topic. He explains how the personal image of the candidate can be influenced in a televised setting by addressing not only what the candidate does but how he or she represents themselves in this artificial environment.

Weise argues that although the Internet has been hailed as a vehicle for direct democracy, it has failed to live up to its promise. She discusses how political handlers have "botched" the effective use of up-to-date Web sites and the control of Internet addresses (URLs), concluding that they apparently fail to understand how the Internet might be best used to reach potential contributors and voters. She does, however, caution that the ability to reference campaign contributors through Internet solicitations could also influence voters' opinions, if they knew which organizations and/or individuals were supporting a candidate.

The number of experiments with using online services for voting is continuing to grow. It is conceivable that the actual process of voting in the future could involve people voting from home, or at centralized agencies, and the votes immediately being tallied for response. Still, the traditions of how certain democratic practices are enacted ask us to consider whether a newer mode of making decisions is facilitated or harmed by the use of instant communication —particularly that which relies more heavily on visual images.

For some years, the tradition of the political debate has been changing from one in which the candidates used the format of a formal debate to that of a public relations spectacle. What difference does it make who asks the questions or how those questions are asked? How much control is exercised in terms of who gets to ask questions? How many people use the media to form their political opinions, and what role do interpersonal channels play in influencing their actions?

As you read Herbeck's selection, you will be prompted to think about how "slick" certain political candidates may be in effectively using the media. Does this mean that only those candidates who know how the media work have a chance for political leadership? What role does the press play in reformulating and reporting what goes on in a campaign? How can the Internet be used to prevent some problems and not cause others?

Media are now an integral component to the effective maintenance of democracy, but are they given too much power? Is it possible to reverse the direction of more media, reaching even more specialized audiences, or should we accept that democratic practices will continue to evolve in conjunction with new ways of distributing information?

Democratic Delusions:
The Town Meeting in
an Electronic Age

Many thoughtful commentators have lamented over the death of public argument in American politics. Even as the quantity of political speech has increased, the quality of argument in the public sphere has grown noticeably more impoverished. Nowhere is this paradox more evident than in presidential campaigns. The length of these campaigns has increased in recent years, yet there seems to be less and less discussion of the issues. Spending on these campaigns has reached record highs, but the amount of meaningful information provided to voters to assess the candidates has decreased. Opinion polls have become more common, and reporting on poll results has become a substitute for substantive coverage of the campaigns. Candidates are seemingly always in the media, but the length of each exposure has decreased as sound bites have grown shorter and shorter. No personal narrative is too tragic, no personal matter too private, when candidates are appealing for votes.

Given the absence of meaningful discourse in contemporary presidential campaigns, debates between candidates for the highest national office seem to provide a unique opportunity for public argument. Debates offer an extended opportunity for the candidates to communicate with millions of eligible voters for an extended period of time. Highlighting the potential implicit in presidential debates, Kathleen Hall Jamieson and David Birdsell have suggested that "debates offer the longest, most intense views of the candidates available to the electorate. Uninterrupted by ads, uncontaminated by the devices programmers use to ensnare and hold prime-time attention, the debates offer sustained and serious encounters with candidates."

Unfortunately, the potential implicit in debates among the presidential candidates has gone largely unrealized. Instead of affording observers a rich discussion of the issues and the candidates' respective positions, presidential debates have become shallow political spectacles, media events virtually devoid of intellectual substance or merit. Unfortunately, all too many explanations have been posed for why debates have failed to realize our expectations. Representatives of the political parties have skillfully negotiated formats that allow the candidates routinely to avoid answering important questions and to evade meaningful discussion. For their part, candidates have learned to recite memorized or scripted passages, to display appropriate emotions and act "presidential," and artfully to avoid discussion of troublesome topics. The media have played an equally dubious role, often reducing a 90-minute debate to a memorable clip appearing later on the news, using questionable polls and devices to declare winners and losers instantly, and trivializing the substance of debate with insipid commentary.

Despite this record of futility, interest in political debates has remained high in recent years because of the penultimate nature of the spectacle and innovative formats. One of the most heralded changes has been to model presidential after a New England town meeting. The first of these so-called town hall debates between presidential candidates occurred in 1992, when President George Bush, Bill Clinton, and Ross Perot used a format that allowed citizens to question the candidates directly. The result was a lively debate, and given the success of the format, it is not surprising that 4 years later one of the two debates between President Clinton and Bob Dole used the town hall format.

Through such town halls, presidential campaigns have attempted to create a means to reach through the media and directly connect with the voters. All across America, candidates for lesser offices have recognized the powerful political appeal implicit in such meetings and adopted similar strategies. Although such forums seem to offer the possibility of meaningful interaction, . . . I argue that the town hall debate is a democratic fiction, an appeal to a cherished political institution designed to mask the mediocrity of contemporary political discourse. To prove this contention, the 1992 town hall debate among Bush, Clinton, and Perot is offered as an illustration. In the pages that follow, I consider the decision to adopt a town hall format . . . and conclude by arguing that the first town hall debate between presidential nominees was more of a political spectacle than an exercise in democratic self-government. Working from this experience, I briefly consider the possibility of an "electronic town square," a powerful democratic image invoked by President Clinton in his 1996 State of the Union Address.

The Changing Face of Presidential Elections

Debates between competing candidates have become a major event in presidential election campaigns. In 1960, 1976, 1980, 1984, 1988, 1992, and 1996, the leading presidential candidates met in televised debates before the general election. Although a variety of formats have been used for these exchanges, the most common until recently featured the candidates responding to questions posed by a panel of journalists: A journalist's question is directed to one of the candidates, then the opposing candidate is given the opportunity to respond, after which time may be allotted for a rebuttal.

From the outset of the debates, argumentation scholars have known that the panel format forces the candidate to choose between answering the questions asked by a panelist and debating the opposing candidates. These scholars have also recognized that the panelists are not objective intermediaries, but rather have rightly observed that panelists necessarily play an adversarial role with the candidates in presidential debates. . . .

Criticism of the panel format has not been restricted to academicians or academic journals. At a practical level, anyone can see that having four journalists interrogate two or more candidates, with each candidate having the right of reply or rebuttal, will produce shallow discussion unlikely to provide much insight into what each candidate would actually do to cope with the nation's most pressing problems. Looking beyond the logistical problems posed by a panel of journalists, critics have also criticized the actual questions asked by the panelists. More than a few commentators have lamented that the journalists on the panels tend to trip over their egos in their eagerness to ask their own questions —leaving gaps and evasions in the previous answer without a follow-up. Even campaign officials and political consultants have questioned whether political debates involving panels of journalists truly produce any useful information. Although criticism of the panel format has been widespread for years, it took the 1992 campaign to break with tradition and adopt a new format.

The 1992 campaign was unique, as two of the candidates, Democratic challenger Bill Clinton and Independent candidate Ross Perot, both displayed a willingness to use innovative means to reach the voters. Bill Clinton in particular made strategic use of the media in his successful campaign. Immediately before the New Hampshire primary, for example, Clinton responded to widespread allegations of marital infidelity by appearing on *60 Minutes* with his wife, Hillary. When questions subsequently arose about how he had avoided serving in the Vietnam War, Clinton responded through a televised town hall meeting in New Hampshire. Still later in the campaign, Clinton appeared in dark glasses with his saxophone on *The Arsenio Hall Show*. Although the viewing audience for the actual show was minuscule, Clinton received extensive coverage in the mainstream media for his rendition of "Heartbreak Hotel."

In his independent campaign for the presidency, Ross Perot also used nontraditional techniques to appeal for support. Although his populist campaign themes were markedly different from those of Clinton, Perot was equally willing to explore opportunities previously spurned by presidential candidates. In February, during an interview on "Larry King Live," Perot intimated that he might be persuaded to run for president if there was enough citizen support to have his name placed on the ballot in all 50 states. After formally declaring his candidacy, Perot made frequent use of half-hour infomercials on television to explain his policy positions and to solicit support. Finally, like Clinton, Perot was always willing to appear on television talk shows and to participate in town hall meetings.

As the campaign reached its climax, the Commission on Presidential Debates proposed four debates—three presidential contests and a single contest between the vice presidential candidates. The bipartisan commission, which had been created to negotiate the logistics of the debates, recommended a single-moderator format. This format, the commission believed, would promote more substantive answers by allowing follow-up questions from the moderator while simultaneously creating the possibility of direct confrontation between the candidates. The Clinton campaign readily agreed to the scheme proposed by the commission, but the Bush campaign was unwilling to accept this plan. Apparently believing that agreeing to debate too early would freeze any momentum toward Bush while also fearing that the format would work to Clinton's advantage, the Bush campaign summarily rejected the commission's recommendations. The inability to agree on a format forced the cancellation of the first debate, and for a time it appeared that no presidential debates would take place in 1992. Finally, after months of posturing, the Bush and Clinton campaigns agreed to a series of debates featuring a variety of formats and invited Ross Perot to participate. Given the competing interests, it is not surprising that the presidential debates held in 1992 reflected a series of compromises. One compromise was the second debate, scheduled for Richmond, Virginia, which featured a town hall format. Under this format, an audience composed of undecided voters would symbolically represent the body politic as they engaged the candidates in a discussion of the issues. The format was unique, and it is doubtful that the Richmond town hall would have occurred were it not for the unusual juxtaposition of politicians, campaigns, and events.…

The 1992 Town Hall Debate: Democratic Ritual or Political Spectacle?

The second presidential debate in 1992 was held on October 15 at the University of Richmond in Richmond, Virginia. The debate was unique, as it was loosely modeled after a New England town meeting in which candidates responded to questions from the audience. To facilitate interaction, the traditional podiums were removed and each candidate was provided with a tall stool. Candidates were permitted to move about the stage when responding to questions. Carole Simpson of *ABC News* played the role of moderator, roaming through the audience to solicit questions from 209 undecided voters empaneled by an independent polling organization. Each question was directed to a particular candidate, but the other candidates were also given the opportunity to respond. Simpson was allowed to clarify and follow up on questions asked by the audience. No order of response was mandated, nor was the debate balanced to guarantee equal time to all three participants. The debate concluded with a 2-minute closing statement from each candidate.

It was clear from the outset that the town hall debate would be different from previous presidential debates. In her opening remarks, Carole Simpson prognosticated that "tonight's program is unlike any presidential debate in history—we're making history here now, and it's pretty exciting." Questions from the citizens that evening were noteworthy, partly because for the first time citizens were involved in a presidential debate, and partly because the citizens insisted that the candidates focus on substantive issues. One of the first questioners complained, "The amount of time the candidates have spent in this campaign trashing their opponents' character and their programs is depressingly large. Why can't your discussions and proposals reflect the genuine complexity and the difficulty of the issues to try to build a consensus around the best aspects of all proposals?" The very next questioner asked, "Can we focus on the issues and not the personalities and the mud?"

The questions dealt almost exclusively with domestic issues; a single query was made about America's role as a superpower. To the surprise of many commentators, the citizen questioners ignored the character issues associated with Clinton's draft record and his antiwar activities in Europe that had been such a large part of the first debate. Although the debate did produce a notable exchange between the candidates about Clinton's character, the most poignant moment of the debate occurred when a young black woman asked, "How has the national debt personally affected each of your lives? And if it hasn't, how can you honestly find a cure for the economic problems of the common people if you have no experience in what's ailing them?"

Answers to this question varied, but they are worth studying because they reveal a great deal about both the town hall format and how the media portrayed the debate. Ross Perot, the first to enter the fray, responded as follows:

> It caused me to disrupt my private life and my business to get involved in this activity. That's how much I care about it. And believe me, if you knew my family and if you knew the private life I have, you would agree in a minute that that's a whole lot more fun than getting involved in politics. But I have lived the American dream, I came from a very modest background. Nobody's been luckier than I've been, all the way across the spectrum, and the greatest riches of all are my wife and children. That's true of any family. But I want all the children—I want these young people up here to be able to start with nothing but an idea like I did and build a business. But they've got to have a strong basic economy and if you're in debt, it's like having a ball and chain around you. I just figure, as lucky as I've been, I owe it to them and I owe it to the future generations and on a very personal basis, I owe it to my children and grandchildren.

After Perot, the question fell to President Bush. "Well, I think the national debt affects everybody," Bush began. The questioner interrupted, "You personally." Flustered, Bush tried again, "Obviously, it has a lot to do with interest rates." This time, moderator Simpson interrupted, "She's saying, you personally." The questioner quickly interjected, "You, on a personal basis—how has it affected you?" before Simpson could ask, "Has it affected you personally?" Clearly flustered, Bush replied, "I'm sure it has. I love my grandchildren.... I want to think that they're going to be able to afford an education. I think that that's an important part of being a parent. If the question—maybe I—get it wrong. Are you suggesting that if somebody has means that the national debt doesn't affect them?" The questioner tried to clarify, suggesting, "I know people who cannot afford to pay the mortgage on their homes, their car payment. I have personal problems with the national debt. But how has it affected you, and if you have no experience in it, how can you help us, if you don't know what we're feeling?" Bush tried one final time:

> Well, listen, you ought to be in the White House for a day and hear what I hear and see what I see and read the mail I read and touch the people that I touch from time to time. I was in the Lomax AME Church. It's a black church just outside of Washington, D.C. And I read in the bulletin about teenage pregnancies, about the difficulties that families are having to make ends meet. I talk to parents. I mean, you've got to care. Everybody cares if

people aren't doing well. But I don't think it's fair to say, you haven't had cancer. Therefore, you don't know what's it like. I don't think it's fair to say, you know, whatever it is, that if you haven't been hit by it personally. But everybody's affected by the debt because of the tremendous interest that goes into paying on that debt everything's more expensive. Everything comes out of your pocket and my pocket. So it's that. But I think in terms of the recession, of course, you feel it when you're president of the U.S. And that's why I'm trying to do something about it by stimulating the export, vesting more, better education systems. Thank you. I'm glad you clarified it.

When presented with the opportunity to answer the same question, Clinton pounced. As he began to respond, he moved toward the front of the stage while simultaneously engaging the questioner, "Tell me how it's affected you again." Before the questioner could internalize the query and respond, Clinton intuitively asked, "You know people who've lost their jobs and lost their homes?" Not allowing time for a response, Clinton instead offered his own answer:

Well, I've been governor of a small state for 12 years. I'll tell you how it's affected me. Every year, Congress and the president sign laws that make us do more things and give us less money to do it with. I see people in my state, middle-class people—their taxes have gone up in Washington and their services have gone down while the wealthy have gotten tax cuts. I have seen what's happened in this last 4 years when—in my state, when people lose their jobs there's a good chance I'll know them by their names. When a factory closes, I know the people who ran it. When the businesses go bankrupt, I know them. And I've been out here for 13 months meeting in meetings just like this ever since October, with people like you all over America, people that have lost their jobs, lost their livelihood, lost their health insurance. What I want you to understand is the national debt is not the only cause of that. It is because America has not invested in its people. It is because we have not grown. It is because we've had 12 years of trickle down economics. We've gone from 1st to 12th in the world in wages. We've had 4 years where we've produced no private sector jobs. Most people are working harder for less money than they were making 10 years ago. It is because we are in the grip of a failed economic theory. And this decision you're about to make better be about what kind of economic theory you want, not just people saying I'm going to go fix it but what are we going to do? I think what we have to do is invest in American jobs, American education, control American health care costs and bring the American people together again.

Response to the town hall format was enthusiastic. Reporting on a research project involving groups of voters assembled to view the debate together, John Meyer and Diana Carlin found, "The focus group members' reactions to this debate format were strongly positive; it was seen as more relaxed and more democratic, and allowed for more openness, honesty, and personality exposure for the candidates." Although focus group members offered a variety of explanations for why they preferred the town hall format to the panel of journalists, it was clear that they preferred the format by a substantial margin. Some members of the focus group thought the questions were less predictable, others believed they could identify with the questioners, and finally, many claimed the candidates had to respond to the concerns of the audiences (those asking questions and those watching the exchange on their televisions) more directly.

Although there was some criticism . . . in general, reaction to the town hall format in the media was equally enthusiastic. Commentators observed that the Richmond debate had the candidates on literally the same level as the electorate and suggested that ordinary citizens, much more effectively than journalists, could force the candidates to address the issues and avoid negative attacks. In accounts pregnant with irony, commentators praised the debate for its substance even as they worked to reduce the debate into a short series of video highlights.

The Death of Discourse: The Myth of the Town Meeting

To liken town hall debates between presidential candidates to a traditional New England town meeting is akin to analogizing watching an athletic contest on television to actually participating in the contest. Although it is true that the candidates submitted themselves to the public by consenting to the debate, their participation in the town hall was more symbolic than substantive. Instead of using the debate as an opportunity to engage those present on the issues, all three candidates used the town hall as a forum for reiterating campaign themes to the tens of millions viewing the debate on television. Simply put, the town hall format was a cynical product of the candidates' calculation of their own strategic interest. As a result, the town hall was structured to discourage argument and media coverage of the debate, further reducing the importance of what the candidates said in Richmond.

The Format

A careful review of the transcript of the debate suggests that the town hall format prevented the citizens from arguing with the candidates. Carole Simpson, playing the role of moderator, circulated through the audience, selecting citizens to ask questions. Each questioner had the opportunity to ask a single question, whereas each candidate claimed the right to respond to all questions. Because audience members had no opportunity to ask follow-up questions, true interaction between the candidates and the questioners was impossible. The debate had none of the public argument characteristic of the traditional New England town meeting because the format devised by the candidates prevented any possibility of dialogue. Even though all the citizens had a chance to ask questions, no one was able to engage the candidates on a particular issue.

Further, the town hall format encouraged a cursory treatment of the widest possible breadth of topics at the expense of in-depth analysis. Instead of focusing on a single topic in the tradition of the New England town meeting, the Richmond format allowed questions on any subject of interest to the questioners. Although this created the impression that no topics were precluded, the practical result was a town hall that featured questions about access to foreign markets, the national deficit, physical infrastructure, crime in cities, term limits, health care, the national debt, Social Security, America's role in the new world order, creating jobs, and the prospect of an African American and female ticket winning the presidency. Given the number of issues addressed in 90 minutes, it is not surprising that the treatment of any specific issue was extremely superficial.

Watching a mediated town hall is not akin to participating in a town meeting. Even though citizens were present in the audience, they did not have the opportunity to argue with the candidates. At the same time, the number of issues addressed necessarily kept the discussion superficial, and the format prevented the citizens from focusing on a particular theme. The Richmond debate may have been good television, but it is surely a misnomer to liken it to the New England town meeting.

The Broadcast Media

Although the debate was not a New England town meeting, media coverage of the debate helped transform what transpired in Richmond into a spectacle. Before the debate, the new format was hyped as a dramatic confrontation between the candidates and the voters. On the eve of the event, democratic appeals and rousing music were used to set the stage. Although television carried the unedited debate to the viewers, the moment the debate ended, commentators switched from observers to participants as they offered judgments regarding the outcome and the likely impact the debate would have on the election.

There may have been much to criticize, but many commentators were quick to highlight the fact that President Bush was unable to answer the question about the personal impact of the national debt, when in fact Bush had responded to the question. Bush was correct; in a personal sense, the national debt had not affected him. Further, Bush was able to invoke the cancer analogy to challenge the premise of the question. The fact that he was not personally affected by the national debt did not mean he was either unaware of the economic hardship being suffered or unqualified to solve the problem.

At the same time the media criticized Bush's answer, Clinton was praised for his emotive response. Commentators noted that Clinton had convinced the audience that he could feel the pain. Yet although Arkansas is a small state, it defies credibility to believe that Clinton knew the names of all the individuals who lost their jobs or who had lost their businesses to bankruptcy. Clinton's response was a flagrant appeal to emotion, but he was rewarded by a medium that privileges such warm pleas over cold facts.

In addition to interpreting the town hall, broadcast accounts immediately assessed the outcome of the debate. On the basis of an instant poll conducted immediately after the debate, for example, *CBS News* reported that 53% of the respondents thought Clinton had won, more than double the 25% who chose Bush, with Perot trailing closely behind at 21%. This outcome, of course, was integrated into coverage of the larger election story. According to these accounts, Bush was trailing badly and he had squandered a late opportunity to close the gap, throw the knockout punch, or hit a home run.

. . . In retrospect, it is clear that the candidates created a town hall format uniquely suited for television. They came to a historic American city, they sat on stools, and they promised to interact with the voters. To make the format entertaining, the candidates developed sophisticated techniques for moving on the stage, appearing empathic, and reaching out to the viewers. The broadcast media cooperated in this enterprise, treating the debate as a major political event. By the time the story reached the evening news, it had been reduced to a brief series of predigested sound bites. As the event receded from the news, it congealed in the public memory as a story told by the broadcast media.

The Print Media

Whereas the broadcast media contextualized the debate, the print media further trivialized the discussion of substantive issues raised during the town hall. Instead of commenting on a particular issue addressed in the debate, the dominant themes in the media were visual or stylistic. Consider, for example, the following characterizations of the town hall debate in Richmond that appeared in some of the leading national newspapers the following day:

> *Los Angeles Times—*
>
> It was perhaps inevitable, in this odd election year, that George Bush, Bill Clinton and Ross Perot would at least meet knee-to-knee on a set modeled after an afternoon talk show.
>
> That was no debate Thursday night between the presidential candidates. That was the triumph of the talk show format over substantive political discourse. Oprah Winfrey and Phil Donahue should sue for the hijacking of their format....

Such characterizations functioned to trivialize the town hall as a political event. Whereas the town hall format was clearly intended to invoke the democratic image of the New England town meeting, the commentary offered by the media shattered the analogy by analogizing the debate to the most common form of entertainment. If the debate was less than the analogy, the media coverage of the debate only magnified the disappointment.

Along with denigrating the town hall format, media accounts also marginalized the participants. Although all agreed that Clinton's performance had been exemplary, accounts of the debate praised him for his acumen as an entertainer and not for the quality of his discourse or policy initiatives. Clinton was favorably compared with Ronald Reagan, a talk show host, and a performer. Throughout print accounts, Clinton was praised for being a good entertainer, not for the originality or substance of his responses. Commentators were impressed by his ability to work the crowd like Donahue, for moving toward the audience when he answered questions, and for his skillful use of eye contact with questioners. These characterizations may be accurate, but taken together they had the unfortunate effect of reducing the town hall meeting to a political beauty pageant.

Whereas these accounts praised Clinton, print accounts of the debate highlighted visual elements to discount the performance of George Bush. In particular, commentators suggested that Bush seemed distant, unable to connect emotively with the audience. Worse yet, during the debate Bush made the inadvertent mistake of looking at his watch. These unfortunate glances, captured by the camera and used in stories to summarize the debate, took on their own political significance. An article in the *Houston Chronicle* claimed, "Restrained from the low blow and not as adept as Clinton at the up-close-and-personal, Bush fumbled. Three times he glanced at his watch. Was he bored? Was he fitful? Or was he just out of his element?" ...

Although the media had praised Ross Perot for his pithy one-liners ("If there's a fairer way, I'm all ears") in the first presidential debate in 1992, accounts of his town hall performance were less charitable. Within days, Perot's act had grown old, and commentators now complained that his performance was old and tired. Just as Bush had been chided for glancing at his watch, Perot was faulted for his inability to occupy his stool completely. An article in the *Washington Post* observed, "Even the crabby Munchkin, Ross Perot, who got several laughs with his one-liners at Sunday night's opener, seemed enervated and spent... Perot may have avoided actually sitting on his stool because, if he did sit on it, his feet wouldn't touch the ground." Given these characterizations, it is not surprising that anyone who read print accounts of the debate would agree with the broadcast pronouncements that Clinton was the obvious winner.

In defense of the media, it might be argued that these accounts accurately represent what transpired in Richmond. Although this claim may hold some truth, a growing body of quantitative evidence suggests that impressions are shaped more by commentary than by actual performance in the debates. Each presidential debate has been summarized, reduced to a defining story, and remembered by the media. According to these chronicles, the 1960 debate between Richard Nixon and John F. Kennedy is notable for images of a youthful Kennedy confronting a sweaty Nixon whose face bore a suspicious five o'clock shadow. President Gerald Ford is still remembered for emphatically stating in a 1976 debate with Jimmy Carter that there was no Soviet domination of Eastern Europe. President Jimmy Carter will likewise be remembered from the 1980 debate against Ronald Reagan for admitting that he discussed nuclear doctrine with his daughter, Amy. The same Ronald Reagan lives in debate infamy for an incoherent trip down a California highway in his 1984 debate with Walter Mondale. Michael Dukakis, the Democrats' candidate in 1988, is notable for his clinical and detached response to Bernard Shaw's emotionally charged question about the hypothetical rape of his wife.

In retrospect, it is apparent that Bill Clinton capitalized on the town hall format because it fit his style and his message. This town hall format also reinforced the implicit campaign theme that Clinton was in touch with the common people, whereas Bush had lost touch. At the same time, it is also clear that the Richmond town hall bears little relation to the New England town meeting. The town hall debate was not an exercise in self-government, but rather a political spectacle. The candidates created the format because it fit their political interest, and the format made true argument impossible. Media accounts of the debate, though celebrating the democratic tradition, functioned to trivialize what little discourse actually occurred in Richmond.

The Future of the Past:
The Electronic Town Meeting

In his 1996 State of the Union Address, President Bill Clinton offered the vision of an America connected by a national computer network. According to Clinton, "As the Internet becomes our new town square, a computer in every home —a teacher of all subjects, a connection to all cultures—this will no longer be a dream, but a necessity." Should such a vision ever become a reality, it would be possible to have an ongoing town meeting. Anyone connected with the Internet could, theoretically, engage in dialogue about local, state, and national issues.

Those who have paused to consider the relationship between democracy and politics seem to agree that the Internet will provide the opportunity for direct—as opposed to representative—democracy. Janette Kenner Muir, for example, has observed, "As electronic media further develop, so does the capacity to reach many more people, and in turn, to increase public participation." According to proponents, herein likes the unique opportunity of the electronic town hall. Because the Internet can accommodate a multitude of users, it should be possible for thousands of citizens to interact simultaneously with each other, government agencies, and elected officials.

The mediated town hall debate in 1992 was a campaign event, and as such it was firmly rooted in a representative understanding of democracy. What happened in Richmond was part of an election process that asked the voters to think about politics, to assess the competing candidates, and then to render a decision. Once the vote was cast, the body politic dissolved, the voters returned home, and those candidates who were elected to govern functioned as the citizens' representatives. Between elections, these elected leaders interact with their constituents on an irregular basis. Aside from the referendum on issues provided by public opinion polls and personal communication, the people's representatives have limited opportunities to consult the citizenry on questions of public policy.

In marked contrast, the electronic town hall offers the promise of both perpetual and instantaneous dialogue between those governing and those being governed. The Internet creates the possibility of direct democracy by linking the government directly with individual citizens. It seems to create a unique "public space," a forum that creates the possibility of substantive dialogue on all questions of public concern. Communication in such space requires genuine interaction, not the pandering common in campaign rhetoric or political spots. The result of such exchanges, proponents of the electronic town hall argue, would be a public argument that tests ideas and produces consensus on policy. If this vision becomes a reality, the "electronic town square" will become one defining element of American democracy.

At the same time that it offers such revolutionary potential, the possibility of an electronic town hall might prove to be the ultimate of political illusions. Because the technology creates the opportunity for direct interaction, those participating in the dialogue may come to believe that their electronic speech is heard, that their opinion is valued. A more cynical response would remember what happened at the town hall debate at Richmond. Although Bush, Clinton, and Perot did come before the voters, their participation was more strategic than democratic. Further, a close inspection of the debate reveals no real interaction between the candidates and the citizen questioners. The candidates' answers were stylized responses, carefully crafted appeals intended to produce votes disguised as answers to the questions being asked. The media further reduced the town hall by filtering out the content while highlighting the visual elements in stories about the debate.

Although some have warned that the Internet might create a form of "hyperactive democracy," with candidates constantly calibrating political positions and legislative votes to react to the smallest or latest shift in public opinion, a more likely scenario suggests that the candidates will co-opt the electronic town hall into another opportunity to broadcast their messages to voters. Given the experience with the town hall debate in 1992, it is clear that politics shapes the forum more than the forum shapes the politics.

As the presidential election in the year 2000 approaches, the leading presidential contenders will loudly announce that they intend to use the Internet to interact directly with the voters. Because genuine interaction between the candidates and millions of computer users is impossible, the campaigns will strategically offer the candidates at well-publicized times to answer questions. Aside from these occasional forums, voter inquiries at the town hall will be "processed" to create the appearance of interaction. Each citizen will receive a prompt and courteous reply, the relevant assurances and information will be provided, and the citizen's e-mail address will be added to the appropriate file for future mailings.

As politicians grow more proficient at using the new medium, campaigns will be able to use the Internet to give the illusion of direct democracy. There is every reason to expect, on the basis of past experience, that politicians will use the electronic town hall to respond to inquires from the voters. Much as they did in Richmond, the candidates will come before the voters and offer the appropriate responses. The mainstream media, angered by their exclusion, will respond with predictably condescending language about happenings in the electronic town square. The result will be a political spectacle, a campaign event carefully staged to create the illusion of democratic self-government.

It might be argued that this progression is inevitable as the political parties assimilate a new form of technology. There is a danger in the electronic town hall, however, because it implies that voters are using the Internet to direct their elected public officials, when in reality, the elected public officials will be using the Internet to create the illusion of participation and manage their constituents. The proof of this can be seen, ever so clearly, in the legacy of the town hall debate of 1992. Although the Richmond debate invoked the imagery of the New England town meeting, the result was a desecration of a long-standing democratic tradition. Unless we are vigilant, the electronic town square of the future may prove to be the ultimate democratic delusion.

Elizabeth Weise

 **NO**

Not Yet for the Net

W hen Bill Clinton became the first president to participate in a live Internet chat on November 8, 1999, history was not made. Although an estimated 30,000 users logged in over the course of the two-hour feed to watch a transcript of the event scroll down their computers, only 27 actually were able to get their questions answered, and those only after their questions were triple-screened.

For the first hour, participants had the thrill of watching a secretary transcribe, word for word, prepared remarks Clinton read off a teleprompter. For the second, they saw a series of softball questions and answers roll by, interrupted at times by technical difficulties. Those with extremely fast connections could also add fuzzy sound and a postage stamp-sized streaming video image of Clinton sipping a soda while he read. This fairly dull experience stood in sharp contrast to press reports of the hilarity in the room at George Washington University where Clinton, various technologists and members of the Democratic Leadership Council dealt with the glitches that kept San Jose, California, Mayor Ron Gonzales from connecting to give his "speech" and caused the group to "lose" Netscape co-founder Marc Andreessen for awhile.

The 2000 election cycle is already being spoken of as the year the Internet will "break through" into politics. It's even been compared to the breakthrough television made in 1960 in the Kennedy-Nixon race. But then again we heard the same pronouncement in 1998, merely because most candidates at least had put up Web sites, and we're likely to hear it again come 2002 and even 2004 before it actually comes to pass.

Call it the "Christmas effect." Every year for the last four, analysts, retailers and journalists have been writing that "this is the holiday shopping season electronic commerce will really break through!" In 1998 everyone finally acknowledged that it actually had, but there was a catch that is often overlooked. Even the $9 billion estimated to be spent on-line in the 1999 holiday season is small potatoes compared with the estimated $185 billion that will be spent in brick-and-mortar stores during the month of December.

Too often, Internet boosters are eager to declare cyber victory in every arena, often years before it happens. Even when victory comes, it actually often means that a fairly minor—though very demographically desirable—portion of the population has begun to do something on-line.

So it is with politics. At a ... panel on Democracy and New Media at MIT, Phil Agre, a professor of information studies at UCLA, lauded the possibility the Internet held to overcome the unequal access to forms of association that impede true democracy. "The power of the network is to connect anyone to anyone and therefore destroy all hierarchies," he told the audience. The Internet does hold that power. But only for those who are actually on it. Figures for Internet access in the United States vary tremendously. DataQuest estimates 37 percent of households are on-line. The Strategis Group says 100 million U.S. adults, or 51 percent, were on-line as of mid-1999. But whichever data you believe, it still leaves half, if not more, of America out of the revolution.

⊷⊙⊷

This is not to say the political promise of the Internet isn't valid, as long as we acknowledge it's still early days. The technology is clunky, the databases sometimes lacking crucial information, the links too often dead, the sites tedious. And yet somewhere down the line it offers us the possibility of power returning to the public in the way the Greeks originally imagined a democracy back in the days when the entire electorate could gather together to debate in the agora.

Sites making use of the information and computing power available are springing up all over. There's Politics.com, which lets voters search the Federal Election Commission database by ZIP code to see who's funding whom. There's Voter.com, which allows users to fill out a questionnaire and then find the candidates with whom they most agree. At Vote.com, citizens fill out a poll to determine their positions, which are then automatically e-mailed to their congresspeople (this the brainchild of former Clinton advisor Dick Morris), as well as FreedomChannel.com, the C-SPAN of Internet political coverage, offering users video on demand, the opportunity to click and pick "the candidates you want, on the issues you want, whenever you want them."

Surprisingly, amidst this upwelling of possibility, both the candidates and the media are among those making the worst use of the possibilities. Candidate Web sites are almost uniformly dull, seldom more than static versions of the brochures that will fill mailboxes come October. Beyond a few high-profile races "most people [politicians] doing Web sites are spending less than $500," says Ron Faucheux, editor in chief of *Campaigns & Elections*. The figure is based on several surveys the magazine has conducted.

Really, how many voters are going to bother to log in if it means reading stories that began "Marshalltown, Iowa—Today, at a local Veterans' Day ceremony, Al Gore honored the sacrifices and contributions of our nation's veterans, and outlined his vision for the use of American diplomacy and force in the post-Cold War era."? Then there's the hard-to-categorize Republican "portal" site at GOPNet.com ... for only $19.95 a month. Meant to lure subscribers with all the comforts of their usual home page, it is to include an @GOPnet.com address, personalized calendars, custom news and instant polling. It will also be "family friendly" in that pornographic content will be filtered. The Democrats are also working on their own "e-Party" initiative.

But however much politicians salivate over the notion of being able to deliver their platform points and messages to everyone with an Internet connection, they'll only be preaching to the converted. No one else is going to slog through the stuff. The GOP says its site will feature television-quality, full-screen video of candidate speeches. But people don't tune in to the speeches when they're shown on TV, so it seems unlikely they'll sit around at home whiling away the hours watching them.

A 1998 survey by Elaine Kamarck, director of the research program Visions of Governance for the 21st Century at Harvard's Kennedy School of Government, found only two candidates, Rep. Tom Campbell of California and Gov. Tom Ridge of Pennsylvania, who truly made use of the interactive capacity of the Internet by holding real-time virtual town meetings. Only in this arena did the promise of the Net actually come to fruition. During one meeting, someone wrote in asking for clarification about a statement the candidate had made on the radio. The candidate wrote back two paragraphs explaining. This, says Kamarck, is "real, meaningful, democracy at work."

⎯⎯◉⎯⎯

As we swing into the 2000 election season, it seems that such direct contact between politicians and voters will be the last hurdle, and one that doesn't seem likely to be leapt in this cycle. The Clinton Virtual Town Hall experience will no doubt be repeated, but true interaction is rare. Politicians are too wary of unrehearsed venues, and the public has lost the notion of the town hall meeting as anything but a televised spectacle. We don't see candidates staying up until late at night answering e-mails from potential voters.

And it's unclear if we ever will. The problem (and the blessing) of the Net is that it is most potent in its original one-to-one form. E-mail was and is likely always to be the killer app. It's e-mail, instant messaging and chat rooms that lure most people on-line, not the chance to shop, whatever retailers want to believe.

But except in small local elections, there's been almost none of that kind of one-on-one interaction happening between candidates and the electorate. Instead, we're given what in Web parlance is called "shovel-ware," repurposed (think regurgitated) speeches, position papers and photos shoveled onto Web sites to fill them up.

Not only are the sites dull, but the campaigns don't get how important the Net is. One way that's obvious is in the issue of domain names. Any Internet company worth its IPO [initial public offering] knows there's only one thing that matters on-line: location, location, location. And in cyberspace, location = address = URL. But the older duck-and-cover mentality still holds, at least with the Gore and Bush campaigns. I know this because last year I became part of a small cyber-squatting syndicate that collectively holds 18 variations on possible 2000 campaign Web sites for both Gore and Bush.

The syndicate was begun by a Democratic friend named Ted Weinstein, who works in the on-line world. During a family discussion someone wondered if the Gore campaign had locked up potentially important URLs, such as Gore-Feinstein.com, Gore-Brady.com and other possible vice presidential candidates. Weinstein checked, and to his surprise they hadn't. To protect the addresses, he put a hold on them. While he was there he picked up a few Bush URLs that hadn't been taken as well.

Next he called the Gore campaign to offer them up, but they didn't want to talk about it. A campaign worker told him they couldn't spend money because of Federal Election Campaign rules since Gore wasn't yet a declared candidate. More likely, they didn't want to make it appear to anyone trolling the Network Solutions database that they were thinking about any one specific running mate for their candidate that far out. Stupid thinking. The first thing any company that goes on-line does even before it incorporates is to tie up every possible URL that might bring people to them, if only to keep their enemies from doing so. "The Bush people went out and bought all the negative names, which was smart thinking. I give them a lot of credit for that," Weinstein said.

As Weinstein didn't want to get stuck paying the almost $1,500 it would cost to reserve the URLs, he e-mailed a bunch of friends and family and suggested if they each put in $100 they could hold the names for a year, or until Gore figured out who his running mate was going to be, and then give the URL to the campaign. As for the Bush URLs, Weinstein wasn't positive what he would do with them; at the time he was mostly fascinated that they hadn't been snapped up.

After checking with my editor, I joined the group so I could write about the experience. Thus far it's been an exercise in the cluelessness of campaign workers. Gore's people still don't want to talk about it, and the Bush folks never even answered Weinstein's e-mails. It's a mistake that would get you fired from a .com company so fast you wouldn't even be able to see your stock options expiring. It's a mistake that shows the campaigns aren't taking the Net seriously.

⋘◉⋙

Thus far this cycle, politicians aren't doing much to engage voters on-line, and most media are only marginally better. Collections of past stories are useful, but few newspaper or television Web sites take advantage of the interactive capabilities of the Net. Some of the best reporting, not surprisingly, is being done on the Web. Excellent work can be found at PoliticalAccess.com, PoliticalJunkie.com, Rough & Tumble (Rtumble.com) and the NetElection coverage being done as a collaboration between The Industry Standard and Slate. (Though because this is the Internet after all, if you try www.netelection.com, you'll end up at www.whitehouse.com, the porn site that very definitely is not www.whitehouse.gov.)

While great reporting can be found at the best political sites, the best use of the Internet as a medium can be found at the interactive Web sites that are popping up everywhere. Suddenly the investigative journalists aren't the gatekeepers—or even the finders—of the juiciest facts about campaigns. That's being left to individuals making use of searchable databases supplied for the most part by not-for-profit organizations.

The seeds are there. Take the issue of campaign fund raising. While the inability of politicians to agree to meaningful campaign finance reform is a stumbling block, the emergence of readily accessible and easy to use databases holds the potential to redefine the discussion.

The Internet, powerful database programs and the Federal Election Commission's site at Fec.gov have given the public the ability to connect the dots between politicians and those who fund them. Sites like Tray.com, Followthemoney.org, OpenSecrets.org and PublicIntegrity.org allow anyone with access to the Web the chance to see exactly who's donated what to whom in a way that was never before possible for ordinary citizens.

Again, it's the nonprofits that are leading the charge. The chance to make clear the trajectories of influence is one of the reasons the Markle Foundation this year launched a major drive to underwrite projects to build democracy on-line. "Now you can enter your ZIP code on a Web site and find out what environmental hazards there are in your area. And when you see the biggest problem is a local car dealership, you can find out if they contributed money" to the campaign of whoever is supposed to be in charge of enforcement, said executive director Zoë Baird.

Watching where money comes from isn't the only thing the Net will change, however. It also carries the potential to change the form the money comes in. In 1998, only 11 percent of the Web sites of candidates at the state and federal level were able to take contributions over the Net. In 2000, Harvard's Kamarck expects that number to be closer to 95 percent.

If, and this is a big if, the electorate truly becomes connected to the election process via the Internet, there's the possibility of overcoming the stranglehold of big money interests, she said. "One of the reasons we've had such problems with big money in campaigns is that it's very expensive to raise small money. The rubber chicken dinner is more efficient than direct mail. The Internet is one possibility to overturn that," she said.

Indeed, turning the Internet into a direct-mail fund-raising medium could not only offset the impact of other sources of funding candidates receive but also cut back on the cost of fund raising itself. *Campaigns & Elections* estimates that about $3 billion will be spent on all political direct mail in the current four-year election cycle. Moving some of the fund raising to the virtually free medium of e-mail could mean millions a candidate won't have to raise.

There may turn out to be no difference between political direct marketing in the real world or in cyberspace. But stranger things have happened. National politics is beginning to move towards Internet time: in December 1999 in San Mateo County, California, the county clerk solicited bids to create on-line voting for 2000. Looking at today's political Web sites with their open maws for voters' VISA and MasterCard numbers, it's hard to believe it was only in June of 1999 that the federal government agreed to match on-line credit card contributions with public funds.

POSTSCRIPT

Has Democracy Been Transformed by New Uses of Media?

This issue examines how the electronic town hall has changed the face of traditional politics in the United States. As a form of direct democracy, meaning that the public can directly address candidates with questions and issues, the highly structured mediated town hall has undoubtedly changed. The real questions, though, are whether or not the meaning of democracy has also been forced to change and whether or not American democratic principles have been altered.

This issue brings up a different dimension of the role of media in a democracy and media as an integral part of democracy. Other key issues to examine might include the question of who pays attention to certain political messages. For example, there was a time when any major political debate would be carried simultaneously by all national television networks. This is no longer the case, largely because ratings show that fewer people are interested in tuning into the debates. When it comes to the Internet, we need to be aware of who, if anyone, accesses the information on political Web sites and what type of response they expect when they post a question.

As we learn more about the way people use the Internet, we might be able to form some theories about how instantaneous messaging influences peoples' long-term beliefs and values, but for now, there is little data to support how people make decisions based on different criteria when interacting with the Internet. We do know, however, that since the Internet can be accessed from the home, the comfort of the home environment may change the way in which people frame their own questions and make decisions. The answers to these, and many other important questions for the continued use of new media, will undoubtedly be with us for some time.

The edited collection of writings, from which the Herbeck selection has been taken, offers a number of contexts for the examination of politics today. Edited by David Slayden and Rita Kirk Whillock, *Soundbite Culture: The Death of Discourse in a Wired World* (Sage Publications, 1999) contains articles ranging from the role of other genres of media and their effect on democracy to the role of graffiti and race as an expression of political opinion.

Similarly, the Web sites mentioned in the Weise selection are great sources for the expression of certain viewpoints. As the author mentions, one in particular, http://www.vote.com, is the project of former Clinton aide Dick Morris.

On the Internet...

DUSHKIN ONLINE

American Civil Liberties Union

This official site of the American Civil Liberties Union (ACLU) provides a general introduction of issues involving individual rights.

http://aclu.org

The Federal Communications Commission

This official site of the Federal Communications Commission (FCC) provides comprehensive information about U.S. federal media rules and guidelines.

http://www.fcc.gov

Federal Communications Law Journal

This site is an online communications journal maintained by the Indiana University School of Law–Bloomington. See the newest issue of the journal, surf the archive, and check out extensive listings of other telecommunications sites.

http://www.law.indiana.edu/fclj/fclj.html

Law Journal Extra! Media Law

This site features abundant resources in media law, including the most recent developments, columns, and reviews of decisions.

http://www.ljx.com/practice/media/index.html

PART 4

Regulation

*F*or the media, the First Amendment entails both rights and responsibilities. How to ensure that these responsibilities will be met is the subject
of much of communications law and legislative action. What are the
valid limits of the rights of free speech and the press? How should society
respond when First Amendment rights are in conflict with other individual rights? What changes will new technology force upon our operation
of these rights? The issues in this section deal with who should be responsible for media content and with the rights of groups who find that
content inappropriate.

- Should Internet Access Be Regulated?

- Do Ratings Work?

- Should the FCC Be Abolished?

ISSUE 11

Should Internet Access Be Regulated?

YES: Michael A. Banks, from "Filtering the Net in Libraries: The Case (Mostly) in Favor," *Computers in Libraries* (March 1998)

NO: American Civil Liberties Union, from "Censorship in a Box: Why Blocking Software Is Wrong for Public Libraries," in David Sobel, ed., *Filters and Freedom: Free Speech Perspectives on Internet Content Controls* (Electronic Privacy Information Center, 1999)

ISSUE SUMMARY

YES: Author Michael A. Banks explains that as more people turn to libraries for Internet access, libraries and communities have been forced to come to grips with the conflict between freedom of speech and objectional material on the World Wide Web and in Usenet newsgroups. He adds that software filters are tools that help librarians keep inappropriate materials out of the library.

NO: The American Civil Liberties Union (ACLU) concludes that mandatory blocking software in libraries is both inappropriate and unconstitutional. Blocking censors valuable speech and gives librarians, educators, and parents a false sense of security when providing minors with Internet access, argues the ACLU.

This is an issue that becomes more complex the more one thinks about it. Should public libraries make adult pornography sites available to minor children? Obviously no would be most people's first response. Should software that blocks or filters objectionable material on the Internet be installed in public libraries? Obviously yes would again be the first response. So, is it okay to limit the sites available within a library for adults and children? Or, should only children be limited? Should children only be allowed access to terminals in the children's section? If so, then shouldn't children also be denied access to the many books in the library that cover the same topics?

Beyond these thorny philosophical questions of what constitutes censorship and what constitutes protection lurk some surprisingly practical issues. If software that filters out "unacceptable" sites is adopted, then who controls what children or adults can download from the "information superhighway"? Who determines what children should and should not access and what is offensive? In short, who writes the filtering programs, and what is eliminated? This is a case in which an easy solution—filtering software—has long-term consequences for repressing freedom of speech and access to information.

Teens present a particularly difficult age group when considering this issue. They are interested in many of the sites that would be blocked by filtering software, and most would agree that teens need to know information about sexual issues that would certainly be blocked by most existing filters.

Libraries face engrossing issues. Long the champion of freedom of speech, they have generally fought attempts to ban books. Although the Internet presents similar issues, libraries can lose big with their constituents by their actions. And the political climate that produced the Communications Decency Act, which made transmission of indecent material over the Internet a criminal act, has spawned many suits against libraries for decisions made in the online arena. Some have installed filtering software and have faced suits by the American Civil Liberties Union (ACLU). Others have kept access open and faced community outrage. Although the Communications Decency Act was declared unconstitutional by the Supreme Court, libraries do not know what liabilities they may face from patrons offended by what they see others access in public areas. In one case, a university library posted a notice that it could not control or censor what individual university students viewed but that those students should be aware that if other nearby library patrons found the material offensive, the viewer could be liable for charges of sexual harassment.

The case of libraries facing online access issues is only one specific example in the larger debate on the issues that we face as technology becomes more accessible in public institutions. In the following selection, Michael A. Banks argues for filtering the Internet; not everything there is appropriate for everybody. Some discrimination is called for, he asserts, and filtering software is the least intrusive manner of accomplishing that goal. The ACLU argues against filters as a voluntary alternative to government regulation of Internet content. Filters are now viewed as architectural changes that may facilitate the suppression of speech far more effectively than congressional lawmaking ever could.

211

Michael A. Banks

 **YES**

Filtering the Net in Libraries

The year is 1967. A patron finds a book in your library containing detailed instructions for making dynamite, and uses that information to build a bomb that he uses to destroy a neighbor's house. Now, you are being sued—and you may be charged with complicity in a crime.

Or, it's 1972, and last month you refused to allow a young patron to withdraw books from the "adult" section of your library. Despite the long-standing rule that anyone under 12 is restricted to the juvenile and reference sections, a lawsuit is brought, naming you, library staff, and trustees as defendants.

Absurd? Unthinkable? Indeed, yes—in those times. But such scenarios are possible now, with one major difference. Rather than allowing access to the "wrong" sort of books, or denying access to certain books, today's focus is on whether to allow Internet access. As more and more people turn to local libraries for Internet access, the possibility of such conflicts becomes more probable. This situation has forced more than a few libraries to pass judgment on what Internet content is appropriate for adults and children to see. The task is simple in theory, but complex in practice. Exactly what should you permit, and what should you block? And why?

At the same time, some communities and/or individuals are demanding that libraries abstain from such judgment. For example, late in December 1997 a community group in Virginia filed suit against the public library system in Louden County in order to block an Internet usage policy. Among other things, the police specified that library computers used for Internet access be equipped with filtering software, to protect children from pornography and other objectionable material on the Web and in Usenet newsgroups. The lawsuit claims that the use of such software is a violation of free speech rights since material that adults may want to access is also blocked.

In short, even though you are not expected to have on hand every magazine and every book in the world, you are expected by many to provide access to the full Internet. Since, as the Virginia case proves, there are no hard and fast definitions of what constitutes community standards, the judgment calls are difficult, to say the least. Then there are the widely varying expectations of patrons as to their rights in using library equipment—often quite independent of any perceived community standards. All of this leaves some librarians trying to answer the question: Do you prefer to be liable for "infringing" on freedom of speech, or do you prefer to be liable for the effects of exposure to objectionable text and images?

To Block, or Not to Block

The decision to apply blocks is an unfortunate situation, indeed, but one that may libraries will have to face over the next few years. With fewer than 40 percent of American households on the Internet, more and more people are turning to libraries for Internet access. Even patrons who have Internet access at home also use library computers to get online, a matter of convenience during library visits. This means that, sooner or later, someone is going to have a problem with what they or others can or cannot access on the Internet. So, what do you do? Allow everyone access to everything, or try to control what is available?

On the whole, I feel that it is simpler to opt for blocking or filtering Internet access. That way, you don't risk offending employees and patrons who don't want to see objectionable material. This is to say, the "liability" is less than if you permit wide-open Internet access because once that genie is out of the bottle, there is no turning back. If there are objections to blocking in your community, they can be sorted out and problems rectified (not the case if you don't block and minors are accessing Internet pornography through your system). The only questions that remain are what you filter out, and how.

No Newsgroups Is Good Newsgroups?

For those concerned about Internet security, I advise blocking all Usenet newsgroup access. Usenet newsgroups, in existence since 1979, are one of the oldest components of the Internet. Today, this venerable element is fast becoming all but useless. Why? Because nearly all of the 20,000-plus newsgroups are clogged and choked with "spam," mass advertising of useless moneymaking schemes, con games, and porno sites. In some newsgroups, it is impossible to sort out the worthwhile postings from the spam, thanks to the perpetrators' attempts to disguise the true nature of their postings. Also, many postings are literal traps and ambushes. As I'll show you below, the simple act of opening a newsgroup posting can cause your browser to be taken over completely. Certain Web pages can do the same thing but, fortunately, there are ways to defend against this happening—but only if you use Netscape.

This is why you might be wise to block all Usenet newsgroup access. Simply not installing the newsgroup reader element of your Web browser will do the trick. Or, you can rely on filtering software that blocks objectionable newsgroups. Remember, though, that almost any newsgroup can contain objectionable material—or the ambushes to which I referred above.

What About Filters?

I see filters as part of a complete Internet security program. There are a dozen or more good Web/newsgroup filters available, each as good as the next in certain respects. There's not enough room to cover all of them here, but I will provide an overview of a few of the better products. Before I do that, though, let's take a quick look at what filtering programs do.

Acting as a Web browser "supervisor," a filtering program prevents access to sites considered inappropriate for the person using the browser. The decision as to what is inappropriate is usually based on listings compiled by the software manufacturer or by one of the Internet rating services. (Some companies also accept recommendations from users for sites to be blocked or unblocked.) Most programs block "adult" or sexual material, as well as sites with racist or bigotry-oriented themes. Sites promoting drug abuse are also blocked, along with adult online chat rooms. Various criteria are used to select sites to block, including the use of keywords, selective filtering of domains, and manual selection.

Unfortunately, filtering programs can be quite literal. At least one will not let you access a site or page carrying the surname or title "Sexton," because the word "sex" is contained in that name. However, if the software allows you to unblock sites manually, this problem can be overcome easily enough. With that in mind, you will want to ask yourself these questions when selecting a filtering program:

- Is the program updatable? Most filtering programs provide online updates of blocked site lists, sometimes by subscription. Relying on such updates is a good idea, as thousands of new potentially objectionable sites come online each month. The publishers that provide updates can catch almost all of these, and they do all the work for you.
- Can I unblock selected sites? Sometimes a filtering program mistakenly blocks a site that is not offensive. When this is the case, you should be able to unblock that site.
- Can I block selected sites? Despite all their efforts, the companies that publish blocking software cannot catch every objectionable site. Thus, you will want to be able to add sites to the blocked list.

In addition to altering lists of blocked sites, you may want to be able to alter the criteria that a filtering program uses to block sites on its own. This allows you to make up your own rules as to what is blocked, and why. The more versatility in this area, the better.

The following programs are among the better ones available. Since most blocking programs feature explanations of their blocking criteria at their Web sites, and some provide lists of blocked sites, I urge you to visit the Web site for each.

Cyber Patrol: Cyber Patrol is among the more successful Web filtering programs. It is used by America Online, AT&T WorldNet, Bell Atlantic, British Telecom, and CompuServe, among other online services and Internet service providers (ISPs), and it is bundled with some PCs. You can set up Cyber Patrol to control access to the Internet and newsgroups based on a variety of criteria. Or, you can grant access only to Cyber Patrol's list of approved sites (some 40,000) and block the rest of the Web. A particularly interesting feature of the program is an option that blocks users from typing in or viewing objectionable words or phrases, based in part on a default list of profanity. A special subscription service provides online updates to Cyper Patrol's blocked site lists. For more information, and to download a free trial version, visit http://www.cyberpatrol.com.

CYBERsitter: CYBERsitter is an interesting filtering/blocking program that runs in the background at all times and claims to be virtually impossible to detect or defeat. It works on several fronts. By default, it not only blocks access to adult-oriented Web sites, but also to newsgroups and images. In addition, Web pages and newsgroup posting are filtered to remove offensive language. Blocking and filtering are based on lists provided with the program, but you can add you own words to the lists. When filtering, CYBERsitter examines words and phrases in context, in order to eliminate some of the ambiguity of blocking. For more information about CYBERsitter, or to download a free trial version of the program, visit http://www.solidoak.com.

NetNanny: NetNanny is designed to manage Internet and computer access. You can use it to monitor, screen, or block access to anything that is on or running into, out of, or through a computer, online or off. The outgoing block can be useful in preventing users from using search engines to find and link to objectionable sites.

The program comes with a list of blocked Internet sites and other parameters that it uses to block still more sites. The list and parameters can be updated at no charge at the NetNanny Web site, and you can add your own screening specifications. NetNanny is available for Windows or DOS. See http://www.netnanny.com for more information.

Net Shepherd: Net Shepherd is an Internet content rating service that filters the results of Alta Vista searches. Its PICS-compliant ratings database can be used with Microsoft Internet Explorer or Net Shepherd's own daxHOUND program, a content filtering tool. For additional information on Net Shepherd, visit http://www.netshepherd.com. Information about daxHOUND (and a download) can be found at http://www.netshepherd.com/products/daxHOUND2.0/daxhound.htm.

SurfWatch: SurfWatch is a filter that screens for unwanted material on the Internet. As with other filter and blocking programs, SurfWatch can be used with almost any Web browser. Various levels of access control are available, and the program cannot be easily disarmed by deleting it or by other means. SurfWatch screens Web sites, newsgroups, ftp and gopher sites, and Web chat rooms. Blocking is based on a list of sites generated by in-house research and customer reports. Online updates are available via subscription.

SurfWatch alone doesn't permit you to modify the list of sites, nor does it attempt to block sites that are violent in nature or include material that is hateful or otherwise potentially inappropriate. A free add-on called SurfWatch Manager lets you edit the list of blocked sites. Full information on SurfWatch, along with its list of blocked sites, is available at http://www.surfwatch.com.

X-STOP: The appropriately named X-STOP is a program designed for use by libraries and other institutions and businesses that provide Internet access. It selectively blocks and filters sites based on a variety of criteria. The program allows you to alter the criteria it uses for filtering. It also monitors outgoing words in order to prevent users from looking up objectionable sites with search engines. For more information, see http://www.xstop.com.

Ambushed by Java and JavaScript Risks

Even if you use a filtering program with your computer systems, you can still run into security problems, thanks to Java and JavaScript. You are probably aware of the many security risks associated with Java, a programming language that is used to transmit small computer programs, called "applets" to Internet users' computers, where they are free to run and do things like collect data from hard drives. Filtering programs cannot detect everything a Java program will do, so it is possible to transmit objectionable content with a Java applet. Thus, it is usually a good idea to disable Java on your browsers. It is true that Java-related risks are fewer since so many "loopholes" involving Java have been exposed. But you never know what someone is cooking up. Besides, the Java-less Web surfer usually misses nothing more than animations that slow down browsing anyway.

JavaScript can pose a slightly greater risk, for two reasons. First, there have been no warnings about problems created by JavaScript. Indeed, I expect this to be the first you've heard of such problems. JavaScript can be used to direct your browser to any page on the Web, alter its configuration, and pull other nasty tricks. This being the case, it is best to disable JavaScript when visiting Web sites unfamiliar to you, and when reading newsgroup messages, in which JavaScript can be used to take over browsers.

Second, the JavaScript language is far easier to use, and thus accessible to more people, than Java. This means that the risk of exposure to malevolent JavaScript code is greater. What can JavaScript do to your system? For openers, JavaScript can be used to take control of a browser from a Web page or a Usenet newsgroup posting in two different ways. With a simple line of code, someone can set up a page so that, should your mouse cursor pass over a link or an image (loaded or not), your browser will be forced to "go to" (load) a specified page on the Web. This happens without clicking on anything.

A more insidious JavaScript trick can take over your browser and re-open it without menus or controls, on top of all other applications. Here again, the perpetrator of this trick can put anything he or she wants to appear in your browser window. This not only forces you to look at the perpetrator's message or images, but also disrupts your browsing session. And it can get worse. I have seen this set up so that you are forced to see the same page—or a series of pages —over and over again. Even if you exit the browser, it will reopen and display whatever the perpetrator wants it to display. This has been used extensively by pornography site purveyors to force Web surfers to their sites and to keep them there. Worse, the code required to do the things just described can be hidden, so that you cannot see it even if you view a Web page's source.

The only defense against this is to disable JavaScript. This is easily done with Netscape. Unfortunately, you cannot disable JavaScript if you are using Microsoft Internet Explorer 4. Mircosoft does not "support" JavaScript, and so does not allow you to turn it off.

Summing Up My Position

The argument against restricting Internet access are many, and at times they sound shrill. However, the fact remains that not everything on the Internet is appropriate for everybody, just as not every book or magazine published is appropriate for everybody. This being the case, some discrimination is called for in choosing what a public institution makes available from the Internet. For example, even though libraries make many magazines available, they do not subscribe to *Hustler* because that would be an inappropriate addition to their collections. In this same vein, just because libraries provide access to the Internet, they do not need to provide access to the entire Internet.

I believe that much of the problem here stems from the differences between not subscribing to *Hustler* and not receiving Internet content that is pornographic, racist, or otherwise objectionable. In the former instance, you need do nothing to avoid a subscription; in the latter, action is necessary to keep pornographic content out of the library. The need to take action in order to avoid questionable Internet material unfortunately confuses some people into mistaking positive proaction for repressing action. No one demands that libraries subscribe to *Hustler,* and so I feel that no one should demand that libraries grant full and unrestricted access to the Internet to everyone.

Obviously, posted rules are not enough to limit access to pornography or other objectionable Internet content. Even those who do not want to access such content may have it forced on them. All this being the case, it behooves libraries to provide practical limits to Internet access. At present, filtering and/or blocking Internet content is the only means of even partially controlling access to offensive or objectionable material. Even though filtering sometimes results in legitimate sites being blocked—a problem that can be rectified manually—it is a practical action.

Those who might object on the basis of some specious "freedom of speech" issue should consider the Internet as an analog to real-world books and magazines. In this light, it is easy to see the absurdity of uncontrolled Internet access for children and other patrons. If the sort of content access that some advocate for the Internet were to be applied to conventional library content, *Hustler* magazine, neo-Nazi books and pamphlets, and worse objectionable material would have to be placed in juvenile and children's as well as general library collections. This is what uncontrolled access to the Internet in a public venue can be.

Censorship in a Box

Introduction

In libraries and schools across the nation, the Internet is rapidly becoming an essential tool for learning and communication. According to the American Library Association, of the nearly 9,000 public libraries in America, 60.4 percent offer Internet access to the public, up from 27.8 percent in 1996. And a recent survey of 1,400 teachers revealed that almost half use the Internet as a teaching tool. But today, unfettered access to the Internet is being threatened by the proliferation of blocking software in libraries.

America's libraries have always been a great equalizer, providing books and other information resources to help people of all ages and backgrounds live, learn, work and govern in a democratic society. Today more than ever, our nation's libraries are vibrant multi-cultural institutions that connect people in the smallest and most remote communities with global information resources.

In 1995, the National Telecommunications and Information Administration of the U.S. Department of Commerce concluded that "public libraries can play a vital role in assuring that advanced information services are universally available to all segments of the American population on an equitable basis. Just as libraries traditionally make available the marvels and imagination of the human mind to all, libraries of the future are planning to allow everyone to participate in the electronic renaissance."

Today, the dream of universal access will remain only a dream if politicians force libraries and other institutions to use blocking software whenever patrons access the Internet. Blocking software prevents users from accessing a wide range of valuable information, including such topics as art, literature, women's health, politics, religion and free speech. Without free and unfettered access to the Internet, this exciting new medium could become, for many Americans, little more than a souped-up, G-rated television network.

This special report by the American Civil Liberties Union [ACLU] provides an in depth look at why mandatory blocking software is both inappropriate and unconstitutional in libraries. We do not offer an opinion about any particular blocking product, but we will demonstrate how all blocking software censors valuable speech and gives libraries, educators and parents a false sense of security when providing minors with Internet access.

Like any technology, blocking software can be used for constructive or destructive purposes. In the hands of parents and others who voluntarily use it, it is a tool that can be somewhat useful in blocking access to some inappropriate material online. But in the hands of government, blocking software is nothing more than censorship in a box.

The ACLU believes that government has a necessary role to play in promoting universal Internet access. But that role should focus on expanding, not restricting, access to online speech.

Reno v. ACLU: A Momentous Decision

Our vision of an uncensored Internet was clearly shared by the U.S. Supreme Court when it struck down the 1996 Communications Decency Act (CDA), a federal law that outlawed "indecent" communications online.

Ruling unanimously in *Reno v. ACLU,* the Court declared the Internet to be a free speech zone, deserving of at least as much First Amendment protection as that afforded to books, newspapers and magazines. The government, the Court said, can no more restrict a person's access to words or images on the Internet than it could be allowed to snatch a book out of a reader's hands in the library, or cover over a statue of a nude in a museum.

The nine Justices were clearly persuaded by the unique nature of the medium itself, citing with approval the lower federal court's conclusion that the Internet is "the most participatory form of mass speech yet developed," entitled to "the highest protection from governmental intrusion." The Internet, the Court concluded, is like "a vast library including millions of readily available and indexed publications," the content of which "is as diverse as human thought."

Blocking Software: For Parents, Not the Government

In striking down the CDA on constitutional grounds, the Supreme Court emphasized that if a statute burdens adult speech—as any censorship law must—it "is unacceptable if less restrictive alternatives were available."

Commenting on the availability of user-based blocking software as a possible alternative, the Court concluded that the use of such software was appropriate for *parents.* Blocking software, the Court wrote, is a "reasonably effective method by which parents can prevent their children from accessing material which the *parents* believe is inappropriate." [Emphasis in the original]

The rest of the Court's decision firmly holds that government censorship of the Internet violates the First Amendment, and that holding applies to government use of blocking software just as it applied when the Court struck down the CDA's criminal ban.

In the months since that ruling, the blocking software market has experienced explosive growth, as parents exercise their prerogative to guide their children's Internet experience. According to analysts at International Data Corporation, a technology consulting firm, software makers sold an estimated $14 million in blocking software last year, and over the next three years, sales of blocking products are expected to grow to more than $75 million.

An increasing number of city and country library boards have recently forced libraries to install blocking programs, over the objections of the American Library Association and library patrons, and the use of blocking software in libraries is fast becoming the biggest free speech controversy since the legal challenge to the CDA.

How Does Blocking Software Work?

The best known Internet platform is the World Wide Web, which allows users to search for and retrieve information stored in remote computers. The Web currently contains over 100 million documents, with thousands added each day. Because of the ease with which material can be added and manipulated, the content on existing Web sites is constantly changing. Links from one computer to another and from one document to another across the Internet are what unify the Web into a single body of knowledge, and what makes the Web unique.

To gain access to the information available on the Web, a person uses a Web "browser"—software such as Netscape Navigator or Microsoft's Internet Explorer—to display, print and download documents. Each document on the Web has an address that allows users to find and retrieve it.

A variety of systems allow users of the Web to search for particular information among all of the public sites that are part of the Web. Services such as Yahoo, Magellan, Alta Vista, Webcrawler, Lycos and Infoseek provide tools called "search engines." Once a user has accessed the search service she simply types a word or string of words as a search request and the search engine provides a list of matching sites.

Blocking software is configured to hide or prevent access to certain Internet sites. Most blocking software comes packaged in a box and can be purchased at retail computer stores. It is installed on individual and/or networked computers that have access to the Internet, and works in conjunction with a Web browser to block information and sites on the Internet that would otherwise be available.

What Kind of Speech Is Being Blocked?

Most blocking software prevents access to sites based on criteria provided by the vendor. To conduct site-based blocking, a vendor establishes criteria to identify specified categories of speech on the Internet and configures the blocking software to block sites containing those categories of speech. Some Internet blocking software blocks as few as six categories of information, while others block many more.

Blocked categories may include hate speech, criminal activity, sexually explicit speech, "adult" speech, violent speech, religious speech, and even sports and entertainment.

Using its list of criteria, the software vendor compiles and maintains lists of "unacceptable" sites. Some software vendors employ individuals who browse the Internet for sites to block. Others use automated searching tools to identify which sites to block. These methods may be used in combination. (Examples of blocked sites can be found below.) . . .

Typical examples of blocked words and letters include "xxx," which blocks out Superbowl XXX sites; "breast," which blocks website and discussion groups about breast cancer; and the consecutive letters "s," "e" and "x," which block sites containing the words "sexton" and "Mars exploration," among many others. Some software blocks categories of expression along blatantly ideological lines, such as information about feminism or gay and lesbian issues. Yet most websites offering opposing views on these issues are not blocked. For example, the same software does not block sites expressing opposition to homosexuality and women working outside the home.

Clearly, the answer to blocking based on ideological viewpoint is not more blocking, any more than the answer to unpopular speech is to prevent everyone from speaking, because then no viewpoint of any kind will be heard. The American Family Association [AFA], a conservative religious organization, recently learned this lesson when it found that CyberPatrol, a popular brand of blocking software, had placed AFA on its "Cybernot" list because of the group's opposition to homosexuality.

AFA's site was blocked under the category "intolerance," defined as "pictures or text advocating prejudice or discrimination against any race, color, national origin, religion, disability or handicap, gender or sexual orientation. Any picture or text that elevates one group over another. Also includes intolerance jokes or slurs." Other "Cybernot" categories include "violence/profanity," "nudity," "sexual acts," "satanic/cult," and "drugs/drug culture."

In a May 28th [1999] news release excoriating CyberPatrol, AFA said, "CyberPatrol has elected to block the AFA website with their filter because we have simply taken an opposing viewpoint to the political and cultural agenda of the homosexual rights movement." As one AFA spokesman told reporters, "Basically we're being blocked for free speech."

The AFA said they are planning to appeal the blocking decision at a June 9th meeting of CyberPatrol's Cybernot Oversight Committee, but expressed doubt that the decision would be overturned. The conservative Family Research Council also joined in the fight, saying they had "learned that the Gay Lesbian Alliance Against Defamation (GLAAD) is a charter member of CyberPatrol's oversight committee," and that "it was pressure by GLAAD that turned CyberPatrol around."

Until, now, AFA, FRC and similar groups had been strong advocates for filtering software, and AFA has even assisted in the marketing of another product, X-Stop. AFA has said that they still support blocking but believe their group was unfairly singled out.

Indeed, as the AFA and others have learned, there is no avoiding the fact that somebody out there is making judgments about what is offensive and controversial, judgments that may not coincide with their own. The First Amendment exists precisely to protect the most offensive and controversial speech from government suppression. If blocking software is made mandatory in schools and libraries, that "somebody" making the judgments becomes the government.

To Block or Not to Block: You Decide

According to a recent story in The Washington Post, a software vendor's "own test of a sample of Web sites found that the software allowed pornographic sites to get through and blocked 57 sites that did not contain anything objectionable."

And in a current lawsuit in Virginia over the use of blocking software in libraries, the ACLU argues that the software blocks "a wide variety of other Web sites that contain valuable and constitutionally protected speech, such as the entire Web site of Glide Memorial United Methodist Church, located in San Francisco, California, and the entire Web site of The San Francisco Chronicle."

Following are real-world examples of the kind of speech that has been found to be inaccessible in libraries where blocking software is installed. Read through them—or look at them online—and then decide for yourself: Do you want the government telling you whether you can access these sites in the library?

www.afa.net   The American Family is a non-profit group founded in 1977 by the Rev. Donald Wildmon. According to their website, the AFA "stands for traditional family values, focusing primarily on the influence of television and other media—including pornography—on our society."

www.cmu.edu   Banned Books On-Line offers the full text of over thirty books that have been the object of censorship or censorship attempts, from James Joyce's Ulysses to Little Red Riding Hood.

www.quaker.org   The Religious Society of Friends describes itself as "an Alternative Christianity which emphasizes the personal experience of God in one's life." Their site boasts the slogan, "Proud to Be Censored by X-Stop, a popular brand of blocking software."

www.safersex.org   The Safer Sex Page includes brochures about safer sex, HIV transmission, and condoms, as well as resources for health educators and counselors. X-Stop, the software that blocks these pages, does not block the "The Safest Sex Home Page," which promotes abstinence before marriage as the only protection against sexually transmitted diseases.

www.iatnet.com.aauw   The American Association of University Women Maryland provides information about its activities to promote equity for women. The Web site discusses AAUW's leadership role in civil rights issues; work and family issues such as pay equity, family and medical leave, and dependent care; sex discrimination; and reproductive rights.

www.sfgate.com/columnists/morse Rob Morse, an award-winning columnist for The San Francisco Examiner, has written more than four hundred columns on a variety of issues ranging from national politics, homelessness, urban violence, computer news, and the Superbowl, to human cloning. Because his section is considered off limits, the entire www.sfgate.com site is blocked to viewers.

http://www.youth.org/yao/docs/books.html Books for Gay and Lesbian Teens/Youth provides information about books of interest to gay and lesbian youth. The site was created by Jeremy Meyers, an 18-year-old senior in high school who lives in New York City. X-Stop, the software that blocks this page, does not block web pages condemning homosexuality....

In addition to these examples, a growing body of research compiled by educators, public interest organizations and other interested groups demonstrates the extent to which this software inappropriately blocks valuable, protected speech, and does not effectively block the sites they claim to block....

Teaching Responsibility: Solutions That Work...

Instead of requiring unconstitutional blocking software, schools and libraries should establish content-neutral rules about when and how young people should use the Internet, and hold educational seminars on responsible use of the Internet.

For instance, schools could request that Internet access be limited to school-related work and develop carefully worded acceptable use policies (AUPs), that provide instructions for parents, teachers, students, librarians and patrons on use of the Internet....

Successful completion of a seminar similar to a driver's education course could be required of minors who seek Internet privileges in the classroom or library. Such seminars could emphasize the dangers of disclosing personally identifiable information such as one's address, communicating with strangers about personal or intimate matters, or relying on inaccurate resources on the Net.

Whether the use of blocking software is mandatory or not, parents should always be informed that blind reliance on blocking programs cannot effectively safeguard children.

Libraries can and should take other actions that are more protective of online free speech principles. For instance, libraries can publicize and provide links to particular sites that have been recommended for children.

Not all solutions are necessarily "high tech." To avoid unwanted viewing by passers-by, for instance, libraries can place privacy screens around Internet access terminals in ways that minimize pubic view. Libraries can also impose content-neutral time limits on Internet use.

These positive approaches work much better than restrictive software that works only when students are using school or library computers, and teaches no critical thinking skills. After all, sooner or later students graduate to the real world, or use a computer without blocking software. An educational program could teach students how to use the technology to find information quickly and efficiently, and how to exercise their own judgment to assess the quality and reliability of information they receive.

... and Don't Work

In an effort to avoid installing blocking software, some libraries have instituted a "tap on the shoulder" policy that is, in many ways, more intrusive and unconstitutional than a computer program. This authorizes librarians to peer at the patron's computer screen and tap anyone on the shoulder who is viewing "inappropriate" material.

The ACLU recently contacted a library in Newburgh, New York to advise against a proposed policy that would permit librarians to stop patrons from accessing "offensive" and "racially or sexually inappropriate material." In a letter to the Newburgh Board of Education, the ACLU wrote: "The Constitution protects dirty words, racial epithets, and sexually explicit speech, even though that speech may be offensive to some." The letter also noted that the broad language of the policy would allow a librarian to prevent a patron from viewing on the Internet such classic works of fiction as Chaucer's Canterbury Tales and Mark Twain's Adventures of Huckleberry Finn, and such classic works of art as Manet's Olympia and Michelangelo's David.

"This thrusts the librarian into the role of Big Brother and allows for arbitrary and discriminatory enforcement since each librarian will have a different opinion about what is offensive," the ACLU said.

The First Amendment prohibits librarians from directly censoring protected speech in the library, just as it prevents indirect censorship through blocking software.

Battling Big Brother in the Library

In Loudoun County, Virginia, the ACLU is currently involved in the first court challenge to the use of blocking software in a library. Recently, the judge in that case forcefully rejected a motion to dismiss the lawsuit, saying that the government had "misconstrued the nature of the Internet" and warning that Internet blocking requires the strictest level of constitutional scrutiny. The case is now set to go to trial. . . .

Earlier this year, the ACLU was involved in a local controversy over the mandatory use of Internet blocking programs in California's public libraries. County officials had decided to use a blocking program called "Bess" on every library Internet terminal, despite an admission by Bess's creators that it was impossible to customize the program to filter only material deemed "harmful to minors" by state law.

After months of negotiation, the ACLU warned the county that it would take legal action if officials did not remove Internet blocking software from public library computers. Ultimately, the library conceded that the filters presented an unconstitutional barrier to patrons seeking access to materials including legal opinions, medical information, political commentary, art, literature, information from women's organizations, and even portions of the ACLU Freedom Network website.

Today, under a new policy, the county provides a choice of an unfiltered or a filtered computer to both adult and minor patrons. No parental consent will be required for minors to access unfiltered computers.

The ACLU has also advocated successfully against mandatory blocking software in libraries in San Jose and in Santa Clara County, California. The ACLU continues to monitor the use of blocking software in many libraries across the nation, including communities in Massachusetts, Texas, Illinois, Ohio and Pennsylvania.

The Fight in Congress: Marshaling the Cyber-Troops Against Censorship

In February of this year, Senator John McCain (R-AZ) introduced the "Internet School Filtering Act," a law that requires all public libraries and schools to use blocking software in order to qualify for "e-rate," a federal funding program to promote universal Internet access. An amendment that would have allowed schools and libraries to qualify by presenting their own plan to regulate Internet access—not necessarily by commercial filter—failed in committee.

Another bill sponsored by Senator Dan Coats (R-IN) was dubbed "Son of CDA," because much of it is identical to the ill-fated Communications Decency Act.

The ACLU and others are lobbying against these bills, which have not yet come up for a vote as of this writing.

Censorship in the States: A Continuing Battle

Federal lawmakers are not the only politicians jumping on the censorship bandwagon. In the last three years, at least 25 states have considered or passed Internet censorship laws. This year, at least seven states are considering bills that require libraries and/or schools to use blocking software.

These censorship laws have not held up to constitutional scrutiny. Federal district courts in New York, Georgia and Virginia have found Internet censorship laws unconstitutional on First Amendment grounds in challenges brought by the ACLU. In April, the ACLU filed a challenge to an Internet censorship law in New Mexico that is remarkably similar to the failed New York law.

Conclusion

The advent of new forms of communication technology is always a cause for public anxiety and unease. This was as true for the printing press and the telephone as it was for the radio and the television. But the constitutional ideal is immutable regardless of the medium: a free society is based on the principle that each and every individual has the right to decide what kind of information he or she wants—or does not want—to receive or create. Once you allow the government to censor material you don't like, you cede to it the power to censor something you do like—even your own speech.

Censorship, like poison gas, can be highly effective when the wind is blowing the right way. But the wind has a way of shifting, and sooner or later, it blows back upon the user. Whether it comes in a box or is accessed online, in the hands of the government, blocking software is toxic to a democratic society.

Questions and Answers About Blocking Software

In the interest of "unblocking" the truth, here are answers to some of the questions the ACLU most often encounters on the issue of blocking software:

Q: Why does it matter whether Internet sites are blocked at the library when people who want to see them can just access them at home?

A: According to a recent Nielsen Survey, 45 percent of Internet users go to public libraries for Internet access. For users seeking controversial or personal information, the library is often their only opportunity for privacy. A Mormon teenager in Utah seeking information about other religions may not want a parent in the home, or a teacher at school, looking over her shoulder as she surfs the web.

Q: What about library policies that allow patrons to request that certain sites be unblocked?

A: The stigma of requesting access to a blocked site deters many people from making that request. Library patrons may be deterred from filling out a form seeking access, because the sites they wish to visit contain sensitive information. For instance, a woman seeking to access the Planned Parenthood website to find out about birth control may feel embarrassed about justifying the request to a librarian.

Q: But as long as a library patron can ask for a site to be unblocked, no one's speech is really being censored, right?

A: Wrong. Web providers who want their speech to reach library patrons have no way to request that their site be unblocked in thousands of libraries around the country. They fear patrons will be stigmatized for requesting that the site be unblocked, or simply won't brother to make the request. If public libraries around the country continue to use blocking software, speakers will be forced to self-censor in order to avoid being blocked in libraries.

Q: Isn't it true that libraries can use blocking software in the same way they select books for circulation?

A: The unique nature of the Internet means that librarians do not to have to consider the limitations of shelf space in providing access to online material. In a recent ruling concerning the use of blocking software in Virginia libraries, a federal judge agreed with the analogy of the Internet as "a collection of encyclopedias from which defendants [the government] have laboriously redacted [or crossed out] portions deemed unfit for library patrons."

Q: Doesn't blocking software help a librarian control what children see online?

A: The ability to choose which software is installed does not empower a school board or librarian to determine what is "inappropriate for minors." Instead, that determination is made by a software vendor who regards the lists of blocked sites as secret, proprietary information.

Q: Why shouldn't librarians be involved in preventing minors from accessing inappropriate material on the Internet?

A: It is the domain of parents, not librarians, to oversee their children's library use. This approach preserves the integrity of the library as a storehouse of ideas available to all regardless of age or income. As stated by the American Library Association's Office of Intellectual Freedom: "Parents and only parents have the right and responsibility to restrict their own children's access—and only their own children's access—to library resources, including the Internet. Librarians do not serve *in loco parentis.*"

Q: What do librarians themselves think about blocking software?

A: The overwhelming majority of librarians are opposed to the mandatory use of blocking software. However some, under pressure from individuals or local officials, have installed blocking software. The ALA has a Library Bill of Rights, which maintains that filters should not be used "to block access to constitutionally protected speech." ...

Q: Are libraries required to use blocking software in order to avoid criminal liability for providing minors access to speech that may not be protected by the Constitution?

A: No. The First Amendment prohibits imposing criminal or civil liability on librarians merely for providing minors with access to the Internet. The knowledge that some websites on the Internet may contain "harmful" matter is not sufficient grounds for prosecution. In fact, an attempt to avoid any liability by installing blocking software or otherwise limiting minors' access to the Internet would, itself, violate the First Amendment.

Q: Would libraries that do not use blocking software be liable for sexual harassment in the library?

A: No. Workplace sexual harassment laws apply only to employees, not to patrons. The remote possibility that a library employee might inadvertently view an objectionable site does not constitute sexual harassment under current law.

Q: Can't blocking programs be fixed so they block only illegal speech that is not protected by the Constitution?

A: There is simply no way for a computer software program to make distinctions between protected and unprotected speech. This is not a design flaw that may be "fixed" at some future point but a simple human truth....

Q: What if blocking software is only made mandatory for kids?

A: Even if only minors are forced to use blocking programs, constitutional problems remain. The Supreme Court has agreed that minors have rights too, and the fact that a 15-year-old rather than an 18-year-old seeks access online to valuable information on subjects such as religion or gay and lesbian resources does not mean that the First Amendment no longer applies. In any case, it is impossible for a computer program to distinguish what is appropriate for different age levels, or the age of the patron using the computer.

Q: Is using blocking software at schools any different than using it in public libraries?

A: Unlike libraries, schools do act in place of parents, and play a role in teaching civic values. Students do have First Amendment rights, however, and blocking software is inappropriate, especially for junior and high school students.

   In addition, because the software often blocks valuable information while allowing access to objectionable material, parents are given a false sense of security about what their children are viewing. A less restrictive—and more effective—alternative is the establishment of content-neutral "Acceptable Use Policies" (AUPs).

Q: Despite all these problems, isn't blocking software worth it if it keep some pornography from reaching kids?

A: Even though sexually explicit sites only make up a very small percentage of content on the Internet, it is impossible for any one program to block out every conceivable web page with "inappropriate" material.

   When blocking software is made mandatory, adults as well as minors are prevented from communicating online, even in schools. According to a recent news story in the Los Angeles Times, a restrictive blocking program at a California school district meant coaches couldn't access the University of Notre Dame's website, and math instructors were cut off from information about Wall Street because of a block on references to money and finance.

POSTSCRIPT

Should Internet Access Be Regulated?

There will probably be many attempts to create some types of controls over content on the Internet, and these attempts will be controversial. While the initial concept of blocking technology was simple, its introduction into the realm of public institutions has raised many troubling questions. Here are a few that have emerged: If information is to be evaluated, who should do the evaluation—the authors/distributors, the public institution, the government, or the public? In a society barraged by information, how feasibly can a ratings system protect vulnerable audiences? Are there information sites that should be exempt from filtering, such as news organizations? What forms of assessment exist to test the effectiveness of such a filter? What should the criteria be for labeling a filtering experience a success or a failure? There is much material on the Internet that most of us would decry. In addition to graphic sexual images, one can find out how to make a bomb or how to join a hate group. In most cases, there are books in the library that contain the same information. It offends many people that individuals can go into a library and find hate groups online. Yet, anyone can check out books with similar information. Of course, the library can control its inventory in a way that cannot be done with unfiltered Internet access.

Extensive writing on this issue can be accessed by any Internet search engine. The ACLU volume from which the No-side selection was obtained can be further researched at the Electronic Privacy Information Center's Internet site: www.epic.org. Parents' organizations and child advocacy groups have argued for some form of protection for children. *Wired* magazine is an excellent resource for a number of perspectives on issues dealing with computers and the Internet. A different perspective is offered by Brian Kahin and James Keller, who have edited *Public Access to the Internet* (MIT Press, 1995), which features articles that focus on the benefits of Internet use.

Undergirding much of this debate is concern about pornography, which is an important topic for thought. How accessible is it, and should it be controlled on the Internet? Some recent publications dealing with this subject include Nicholas Wolfson's *Hate Speech, Sex Speech, Free Speech* (Praeger, 1997) and James M. Ussher's *Fantasies of Feminity: Reframing the Boundaries of Sex* (Rutgers University Press, 1997).

ISSUE 12

Do Ratings Work?

YES: Paul Simon, Sam Brownback, and Joseph Lieberman, from "Three U.S. Senators Speak Out: Why Cleaning up Television Is Important to the Nation," *The American Enterprise* (March/April 1999)

NO: Marjorie Heins, from "Three Questions About Television Ratings," in Monroe E. Price, ed., *The V-Chip Debate: Content Filtering from Television to the Internet* (Lawrence Erlbaum Associates, 1998)

ISSUE SUMMARY

YES: Senators Paul Simon, Sam Brownback, and Joseph Lieberman speak up on why cleaning up television is important to the nation. They detail the frustrating experiences that caused them to support legislation to clean up television.

NO: Marjorie Heins, founding director of the American Civil Liberties Union's Arts Censorship Project, poses three questions about television ratings: First, what is the ratings system meant to accomplish? Second, who will rate programming, and how? Third, what are the likely political and artistic effects of the ratings scheme? The V-chip and television ratings will do nothing, she argues, to solve the problems of American youth and society.

The most obvious consequence of the massive 1996 Telecommunications Act was the extensive restructuring of the industry as corporations took advantage of relaxed ownership regulation to bolster their organizational reach. One other consequence, mysterious to many people, is the ratings that appear in the corner of the television screen at the beginning of programs. Not only did the 1996 Telecommunications Act force the industry to implement a ratings system, it required the installation of a V-chip in television sets, which would "read" violent ratings so families could block violent programming.

Controversy raged over the implementation of the ratings and V-chip system. Are such ratings an infringement of the free speech rights of broadcasters? Government mandated this system; should it be involved in the creation and application of the system? Does this attempt to protect children infringe on the rights of adults? Will it have a chilling effect on production? Will it encourage more explicit programming, with more shows rated "M" for mature audiences? Will ratings create a "forbidden fruit" appeal for some children?

Now a ratings system is in effect. After much controversy over whether ratings should be age- or content-based, most networks are using a combination of age and content systems. The original system had only age guidelines, but extensive debate produced a system that not only provided age guidelines but also descriptive labels upon which parents can base informed decisions. For children's programs the designation TV-Y is for all children, and TV-Y7 indicates a show for older children. TV-G, and TV-PG are easily understood, but TV-14 is used for general programs where parents may find material unsuitable for children under 14. TV-MA programs are designed for adults and are deemed unsuitable for children under 17. Content labels are also attached to many of the age designations: FV for fantasy violence in children's programs, V for violence, S for sexual situations, L for coarse language, and D for suggestive dialogue. Only in the past year have V-chip–equipped sets become widely available. Now parents can program into the set what levels of ratings will be used to block the set. When that is done and a program with an unacceptable rating is scheduled, a blank screen, sometimes with the words "this is a blocked program," will show up on the screen. For the first time, the pieces are in place to implement the 1996 Communications Decency Act. Now is the time to begin assessment. Does the ratings system work?

Paul Simon, Sam Brownback, and Joseph Lieberman each discuss why they are convinced that television can only be cleaned up through legislative action. They outline the frustration of parents and child advocates and the failure of self-regulative efforts. They assert that ratings exist to provide parents with information they need to monitor their children's exposure. Marjorie Heins questions the consequences of the ratings. Will they actually be used? And, if used, what will the consequences be for children and for society? What problems might arise from the fact that the entertainment industry governs the ratings? Finally, Heins fears the artistic and political effects of such regulation on a creative industry.

Paul Simon, Sam Brownback,
and Joseph Lieberman

 **YES**

Three U.S. Senators Speak Out: Why Cleaning up Television Is Important to the Nation

These remarks are from presentations to the conference on TV program-ming held in Washington, D.C. in December by the Center for Media & Public Affairs and The American Enterprise.

Senator Paul Simon
(D-Illinois, Retired)

I got into the effort to clean up TV accidentally. I checked into a motel in Lasalle County, Illinois, and turned on my television set. All of a sudden there in front of me in living color someone was being cut in half by a chainsaw. Now, I'm old enough to know it wasn't real, but it bothered me that night. I thought, what happens to a ten-year-old who watches this?

So I called my office the next morning and said, "Someone has to have done research on this; find out what research has taken place." My staff came back with all kinds of research showing that entertainment violence harms us.

I called a meeting of representatives of the TV industry and said, "I don't want government censorship, but I think we have to recognize we have a prob-lem, and I'd like you to come up with the answers." One of those present said, "Violence on television doesn't do any harm." I replied, "You remind me of the Tobacco Institute people who come into my office saying they have research that cigarettes don't do any harm." Then they said, "Well, we can't collaborate on this because it would violate the antitrust laws."

That led me to introduce a bill that included an exemption in the antitrust laws for television violence, and to give you some sense of the breadth of in-terest in this, my co-sponsors eventually included Senator Jesse Helms (R-N.C.) and Senator Howard Metzenbaum (D-Ohio). Now that's a broad philosophical spectrum.

The industry opposed my bill. The ACLU [the American Civil Liberties Union] opposed my bill. But we finally got the bill passed. George Bush signed it. And both broadcasters and cable operators began to adopt standards. I have to say they were fairly anemic, but they were better than nothing.

On the broadcast side, there has been progress. Arthur Nielsen of the Nielsen ratings says there have been significant improvements in terms of violence on the broadcast side—not going as far as needed, but still improvements. On the cable side, improvement is not perceptible.

At a meeting of about 700 TV and movie executives where I spoke, I said,"Many of you disagree with my conclusions. Why don't you do your own analysis of TV violence." And to their credit, both the broadcast and the cable industries authorized three-year studies. That research has recently come back, and I think they got more than they bargained for. The many damaging findings included the fact that three-quarters of all entertainment violence shows no immediate adverse consequences for the person committing the violence. The lessons for children and for adults, but particularly for children, is that violence pays.

The entertainment industry has periodically changed what it does and improved our society. For instance, if you look back at old movies and TV clips, you'll see the heros and heroines smoking and drinking much more heavily than they do today. I think this change is one of the reasons there has been a diminution in smoking and drinking in our society.

When television glamorizes violence, we imitate that. We have the most violent television of any nation on the earth with the possible exception of Japan, and there is one huge difference: In Japan, the people who commit the violence are the bad guys; people one wouldn't want to associate with. In American television, too frequently, those who commit the violence are the good guys.

The V-chip and ratings can offer an assist against objectionable TV content, but they are not a substitute for the industry's being responsible. First of all because children are technologically adept. I can't even program my VCR to tape a program. I have my son-in-law do it for me.

Second, the Nielsen ratings clearly show that in the impoverished areas in our country, which are also the high-crime areas, children watch 50 percent more television than they do in other areas; the TV set becomes a companion and babysitter.

Third, you're an unusual parent if, when Johnny or Jane go next door to play, you say, "Just a second. I want to find out what the neighbors have on television."

Finally, as a recent University of Wisconsin study shows, adult ratings, instead of repelling, frequently have an appeal for TV-watching children.

Another argument favored by the TV industry is, "We're just giving the public what it wants." That's the worst excuse of all. It is the same excuse that people in politics, business, and other fields use to rationalize irresponsible decisions. We ought to expect from the leaders in any field some sense of responsibility, some long-term social outlook.

I am not suggesting there be no violence on television. If you do a story on the Civil War, there's going to be some violence. *Schindler's List,* the most moving film I've ever seen, was on television, but it was on television late at night, when it should have been. And it didn't glorify violence. It associated violence with hurt, people crying. That's truthful.

Senator Sam Brownback
(R-Kansas)

TV content has attracted Congress's attention for the past several years because a lot of people across the country are upset.

The main problem with TV is not that a few scenes or even a few shows are horrifically shocking, but rather the near-constant stream of sleaze. Violence, irresponsibility, and vulgarity are staples of prime time. The majority of sexual relationships portrayed are extra-marital or pre-marital, and have no negative consequences. TV scenes of illicit sex rarely include AIDS, unwanted pregnancy, or heartbreak. Television strongly implies that adultery and teen sex are normal, even desirable, when the truth is that such things easily lead to grief, poverty, and shattered lives.

Senator Lieberman and I have co-hosted hearings the past two years on the impact of television sex and violence. We've been struggling with exactly what to do about this problem. I think it's critical that we talk a lot about it, that we put it high on the priority list, and that we look for solutions.

One idea several senators have put forward, so far with little success, is encouraging a voluntary code of conduct within the industry. We'd like to help reinvigorate and bring back the voluntary code that the broadcasting industry abided by until a 1982 ruling by the courts suggested that cooperating on standards might violate antitrust laws. Last year I introduced a bill that would remove this potential violation of antitrust laws and let the industry work together on standards. We're going to try again this year.

Entertainment companies have fought me on this. It's a strange situation for an industry to resist being given new powers, but so far the National Association of Broadcasters [NAB] and others have been uncooperative. They don't want the authority and responsibility to control their programming. But we're not giving up, because this project is very important.

Some people in the industry assert, "We don't make the culture. We just reflect it." But actually, television is a very powerful culture-shaping medium. As a candidate for public office, I've found that TV advertising is the key to transmitting a message today. If I could get by without buying it, I would in a heartbeat. But I can't.

What today's TV programmers are actually holding up is not a mirror but a mirage. The world of TV characters is, thank goodness, far more violent, disturbed, and perverse than typical American life. There are more Amish people in the United States than there are serial murderers. There are far more pastors than prostitutes. But you'd never know it from TV.

Does this matter? Of course. Television is the dominant influence on our culture. It rules the world because of its invasiveness, because of the impact it has on people. We all know by watching our own children watch television that

TV has clear effects, and studies confirm this. Consider just a couple of current examples:

- A recent study by Professor Mark Singer at Case Western University found that sustained TV viewing was linked to aggression, anxiety, and anger and violent behavior in children.
- The American Medical Association recently concluded that "exposure to violence in entertainment increases aggressive behavior... and contributes to Americans' sense that they live in a 'mean society.'"

These kinds of findings keep building and building.

We have to be much more aggressive in combating this problem. Abraham Lincoln taught that "He who molds public sentiment goes deeper than he who enacts statutes or pronounces decisions." I think what we have to do is mold public sentiment, inform people that television is hurting our children, and start moving to correct that.

My office stands ready and willing to do anything we can to help this effort, but I don't think you can legislate the problem out of existence: The First Amendment's protections on speech are clear and appropriate, and I wouldn't want to try. Instead, we have to change behavior in this area the old-fashioned way, the hard way, where you just continually talk, tell the story, push and encourage.

We need to tell the TV industry, "You are influencing our young and our nation, and it's not for the good. And we can't afford it as a people."

Sen. Joseph Lieberman (D-Connecticut)

We can't expect individual broadcasters to unilaterally institute controls on the kind of material they put out—not with the competitive pressures being what they are. That is why I strongly believe that one of the best things the industry could do to address the concern over exploitative shows would be to bring back a set of basic standards that would insulate programmers from the temptation to be more shocking or titillating than their competitors.

The National Association of Broadcasters maintained such a code for more than three decades and then chose to abandon it after a few of its provisions (restricting advertising only) were struck down by the courts on antitrust grounds. Re-reading the NAB standards today, I am struck by what a powerful statement of citizenship and community responsibility it was, and what a mistake it was to scrap it. America's families have paid the price for that decision, by way of sinking standards and vanishing values.

My argument is the same one made [in 1998] by ABC president Bob Iger, who said in a speech:

> The thing that differentiates television from other businesses is that so many of our program decisions impact the public in a powerful way. I believe there is room on the air for adult-oriented programs, provided they are high in quality. Programs like "Jerry Springer" are another matter. I question the logic of putting him on the air, and I believe the entire industry suffers from the association. Programs that are embarrassments to our business will, in the long run, alienate our viewers. Let's make these improvements—without any government intervention.

Good idea.

Despite the troubling direction the industry has been heading in, I still believe that the lion's share of local broadcasters take seriously their obligation to serve the public interest. And it is in that spirit that we are asking for their help in making television a safer place for children, by beginning to work together to develop a new code of standards for the next century. If help from Capitol Hill is necessary, rest assured such a measure would fly through both houses of Congress.

We are not calling for a return to the 1950s, but simply a respite from the graphic gunplay and foreplay that increasingly dominate the tube and send the worst messages to the public. We don't want to take away broadcaster discretion. We simply want them to take it back and use it responsibly.

NO ◀

Marjorie Heins

Three Questions About Television Ratings

In the 1996 Communications Decency Act [CDA], Congress mandated that all television sets manufactured or distributed in the United States after February 1998 contain "a feature designed to enable viewers to block display of all programs with a common rating"—that is, to have a so-called V-chip.[1] A chip enabling viewers "to block display of all programs with a common rating" is, of course, meaningless without someone to sit down and actually rate programming. Who will rate, how, and with what effect, have thus become critical issues for television producers and artists, for parents, children and teenagers, and for others who may rely upon the ratings. This article poses three questions worth pondering as the United States for the first time embarks upon a massive program of evaluating, labeling, and blocking hundreds of thousands of broadcast and cable television productions.

First, what exactly is the TV rating system that the industry created in response to the CDA[2] meant to accomplish? The answer is not so obvious, and looking beyond the conventional answer ("parental empowerment"), it becomes clear that the congressional purpose was to disfavor, and hopefully chill, broad categories of speech of which Congress disapproved.

Second, who will rate programming, and how will they decide? Unless one believes that the mandated V-chip combined with the industry's rating system will have no effect whatsoever on what is produced or viewed, these procedural questions are critical.

Finally, what are the likely political and artistic effects of the U.S. ratings scheme? The evidence is just beginning to come in, but it tends to confirm that the ratings will indeed be used to censor, chill, and pressure the industry into dropping controversial shows.

I. What Exactly Is the Rating System Meant to Accomplish?

The V-chip law, which forced the TV industry's creation of the rating system, is often touted as a form of parental empowerment; that is, its proponents characterize it as an innocent means of giving information to parents that will enable them to decide for themselves what programs their children should and should not watch. But the law is not quite so benign and noncensorial as its defenders sometimes would have it appear. For the CDA singles out certain categories of television content that Congress disliked (primarily violence and sexuality), and imposes, or at least very strongly encourages, the creation of a rating system to identify, and facilitate the blocking of, programs with just this content. The V-chip law is thus not simply an attempt to inform parents generally about the content of television programming.

Indeed, the "findings" portion of the law is quite explicit on this point. It reads, in pertinent part:

The Congress makes the following findings:

> (1) Television influences children's perception of the values and behavior that are common and acceptable in society....

> (4) Studies have shown that children exposed to violent video programming at a young age have a higher tendency for violent and aggressive behavior later in life than children not so exposed, and that children exposed to violent video programing are prone to assume that acts of violence are acceptable behavior....

> (6) Studies indicate that children are affected by the pervasiveness and casual treatment of sexual material on television, eroding the ability of parents to develop responsible attitudes and behavior in their children....[3]

These findings make clear that the purpose of the V-chip legislation was to target certain subjects and ideas with plainly stated censorial purposes. Those subjects and ideas, as spelled out in the law, are "sexual, violent, or other indecent material about which parents should be informed before it is displayed to children."[4]

But what is the basis for Congress's conclusions that "children exposed to violent video programming at a young age have a higher tendency for violent and aggressive behavior later in life," or that "casual treatment of sexual material on television [erodes] the ability of parents to develop responsible attitudes and behavior in their children"? Putting aside the constitutional questions raised by a law that imposes congressional value judgments about "responsible attitudes and behavior,"[5] what precisely are the subjects or ideas that Congress thought to be harmful, and what is the nature of the social science evidence that is said to prove the point? The two questions are related, for without defining what we are talking about (*all* violence? only "excessive" or "gratuitous" violence? explicit sex? implied sex? irresponsible attitudes *about* sex?), it is impossible to say whether "violence" or "sex" cause harm, or whether labeling and blocking TV programs is likely to reduce such harm.

One of the weaknesses in the social science literature on minors, television, and violence is precisely the inconsistency among researchers in defining these terms. Some studies attempt to identify the effects of films or TV shows with realistic physical violence; others look at make-believe play or cartoon violence; still others include verbal aggression. Some researchers attempt to distinguish "good" from "bad" violence—that is, they would excuse war movies, educational documentaries, or situations in which the hero uses force in self-defense. As a recent report by the Committee on Communications and Media Law of the Association of the Bar of the City of New York points out,

> The subject of violence and aggression in psychology is vast. These topics are fundamental to the models and theories created in the fields of psychology, biology, ethnology and evolution. One author estimated that there were 20,000 to 30,000 references on the subject of human aggression. What is most striking, even after sampling only a small part of this literature and thought, is how little agreement there is among experts in human behavior about the nature of aggression and violence, and what causes humans to act aggressively or violently. There is even difficulty defining the words "aggression" and "violence."[6]

The report goes on to note that aggression and violence themselves

> are necessarily defined relative to culture, intent, and context. While all societies condemn murder, the same act may be seen as treason or heroism. Physical discipline of a child may be viewed as appropriate or abusive, depending on viewpoint and culture. Physical assault may be viewed as reprehensible conduct or as an appropriate part of a sport or entertainment, like hockey or boxing.[7]

Thus, despite numerous pronouncements over the past decade that a causative link between television violence and social or psychological harm has been definitively proven, the ambiguities in scientists' own use of definitional terms is in itself enough to raise questions about the "findings" that Congress made.

The social science literature is too vast and technical to review in detail here; in any event, excellent critiques have been published elsewhere.[8] The report of the Association of the Bar of the City of New York, however, does provide a useful summary of the types of studies that have been done and of what, if any, political, scientific, and legal conclusions can reasonably be drawn from them. The report notes first that there are many schools of psychology, only one of which considers "social learning" to be the primary cause of aggressive or violent behavior:

> [P]sychologists do not even agree on the basic mechanisms that cause aggression—and therefore on the possible role of stimuli such as media depictions of violence in contributing to it. Some see aggression as innate in human beings, a drive which demands discharge in some form. Evolutionary psychologists see human aggressiveness and destructive violence as a naturally evolved response to particular environments. Violence is simply the route to status in certain social environments. Another psychologist sees human destructiveness and cruelty not as an instinct but as a part of character, as "passions rooted in the total existence of man." For psychologists who emphasize the social needs of humans, violence is a reflection of psychological trauma in establishing relations to others. The failure to develop a mediating conscience because of a deficient family structure may lead to an inability to control aggressive impulses which arise.
>
> Finally, there are psychologists who believe aggressive behavior is learned from the environment. It is primarily these theorists who have

looked particularly at television and violence. But, although it is sometimes sweepingly said that television violence causes violence in society, the research of these psychologists by no means supports so broad a statement. For over thirty years researchers have been attempting to discern the relationship, if any, between aggressive behavior and viewing television violence. The results remain controversial and skeptics abound.[9]

The report then describes the four basic methodological approaches that have been used by this last category of social scientists, who believe that "aggressive behavior is learned from the environment." These four are laboratory experiments, field experiments, quasi or natural experiments, and longitudinal studies. After examining the strengths and weaknesses of each method, the report concludes that the results of empirical research

offer only modest support, and to a greater extent contradict, the legislative findings drawing connections between media violence and violent conduct or predispositions that underlie most of the efforts to regulate violent media content.

This is because, first,

most psychological studies of the effects of television are studies of aggression or aggressive attitudes, not violence. The distinction is significant: many behaviors which few would deem "violent" may be counted and measured by psychologists as aggressive. Yet the purported focus of most legislative efforts is violent behavior caused by media content. It would therefore be erroneous to rely on psychological studies of aggression to justify such regulations.

Second, as the report noted,

research studies are generally influenced by more fundamental, underlying conceptions of the causes of human social behavior—issues on which there is little agreement. For example, theorists who believe that behavior is learned by children from what they observe are more inclined to construct studies focusing on television or media than theorists who place more weight on the child's family structure or position in a social pecking order.

Finally,

determining psychological causation is problematic, difficult and the subject of a considerable amount of disagreement. The empirical findings normally speak in terms of correlation of events and not causation; the researchers' findings are usually carefully limited and, in general, do not make broad or definitive assertions about the causes of particular behavior. For many reasons, generalizing from research results to everyday experience can be perilous. It is difficult, for example, for psychologists to duplicate the mix and range of violent and non-violent programming that an individual may choose. There is also great variation in the population viewing violent programming: some persons may be unusually susceptible to imitation of violent media portrayals, and research populations may be skewed by over-representation of such individuals. It is also difficult to isolate everyday viewing of violent media portrayals from other experiences that psychologists believe may contribute to violent behavior. There is no consensus among even the researchers who have found some correlations that there is any clear causal link between media violence and violent behavior. Many psychologists point to other factors—such as watching television in general, or watching fast-paced programming—as the most likely causes of any aggressiveness associated with television viewing. And no researcher, to our knowledge, purports to demonstrate that eliminating media violence is necessary to reducing violent behavior.[10]

In short, Congress's "findings" about exposure to TV violence and subsequent behavior do not hold up to even the most cursory examination. The effects of art and entertainment on the complex and idiosyncratic human mind are still largely a mystery. The unavoidable conclusion is that Congress seized upon social science literature to cloak what was essentially a political and moral judgment that large, vague categories of television programming are offensive or at least inappropriate for youth.[11]

II. Who Will Rate Programming, and How Will They Decide?

The V-chip puts significant power in the hands of the people who will actually rate TV programming. Those parents who choose to activate the chip will not be evaluating programs themselves to determine if they are consonant with their own values or appropriate for the age and maturity levels of their children. Instead, parents will be blocking programs based on simple, conclusory V, S, L (for language), or D (for dialogue) labels, combined with the industry's originally proposed TV-G, TV-PG, TV-14, and TV-MA age-based recommendations.[12] The system will give no further information about the multitude of shows subject to the rating system—their context, purpose, viewpoint, quality, or educational value.

Those parents who block will thus do so based on *Congress's* determination that it is sex, "indecency," and violence that must be restrained, and the industry's apparent interpretation of "indecent," to the extent it differs from "sexual," to mean primarily "coarse" language (L) or "suggestive dialogue" (D).[13] Other types of content that have occasionally been blamed for juvenile delinquency or other ills—for example, racist speech, discussions of drug use, or paeans to "Satanism" or other disapproved religious beliefs—are not included.

Critics of ratings systems have pointed out the dangers of using broad, conclusory labels as measures of the value of speech, or of the harm it may cause. An often cited, and still powerful, example is Steven Spielberg's film *Schindler's List*, which will presumably receive V, S, L, and D labels because of its violent content (it is, after all, about the Holocaust) and occasional nudity (Schindler has affairs—sexual nudity—and the Jews who are being rounded up for slaughter are frequently deprived of their clothing—nonsexual nudity). Yet *Schindler's List* is probably among the most important and educational of commercial films in recent years. Whatever arguments might be made about the psychological effects on children of *gratuitous* violence, the violence shown in *Schindler's List* can hardly be deemed gratuitous, and indeed the film has been criticized in some quarters for not giving a vivid *enough* depiction of the horrors of the Nazi regime. What then, is the point exactly of shielding minors, particularly teenagers, from the knowledge of human pain and brutality imparted by this and other historical films? How are they to learn about human history without studying the evil that characterized one of its most gruesome episodes? Does it really help educate young people to airbrush the atrocities of history— or, for that matter, to pretend that the powerful force of human sexuality does not exist? Certainly, there is little basis to believe that viewing *Schindler's List* will cause young people to develop greater tolerance for violence, to behave more aggressively, or to acquire irresponsible attitudes about sex.[14]

Eyes on the Prize, to cite an example of a program specifically designed for TV, is a powerful documentary of the American civil rights movement, and contains violence galore—most of it visited by Southern white citizens or law enforcement officers against black protesters. The film would be historically false if it did not. Yet its educational value and dramatic power cannot be doubted. What is the justification for labeling with a V—and therefore suggesting to parents that they block it as unsuitable—this masterwork of documentary filmmaking?

On a more mundane level, the process of deciding whether a program merits a V, D, S, or L—or a TV-14 or TV-MA—will inevitably be subjective, value-laden and time consuming, as a Fox Broadcasting executive noted in September 1997.[15] Ellen DeGeneres, the recently "out" lesbian of the popular eponymous ABC sitcom, discovered in October 1997, that her completely nonviolent and nonsexually explicit show was slated to receive a TV-14, presumably because it deals approvingly with homosexuality. "How can I go forward?" DeGeneres was quoted as asking. "This is blatant discrimination. . . . This advisory is telling kids something's wrong with being gay."[16]

A December 1993 report from North Dakota Senator Byron Dorgan is pertinent here. The report summarized the results of a one-week survey of violence on prime time television conducted by college students earlier that year. Among the shows found to contain the highest number of violent acts per hours were *The Miracle Worker, Civil War Journal, Star Trek 9, The Untouchables, Murder She Wrote, Back to the Future, Our Century: Combat at Sea, Teenage Mutant Ninja Turtles,* and Alfred Hitchcock's classic *North by Northwest*.[17] Even if a TV ratings system purported to give pejorative V labels to only the programs on this list deemed to contain "bad" violence, which the industry's current plan does not, it would be difficult for a team of raters to make those judgments, expected as they will be to decide upon labels for dozens of programs daily. Indeed, the subjectivity of judgments about "value" or about the meaning or propriety of the messages contained in creative works, as well as long-standing First Amendment rules against "viewpoint discrimination,"[18] are one reason that the ratings, like the Communications Decency Act itself, do not distinguish between "good" and "bad" violence or sex.

But if making value judgments of this type is both difficult and offensive to our anticensorship instincts, a system that fails to do so, and thus encompasses *all* programming bearing on large subjects like sexuality or violence, is hopelessly overbroad. As Professor Burt Neuborne recently pointed out:

> The impossibly broad reach of a literal ban on all speech depicting violence inevitably requires a narrowing set of criteria designed to distinguish *Hamlet* from forbidden speech depicting violence. But any effort by the FCC, or anyone else, to decide when speech depicting violence crosses the line from an acceptable exercise in artistic creation, as in *Hamlet*, or *Oedipus Rex*, or *Antigone*, or *The Crucible*, to a forbidden depiction of "gratuitous" or "excessive" violence must involve purely subjective notions of taste and aesthetic judgment. Indeed, once it is recognized that the ban on violence cannot be applied literally, any effort to apply a narrower ban is utterly without objective guidance. In effect, efforts to ban violent programming would turn the FCC into a drama critic, forced to pass judgment on the artistic merits of any effort to depict a violent act.[19]

The problems Professor Neuborne identifies with respect to a ban are equally present in a ratings system. The American Psychological Association has acknowledged that "[t]elevision violence per se is not the problem; rather, it is the manner in which most violence on television is shown that should concern us."[20] But as Professor Neuborne points out, trying to distinguish between "excessive" or "gratuitous" violence on the one hand, and violent material presented in an instructive or morally approved way, as the APA suggests, would enmesh whoever is responsible for the ratings in a vast process of policing thought and censoring ideas.

Nor are these problems resolved if television companies decide not to assign the task of rating to in-house staff but instead force producers or directors to evaluate and label their own programs. Many of those on the creative side of the industry will object to being compelled to attached pejorative ratings to their works, or will bridle at the constraints of a system that substitutes overgeneralized and fundamentally uninformative labels for real contextual information about programs.[21] If, despite their objections, they are forced to label, the results are likely to be arbitrary and idiosyncratic. For example, the distinction between "strong, coarse language," requiring a TV-14 rating, and "crude indecent language," requiring a TV-MA,[22] is likely to elude many raters and lead to inconsistent results.

On the other end of the television continuum, there are countless programs with no violence, sex, "coarse language," or "suggestive dialogue," and also with little educational or artistic value. Mindless entertainment—the "idiot box" of popular discourse—may be a greater threat to healthy child development, to the nurturing of thoughtful young people who are knowledgeable about and capable of dealing with the complexities and tragedies of human life, than violent or sexual content per se. Justice Brandeis's much-quoted rhetoric about "more speech"[23] is pertinent here: teaching young people about responsible sexuality or other aspects of human behavior requires education and discussion, not censorship.

III. What Are the Likely Political and Artistic Effects of the U.S. Ratings Scheme?

Regardless of its unambiguously stated censorial purposes,[24] the 1996 V-chip law, it is sometimes said, will not have any speech-suppressive effect, or at least none attributable to the government. Parents will make their own decisions based on accurate information about programming—an outcome no more repressive of free speech than the existing operation of market forces as consumers choose some programs and reject others.

Let's examine this seductively simple proposition. First, even in the constitutional sense (as the First Amendment generally applies only to government), the television ratings are not likely to operate wholly in the unregulated sphere of private choice. Some public schools will rely upon the ratings in choosing—or, more accurately, disqualifying—what may be worthy and valuable TV programs for homework assignments or in-class viewing. Indeed, there are school districts that already rely upon the familiar Motion Picture Association of America/Classification and Rating Administration movie ratings in just this fashion,[25] despite the fact that MPAA/CARA raters have no background or expertise in education or child development.[26] Just as numerous students have been deprived of *Schindler's List* as part of their high school history courses because of its R rating from CARA, so *The Accused, The Miracle Worker, The Civil War*, and countless other educationally profitable TV movies or other shows with violent content will receive V ratings and be subject to at least a presumption against curricular use in many public schools.

Second, ratings necessarily imply that certain programs contain themes that are morally disapproved or psychologically harmful to minors. They thus provide an easy set of symbols for "family values" activists in local communities to seize upon. The average public school administration will not be particularly eager to countenance curricular use of S-, V-, L-, or D-rated material in the face of likely protest from such groups. Ratings thus advance censorship by giving private pressure groups easy red flags to wave in the faces of nervous government officials.

Moving from the local to the national government level, it is difficult to imagine that the Federal Communications Commission, which is so enmeshed in the regulation of "indecency" in broadcasting,[27] will not be drawn into disputes over ratings as well. It will no doubt receive complaints from politicians, members of the public, and perhaps rival broadcasters, that some companies are not accurately rating their programming, or are refusing to rate at all. Indeed, one member of Congress has already made such a threat explicitly. In September 1997, Senator John McCain wrote to NBC, which had so far resisted the addition of content-based letter labels to the original age-based industry ratings plan, that if NBC continued to "refuse to join with the rest of the television industry,"

> I will pursue a series of alternative ways of safeguarding, by law and regulation, the interests that NBC refuses to safeguard voluntarily. These will include, but not be limited to, the legislation offered by Senator Hollings to channel violent programming to later hours, as well as urging the Federal

Communications Commission to examine in a full evidentiary hearing the renewal application of any television station not implementing the revised TV ratings system.[28]

Is the FCC to ignore the complaints of Senator McCain and others? It may, to be sure, be wary of initiating formal reviews of allegedly inaccurate or deceptive ratings, for fear of establishing the very "state action," and consequent vulnerability to a First Amendment court challenge, that the authors of the V-chip legislation attempted to avoid. Nevertheless, the agency is charged by law with evaluating a broadcast licensee's record of contribution to the "public interest" when reviewing requests for license renewals, transfers, or acquisitions.[29] Just as the commission has long considered broadcasters' records on community programming and their capacity to disseminate diverse points of view,[30] and just as it has threatened adverse licensing action based on complaints of "indecency,"[31] it is likely to consider allegations that broadcasters have rated programs improperly when it makes licensing decisions. At the very least, the possibility that it may do so, and the power of economic life and death that the FCC holds over broadcasters, will make the television industry cautious about displeasing the agency.

What about private censorship? Putting aside the legal question whether private marketplace choices made as a result of the V-chip law create First Amendment concerns,[32] it cannot be doubted that such private choices do have an effect on artistic freedom. Again, the analogy to movie ratings is instructive. Just as many theaters are reluctant to book NC-17 movies, some advertisers will be reluctant to support V-, S-, L-, or D-rated TV shows. Less advertising means less revenue, which in turn means less likelihood that the show will survive —unless, of course, its content is toned down. In many situations, advertisers' threats of withdrawal will not even be necessary, since for large entertainment companies the mere prospect of pejorative ratings may be daunting enough in terms of public relations to cause them to instruct producers to self-censor their material.

In recent years, the MPAA/CARA film ratings system has had just this effect. Leading directors like the late Louis Malle have been forced to eliminate artistically important scenes from their work because of the studios' insistence on obtaining at least nothing more pejorative and audience-thinning than an R rating.[33] Self-censorship will thus be a predictable and intended effect of the V-chip law.

I have discussed in the previous two sections whether such pressures to self-censor are justifiable, given the ambiguity of the social science literature, the difficulty of defining what it is that is supposed to be harmful, and the dangers of reposing discretionary ratings powers in either program producers themselves or large numbers of industry-employed functionaries. The point here is that, regardless of the strength of the justifications or the fairness of the procedures, the inevitable pressures of the ratings system will in many instances lead to blander, less provocative programming—less coverage of controversial but important issues like sexuality, and less artistic freedom.[34]

V-chips and ratings will do nothing to solve the tough, persistent social problems we associate with youth: poor education, violence, alienation, high teen pregnancy rates. American political leaders, however, seem increasingly devoted to the art of making symbolic gestures while ignoring serious solutions to social problems. V-chips and ratings are such gestures, but they are not entirely empty ones. For although they will do nothing to reduce irresponsible sexual activity or violence, they will restrain artistic freedom. Moreover, they create the illusion that "something is being done," and reinforce the pernicious notion that information about such complex human phenomena as sexuality and aggression is better suppressed than examined.

Notes

1. 47 U.S.C. §303(x), Public Law 104–104, Title V, §551(c). The law only applies to TV sets with screens 13 inches or larger, and allows the FCC to alter the requirement consistent with advances in technology. *Id.*, §551(c)(4).

2. The law provided that if the television industry did not within a year develop a ratings system satisfactory to the Federal Communications Commission, the FCC must "prescribe" one that would identify "sexual, violent, or other indecent material," and then, "in consultation" with the industry, must establish rules requiring programmers to transmit the ratings in a manner allowing parents to block rated shows. 47 U.S.C. §303(w). Despite initial protests, the industry responded promptly by setting up a committee to design a ratings system. See n. 12, *infra*.

3. Section 551(a), Public Law 104–104 (1996), published in the Historical and Statutory Notes to 47 U.S.C. §303(w). Congressional "findings" may or may not be based on accurate empirical evidence, and in any event are not binding on courts, particularly not in First Amendment cases, where the judicial branch must make its own judgment about the facts on which the government relies to justify restrictions on free speech. See, e.g. *Sable Communications, Inc. V. FCC*, 492 U.S. 115, 129 (1989); *Landmark Communications v. Virginia*, 435 U.S. 829, 843 (1978).

4. 47 U.S.C. §303(w). The section goes on to assure that "nothing in this paragraph shall be construed to authorize any rating of video programming on the basis of its political or religious content." *Id.*

5. A fundamental First Amendment principle is that government cannot suppress ideas because it thinks them dangerous. See Marjorie Heins, "Viewpoint Discrimination," 24 *Hastings Con.L.Q.* 99 (1996); *American Booksellers Association v. Hudnut*, 771 F.2d 323 (7th Cir.) aff'd mem., 475 U.S. 1001 (1985).

6. "Violence in the Media: A Position Paper," *The Record of The Association of the Bar of the City of New York*, vol. 52, no. 3 (April 1997), at 283–84 (citations omitted). Reprinted with permission from *The Record* of The Association of the Bar of the City of New York, copyright 1997, 52 *The Record* 273, 283–84.

7. *Id.* at 284.

8. See e.g., Jonathan Freedman, "Television Violence and Aggression: A Rejoinder," *Psychological Bulletin*, Vol. 100(3), 372–78 (1986); Robert Kaplan, "Television Violence and Viewer Aggression: A Reexamination of the Evidence," *Journal of Social Issues*, vol. 32, no. 4, 35–70 (1976); Robert Kaplan, "TV Violence and Aggression Revisited Again," *American Psychologist*, vol. 37, no. 5, 589 (May 1982); O. Wiegman, M. Kuttschreuter & B. Baarda, "A Longitudinal Study of the Effects of Television Viewing on Aggressive and Prosocial Behaviours," *British Journal of Social Psychology*, vol. 31, 147–64 (1992).

9. "Violence in the Media," *Record of The Association of the Bar of the City of New York*, *supra* n. 6, at 286 (citations omitted).

10. *Id.* at 296–97 (citations omitted).

11. Social science studies with respect to sexual situations on television are quite limited compared to the extensive, if inconclusive, literature on violence. The few studies that do exist are at best suggestive of a correlation, not necessarily a causal relation, between viewing habits and sexual behavior. See, e.g., Charles Corder-Bolz, "Television and Adolescents' Sexual Behavior," *Sex Education News*, vol. 3 (Jan. 1981), p. 3 (survey showed that of seventy-five adolescent girls, half of them pregnant, the pregnant ones watched more TV soap operas and were less likely to think that their favorite characters used contraceptives). As the American Academy of Pediatrics, a proponent of more sexually responsible TV programming, acknowledges, "there is no clear documentation that the relationship between television viewing and sexual activity [among teenagers] is causal." American Academy of Pediatrics, "Children, Adolescents, and Television," *Pediatrics*, vol. 96, no. 4 (Oct. 1995), p. 786.

12. The industry's original plan, submitted by the National Association of Broadcasters (NAB), the Motion Picture Association of America (MPAA), and the National Cable Television Association (NCTA) to the FCC for its approval on January 17, 1997, was wholly age-based and gave no information about the content of specific programs. It encountered widespread criticism from politicians and advocacy groups. After a six-month period of negotiations with these groups, the three industry associations agreed to add V, S, L, and D labels to the scheme. See Letter Submission of Jack Valenti, President and CEO of the MPAA, Decker Anstrom, President and CEO of the NCTA, and Eddie Fritts, president and CEO of the NAB, to William Caton, FCC Secretary, Aug. 1, 1997 (hereinafter, "Valenti letter").

13. *Id.*, p. 2. As a legal term "indecency" derives from the Federal Communications Commission's policing of radio and television broadcasting, as approved by the Supreme Court in *FCC v. Pacifica Foundation*, 438 U.S. 726 (1978). The monologue by comedian George Carlin found to be indecent in *Pacifica* consisted of the repetitive use of the so-called seven dirty words, not of any explicit description of sexual activity.

     Under the industry's plan, news and sports are to be exempt from labeling requirements. See Valenti letter, p. 3. Disputes may easily be anticipated about what programming qualifies as "news."

14. Many other examples of fine films with violent content could, of course, be cited: *The Accused, Bonnie and Clyde, The Burning Bed, Psycho,* and almost any war story or Biblical epic.

15. Lawrie Mifflin, "Helping or Confusing, TV Labels are Widening," *New York Times*, Sept. 30, 1997, p. E1 (quoting Roland McFarland, Vice President for Broadcast Standards and Practices at Fox, as stating that "the process had become much more time-consuming now that D, L, S, and V had to be considered." "Is it a punch? A gunshot? A gunshot plus killing? These are all subjective interpretations. The classic discussion here is around shows where there's heavy jeopardy involved, but not real on-screen violence. You might see a body, the aftermath of violence.... Where's the tilt factor, as far as giving it a V?" *Id.*, p. E8.

16. Bill Carter, "Star of 'Ellen' Threatens to Quite Over Advisory," *New York Times*, Oct. 9, 1997, p. E3.

17. Press Release from U.S. Senator Byron L. Dorgan (North Dakota), "Report on Television Violence Shows Fox Network Has the Most Violence Programming," Dec. 16, 1993, and attached report, "Television Violence Demonstration Project Conducted at Concordia College, Moorhead, Minnesota, Sept.–Dec. 1993."

18. See n. 5, *supra.*

19. Television Rating System: Hearings on S.409 Before the Senate Comm. on Commerce, Science and Transp., 105th Cong. (1997) (testimony of Burt Neuborne, Professor of Law, New York University).

20. Comments of the American Psychological Association to the Federal Communications Commission 3 (April 8, 1997) (in the matter of Industry Proposal for Rating Video Programming, No. 97–55).

21. In the analogous context of Internet ratings, producers of online information have loudly objected to proposals that they "self-rate" their sites: as one editor explained, "The rating of content, particularly in the area of violence—to tell people whether they should or shouldn't read about war in Bosnia—takes news and turns it into a form of entertainment." Amy Harmon, "Technology," *New York Times*, Sept. 1, 1997, p. D3.

22. As set out in the Valenti Letter, *supra* n. 12, p. 2.

23. "Those who won our independence . . . believed that freedom to think as you will and to speak as you think are means indispensable to the discovery and spread of political truth; that without free speech and assembly, discussion would be futile; that with them, discussion affords ordinarily adequate protection against the dissemination of noxious doctrine. . . . [T]hey knew that . . . the path of safety lies in the opportunity to discuss freely supposed grievances and proposed remedies; and that the fitting remedy for evil counsels is good ones." *Whitney v. California*, 274 U.S. 357, 375 (1927) (Brandeis, J., concurring).

24. See *supra*, text accompanying notes 2–3.

25. See *Borger v. Bisciglia*, 888 F.Supp. 97 (W.D.Wis. 1995) (rejecting First Amendment challenge to school district's ban on showing any R-rated film as part of curriculum, which resulted in inability of students to see *Schindler's List* as part of their study of the Holocaust); *Desilets v. Clearview Regional Board of Education*, 137 N.J. 584 (1994) (striking down school authorities' refusal to allow student newspaper to review R-rated films, *Rain Man* and *Mississippi Burning*); " 'Schindler' Blacklisted," *New York Times*, March 18, 1994, p. A28 (Letters to the Editor) (describing Plymouth, Massachusetts's school board's decision not to allow high school students to see *Schindler's List* because of R rating); "Twin Falls, Ohio," American Library Association *Newsletter on Intellectual Freedom* (Sept. 1997), p. 127 (describing parent's challenge to use of films *Schindler's List* and *Macbeth* because of their R ratings).

26. See Richard M. Mosk, "Motion Picture Ratings in the United States," in this volume. I do not mean to suggest that a ratings board composed of literary or psychological experts, as is found, for example, in Britain, would necessarily be an improvement.

27. See *FCC v. Pacifica Foundation*, 438 U.S. 726 (1978); *Action for Children's Television v. FCC* ("ACT III"), 58 F.3d 654 (D.C. Cir. 1995), cert. denied, 116 S.Ct. 701 (1996).

28. Letter from Senator John McCain, chairman, Senate Committee on Commerce, Science and Transportation, to Robert Wright, President and CEO, National Broadcasting Company, Sept. 29, 1997. At around the same time, Senator McCain asked each of four new FCC commissioner candidates "to agree to consider a station's use or nonuse of the revised ratings-code as a factor in deciding whether to renew a station's license." Lawrie Mifflin, "Media," *New York Times*, Oct. 6, 1997, p. D11. Although refusing to use the letter labels, NBC was already giving "full-sentence advisories" about violent content at the start of some shows. *Id.*

29. See 47 U.S.C. §§303–309.

30. *See Metro Broadcasting, Inc. v. FCC*, 497 U.S. 547 (1990) (approving FCC's consideration of diversity of viewpoint in awarding licenses), overruled on other grounds in *Adarand Constructors, Inc. v. Peña*, 515 U.S. 200 (1995).

31. See *Action for Children's Television v. FCC* ("ACT IV"), 59 F.3d 1249, 1266 (D.C. Cir 1995), cert. denied, 116 S.Ct. 773 (1996) (Tatel, J., dissenting) (noting FCC use of administrative "indecency" determinations to threaten loss of broadcast licenses).

32. In *Denver Area Educational Telecommunications Consortium v. FCC*, 116 S.Ct. 2374 (1966), Justice Stephen Breyer, writing for a plurality of four members of the Supreme Court, asserted that although a law authorizing private cable companies to censor "indecent" leased access cable programming was clearly "state action," it did not violate the First Amendment because, among other things, the law addressed "an extremely important problem"—"protecting children from exposure to patently offensive depictions of sex"—and it reflected a balancing of cable companies' and leased access programmers' free speech rights. *Id.* at 2385, 2382-88. As to public, educational, and governmental access cable programming, the Court reached the opposite conclusion. *Id.* at 2394-97.

33. *See* Marjorie Heins, *Sex, Sin and Blasphemy: A Guide to America's Censorship Wars* 58-59 (1993) (describing Malle's cutting, over protest, of his controversial film, *Damage*); Stephen Farber, *The Movie Rating Game* 71 (1972) (recounting how line about pubic hair was cut from *The Reivers* to obtain GP rating and how pot-smoking scene and two short love-making scenes were eliminated from *Alice's Restaurant* for the same reason); see also *Miramax Films Corp. v. Motion Picture Association of America*, 560 N.Y.S. 730, 734 (Supreme Ct., NY County 1990) ("[t]he record also reveals that films are produced and *negotiated* to fit the ratings. After an initial 'X' rating of a film whole scenes or parts thereof are cut in order to fit within the 'R' category. Contrary to our jurisprudence which protects all forms of expression, the rating system censors serious films by the force of economic pressure"). Since the decision in *Miramax*, CARA's dreaded X has been replaced with the almost equally undesirable NC-17.

34. Some critics of ratings claim that the censorial purpose may backfire—that is, the quest for adventuresome (especially teenage) audiences may in some cases cause producers gratuitously to *add* sexual or violent content to their work, for what self-respecting adolescent wants to attend a G-rated movie? Whatever the accuracy of this speculation, it seems evident that television ratings, like movie ratings, will distort artistic judgments and introduce extraneous pressures into the creative process.

POSTSCRIPT

Do Ratings Work?

From the earliest years of television broadcasting, parents and educators have expressed concerns that television is harmful, particularly to such a vulnerable population as children. These concerns have become important public policy issues. Groups, such as Action for Children's Television (ACT), have lobbied the Federal Communications Commission (FCC) for guidelines on appropriate practices for entertaining and advertising to young audiences. In addition to the 1996 Telecommunications Act, the 1990 Children's Television Act imposed an obligation on broadcasters to serve the educational and informational needs of children. Broadcasters are now required to schedule at least three hours of educational and informational (ELI) programming for children per week. And that regulation accounts for another piece of information appearing on television screens at the beginning of programs, often an ELI symbol indicating that the program fulfills the educational or informational needs of children.

A common theme of arguments for and against regulation has to do with the responsibility of parents. To monitor children's viewing, parents have to be full-time television watchdogs, states George Gerbner, head of the Violence Index project. Those on the other side of the argument say that monitoring children is exactly what parents should do; television is not a babysitter. Some worry that concern over ratings will produce homogenous, uninteresting entertainment fare.

The Annenberg Public Policy Center (APPC) has been studying the state of children's television for the past four years. The aims of this research have been to determine the availability of high-quality choices for children of different age groups with different resources, to identify the high-quality programs that exist on broadcast and cable, and to track the impact of government regulation of children's television programs. *The 1998 State of Children's Television report* notes that many programs do not contain appropriate labels previewing violent content. They particularly argued for the more common use of the FV rating (for fantasy violence) rather than the less informative TV-Y7, which was more commonly used. This report seems to have been heard, as the FV rating is showing up considerably more frequently than it used to in children's programs. The 1999 APPC report notes that 64 percent of parents and 72 percent of children are aware of the existence of a TV ratings system; even fewer know of the ELI designation. Over half of parents indicated that they would use the V-chip system if they had it, but also over half of children have a television in their own bedroom, which presumably limits parental monitoring.

Much has been written on this subject. One place to start is with the volume edited by Monroe E. Price, *The V-chip Debate: Content Filtering from*

Television to the Internet (Lawrence Erlbaum Associates, 1998). The bibliography and appendices are particularly useful. In the debate over the potentials and problems of the V-chip, the Canadian experiment with the technology is frequently mentioned. Two essays, one by Al MacKay and another by Stephen D. McDowell and Carleen Maitland in the Price volume, explore the Canadian experience with the V-chip.

ISSUE 13

Should the FCC Be Abolished?

YES: Peter Huber, from *Law and Disorder in Cyberspace* (Oxford University Press, 1997)

NO: William E. Kennard, from Statement Before the Federal Communications Commission, Washington, D.C. (January 19, 2000)

ISSUE SUMMARY

YES: Professor Peter Huber writes that the Federal Communications Commission (FCC) is no longer adequate as an organization to oversee telecommunications in the United States. Because technologies are emerging so quickly, and because of the effect of deregulation as a philosophy and practice, he argues that the FCC can no longer be an effective agency and therefore should be abolished.

NO: William E. Kennard, chairman of the FCC, embraces the effect of deregulation in telecommunications but says that the role of the FCC has changed to accommodate the current climate of communications development. He outlines how the FCC will continue to operate as a legislative body to encourage continued growth in telecommunications.

W hen the Federal Communications Commission (FCC) was officially established in 1934, it served as a government agency to address issues of the relationship among the government, the public, and the companies involved in technology development and content distribution. Throughout the 1980s, deregulation of many important industries in the United States changed the relationship between government and industry and effectively limited the role of government as a "regulator" of business. Instead, "marketplace rules" were allowed to gain preeminence, and the power of business and industry to set its own rules was seen as the most effective means of spurring economic growth and competition. The passage of the Telecommunications Act of 1996 was the culmination of the new relationship of business and government, which fully complied with deregulation and marketplace rules. With less of a need for the government agency of the FCC to monitor and control telecommunications practices, the agency's mission has changed.

Peter Huber outlines how the establishment of the FCC came from a tradition of government control over communications industries. He cites how the evolution of communication technologies has now bypassed the ability of the government to be an effective monitor of change, and he asserts that deregulation has made many government agencies obsolete. Based on his evaluation of past evidence, he argues that the FCC is no longer necessary to the effective operation of the telecommunications industries.

William E. Kennard contends that the FCC has redefined its goals and mission and that it now acts in the interest of encouraging competition. In his view, the FCC is more vital today as a catalyst for business than it was in the past. His selection outlines the FCC's goals for the new millennium and predicts what the FCC's agenda will be, so that this agenda is indeed compatible with deregulatory practices and the Telecommunications Act.

In Kennard's remarks, he mentions Mark Fowler, former FCC chair under President Ronald Reagan, who also engineered the deregulation of the media industries. In a famous and often quoted statement, Fowler described the television set as an appliance that functioned as a "toaster," meaning that it was an artifact in the home that warranted no more consideration than any other appliance. His remark has been criticized heavily over the years by people who say that communications technologies play a greater role in defining the relationship among media providers and audiences and that some agency (like the FCC) should exercise control over such powerful forms of communication.

This fundamental social issue of who, if anyone, should oversee such important media underscores the debates concerning the effectiveness of the FCC. When George Bush was president, he began a move to eliminate the FCC and place jurisdiction for communications media under the Commerce Department. Because the president appoints all five members of the FCC and names the chair, presidential and party philosophy has much to do with the direction of the FCC and its status as a government agency.

This issue warrants discussion on the effectiveness of governmental agencies and the role they play in creating the content, technologies, and business operations surrounding all communication media. While the FCC is powerless to create law, it does suggest and recommend actions to Congress for enactment.

Can any organization adapt to a world in which the media technologies are being developed faster than any bureaucratic organization can cope with suggested changes? Will the FCC be able to encourage competition in an age in which market forces tend to eliminate the smaller, less powerful companies? Can the FCC be an effective agency in a world that increasingly sees telecommunications issues expanding beyond the boundaries of the United States?

Law and Disorder in Cyberspace

Until 1996 the telecosm was governed by laws written half a century ago. The rules for the telephone industry dated back to 1887. They had been written at a time when land, air, water, and energy all seemed abundant, while the telecosm seemed small and crowded, a place of scarcity, cartel, and monopoly, one that required strict rationing and tight, central control.

In the last decade, however, glass and silicon have amplified beyond all prior recognition our power to communicate. Engineers double the capacity of the wires and the radios about every two years, again and again and again. New technology has replaced scarcity with abundance and cartels with competition.

The electronic web of connection that is now being woven amongst us all is a catalyst for change more powerful than Gutenberg's press or Goebbels's radio. Every constraint of the old order is crumbling. The limitless, anarchic possibilities of the telecosm contrast sharply with the limits to growth we now encounter at every turn in the physical world.

In early 1996 Congress passed the most important piece of economic legislation of the twentieth century. The Telecommunications Act of 1996 runs some one hundred pages. The Act's ostensible purpose is to open markets to competition and deregulate them. It may eventually have that effect. The process of deregulating, however, seems to require more regulation than ever. The FCC [Federal Communications Commission] no longer aspires to immortality through its work. Like Woody Allen, it aspires to immortality through not dying.

It is time for fundamental change. It is time for the Federal Communications Commission to go.

The Future and the Past

The telecosm—the universe of communications and computers—is expanding faster than any other technocosm has ever expanded before. It is the telephone unleashed, the personal computer connected, and the television brought down to human scale at last. Its capacity to carry information has expanded a millionfold in the last decade or two. It will expand another millionfold in our lifetime—or perhaps a billionfold. No one really knows. The only certainty is that the change will be enormous.

This change is characterized by a paradox: It is both fragmentation and convergence.

The old integrated, centralized media are being broken apart. Terminals—dumb endpoints to the network—are giving way to "seminals"—nodes of equal rank that can process, switch, store, and retrieve information with a power that was once lodged exclusively in the massive switches and mainframe computers housed in fortified basements. This is the fragmentation.

At the same time the functions of these nodes are coming together. In digital systems a bit is a bit, whether it represents a hiccup in a voice conversation, a digit in a stock quote, or a pixel of light in a rerun of *I Love Lucy*. This is the convergence.

Then there is the law. Until 1996 most of telephony was viewed as a "natural monopoly." The high cost of fixed plant, the steadily declining average cost of service, and the need for all customers to interconnect with one another made monopoly seem inevitable. The broadcast industry was viewed as a natural oligopoly. It depended on inherently "scarce" airwaves, and was therefore populated by a small, government-appointed elite.

The FCC and comparable state-level commissions were established in the 1920s and 1930s to ration the scarcity and police the monopoly. The administrative structures, their statutory mandates, and the whole logic of commission control reflected the political attitudes of the New Deal. Markets didn't work; government did. Competition was wasteful; central planning was efficient. A fateful choice was made: Marketplace and common law were rejected. Central planning and the commission were embraced.

The common law evolves from the bottom up. Private action comes first. Rules follow, when private conflicts arise and are brought to court. Commission law was to be top-down. A government corps of managers, lawyers, economists, and technicians would settle in at the FCC first. Private action would follow later, when authorized. Common law is created by the accretion of small rulings in discrete, crystallized controversies. Commission law would be published in elaborate statutes and ten-thousand-page rule books; while these were being written, the world would wait. Common law centers on contract and property, legal concepts that are themselves creations of the common law. Commission law would center on public edicts, licenses, and permits. Common law is developed and enforced largely by private litigants. Commission law would come to court only at the end of the process, when public prosecutors filed suits against private miscreants.

Common law would have suited the American ethic of governance far better, particularly in matters so directly related to free speech. But between 1927 and 1934, when the FCC was erected, the winds of history were blowing in the opposite direction. National socialism, right-wing or left, seemed more efficient, the only workable approach to modern industrialism. Around the globe, people in power persuaded themselves that the technical complexities of broadcasting, and the natural-monopoly economics of telephony, had to be managed through centralized control. The night of totalitarian government, always said to be descending on America, came to earth only in Europe. But America was darkened by some of the same shadows. One was the FCC.

Once in place, the FCC grew and grew. Today it has 2,200 full-time employees and a $200 million budget—more offices, more employees, and more money than at any other time in its history. As competition increases, monopolies fade, and the supposed scarcity of spectrum is engineered into vast abundance, the Commission just gets bigger. An institution created to ration scarcity now thrives by brokering plenty. It is an Alice-in-Wonderland sort of world, in which the less reason the Queen has to exist at all, the more corpulent and powerful she becomes.

For the next several years at least, the FCC will have the most important mission in Washington. Wireline and wireless telephony, broadcasting, cable, and significant aspects of network computing together generate some $200 billion in revenues a year. For better or worse, the FCC will profoundly influence how they all develop. And in so doing it will exert a pivotal influence over the entire infrastructure of the information age and thus the economy, culture, and society of the twenty-first century.

The faster that power is dissipated, the better it will be for America.

Deconstructing the Telecosm

The beginning of the end was cable television. Cable demonstrated that spectrum could be bottled, and made abundant. Cable refused to be merely "broadcaster" or merely "carrier." It threatened all the old regulatory paradigms. It was just too capacious and flexible for regulators, even with the relatively primitive technology it used at that time. Now cable is moving into telephony. Meanwhile, by boosting the capacities of their wires, phone companies are poised to move into video. They already carry most of the Internet traffic, which is television in slow motion.

Wireless services are changing even faster. Once dedicated largely to feeding the idiot box, wireless is now the flourishing center of cellular telephony, direct broadcast satellite, wireless cable, and personal communications services. Spectrum is gradually being privatized and dezoned. The new owners are using their wireless bandwidth to provide whatever services they like, to whichever customers they choose.

The fundamentals of deregulation are now clear. The concepts are simple. They can be implemented quickly.

First, throw open the markets. For wireless, this means privatizing the critical asset—spectrum—by giving it away or (better still) selling it. For wires, it means letting anyone deploy new metal and glass alongside the old. Contrary to what Congress assumed for half a century, no commission is needed to protect against "wasteful duplication," "ruinous competition," or "inefficient deployment of resources." Markets take care of that.

Second, dezone the bandwidth. On wire or wireless, a bit is a bit. No government office should zone some bandwidth for pictures, some for voice, some for data. The market can work this out far better than any central planner.

Won't new robber barons then buy up all the wires, corner the spectrum, jack up prices, ruin service, and impoverish consumers? With the entire industry in ferment, with engineers doubling the capacity of every medium every few years, and with the telecosm expanding at big-bang rates, these fears are utterly implausible. But in any event, the traditional antitrust laws will remain in place. For all practical purposes, antitrust law is common law. It addresses specific problems in courts, not commissions. It is decentralized, adaptable, and resilient. Sclerotic commissions just get in the way. Indeed, for decades the FCC has legitimized telecom practices that antitrust courts would never have tolerated in its absence.

Ironically, the Commission can justify much of its current frenetic activity by blaming its predecessors. If the airwaves hadn't been nationalized in 1927, they wouldn't have to be sold off today. If the FCC hadn't spent half a century protecting telephone monopolies, it wouldn't have to dismantle them now. If the Commission hadn't spent so long separating carriage from broadcast, broadcast from cable, and cable from carriage, it wouldn't have to be desegregating those media today. If it hadn't worked so diligently to outlaw competitive entry back then, it wouldn't have to labor so hard to promote it now.

I-broke-it-then-so-I'll-fix-it-now has a certain logic to it, even if the confession of past breaking is always much less emphatic than the promise of future fix. But the fixing somehow always seems to take as long, or longer, than the breaking. And while the Commission plans and plans for perfect competition, competition itself waits uselessly in the wings.

The telecosm would be vastly more competitive today if Congress had just stayed out of session in 1927, in 1934, in 1984, and again in 1992—if Congress had never created the Federal Radio Commission, never folded it into the FCC, never extended the Commission's jurisdiction to cable, and never expanded the Commission's powers over cable further still. The 1996 legislation guarantees that the Commission will grow in size and influence for the rest of this decade while it uproots the anticompetitive vineyard planted and cultivated by its predecessors.

But the uprooting should be done quickly. Five years is time enough; ten would be too long. And then? Then the Commission should shut its doors, once and for all, and never darken American liberty again.

Common Law for the Telecosm

Who, then, will maintain order in all these areas when the Commission is gone? Private actors and private litigants, common-law courts, and the market. It is the Commission that must go, not the rule of law.

We still need laws to defend the property rights of people who lay wires and build transmitters, to enforce contracts and carriage agreements, to defend the freedom to speak and to listen, and to protect copyright and privacy. Anarchy works no better in virtuality than in actuality. The question is not whether there will be rules of law, but where they will come from.

Commissions proclaim the "public interest, convenience, and necessity." They issue general edicts. They publish rules in a massive Code of Federal Regulations. Common law, by contrast, evolves out of rulings handed down by many different judges in many different courtrooms. The good rules gain acceptance by the community at large, as people conform their conduct to rulings that make practical sense. In this kind of jurisprudence, constitutions and codes provide, at most, a broad, general mandate to develop the law by adjudication. They operate like the Bill of Rights or the Sherman Act.

Commission law has been tried. Not just in the telecosm but in command-and-control economies around the globe. Like Communism, commission law has failed. It is rigid, slow, and—despite all the earnest expertise of bureaucrats—ignorant. Market forces, mediated by common law, elicit information faster and more reliably. Markets constantly probe new technology, try out new forms of supply, and assess demand with a determination, precision, and persistence that no commission can ever match. Property-centered, contract-centered, common-law markets allow people to get on with life first and litigate later, if they have to. Most of the time they don't. Rules evolve spontaneously in the marketplace and are mostly accepted by common consent. Common-law courts just keep things tidy at the edges.

The one strength of commission law is that it reduces uncertainty all around. But only because the market must wait for the commission to invent a whole framework of law up front. That often takes years, and the framework is always rigid and inadequate. In a universe where technology transforms itself every few months, where supply and demand grow apace, where new trillion-dollar economies can emerge from thin air in a decade or so—in such a universe, uncertainty is a sign of health and vigor. In a place like that, nothing except common law can keep up. The law must build itself the old-fashioned way, through action in the market first and reaction in the courts thereafter.

If that suggestion seems outlandish, it is only because the FCC has been around so long that people can no longer imagine life without it. Once Henry the Eighth's licensing of printing presses had become routine, it would have seemed equally outlandish to suggest that such an unfamiliar, complicated, and important technology might be left to open markets and common-law courts. When it was created in 1887, the Interstate Commerce Commission seemed essential to proper management of railroads. But when it was abolished in early 1996, hardly anyone even noticed. We never did create a Federal Computer Commission. The computer industry has nonetheless developed interconnection rules and open systems, set reasonable prices, and delivered more hardware and more service to more people faster than any other industry in history.

Now, in the 1990s, with the telecosm growing explosively all around us, with the cacophony of free markets already drowning out the reedy proclamations of a senescent Commission, the only outlandish proposal is that we should keep it.

It is time to finish the job. The Commission must go.

NO ↩

William E. Kennard

Statement of William E. Kennard

Introduction

... Thank you for coming this afternoon.

This is my third annual "agenda" statement as Chairman. In preparing for today I looked at my two earlier statements, and, whereas those statements were primarily about promises made, today's statement is about promises kept.

I can report that the state of the network is excellent. Whether wired, wireless, broadcast or satellite, this growing "network of networks" that functions as the nation's central nervous system is ubiquitous, agile and robust.

The network is characterized by compatibility, co-location and interconnection, and it has become a virtual Cuisinart of convergence. It allows competitors to cooperate and compete at the same time, it transmits movies where only voice once traveled, and it provides thousands of different on-ramps to the Internet.

There also are many fewer bottlenecks—clogged arteries—than when I first took office, and we are performing "open network surgery" on those that remain.

American consumers are significantly better off because of this network. For example.

- Directly or indirectly, one-third of our economic growth can be attributed to the digital economy and this network. That translates into jobs and the maintenance of families.
- The entry price to the Internet may drop from a one thousand dollar personal computer to a one hundred dollar palm top.
- Tele-medicine, tele-learning and tele-commuting are no longer speculations, but are real contributors to our daily lives.
- Our offices operate differently because of this network. Ninety percent of electronic commerce is business-to-business commerce, and whole layers of the business world are being replaced by buffers and browsers.
- Now I read that our homes and cars are about to be linked to the Internet, so that my refrigerator will read bar codes, and tell me when I am out of milk.

From Federal Communications Commission. *Agenda 2000 and The Third Millennium Commission.* Statement, January 19, 2000. Washington, D.C.: U.S. Government Printing Office, 2000.

Several years ago one of my predecessors made a remark, controversial at the time, that the television should be regulated just like a toaster, as just another appliance, and that it should be regarded as such.

Now it looks like my house may be just a toaster, but a very intelligent one.

Mark Fowler was more prescient than he knew.

Third Millennium

These phenomena have been variously called part of the Knowledge Age or the Internet Age or the Digital Age, and something larger than Guttenberg.

Whatever the label, we know that something really big is taking place. One observer called it a "10.5" on the Richter scale of social change... and another, a sea change in our culture.

Whether the Internet is a new level in human consciousness, or just a toaster, it did not just happen by chance. We can trace it back to the infrastructure bed of our national network, upon which it rests.

For example, I do not think the Internet explosion would have been possible without the decisions over the last twenty-five years to deregulate customers' premises equipment, such as telephones, or to leave services beyond "basic" telephone services, what we call enhanced services, unregulated.

Similarly, I do not think the Internet would have developed in the way that it has without the divestiture in 1984, because without the divestiture, the competitive long distance networks would not have been laid.

Finally, our decision to leave the Internet itself unregulated allowed the Internet to be open and unfettered, and contributed greatly to its vibrancy today.

My point is that what we do here at the beginning of the Third Millennium really matters. Third Millennium society is being shaped today. Whether it will be an open society and an opportunity society, or some alternative, turns in part on the daily, sometimes technical and prosaic, decisions we make here at the Commission.

Our "network of networks" may be a defining event that marks the beginning of the Third Millennium. It could be a seed-bed that bears fruit for decades to come.

As long as I am Chairman, the Commission will continue to be a part of this vision.

1996 Telecommunications Act

The Telecommunications Act of 1996 has contributed to the success of this network of networks.

There have been three phases to the roll-out of the 1996 Act: rulemaking, testing those rules in court, and implementation.

When I first started serving as Chairman, we had to finish writing the rules, and major parts of the Act were being reviewed by the Supreme Court. Reports of the Act's premature death were rampant.

But we have seen our way into the clear. The rules of the road are virtually complete, we have prevailed in the courts, and our authority is settled. We are now implementing the Act and seeing the results. I can say with pride that the Act is working.

This is nowhere more evident than in the bedrock ABCs of my Chairmanship: Access, Broadband and Competition.

Access: The E-Rate program is bringing its second successful year to a close, and now provides connectivity for one million public school classrooms. This program is a down-payment on our children's futures, and on the skills needed to keep our high-tech economy going. In another area of access, this last year we increased the access to the network by the 54 million Americans with disabilities.

Broadband: The American people want high-speed access to high-quality programming, and broadband to every home is critical to that vision. The Commission wisely withheld regulation of most advanced services, while making sure that certain features, such as the ability of one company to deliver broadband to the home over the same line another company is using to provide basic telephone service, are available to all competitors and incumbents alike. Video competition is still getting underway, but, as demonstrated by our video market competition report last week, progress is being made.

Competition: Local exchange markets are opening to competition, signaled first by Bell Atlantic's demonstration, in its application to provide long distance service in New York, that its New York market is open to competition. More applications are on the way. We have reviewed and approved several mergers over the last year, after we ensured that they will not impair the FCC's responsibility to encourage wider availability of competitive options and the more rapid deployment of advanced services. Finally, this last year we pumped new spectrum into the marketplace, so that today, over 75% of Americans have a choice of five wireless providers.

Promises Kept

Our aggressive implementation of the Act is generating new classes of competitors, new industries and lower prices.

I have just come this morning from a meeting of competitive local exchange carriers, or CLECs. The energy and excitement there were tremendous. Clearly that industry existed before our implementation of the 1996 Act, but never on this scale, and never at this level of intensity.

CLECs invested $18 billion in 1998, and serviced 3.4% of all telephone lines in the second quarter of 1999. This is a small but growing percentage, for they were adding a million lines a quarter in mid-1999. Their revenue share of the local service market was six percent.

In addition to CLECs, there are now DLECs (competitive local data carriers), as well as whole industries of equipment and applications that have suddenly become active players in servicing consumers.

We also have deployed spectrum for thousands of licenses for new and innovative services, such as PCS, LMDS, and DARS.

The forces unleashed by our competitive policies have resulted in more consumer choices at home, such as wireless and video connections; at the office, such as high-speed data networks; and at schools and libraries, such as the connectivity delivered through the E- Rate.

In addition to increased choices, consumers also have benefited from falling prices. Since 1994, wireless prices have dropped 40%, and wireless subscriber-ship has quadrupled.

Long-distance rates have dropped nearly 56% in real terms since divestiture in 1984. In the last two years alone, we have reduced access charges by $3.1 billion, resulting in the five-cents-a-minute offerings available to every American this very day.

Finally, partly because of the downward pressure we have brought to bear on international settlement rates, international call rates dropped 25% from 1996 to 1998.

New York State

For a look at the future of the 1996 Act, look at New York State. That is where the Act is working now. Competitive local carriers there already serve over 1.3 million business and residential telephone lines, and over 55% of those lines are delivered over the competitors' own facilities. Worldcom alone has over 200,000 local unbundled lines. AT&T was scheduled to add 30,000 unbundled lines [in] (December [1999]), for an estimated total of 80,000 unbundled lines.

Incumbents

I also want to tip my hat to the Bell Companies. For all the differences the Commission has had through the years with the incumbent local exchange carriers, we should acknowledge that they laid the marvelous infrastructure that has made many of these competitive advances possible, and that has allowed us to become the first "Internet Nation."

And since the Supreme Court ended the debate as to whether Congress actually meant for the Bell Companies to open their markets, the companies, in a welcome change, have begun to refocus their energies toward doing just that.

I now look forward to working with these same incumbents as vigorous competitors in the new digital economy.

Agenda 2000

Finally, for the year 2000, the pace at the Commission will not slacken.

Again, looking at the ABCs of my agenda . . .

Access: We will initiate the year with Agenda action on Low Power FM and broadcast EEO [equal employment opportunity] rules, both of which increase the access of Americans to the airwaves or to the industry. During the year, we will address additional access by Americans with disabilities, access for under-served areas, and access by the public through the broadcast public interest obligations. We also will be working through the Development Initiative to increase the access to international networks by under-served nations.

Broadband: We will be looking closely at industry's progress in making digital televisions compatible with cable. We also will be taking steps to bring high-speed broadband service to rural areas, and to expand the opportunities for entrepreneurs to build wireless webs.

Competition: We anticipate completing our review of several major merger proposals, including those of USWest/Qwest, Bell Atlantic/GTE, Sprint/Worldcom, CBS/Viacom and AT&T/Media One. We have received an application from SBC [Communications Inc.], and we anticipate receiving an application from Bell South, to provide long distance service. Finally, addressing access charge reform, including a coalition plan, CALLS [Coalition for Affordable Local and Long-Distance Service], is high on our list.

Finally, we are committed to implementing the Strategic Plan we presented to Congress.... We have begun to reinvent the Commission along functional lines, and have launched the Enforcement Bureau and the Consumer Information Bureau. We have a team working on a possible Licensing Bureau. We also have internal teams tackling specific Commission issues, such as electronic filing, merger review, the biennial review, under-served populations and spectrum efficiency.

Closing

In light of these achievements, I think we can say with confidence that in 1999, "We delivered," and that the Third Millennium has begun at the Federal Communications Commission.

POSTSCRIPT

Should the FCC Be Abolished?

The FCC is somewhat unique in its capacity to effect change toward communications technologies and practices. It was established to provide guidance to Congress to enact socially responsible policies and procedures, but because it cannot legislate change itself, it has remained a relatively weak federal agency. In many other countries, the same regulatory role is often given to organizations that have more power to safeguard the public's interest or to be accountable to government. For example, in some countries, the minister of information or head of the post, telegraph, and telecommunication (PTT) organization functions similar to the way a cabinet post would in America's presidential power hierarchy.

The five commissioners of the FCC often have legal backgrounds, which reflect a strong commitment to constitutional law. Increasingly, their familiarity with issues of international trade is becoming a more important component to their effective discussions. While each commissioner serves for a specified term, the appointees tend to favor the political affiliation of the president, who has the power to appoint new commissioners during the presidential term. As a result, as terms expire and new individuals are named to the FCC, political power and industrial policy come to be reflected in the deliberations of each group.

The FCC has a powerful Internet site that allows a user to navigate through such diverse pages as the biographies of the commissioners, to the specific publications produced by the organization. The key topics for discussion at any given time are also available by contacting www.fcc.gov.

Many of the publications of the FCC are available on the Web site, or, at a later date, through the Government Printing Office (GPO). The Telecommunications Act of 1996 is rather cumbersome, but it does constitute the present rules for telecommunications operation. Additionally, the July 10, 1985, House of Representatives publication "Media Mergers and Takeovers: The FCC and the Public Interest: Hearing Before the Subcommittee on Telecommunications Protection and Finance of the Committee on Energy and Commerce" (GPO 1996) has many important points to make with regard to how the FCC envisions its own role as an arbiter of the current flurry of megamergers in U.S. media businesses.

The question of whether or not the FCC should be abolished is likely to remain a key topic in the future. When the presidency is in the hands of the Democrats, one might expect to see that many of the goals outlined by Kennard remain constant. If, however, the Republicans gain the presidency, one might expect to see greater emphasis on competition and marketplace rules, as defined by the Republican agenda.

National Association of Broadcasters

The National Association of Broadcasters (NAB) is dedicated to promoting the interests of broadcasters. Some of the pages found at this site include information on television parental guidelines, laws and regulations, and research on current issues.

http://www.nab.org

The National Cable Television Association

The National Cable Television Association (NCTA) is dedicated to promoting the interests of the cable television industry. This site contains discussions of current issues and updates on issues of importance to the NCTA.

http://www.ncta.com

Telecom Information Resources

This site has over 7,000 links to telecommunication resources throughout the world. At this site you will find information on service providers, government agencies, government policies, economic policies, and much more.

http://china.si.umich.edu/telecom/telecom-info.html

PART 5

Media Business

*F*reedom *of speech and the press makes producing news and enter-tainment content somewhat different from manufacturing widgets. It is important to realize that media industries are businesses and that they must be profitable to be able to thrive. However, are there special stan-dards to which we should hold media industries? Are the structures of media industries responsive to the public's interest? How do monopolies affect media content? What is the primary function of advertising?*

- Media Monopolies: Are the Dangers of Concentration Overstated?

- Should the Internet Facilitate a Free Exchange of Information?

- Do Public Relations Practitioners Provide a Valuable Service to the Public?

ISSUE 14

Media Monopolies: Are the Dangers of Concentration Overstated?

YES: Eli M. Noam and Robert N. Freeman, from "The Media Monopoly and Other Myths," *Television Quarterly* (vol. 29, no. 1, 1997)

NO: Ben H. Bagdikian, from "The Realities of Media Concentration and Control," *Television Quarterly* (vol. 29, no. 3, 1998)

ISSUE SUMMARY

YES: Professors Eli M. Noam and Robert N. Freeman contend that there will be more competition in the future among U.S. media markets, not less. Using U.S. Department of Justice procedures for identifying overly concentrated markets, they demonstrate that media industries are only moderately concentrated and advise that such concern should focus on local, not national, media.

NO: Ben H. Bagdikian, a Pulitzer Prize-winning journalist states that the public needs to be aware of the control that international conglomerates like General Electric and Rupert Murdoch have over the media. One should not assume that technology will be the savior, since it too is subject to the domination of the same conglomerates.

The Telecommunications Act of 1996 was designed to increase telecommunications industry competition, primarily by removing barriers between what are now distinct industries and by reducing restrictions on ownership of multiple stations, sometimes in the same market. Yet the media industry has a special function defined by its journalistic endeavors and protected by the Constitution as freedom of the press. Can this restructuring of the American media industry threaten the ability of that industry to fulfill its surveillance function?

The long tradition of private, rather than governmental, ownership of media in the United States stems from the legacy of libertarian philosophy, which argued that truth would emerge from a diversity of voices in the communication marketplace. These diverse voices, says this traditional philosophy, can best provide the public with information on which to base its decisions. Another important legal foundation for broadcast outlets has been the requirement that broadcast stations "operate in the public interest," which was imposed upon them due to their use of a scarce spectrum—the public airwaves.

In the following selection, Eli M. Noam and Robert N. Freeman question the basic premise of whether or not media are becoming more concentrated. Despite some concerns about concentration with the local media and with companies such as Microsoft, Noam and Freeman maintain that once the initial spate of mergers has been accomplished, the barriers that have reduced competition will foster a new competitive environment.

According to Ben H. Bagdikian in the second selection, large corporations are gaining control of the media at an alarming rate. Control of media by a few giant corporations is tighter than it was when the first edition of his book *The Media Monopoly* (now in its fifth edition) came out in 1983. These dominant corporations, through their control of news and other public information, can censor public awareness of the dangers of information control by the corporate elite. When the central interests of controlling corporations are at stake, Bagdikian further argues, news becomes weighted toward what serves the economic and political interests of the corporations that own the media, not the public interest. The concept of media as public trust seems to be lost in the new era of corporate restructuring.

Note that several issues are intertwined. Is media concentration increasing? If so, is it necessarily a problem? We may not think so if economies of scale reduce the prices we pay for our media. We may, however, have problems if most of the media outlets in our community are owned by the same corporation. What implication does concentration have for news coverage? For example, is a chain owner more likely to impose a one-size-fits-all perspective on its coverage of local events, thus reducing diversity? Is a local or a national corporation more likely to stand up to attempts to control editorial content by advertisers or other powerful people? The Telecommunications Act of 1996 has unleashed a torrent of mergers and acquisitions. Is the promise of erasing traditional monopolies, which will reduce prices for services, being realized? Or has the law opened the door for new forms of monopoly?

Eli M. Noam and
Robert N. Freeman

 **YES**

The Media Monopoly and Other Myths

It's been said that generals always fight the last war, not the new one. And the question is whether media critics sometimes do that, too. For many years, we were worried about the concentration of private power over the media. The fear was a media mogul with a political agenda: a William Randolph Hearst, who started a war and ran himself for Mayor, Governor, and President. And that was just using newspapers. Later, when television was controlled by three networks, all within ten blocks of each other in Manhattan, the fear of control over hearts, minds, pocketbooks, and voting booths was amplified from the left and right. And today, with electronic media becoming smart, powerful, and pervasive, and with media mergers reported every week, the same fear is around more than ever, that in the end there will be only four media companies left in the world, and running the world, half of them owned by a guy named Rupert.

Ben Bagdikian expresses this fear in his article *The Media Monopoly*, published in *Television Quarterly* (Volume 28, Number 4). He pointed to the growing size of media mergers, the shrinking number of major media corporations, and their increasing diversification into multiple branches of media. He discounted the relevance of the diverse and publicly accessible Internet by pointing to the small share of Americans that have the equipment to get online. He also expressed frustration that the Telecommunications Act of 1996 has so far led to more cooperation than competition.

To evaluate all this, it is important to understand how the media world has evolved through stages. In the past of electronic media, twenty years ago, we had *limited* media, with only three networks, one phone company, and one computer company. Today, we are in the stage of multi-channel media, with many dozens of TV channels and with multiple phone networks. But this is still not the end of the story. The third stage, and the one we are entering now, is *cyber-media*. Cyber-text is already established. Cyber-audio is here. And cyber-telephony and cyber-video are emerging. In time, this will led us to an entirely different system of mass media. Yet governments, media companies, and media critics are still looking backward to the good old days of scarcity.

The discussion over media concentration often has that anachronistic flavor. So let's first look at the facts. Yes, there have been lots of mergers. Some are troubling, some are not. Going beyond the specific deal, the more important question is, in the aggregate, have American media become more concentrated?

Despite the conventional wisdom, the answer is not an obvious "yes." First, while the fish in the pond have grown in size, the pond did grow, too, and faster. The growth of the information industry has been 8% faster than inflation since 1987. Second, all these separate ponds are becoming more of a large lake, as the technological and regulatory dikes between them fall.

The combined share of the top 10 companies in the US information industry declined from 59% in 1987 to 39% today. This is a totally different conclusion from those who claim that US media are now controlled by ten firms. In 1979, AT&T alone accounted for a full quarter of the entire media and information industry (*Table 1*). Today, even with two divestitures, AT&T is larger in dollar terms, but now commands only 7% of the total industry. IBM tripled in the past 15 years, but its share in the media and information industry dropped by one third, to less than 10%. CBS used to have 2%.

Table 1

Share of Information Industry

	1979	1987	1997
AT&T	24%	16%	7%
IBM	14%	17%	9%
CBS/Westinghouse	2%	1%	1%
Bell Atlantic		3.2% ↘	
		→	4%
Nynex		3.7% ↗	
Disney	0.5%	1% ↘	
		→	2%
ABC	0.2%	1% ↗	
Microsoft	0.0%	0.1%	0.7%
TCI	0.0%	0.5%	0.7%

A decade later, even after mergers with Westinghouse and Infinity, the new company has only 1%. Bell Atlantic and Nynex both used to have about 3.5% each. A decade later, after their merger, their combined share is barely higher, at 4%. The major exception was Disney/CapCities/ABC, with a share that is now twice the combined share of these firms in 1979. But it's still only 2%. Also, both Microsoft and TCI grew from nothing to each capture 1% of the industry. But little of that growth was due to mergers.

When it comes to concentration, views are strong, talk is cheap, but numbers are scarce. Therefore, we have gotten our hands dirty by collecting the actual market share numbers, industry by industry, company by company, for 60 sub-industries from book publishing to film production to microprocessors, in order to trace the concentration trends over the past 15 years. We then aggregated these data into broader sectors such as telecommunications, video distribution, etc. And we aggregated those sectoral figures again into an overall industry concentration trend. This is probably the most detailed study ever of media concentration in America.

What did we find? Surprisingly, the overall concentration of the information industry did not increase, but declined somewhat in the past decade (*Table 2*).

Table 2

Total Information Sector Concentration (weighted aggregates)

	1986	1990	1995
Top 4 Firms	52%	49%	50%
HH Index	1839	1347	1262

To confirm this result, we used two separate measures of concentration: the combined share of the top four firms in each sector, and the Justice Department's HHI index, a more sensitive but less intuitive measure. An HHI under 1,000 means a market is unconcentrated, an HHI over 1,800 means a market is highly concentrated, between 1,000 and 1,800, a market is moderately concentrated.

If one looks at the classic mass media industries alone (excluding telecommunications, computers, software, and equipment) they did increase in concentration (*Table 3*), but remained unconcentrated by Justice Department standards. The main factors increasing these concentration figures were cable television systems (accounting for half) and home video (accounting for 20%).

Table 3

Mass Media Sector Concentration (weighted aggregates)

	1986	1990	1995
Top 4 Firms	33%	27.5%	40%
HH Index	514	491	574

The greatest drops occurred in telecommunications services, computers, TV programming, and music (*Table 4*). In long distance, AT&T's shares dropped from 80% to just over half. Soon, new entrants into mobile and local telephony will gradually further that trend. In computers, the market shifted away from mainframes to micro computers, where no top firm controls much more than 10%. This shift also lowered entry barriers in the software market, which used to be vertically integrated with hardware, reducing the share of the top four firms to about one third. Concentration in TV programing dropped with the launch of new broadcast and cable networks. The share of the top four cable channel firms dropped from two thirds to about 40%. In pay cable, the share of Time Warner shrank slightly, but it still controls half the market. In music, the share of the top four labels dropped from 80% to 60%.

Table 4

Declining Concentration
(4 firm shares)

	1986	1990	1995
Telecom. Services	77%	76%	73%
Computer Hardware	56%	45%	45%
Computer Software	42%	39%	35%
3 Major TV Networks	70%	63%	53%
Basic Cable Channel Firms	67%	53%	39%
Pay Cable (Time Warner)	57%	57%	51%

On the other hand, concentration *increased* in other industries (*Table 5*). Microsoft controls 90% of the microcomputer operating system market, for all the talk about platform independent Java. This is the Bill Gates problem.

❧

There is also a cable issue. The share of the top four cable firms grew from one-fourth in 1979 to nearly two-thirds today. That's a lot of gatekeeping power, though they now must contend with satellite TV firms. Concentration also increased in TV station ownership and retail bookstores, and more than doubled in radio station ownership and book publishing. But the top four firms still have only about a quarter of these markets, as measured by revenue. In terms of stations, the largest radio firm has 102 stations, which sounds like a lot, but there are over 12,000 stations nationwide.

In other industries, concentration held relatively steady (*Table 6*). Film production remained fairly concentrated, with the top four firms controlling

Table 5

Rising Concentration (4 firm shares)

	1986*	1990	1995
Microcomputer			
Operating Systems	55%	85%	90%
Cable TV Distribution	37%	46%	60%
TV Stations	15%	16%	26%
Radio Stations	8%	9%	20%
Book Publishing	15%	30%	33%
Book Stores	20%	23%	26%

*The 1986 column actually contains Microsoft's 1984 market share.

60%. The movie theater, newspaper and magazine markets remained relatively unconcentrated, with the top four firms accounting for a quarter of sales.

Therefore, it cannot simply be said that US media have become, in general, more concentrated. Still, the next question then must be raised: even if a firm does not dominate any specific market, could it not be overpowering by being a medium sized firm in every market? The fear is that vertically integrated firms will dominate by having their tentacles in each pie. But in economic terms, this can only happen if a firm has real market power in at least one market, which it then extends and leverages into other markets. And such single-firm dominance of a market is becoming rare, as we have seen.

Table 6

Stable Concentration (4 firm shares)

	1986	1990	1995
Film Production	62%	62%	61%
Cinemas	29%	29%	29%
Newspapers	25%	25%	26%
Magazines	23%	22%	22%

One exception is cable TV, where TCI and Time Warner can still favor their own channels over those of competitors. In New York, Time Warner could have shut out Murdoch's Fox News Channel, as a rival to its own CNN. This problem may disappear with satellite TV. The second important exception is Microsoft, which could extend its market power from computer operating systems to become the gatekeeper of other cyber-media. If this control persists with no competitive relief, Microsoft will become the major media policy headache of the 21st century.

But where markets are competitive, vertical integration makes little sense. Disney should not earmark its best programs for ABC if other networks offer more money. Conversely, for Disney to force its lemons on the ABC television network would only hurt the company. This creates major centrifugal forces inside the organization which in a competitive environment will lead to a breakup of the company. In a competitive environment, media firms must divest and focus for optimal efficiency. To attract viewers, content production will separate from distribution, and news writing will separate from political lobbying.

And what about all those famous synergies? These have been more asserted than shown. In announcing its mega-merger, Disney CEO Michael Eisner invoked the word not less than five times in four consecutive sentences, like a mantra. But most of those cross-promotional benefits—film, books, toys, etc.—could be established by simple contracts. You don't need $15 billion mergers to create them.

Twenty years ago, CBS bought the New York Yankees baseball team and the big publisher Simon & Schuster, all to achieve those same vaunted synergies. Nothing came of it. Sony bought Columbia Pictures and Records, to merge film and music with consumer electronics, and lost billions on movies. Its share in music fell from one-fourth to one-sixth. In Time Warner's case, the synergies became negative as the rap music business dragged down the respectability of the news magazines; today, the company is a collection of feuding fiefdoms. Disney, Viacom, and News Corp. will get there too, after their empire-building leaders have left the scene.

Although media companies have become more diversified, they can only exploit cross-ownership for so long as they retain market power in distribution. While the Telecommunications Act of 1996 led to an immediate spurt of media mergers, it also opened the door to competition between cable, wired, and both satellite-based and terrestrial wireless distribution systems. Such developments will not be as instantaneous as the media deals. But in time they will undermine the economic power and rationale for diversified media corporations.

⚜

Does this mean there is no concentration problem? No. But the real problems in media concentration are not national, but local. 98.5% of American cities have only one newspaper. They rarely editoralize about that. 98% of American homes have no choice in their cable provider. Alternative local residential phone service may be coming, but is not here yet. Local radio concentration has increased considerably since the Telecommunications Act of 1996 relaxed local ownership ceilings, and is more of a problem than national radio concentration.

None of this is surprising. Local media are the weak link in the media revolution. Competing national media lead to narrow-casing. Programs are expensive, and must be produced for the world, not just for a town, in order to make money. Media companies must aggregate increasingly scarce eyeballs nationally and internationally. That's also true for cyber-media, which have been world-wide from the beginning. And local media are even more in trouble in the future. In cyber-television, advertising can be customized and targeted, and advertisers will migrate away from local newspapers as advertising vehicles.

But on the national level, to repeat, there will be more competition, more conduits, more content. With the number of channels increasing, smaller firms can enter. The Internet is rapidly becoming an important media outlet. In 1996, somewhere between 9 million and 42 million US residents used the Internet, depending on whose estimate you believe. These estimates have been doubling annually. The current Internet is primarily a medium for text, graphics, and audio information. In the future, small firms will connect their video servers to such cyber-networks, and users will come to them. It will be more like in book publishing today, some big players and many small ones.

Does this solve all of our concerns? Not all of them. Diversity still does not assure openness. Competition can lead to exclusion of unpopular voices in order not to offend. Advertisers have more power. Content becomes more sensationalized. In the past, common carriage was the bedrock of free speech in an environment of private carriers because it prevented a carrier from discriminating against any speaker or lawful speech. But now, the days of common carriage are numbered. Most importantly, the regulatory status of the Internet is up for grabs. And those are the issues we should focus on.

NO ↵

Ben H. Bagdikian

The Realities of Media Concentration and Control

In a recent *Television Quarterly*, Professors Eli Noam and Robert Freeman, of Columbia University, argue against what they call "The Media Monopoly... Myth," citing my Quarterly article which was based on findings in my book, *The Media Monopoly* (5th Ed.). They state that media ownership concentration has actually declined in the last decade and will become even more so in the future, thanks to new media channels and the authors' own expectations for the cyber-media evolution.

I have no doubt about the accuracy and honesty of the numbers they use. But by depending on bare statistics of market shares and numbers of corporations, obviously significant, nevertheless they miss fundamental points about communication channels and mass media evolution. By using their method they have, unfortunately, created a myth of their own and clouded the realities on which a reform of media policies and practices depends.

The methodology of Professors Noam and Freeman sidesteps fundamental problems in present mass media concentration. Some of the predictions that buttress their argument display a surprising naïvéte about the dynamics of the real world of broadcasting and other media. In the end, they take back much of their sweeping initial generalizations but do so only as mere afterthoughts.

Even if one accepted the authors' simple statistical method, they display some of the sins they attribute to others. "Mass media" is universally defined as content designed for the "mass," that is, the general public. The authors' inclusion of "the information industry" is sensible, but under the rubric they sweep undifferentiated items like creators of computer software and manufacturers of computer hardware. This is the equivalent of calculating concentration in newspapers by including manufacturers of printing presses.

Their exclusive use of quantitative statistics without context becomes a crucial weakness. Their analysis ignores the realpolitik that sways the "information industry" and every other technology of any magnitude, an historical and almost inevitable process under which every industry tries to influence public opinion and legislation, and thus conditions (and sometimes governs) its fate in the marketplace.

General Electric, for example, owns NBC, and radio and cable networks, important mass media. But GE also is one of the largest non-media manufacturers in America, making, among other things, nuclear reactors, electrical equipment, and much else. When it lobbies the Congress, FCC and White House, it does so not just with its media clout but with its full economic power in other industries. Rupert Murdoch has used his media power, always a powerful lobbying political weapon all by itself (politicians are kind to controllers of their public images), to obtain stunning exemptions from U.S. law and forgiveness of taxes denied less powerful owners.

Murdoch was permitted to ignore the legal limit of 25% ownership of broadcasting stations for foreign firms (his parent firm, News Corp. is still Australian). Without this exemption he could not have formed the FOX network and become a major multi-media force in the country. GE and Murdoch are only two examples of many that make the one-dimensional statistical approach far too limited. Industries with that kind of political power do what they can, and historically have done to prevent entry of serious new competitors.

The authors seem unaware of the powers of very large media firms to impose corporate censorship that affects a significant portion of public thought and discourse. For example, in March of 1998, Murdoch's HarperCollins canceled its contract to print a book by the former British Governor of Hong Kong, Chris Patten, after the book house editor, Stuart Proffitt, had said it was the most lucid and intelligent book by a politician he had ever read and was sure to be a best seller. When Proffitt refused to cancel the book, he was suspended.

Murdoch clearly canceled the book, as he had the BBC World Service from his satellite broadcasts, because the Patten book, as did the BBC World Service, displeased authorities in China where he has large media investments scheduled for enlargement.

More significantly, according to the *New York Times*, a number of the major media book house editors admitted they practiced self-censorship when it came to accepting or rejecting books that might affect their owner's parent firm. Phyllis Grann, president of Penguin Putnam, said she was told she was the decision maker, but the owning firm's other industrial interests "was in my head." Albert Vitale, head of Random House, said it made "common sense" to cancel a book that parodied one of the house's most profitable authors. An executive of Simon & Schuster, owned by Viacom, said that when a book touched on Viacom's other large interests "we are smart enough to be sensitive to potential problems." And it is taken for granted in the Disney book groups that no book critical of Mickey Mouse will get past the gate.

Typically, Rupert Murdoch made bold and obvious what is a silent process throughout the conglomerate-owned book industry, which is to say publishers of the largest numbers of books—and TV programs—that reach the public. Later, after a settlement with Patten, Murdoch's lawyers issued a full apology on the publisher's behalf, about which the *New York Times* commented that Murdoch is not "known for publicly admitting mistakes...."

Simple counting channels and market shares displays another weakness. Just one conventional existing medium, television, is a powerful self-protecting filter, and the average U.S. home TV set is on seven hours a day. It is a powerful socializing force on the whole population. You cannot count this social and political power by simple channel and market data.

Simple quantitative counting of market shares makes no distinction between marginal trivia and major conventional channel content like news that powerfully influences the country's political and regulatory agenda. Publicly distributed news is not just another program and channel. It is crucial to informing people, helping them decide how to vote, and whether to retain or alter the status quo. (Americans say they get 56% of their news from television, 24% from newspapers, and 14% from radio, the remaining 6% from "other".) Control of news and its market share is very different from market share of say, "Roadrunner" cartoons or "The Three Stooges" re-runs. News that would materially alter the power of existing media is faint to non-existent in commercial broadcasting. But quantitatively by the authors' measure, that power to resist change and buttress the status quo doesn't enter the picture.

Furthermore, when the authors predict even less concentration in the future, they are probably correct in a limited time scale, but their thesis about the present nature of a major medium like commercial broadcasting and cable is naive in ignoring the history of technological innovations that have commercial possibilities.

They say that where markets are competitive, "vertical integration makes little sense." Since vertical integration has been the media investment world's major strategy for the last 20 years, one must conclude either that the investors are stupid or that markets are insufficiently competitive. They concede that the Telecommunications Act of 1996, which was sold politically to increase competition and dilution of control, did the opposite and produced what they call a "spurt" of increased mergers and concentration. But they predict that "in time" the Act will undermine the economic power of the newly merged firms. But the "spurt" continued with even greater magnitude in 1997. The Act's highly touted lowering of household telephone rates has yet to materialize. How long must the public wait?

The authors see new "cyber-media" as introducing new techniques and channels. They are not alone, and not yet proven wrong, but like most people, they display what public reaction has always tended to be with an ingenious invention. In an earlier book, I called it "technological euphoria" (*The Information Machines*, Harper & Row, 1971)—exaggerated expectations that every substantial new invention will have exclusively beneficial social effects. History tells us that we cannot take for granted who will end up controlling most of a new technology and what its ultimate impact will be.

Like others, the authors see the Internet as emblematic of this new salvation. They are correct that it will bring serious changes and already has. But at the moment, it is not clear how much of the Internet will be a point-to-point non-mass medium (personal and in-house corporate messages and highly specialized professional data) and how much intended for mass consumption (web sites of newspapers, magazines, new zines, etc.). At the moment, the Internet is analogous to handing out on a street corner everything from handbills for a coffee house to mathematical monographs to instructions for blowing up your local post office. And it still is not clear through what imminent governmental or dominant commercial funnel all this will be required to pass.

New industries often start with a large number of entrepreneurs and usually, though not always, end in concentrated hands. William Gates' Microsoft is already more than a small cloud in the cyber skies.

⌒◉⌒

The Noam and Freeman thesis provides a statistical snapshot of the present generation of modern channels. Someone could have taken a similar statistical snapshot of the auto industry anytime during the first third of this century when 239 firms entered the auto-making industry. But from 1930 to the 1960s their snapshot would show that two of these original 239 firms, GM and Ford, dominated the market, with Chrysler a poor third.

Closer to technological home, in 1902 there were 3,000 individual telephone companies. There was inevitable consolidation needed to create an integrated national network and AT&T-Western Electric became a legal monopoly. But here, again, size and qualitative factors became important. AT&T's political power delayed innovation and rate reductions until the 1960s when, for the first time, consumers could attach phones by other manufacturers onto the system and from that time on, we have benefited from added features. Here again, Microsoft is an echo of that history.

The authors' view of the dynamics of the present broadcast world is naive. They write, "Disney should not earmark its best programs for ABC if other networks offer more money... [or] force its lemons on... ABC." If ABC did this, the authors' state with certitude "centrifugal forces" will breakup the company. NBC offer first-run *Seinfeld* to a competing network at any price? Never, and for hard-nosed reasons. Big hits are multipurpose assets. They not only attract big ratings and ad revenues, they are audience builders for subsequent programs on the same network the same night; they become ideal carriers for promos for the networks' upcoming shows and sports, and they bring big money for rerun syndication and foreign sales (half of TV show and movie revenues).

The authors ask, "And what about all those famous synergies?" The synergies—clusters of different companies under common control with each company presumed to be helpful to the others—survive in some cases and not others. The classic Gulf & Western mish-mash collection—auto parts to lingerie —made lots of money and was a power in the marketplace, but was unwieldy for investors to analyze. But the new media conglomerates have a coherence that make them work more often than not. GE is a massive conglomerate that has learned, as do other modern synergistic conglomerates, to decentralize units and has centrifugal force all the way to the bank.

Synergy works better in the mass media because, among other reasons, digitalized content can easily transform newspaper features into magazines and consumer computer services. It permits TV programs to be reused in other media, like movies, cassettes, commercials, etc. Murdoch puts the obscure "stars" of FOX's weak programs on the cover of his *TV Guide*. *Time* puts on its cover singers from the Time-Warner-owned Warner records. Disney Tours and theme parks get endless open and sly promos on ABC and Disney cable channels.

<hr/>

I guess every writer is entitled to some hubris. The authors get theirs by saying "we have gotten our hands dirty by collecting the actual numbers," implying others have not. Alas, fellows, there is no other way and other ink-stained wretches have come before you. They add, "This is probably the most detailed study ever made of media concentration in America." Too bad. Landmark encyclopedia studies have been made for years, by Congressional committees, government agencies, anti-trust challenges, civil suits between major media firms, and joint works like the 1978 two-volume, 761-page compendium, "Proceedings of the Symposium on Media Concentration," issued by the Bureau of Competition of the Federal Trade Commission.

In their closing, the authors take much of their best thesis away in an almost offhand manner. They state that while there is no problem nationally, there is in the local markets. They write that "98.5% of American cities have only one newspaper... 98% of homes have no choice of cable provider." (I'm sure the authors meant 98.5% of American cities *that have any daily paper at all* there is only one paper—there are more than 19,000 cities, so with 1500 dailies, more than 17,000 cities have no daily at all.)

Relegating the serious problem exclusively to local ones overlooks the fact that "local" is where people live, and in the United States voters learn from local media what they need to govern themselves because no other industrial democracy leaves so many central decisions to local jurisdictions. With only brief headline news on our national broadcast media, and local TV news a national scandal of nightly visits to fires, shootings and happy talk, local newspapers become important. But now Wall Street pressure for lowered costs and quick returns has caused major dailies to shift from designing themselves more as entertainment rather than news carriers.

There are, as the authors say, 12,000 radio stations, but about seven standard formats are used by most of them and each of these formats is exactly duplicated in all their cities, so Kansas City gets pretty much the same computerized programs as Bangor, Maine.

One ends with the feeling that after the initial sweeping assertions, by the end, the authors have taken back too many exceptions that in fact are major and that dramatically weaken their "Myth" assertion. This happens in the manner of Haydn's Farewell Symphony that starts with the full ensemble but as players start leaving by twos and threes, by the end the stage consists of two lone violinists.

POSTSCRIPT

Media Monopolies: Are the Dangers of Concentration Overstated?

Media mergers are the topic of a special issue of the *Media Studies Journal* (Spring/Summer 1996). Todd Gitlin argues in that special issue that today's deals may weigh on the culture for decades. The potential for harm, he suggests, is as great as the potential for good. In a counterpoint, Steven Rattner predicts benefits for consumers. He foresees the consequences of technology development and corporations that are large enough to fund expensive new undertakings as producing exciting new options for the public. Both agree that attention must be paid to traditional expectations of freedom of expression. They diverge considerably on whether or not large corporations can accomplish that end.

This counterpoint was represented in the debate over the Telecommunications Act. *Congressional Digest* (January 1996) reports the divergent opinions of a number of representatives, including Thomas Bliley, Jr. (R-Virginia), who says, "For the first time, communications policy will be based on competition rather than arbitrary regulation"; John Conyers, Jr. (D-Michigan), who contends, "For American consumers, this is one big sucker punch"; and William Coyne (D-Pennsylvania), who argues, "The rush to deregulate opens the floodgates for companies which already enjoy a monopoly position in one market to expand their dominance to other segments."

A number of authors have examined the issue of concentration of ownership in the media industries. Mark Crispin Miller offers what he calls a guide to our contracting media cosmos in his article "Free the Media," *The Nation* (June 3, 1996). A number of people from the media, the academic world, and public interest groups offer responses to his work. The Center for Media Education's 12-step program for media democracy is presented at the end of the article. A *Columbia Journalism Review* forum on the dangers of corporate control (March 1997) is a nicely balanced representation of varying opinions.

Whatever their persuasion, observers seem to share a concern about the impact of Bill Gates and Microsoft as it enters the media industries. This is reflected in "Will Gates Crush Newspapers?" *Columbia Journalism Review* (November 1997). Some other recent volumes include *Triumph and Erosion in the American Media and Entertainment Industries* by Dan Steinbock (Quorum Books, 1995), *Commercial Culture: The Media System and the Public Interest* by Leo Bogart (Oxford University Press, 1995), and *Conglomerates and the Media* edited by Patricia Aufderheide (New Press, 1997).

ISSUE 15

Should the Internet Facilitate a Free Exchange of Information?

YES: Andrew Sullivan, from "Dot-communist Manifesto," *The New York Times Magazine* (June 11, 2000)

NO: Russell J. Frackman et al., from Notice of Joint Motion and Joint Motion of Plaintiffs for Preliminary Injunction; Memorandum of Points and Authorities, *A&M Records, Inc. et al. v. Napster, Inc.* and *Leiber et al. v. Napster, Inc.*, U.S. District Court, Northern District of California—San Francisco Division (July 26, 2000)

ISSUE SUMMARY

YES: Journalist Andrew Sullivan argues that the Internet makes instant communication between citizens easier than ever before. He presents his argument in Marxist terms, stating that Marx's primary complaint about capitalism was that it reduced everything to money. However, the Internet does not have money at its core, and therefore, can link users to each other without a profit motive.

NO: Attorneys for the plaintiffs Russell J. Frackman et al., writing the Motion on behalf of members of the Recording Industry Association of America (RIAA), argue that peer-to-peer programs, like Napster, infringe upon copyright and also subvert sales and royalties to performers and those in the record distribution chain. Therefore, they argue that it should be illegal for Napster to distribute music via the Internet.

By the time this book is in print, the Napster controversy may be over, but the issues raised by the legal challenges to Napster, Inc., will undoubtedly become part of our existence for many years ahead. Peer-to-peer file sharing is the real process behind many programs that link users together by allowing access to a computer's hard drive. If this type of networking catches on, one can expect to see more attention given to "firewalls" (programs that protect certain files), as well as issues of copyright, ownership, privacy, and personal control over one's own data.

For many years after the Internet began to catch on with home and business users, pundits claimed that it would, in essence, become nothing more than a marketing vehicle. "E-commerce" was heralded as the real purpose of the Internet, and the stock market dramatically rose and fell, making many investors fortunes and sometimes losing those investments all within a few days. But while the stock market was experiencing record highs and lows with e-commerce, some entrepreneurs were developing programs that they wanted to make available to users for free. Napster was one such program that could be downloaded and used to access music files on other peoples' hard drives.

The rock group Metallica brought attention to Napster when they threatened to sue anyone who had downloaded, or "pirated," any of their music. Many Napster users who had traded Metallica music were either prohibited from using the program for ten days, or, they could continue to use it and have their names included in a law suit. So many users decided to fight the Metallica threat that it would have been impractical for the group to fight against them. Instead, publicity about the controversy made many people aware of Napster and other "freeware" programs and how to use them.

Napster and other similar types of programs require high speed connections to the Internet, like those available on most college campuses. The controversy over piracy and copyright, then, has also involved colleges and universities regarding their own policies for how and what Internet connections can be used. This test of traditional legal concept, law, and access provides a benchmark for future development of programs and computer systems for the Internet. Is this a sign of the type of questions we may expect throughout the twenty-first century? If so, communication technology could well be on the threshold of pushing traditional boundaries. As users of these technologies, we bear the responsibility for evaluating our behaviors, and ultimately, influence the institutions that support our communications infrastructure.

In the following selections, Andrew Sullivan maintains that the Internet should be a resource for the free exchange of information. He argues that its value lies in the fact that it is motivated not by profit, but by the exchange of knowledge. Russell J. Frackman et al. counter that unlimited exchange causes irreparable harm to those whose information is shared. Frackman et al. assert that the use of programs such as Napster is piracy.

As you read these selections, ask yourself where your standards and beliefs lie. Do you believe that the Internet should exchange information for free? Should there be limits on the type of information? Once allowed, can these information sharing programs and technologies be controlled, and, if so, by whom?

Andrew Sullivan  **YES**

Dot-communist Manifesto

Asharp, unexpected twang of conscience hit me the other day. It occurred as I was merrily downloading the umpteenth Pet Shop Boys B side from another Napster user's hard drive. Was this theft?

Nobody, I rationalized, was going to be without the Extended Rollo Mix of "New York City Boy" because of my actions. All Napster is, after all, is a huge database of MP3 files, a musical commune dreamed up by a college-freshman geek. And sharing a database isn't theft. If you agree to join the Napster "community," you agree to share every MP3 you have with any other Napsterite who is online at the same time you are. It's worth the tiny loss of privacy, because what you get in return is access to more free music than anyone could listen to in a lifetime.

So whom was I hurting by copying one lousy song? Sure, I'd avoided paying a record company a royalty—but it was rich enough already. Likewise the Pet Shop Boys. And it wasn't as if I'd smuggled a disc out of Tower Records in a knapsack. It wasn't even in any meaningful sense "mine," since other Napster users could now download it from me without my even noticing. Neither had it been in any meaningful sense "theirs"—once they agreed to pool their own MP3 collection with those of other Napsterites.

What exactly was going on here? The only workable definition is communism. What Marx had hoped would occur because of a new dawn in human economic relations has been made possible instead by a new form of human technology. Once we enter the Web, we become like medieval peasants entering their village commons; almost everything is shared. The only difference is that, unlike the Middle Ages, our modern ability to duplicate everything instantly means that property isn't even "shared." It's possessed simultaneously by everyone. By turning physical property into endlessly duplicable e-property, the ancient human problem of "mine-thine" has been essentially solved. There was once the parable of the loaves and the fishes; there is now the parable of copy and paste. For the first time since Plato first dreamed of it in "The Republic," communism is actually feasible. And for the first time since Marx christened it, it makes sense.

By this I don't mean that the real world has changed. We live at a time when the market is the closest thing we have to a civic religion. Money has rarely been as important in determining prospects in life, and economic inequalities are mounting. But the online world is different. Admittedly, even dreamy start-ups like Napster hope to make millions one day—and the Web promises to be an unparalleled way to buy, sell and market products. But alongside this growth of e-capitalism, and inextricable from it, is the tenaciously communistic nature of the Web itself. What the Web is best at, after all, is transmitting information—and what the fledgling years of the Internet have proved is that, in this context, free information has an edge over its pricey competition. Apart from pornography sites and a few business sites, the Web is still largely free to anyone with a modem and a phone line. Many information sites that once charged subscribers (Slate.com comes to mind) have subsequently capitulated to dot-communism. Moreover, virtually any site's content can be copied and pasted by subscribers and sent immediately to nonsubscribers in ways that destroy the tollbooth almost as soon as it is constructed. Private property in this world is about as fashionable as public property outside it.

This is surely good news. Left-leaning intellectuals have long worried about the way in which our public space—shopping malls, urban parks—have become increasingly private. Other liberals have emphasized the dangers to civic life of pervasive economic inequality. But the Web has provided small answers to both of these conundrums. As our public life has shrunk in reality, it has expanded exponentially online. Acting as a critical counterweight to market culture, the Web has made interactions between random, equal citizens far more possible than ever before. In the virtual city that the Web is quickly becoming, you can walk unimpeded into hundreds of thousands of apartments and play any music or read any book you find there. You can pick up almost any publication at the sidewalk newsstand and read it free. You can chat with the best gossip in town and hear the dish as soon as anyone else. There are very few cops, no taxes and, except for a tiny handful of exclusive salons, no keys, locks, tolls or security guards. This is what Marx dreamed of. It is what Plato fantasized about. It's what Thomas More dreamily satirized in "Utopia"— or "nowhere land." Except that E-topia is both nowhere and everywhere at the same time.

Recall Marx's essential gripe about capitalism. It was that by converting everything into money, the market alienated human beings from one another and themselves. Rather than relating directly to one another, we related to money. Rather than doing something meaningful with our lives, we became specialized units of economic production, valued not for what we were but for what we produced and consumed. Part of the dream of communist consciousness was that by abolishing this system, by liberating human beings from the tyranny of being instruments of wealth creation, we would become more fully human. We would finally be ends, not means. We could farm, write poetry, fall in love, make music and listen to Santana—all in the same day! We would be authentic again, valued not for our monetary worth but for our human capacities, which we would share freely and spontaneously with anyone else.

Of course we know now what the consequences are of actually trying to turn this utopia into reality. Unlike easily copied software, physical property tends to be missed when it's pilfered or shared. So the only way of ensuring that human beings commune with one another with sufficient enthusiasm is to create a government big enough and terrifying enough to compel them. Millions of murders later, Marxism has rightly been junked. But this is where the Web comes in. Having dissolved property into thin air, the Web has no need of a police force, and by preying on curiosity and mischief, it harnesses human nature rather than fighting it. Unlike communism, dot-communism is enforced through the impulsive decisions of millions of users. Try charging and you'll wait a long time for traffic; give it away free and they'll come running.

The Web does something else only dreamed of by Marx. It goes further than any previous innovation in alleviating the problem identified by Marx as "bourgeois alienation." For many, market democracy still means that people are being valued for their capacity to generate wealth, not their intrinsic human dignity. For many more, it means jobs they long to leave on Friday afternoon for brief glimpses of pleasure on the weekend. For more still, class and money are never left behind. Wherever they go, their clothes, accent and credit rating subtly keep them in their place.

But on the Internet, a simple screen name will get you almost anywhere free. Suddenly, motives other than the profit motive begin to come into play. People give you music because they actually want you to hear and enjoy it. People set up their own Web sites because they actually want to communicate with others. Chain e-mails pass along jokes for the sheer hell of it. Favorite columns get traded around—and databases are linked together—purely for mutual enlightenment or mutual mischief. By abolishing mine-thine, the Web also helps abolish the alienating, propertied distance between one person and another.

Apart from churches—and even they take donations—the Web is one of the few truly powerful private organizations that does not have money at its core. Again, consider Napster. It sells nothing. It asks nothing but a few personal particulars from its subscribers. You make up a name to join. It's just a means for people to communicate, share, copy. Napster is the favorite of college students everywhere because, like them, it's still dreaming. Eighteen-year-olds may be the last people on earth to still believe in communism, but unlike every previous generation of dreamers, these kids have figured out the technology to make it possible. So what if there's no money in it? That's the point! Indeed, if Napster ever starts charging subscription fees, some teenager will surely invent a rival method for distributing free music.

Sure, more and more Web sites want you to shop, not dream, but as their profit margins increasingly show, this is not what the technology is most comfortable doing. As more and more experiences—musical, literary, erotic—get translated into downloadable, postphysical entities, what scant profits there are now will dwindle away. This won't be as tragic as it sounds. Eventually, musicians will remember that the real reason they started their careers was to express themselves and communicate, rather than actually do it all to make money. And since money will no longer be required to access other artists' music, they will be less desperate to get rich. Dot-communism will help artists get back in touch with their authentic aspirations. Take that, Metallica!

The only drawback, of course, is that many of us quite like our bourgeois individualism. I am somewhat fond of the fact that I will actually get paid for writing this column, rather than sharing it free. So you can see the ideological battle ahead: greed on one side will face a feasible high-tech commune on the other. Big corporations will take on plucky teenagers. But given the track record so far, the teenagers and the commies may well win. Indeed, they already have. Take journalism. I can see the attraction of dot-communism in my own profession—you could call it Hackster—but I'm not sure I want to sign up. But then the more I think about it, the more I realize I already have. Almost every newspaper now gives away online what it used to charge for on paper. The proliferation of links, cybergossip and cyberhype means that articles online soon lose their point of origin, and, like orphaned MP3 files, Love Bug viruses and Al Gore jokes, move around the world with lightning speed. Eventually, even journalists may get used to the Marxist idea of writing for more than a bourgeois readership—and writing for more than a check. Before too long, we may find ourselves setting up a Web site, penning bons mots each day and giving them all away for free! Come to think of it, AndrewSullivan.com will be up and running by Labor Day. I'm serious.

A specter, to put it bluntly, is haunting America: the specter of dot-communism. Of course, the deep problems that Marx identified—the problems of alienation and inequality—are not solved by dot-communism, but they are certainly salved by it, and in ways we are only beginning to appreciate. No revolution is required; and the bourgeoisie doesn't even have to be liquidated. In fact, capitalism made the whole thing possible, just as Marx suspected it would. And what, after all, could be more enticing at the dawn of the new century than a high-tech world solving a very low-tech human problem? So let the capitalist classes and the Recording Industry Association of America tremble. The dot-communists have nothing to lose but their chains. And they have a Web to win.

◀ **NO**

Notice of Joint Motion and Joint Motion of Plaintiffs for Preliminary Injunction; Memorandum of Points and Authorities

This is a joint motion for a preliminary injunction by two sets of plaintiffs. The Record Company Plaintiffs are record companies that spend substantial time, money, and resources to create, manufacture, and sell recorded music, and own the copyrights and other rights in innumerable sound recordings. The Music Publishing Plaintiffs are songwriters and music publishers who own the copyrights and other rights in popular and successful musical compositions. Hundreds of thousands of copyrighted works owned by plaintiffs are being infringed—reproduced and distributed—*every day* by users of defendant Napster's system—infringements that Napster actively enables and encourages, and from which it directly benefits.

There can be no doubt that Napster was designed for the purpose of facilitating piracy, and that Napster knows full well that its users are using its service overwhelmingly to trade pirated MP3 files. . . .

The irreparable harm being suffered by plaintiffs from Napster's conduct is enormous and increasing daily. Each of the Record Company Plaintiffs has engaged in years of planning and has made huge expenditures to establish a legitimate commercial downloading market for its copyrighted music. Napster is attempting to usurp plaintiffs' ability to enter this market by giving away plaintiffs' property. As Congress has recognized, on-line services permitting users to obtain the music they want on demand poses "the greatest threat to traditional sales of records and compact discs." Plaintiffs' surveys of Napster users confirm this fact and show that significant numbers of Napster users report buying fewer CDs as a result of their downloading the music for free on Napster. Empirical analyses of music purchasing data show that, while national sales are increasing, purchases by college students (Napster's core constituency) are *decreasing*. Even more telling, at stores in the vicinity of colleges where Napster use likely is greatest, music sales actually are *sharply declining*.

These analyses are alarming, and are corroborated by countless media reports of consumers eschewing CD purchases in favor of free downloads through Napster, as well as the personal experiences of music retailers describing a drop

From *A&M Records, Inc. et al. v. Napster, Inc.* and *Leiber et al. v. Napster, Inc.*, C-99-5183; C-00-0074 (2000). Notes and references omitted.

in business on account of Napster. These studies and reports confirm what is self-evident: the millions of illicit downloads that Napster enables and encourages are eroding the marketability of recorded music. Indeed, on Napster's own moderated message boards, its users brag about illegally downloading copyrighted music from popular artists, and celebrate the imminent destruction of the recording industry. When plaintiffs' music is copied on the Napster system, no one involved in the creation or sale of that music is compensated—not the copyright owners of the recordings, not the copyright owners of the musical compositions, not the recording artists, not the producers, not the musicians, not the unions, and not the retailers whose opportunity for sales are diminished. . . .

Plaintiffs Are Likely to Succeed on the Merits

Napster's conduct happens to occur on the Internet, but the law of contributory and vicarious infringement is no less applicable to an Internet-based company than any other—such as the swap meet owner in *Fonovisa* [*Inc. v. Cherry Auction, Inc.*, 76 F.3d 259 (9th Cir. 1996)] the leading Ninth Circuit case on contributory and vicarious infringement—and plainly applies to Napster's conduct.

In *Fonovisa*, the defendant operated flea markets where individual vendors sold and offered for sale counterfeit copies of the plaintiffs' copyrighted sound recordings. The owner controlled access to the flea markets, promoted them, supplied general support services such as parking and utilities, retained the right to exclude any vendor from the flea markets for any reason, helped conceal the identities of vendors, and profited from the increased customer traffic resulting from consumers being attracted to cheap counterfeit recordings. These facts, the Ninth Circuit ruled, showed that "it would be difficult for the infringing activity to take place in the massive quantities alleged without the support services provided by the swap meet," and were sufficient to support both contributory and vicarious copyright infringement.

Napster essentially is an Internet swap meet—more technologically sophisticated but in many ways indistinguishable from the swap meet owner in *Fonovisa*—"and the mere fact that [infringement is] clothed in the exotic webbing of the Internet does not disguise its illegality." . . .

Napster is liable for contributory infringement because it has knowledge (actual and constructive) of its users' infringements, and materially contributes to those infringements. . . .

Anyone who uses Napster, even for a few minutes, knows immediately what Napster and every other Napster user knows: massive copyright violations occur on Napster—not sometimes, but all the time. And not by just some users —by all users. Simply enter the name of any well-known musical artist or song into Napster's search engine and you will find dozens, and most likely hundreds, of unauthorized copies of copyrighted sound recordings and musical compositions.

Napster users overwhelmingly use Napster to engage in music piracy, and very little else. Napster told this Court it did not know the level of piracy through its system.... Based on actual user download data obtained from Napster and on independently-gathered data regarding the files being offered for "sharing" by Napster users (collectively more than 24 million files), [Stanford University] Professor Olkin sought to answer two questions: (1) what percentage of Napster users are engaged in some level of music piracy (by offering at least some pirated music) while logged onto Napster?; and (2) what percentage of the MP3 music files actually being downloaded by Napster users are infringing? His findings hardly are surprising:

- First, every single Napster user sampled was offering at least some pirated music for others to download. In other words, no one is using Napster exclusively for non-infringing activities; and
- Second, over 87% of the files actually selected for downloading by Napster users have been conclusively confirmed to be infringing, an additional 3.2% of files are likely (but not yet conclusively verified) to be infringing.

Of course, these facts are not news to Napster. From its earliest design stage, the purpose of Napster was to facilitate music piracy. Napster's chief architect and co-founder, Shawn Fanning, testified that he began work on Napster to put an end to the frustration of his college roommate in finding and downloading MP3 music files. The essential nature of Napster was reaffirmed when the three founders were developing their first business plan. Co-founder Sean Parker, writing to co-founder John Fanning, emphasized the business need to collect user information (to sell to advertisers and other third parties) while at the same time ensuring complete user anonymity:

> "Users will understand that they are improving their experience by providing information about their tastes without linking that information to a name or address or other sensitive data that might endanger them (*especially since they are exchanging pirated music*)."

In a perverse "fox guarding the hen-house" twist, this plan to conceal user identities was written by the same Sean Parker who currently purports to be Napster's officially designated "copyright compliance officer" under the DMCA. His job is to deal with copyright infringement notices received by Napster. Adding to the irony, he himself is a direct infringer of plaintiffs' copyrights, having used Napster to download copyrighted MP3 music files.

Parker's strategy memo—in a section headed "Problems"—also stressed the need for Napster to try to convince the music industry that it is more than just a haven for piracy:

> "Problems
>   The main hurdle I was planning to discuss was RIAA harassment, but that was addressed on the phone. It should be noted however, that many of the strategies I mentioned above (harping CD's, recommendation engine, etc.) will put us in a much better bargaining position with the RIAA when they see that we are not just *making pirated music available* but also pushing demand." (emphasis added)

Indeed, Napster always knew it was building a business based on music piracy—but it always had a plan, and even to this day the plan really hasn't changed:

> "the key is to maintain the hook (Napster users know that by connecting to Napster, they have access to *any music they want, absolutely free*)... to grow our user base, and then use [this] user base coupled with advanced technology to *leverage the record companies into a deal.*" ... (emphasis added)

Napster Has a Direct Financial Interest in Users' Infringing Activities.

The economic benefit Napster receives from the infringement of plaintiffs' music on the Napster service is both enormous and quantifiable. It already has translated into a cash infusion of over *$13 million* from venture capital firm Hummer Winblad (for 20% of the company), among other substantial investors. Napster's current value (even with this lawsuit pending) has been pegged at figures ranging from *$60-80 million to $150 million....*

That Napster has, to date, not earned revenues is immaterial. Napster consciously has decided initially not to pursue revenues, but instead to focus on its most important metric for success and value generation: "new user acquisition." Internal Napster planning documents confirm a deliberate strategy: "early efforts should be directed first toward generating user base, then toward extending the e-commerce possibilities of the product." ("Napster will create the largest, fastest growing and most active user base of digital music enthusiasts *—a population that directly drives revenue.*")...

However, from the very beginning, Napster has been making plans and devising strategies to "monetize" its service. Napster has considered "many, many models" of revenue generation, including sponsorships, advertising, selling artist and Napster merchandise, and compact disc sales. Napster also has considered selling or marketing digital music products "related" to its core service such as compact disc "rippers" and "burners." Napster is exploring and negotiating commercial contracts in many of these areas, and, very recently, has entered into a written agreement with online retailer Amazon.com, pursuant to which Napster will receive a portion of the revenues Amazon receives from users Napster refers....

Over 10 million Napster users currently are "sharing" tens of millions of copies of copyrighted music—and, according to Napster, the number of users is growing at the almost unthinkable rate of "5% to 35% *per day.*" And Napster is still in "Beta." The irreparable harm being inflicted upon plaintiffs is self-evident. Napster is harming sales of CDs. It is undermining the emerging commercial market for downloaded music. It is teaching a generation of music consumers that music has little intrinsic value. These injuries are happening now and are irreparable. This harm also was foreseen and intended by Napster. As an internal Napster business plan concludes: "the key is to coexist with the record industry, *at least temporarily* [and] ultimately *bypass the record industry entirely....*" ...

As for Napster's impact on CD purchases, an internal Napster strategy document effectively puts an end to any suggestion that Napster is intended somehow to promote legitimate sales. Under the heading "Goals," Napster executives wrote:

> "Napster brings about *death of the CD*
>   Record industry may be unwilling to support this transition (*gut their bottom line*)
>   Record stores (Tower records) *obsoleted*."
>   (emphasis added)

Napster's internal prognostications are being borne out in the market, even after just a few months of operation. The evidence demonstrates that Napster users report that they are buying significantly fewer CDs as a result of their Napster use; empirical sales data analyses confirm a decrease in purchases among Napster's core constituency; and retail record stores near college campuses fear that Napster is putting them out of business. This evidence is summarized below:

Survey of Napster Users   Plaintiffs commissioned Dr. Deborah Jay of Field Research to survey Napster users. In response to open-ended questions asking why they use Napster and how it has had an impact on their purchases of CDs, Napster users (answering in their own words and unprompted) report as follows:

- **They are buying few CDs because of Napster.** A full 22% expressly said that, because of Napster, they don't buy CDs anymore or buy fewer CDs. Additionally, a full 41% of Napster users responded with answers that, while not explicit, certainly indicate they are buying fewer CDs or using Napster downloads as a substitute for purchasing CDs, including words to the effect that they use Napster "to get free music" or "to get music I don't have" or "it's easier or better than CDs."
- **The more people download from Napster, the more they report buying fewer CDs.** More than 30% of heavy Napster users (those who have downloaded more than 75 songs) expressly said that, because of Napster, they don't buy CDs anymore or buy fewer CDs. And, 56% gave an answer that fairly suggests they are buying fewer CDs.
- **The longer people use Napster, the more they download.** Of those who had used Napster for more than four months, a majority (51%) had downloaded more than 75 songs. Napster users who have downloaded 25 songs or fewer overwhelmingly (65.1%) had been using Napster for less than three months.

Corroborating these findings, Dr. Jay's research also found that most Napster users don't already own—and do not subsequently purchase—the music they download. Almost half (48.6%) owned less than 10% of the music they were downloading, and almost half (46.6%) subsequently purchased less than 10% of the downloaded music they did not previously own....

A Preliminary Injunction Will Serve the Public Interest

In copyright cases, "the issue of public policy rarely is a genuine issue if the copyright owner has established a likelihood of success," because "the public interest is the interest in upholding copyright protections." "[I]t is virtually axiomatic that the public interest can only be served by upholding copyright protections and, correspondingly, preventing the misappropriation of the skills, creative energies, and resources which are invested in the protected work."

The foregoing observations could not be more pertinent here. In addition, plaintiffs have submitted the declarations of individuals and organizations —from both the online and offline communities—whose interests are being compromised by Napster's disregard for the copyright laws. For example:

- The American Federation of Television and Radio Artists (AFTRA)— which represents approximately 15,000 vocalists on sound recordings, 11,000 of whom are background singers—describes how "[f]or the majority of Artists who do not have lucrative recording contracts, but rather, struggle to make a living at their craft, [Napster] represents nothing less than a brazen assault upon the already shaky economic foundation on which their professional careers are built."
- The Internet site with the largest collection of authorized MP3's available for free download (MP3.com) and the site that is the largest source of authorized MP3 downloads for sale (EMusic.com) both have testified that they have not authorized their MP3 files—over 500,000 MP3 files in total—to be distributed over Napster. They also explain how Napster injures their businesses: "Napster is gaining an unfair competitive advantage over EMusic.com. Every time a Napster user illegally copies a recording that is available in MP3 format from EMusic.com... that is one more person who does not need to visit the EMusic.com site to purchase the recording legally. Each such copy thus potentially deprives EMusic.com of both a visitor to our site and a sale of that recording, our two sources of revenue." ([E]ven though MP3.com offers free MP3 downloads, "[m]any of the benefits that MP3.com provides to its artists —as well as our own revenues—depend on attracting as many people as possible to the [MP3.com] Website.")
- The Chairperson of *The Copyright Assembly*—whose members represent every significant intellectual property industry in the country (including the software industry, the sports industry, film producers, television programmers, broadcast and cable stations and networks, photography, magazine and book publishers, and the creative guilds)—cautions that "any intellectual property that can be digitized is vulnerable to the wholesale piracy enabled by Napster. The owners and creators of copyrighted material will of course be hesitant to offer their works over the Internet if they cannot be protected from this type of unauthorized duplication and dissemination."

Although it undoubtedly will try, Napster cannot invoke the innovation of the Internet or unmet consumer demand to justify its actions. Copyright "is not designed to afford consumer protection or convenience but, rather, to protect the copyrightholders' property interests." In the end, "[c]reative works do not spring from a void. The seed bed of this creativity lies within the imagination, artistry and ingenuity of a community of artists and craftspeople who provide Americans with most of what they read, hear and watch.... But if we cannot protect what we invest in, create and own, then we really don't own anything."

POSTSCRIPT

Should the Internet Facilitate a Free Exchange of Information?

Napster is just one of many Internet programs that circumvents traditional file sharing protocols. Some of the most well-known programs include Onutella and Freenet, both of which have the potential to be far more powerful than Napster, but there are at least 15 other programs that share similarities. Why then, did Napster receive most of the initial attention?

Napster and the other programs mentioned use MP3 technology to link to computer hard drives to transfer music. While initially Napster was available to anyone to download for free, there is evidence in the lawsuit document that eventually there would be ways for Napster to make a profit. Even though Napster executives have refuted that claim, the potential to become a for-profit business can be seen as apparent.

What is far more important, however, is the reality of peer-to-peer file sharing. This raises questions of copyright, ownership, piracy, and privacy. What *could* result from peer-to-peer file sharing? When you consider the other types of information that could be transferred, the question of the technology's impact becomes far more complex.

While new information is published every day, an excellent source of information from the Record Industry's perspective is the Recording Industry Association of America's (RIAA's) website, www.RIAA.com. Other articles praising or decrying peer-to-peer file sharing as revolutionary or dangerous can best be found in general publications like *Time, Newsweek,* and *Rolling Stone.* Arguments on behalf of the programs themselves can best be found on websites sponsored by each program, such as www.napster.com, www.gnutella.com, and www.freeware.com.

ISSUE 16

Do Public Relations Practitioners Provide a Valuable Service to the Public?

YES: James E. Lukaszewski, from "Public Relations Is a Transformational Force," *Vital Speeches of the Day* (August 1, 1999)

NO: Stuart Ewen, from *PR! A Social History of Spin* (BasicBooks, 1996)

ISSUE SUMMARY

YES: James E. Lukaszewski is a public relations practitioner who, in a commencement address to the 1999 Summer Institute on Public Relations Program at New York University (NYU), outlines the practical skills necessary for a successful career in public relations.

NO: Professor Stuart Ewen traces the evolution of the profession and practice of public relations, and cites events in which the field of public relations did not operate in the best interest of the public.

W hile each author represented in this issue is writing for a different audience, together they outline an important issue for discussion. Is public relations a field in which message creators exert influence over an unsuspecting audience, or do practitioners influence social organizations by creating messages that serve or hinder the interests of the public?

Many have strong opinions about the ethical issues that underscore the practice and effect of public relations. Still, it appears that many students want to work in the field. Public relations can be viewed as a legitimate business activity or a practice that is tainted by moral and ethical problems, which results in the perception that practitioners are out to manipulate or dupe the public.

What are the benefits and drawbacks of public relations, and why does this field warrant so much controversy? The following selections give us many topics for debate, or, in public relations terms, *talking points*. As you read these selections it might be useful to consider a number of contexts in which public relations practitioners work. Does the desire for a company to make its products known present different considerations than a politician running for office? Does a government wanting to maintain the current economic policy act in the same way special interest groups do, like the National Rifle Association (NRA)? Is it necessary to acknowledge different motives, actions, or circumstances for each "client"? Is it possible for a public relations professional to serve a variety of clients who might have different agendas?

James E. Lukaszewski does not critically evaluate public relations; instead, he focuses on how a good practitioner can work effectively as an agent of change. The advice he offers to the NYU graduating class might make one think about public relations in a different way. His examples are useful to anyone considering a career in public relations, but his message is something more. He talks about what a good professional in a field like public relations must do to be successful.

Stuart Ewen provides a sense of how the field of public relations has changed throughout the twentieth century. His chronology shows how different social events both shaped and were shaped by public relations practitioners, whether or not they believed they were working ethically and responsibly. He contends that every occupation goes through many changes over time. Ewen reports that an early guiding principle of public relations was that it was to be used for democratic purposes, and he outlines how and why this belief has changed. Ewen also poses several questions for the twenty-first century, which now gives us a different set of social, business, and governmental relations that can influence any field or career in communications.

Can the positions taken by Lukaszewski and Ewen both be right? Has public relations devolved from being an active agent in a vital democracy? Does it contribute to the glossing over of issues that do not emphasize positive images and ideas? If so, is the practice of public relations a good thing? Can people work in public relations and take pride in their work?

James E. Lukaszewski

 **YES**

Public Relations Is a Transformational Force

Delivered to the 1999 NYU Summer Institute Public Relations Program,
New York, New York, June 18, 1999

... It is an extraordinary personal honor to be asked to share ideas and thoughts with professionals who have taken two weeks out of their lives to refocus their careers and professional attitudes about one of the most important functions in society today, how we relate to each other....

This year I've been able to attend or hear a number of commencement addresses. An amazing number of speakers have begun with something like, "I can't remember who the commencement speaker was at my high school or college graduation." One speaker said, "I can't even remember who the speaker was from my graduation from medical school." A rather poor beginning, and virtually every one of them went on to be rather unmemorable.

My goal today is something different. You have just completed a rather intensive two-week professional program leading to a certificate in public relations. So, let's have a personal conversation about what you want to accomplish in your life.

Each year I have the privilege of working with many, many public relations professionals in a variety of settings covering virtually the full spectrum of our professional life: the corporate sector, government, military, non-profit organizations, and more. One powerful driving concept comes through in all these settings, and that is the gut-level desire to transform the organization, or transform the body of thinking, or transform the attitudes of a group of individuals, or transform society as a whole. Public relations—our profession—is a transformation force if we understand how to energize and exert that power through others.

Today, I need to speak with each of you, individually, because we practice our profession quite often by ourselves. It is a lonely profession. Each of us is an individual actor, adding our personal ideas and concepts to the lives of others in the hope of producing a result that benefits them and their world.

The question for each of you is "How can I do that?" And, if you agree with me that somewhere in your soul, the reason you do your professional work every day is to have an impact, to make a mark, to move some part of the world forward, question number two is "How do you do it, personally, from the inside out?" It's this second question that is really what I want to talk about with you....

As I analyze how successful executives, how real leaders, how important people move the process forward, I've identified seven crucial behaviors that add up to transformational power. What I'm saying is that if you take these concepts to heart, personally, the more of them you exercise as a routine part of your professional and personal life, the more transformational power you will gain as an individual.

The seven behaviors are quite simple, quite positive, and very doable. I refer to them as the Be-attitudes of Transformation of Power because, you see, they start with "be":

Be constructive, by this I mean constructive behavior.

Seek to make and solicit positive, constructive suggestions every day.

Seek out useful questions to answer every day.

Critique the performance of others constructively.

Help others benefit more than you do each time you interact with them.

Example: Recently a friend called. She was in charge of evaluating the performance of the new minister in their church after a year's service. She put together a brief note to every one in the congregation asking that they provide some criticism—I believe she even used the words "constructive criticism"—of the minister's performance. What she received was over 150 responses, each of which contained an average of four negative criticisms or comments.

It was devastating. If you added up all of the criticisms there was no way this minister could have possibly survived. Most of the criticisms were negatives; most reflected individual misunderstandings; virtually none of the criticism had the scope of the congregation in mind or the actual work the minister did as a congregational leader. The criticisms boiled down to negative personal commentary.

My friend's problem was, of course, that she had to show this information to the minister. She felt that when she did, if she didn't have something else worked out, he would undoubtedly resign. No one could withstand this level of personal criticism.

I told her about a lesson I learned early in my career from Chester Burger. As a communications consultant he faced similar situations inside corporations. His strategy, which I've followed for years, was to go back to the same people, and rather than asking for criticism, ask them to make one positive constructive suggestion about what the individual might do to achieve the goals of the organization. The application of this technique is incredibly powerful. If asked to say something of a critical nature about virtually any circumstance, we can all think up two or three or four comments quite easily. But when asked to provide a single positive constructive suggestion, out of every 20 people you may get only one or two truly useful constructive suggestions.

My friend did go back and use this technique. Out of the 300 member parish, she received 12 suggestions. Each of these suggestions was implementable and achievable within a 30-day period. My friend went back to the minister in all honesty and showed her preliminary request for assessment from the congregation, but then showed the follow-up work. The minister not only stayed but amazed just about everyone by transforming the life of their congregation through the implementation of the constructive suggestions of his congregation.

The lesson is this: It is how we structure the discussion and the debate as well as the product we're seeking from that work that determines our success and our level of impact. If you are constructive and seek positive, constructive suggestions, you automatically control and therefore powerfully manage how decisions are made in an organization in a positive way.

Be positive; behave in positive ways.

Teach others to have fun and celebrate some success every day.

Use positive declarative language.

Reduce the use of negative language.

Eliminate the use of negative emotional words.

Example: In normal discourse, when someone says something with which we disagree, we invariably respond by saying something like, "You're wrong" or "That's incorrect," or "You don't know what you're talking about," or "It's simply not done that way," or some similar, negative approach. You may well then move ahead and say what is correct, or what the actual routine happens to be, or how you really do things. The problem is, your listener is still dealing with the insult of a negative comment, making it almost impossible for him/her to hear what your constructive language happens to be. In addition, negative comments almost always put us on the defensive even though we have important, positive, constructive things to say.

"The Bad News Eradicator," is a little exercise I do with clients in which I present a list of common negative phrases and simply ask the clients to turn them into positives. While it may be unusual to interact so directly with the audience during a presentation like this, let me try out just a few on you. Take the phrase I'm about to say and turn it into a positive one.

"We don't do it that way."—What's a positive way of saying the same thing?

"That's not our style."—What's a positive way of saying that?

"The boss won't buy it."—How could you make that a positive statement?

"That's a lie."—How can this be made more positive?

The lesson is this: You control your own negative language. Eradicate or eliminate the use of negative and emotional words and you become far more powerful in managing almost any situation. You deny those who are negative the opening they need to throw everything out of control through their negative comments.

Be prompt; be biased for useful, positive action.

Do it now.

Ask it now.

Answer it now.

Fix it now.

Example: Over the years what I've learned is that whether it's an activist group, an angry group of employees, upset neighbors, or competitors who seem to outsmart us, the way to win every time, the way to move things forward, the way to stay in charge and help others do the same, is to act now—and do it now. This often means making smaller decisions and acting on them more quickly.

Ask it now. Rather than waiting for someone else to ask a question about something that's going on, you ask the question to get the answer.

Answer it now. If there are questions, go get the answers and get them now.

Fix it now. If it's broken, move to repair it. If it's breaking down, move to shore it up.

If you know it's going to be a problem, act now to eliminate the cause.

The lesson is this: Those who act promptly—who do it now—are ahead of the competition, foil the most carefully laid plans of the opposition, and can defeat almost any enemy or control the situation.

Be outcome focused, which essentially means to look to the future; select an achievable, understandable, time-sensitive, worthwhile goal; and then go for it.

Focus on today and tomorrow.

Recognize that the past holds very few important lessons.

Commit to generating and maintaining forward momentum.

Example: Five years ago I became involved in negotiations between some powerful corporate forces, groups of labor unions, church groups, and non-governmental organizations. The issues were extraordinarily compelling, in the news, divisive, and to some extent in the streets in various parts of the United States. The challenge was to find a way to sit down face-to-face, put these matters in some perspective, and develop a plan of action to move forward.

Fortunately, someone suggested that we meet with a minister in Brooklyn Heights, New York, just across the East River from here. He was an individual reputed to have the personal presence to manage such a confrontation.

We met in his living room before a roaring fire in December of 1995. This huge, jovial minister greeted us warmly, had us sit down in front of the fire, listen to some music, and asked us to be quiet for a few minutes.

The minister then laid down one ground rule for the day's work: the discussion was to be entirely outcome-focused. This meant that whatever happened between us prior to entering his living room no longer existed or mattered. Disagreements, arguments, behaviors, the truth, fiction, lies, whatever, from the past were completely irrelevant to our current discussions. Each time anyone began a discussion supported by something from the past, Rev. Smith would halt the discussion and get it focused on tomorrow. If we couldn't abide by this fundamental ground rule, he promised to end the discussions, bid us a pleasant day, and get on about his life.

It's hard to convey just how powerful this concept is. At its most fundamental it recognizes that everyone owns yesterday, everyone owns this morning. Each of you owns the minutes leading up to this point in my presentation, from your own perspectives. There is nothing I can do to change that ownership. But none of you own the next 15 minutes. No one inside or outside this room owns the next day, the next week, the next month, the next year. There-fore, we can—if we choose to—establish how we're going to enter it and live through it, together—if we choose to be outcome-focused.

Now back to Brooklyn Heights. By 4:30 that afternoon we had negotiated and signed a one-page agreement that each of these organizations is living up to today, nearly five years later.

The lesson is this: Being outcome focused is one of the most powerful concepts I've ever come across to help move things forward. You see, if you stay in the past, argue the past, try to re-write the past... you'll die in the past and so will your career.

Be reflective: Seek positive lessons from the past.

What could you have done more or less often in the past? What could you have done to make something better?

Could you have conducted yourself differently, more consistently, more positively?

Example: Rev. Smith from Brooklyn Heights, in the course of our dis-cussions, did permit a few references to the past, eventually, if the observer could apply the principle of reflective thinking. In other words, what construc-tive lesson was learned from the past? What useful bit of information could be extracted that would help implement moving forward to achieve a specific goal? Negative lessons were not permitted; emotional conclusions and negative incidents were eliminated.

The lesson is this: The past is of only limited value. It never repeats itself. No scenario from the past is precisely reproducible in the future. There are a few—very, very few—positive lessons that can be mined from that experience.

If you must look backwards, look in the most constructive, positive way possible.

Be pragmatic. Search for the truths everyone can recognize and benefit by.

Make your forecasts achievable.

Help others achieve their goals and forecasts.

Prepare everyone for underwhelming results.

Example: If you want to be a transformational source, transformation will occur in positive and negative increments rather than as blinding, over-blown achievements. Try to do the doable and know the knowable; achieve the achiev-able and get the gettable. Your credibility rests more on what you're actually able to accomplish than on any series of goals or concepts you may choose to announce but only partially achieve.

The lesson is this: A pragmatist matches rhetoric with reality. Put your-self in the other person's shoes, see the world from their perspective, and help them achieve a portion of their goals in ways they recognize—from their own perspective. Dale Carnegie was right, "Help the other guy get what he wants, and he'll help you get what you want."

Relentlessly seek positive, incremental, personal improvement every day.

This is perhaps the most profound lesson I can share with you today, the one I think you'll probably remember most. In fact, I'm going to ask you to say it out loud: "Relentlessly seek positive incremental personal improvement every day."

Example:

Break problems into solvable parts.

Resolve each increment of the problem promptly.

Prepare to be lucky.

Watch for the big break.

Those who are relentlessly incremental in their personal progress every day are the ones who are lucky.

Luck is limited.

Be ready. Capitalize on big things when they happen.

The most credible public relations practitioners I work with every year are those who:

Intentionally and relentlessly grow every day.

Relentlessly and intentionally try to learn new things every day.

Relentlessly and intentionally help those they serve to achieve some positive incremental progress every single day.

Well, there you are, seven powerful transformational attitudes and behaviors:

Be constructive.

Be positive.

Be prompt.

Be outcome-focused.

Be reflective.

Be pragmatic.

Relentlessly seek positive, incremental personal improvement every day.

So now you ask, "How will I know if I'm a transformational factor?" It will be pretty obvious to you as you gain this positive power. You'll be invited to be heard more within your organization and at higher levels. You'll be able to articulate what is truly important, truly useful, and truly helpful as a matter of daily routine. You'll notice that you are doing more important things, from your perspective. This may mean moving to more important work than that which you're currently doing. It may mean evaluating your current environment and determining whether or not you can become a transformational force within the situation in which you currently find yourself.

If you are truly a transformational force, you'll automatically ask yourself these questions everyday:

What did I learn today?

How can I apply that learning to something I'm currently working on or something I want to work on?

How many times today did somebody tell me they heard me quoted in a meeting they attended?

How or what have I improved in some way for someone else today?

Well, this is one commencement address I hope that you will remember. My wish for today is that you and I have touched foreheads for a few minutes and that my personal determination to help you be successful—from your own perspective—is as clear and apparent to you as it is to me.

Let me congratulate each of you on successfully completing this two weeks of intensive study and professional refocusing and, at the same time, urge every one of you to seriously consider becoming a transformational force in your environment. If you do, I believe you will make that contribution you seek to achieve and you will have a happy, productive, and important personal and professional life.

May the transformational force be with you.

NO 👈

Stuart Ewen

The Public and Its Problems

In March, 1995 . . . Edward L. Bernays died in Cambridge, Massachusetts, at the age of 102. Present at the beginning, so to speak, his life (1892–1995) spanned the history [of public relations].

When I visited with Bernays in the autumn of 1990, I encountered two different people. On the one hand, I met a man who—as witnessed in his nostalgic recollection of Dumb Jack—understood public relations as a necessary response to a society in which expanding democratic expectations were forcefully combating the outmoded assumptions of an old, hierarchical social order. According to this Bernays, the modern belief in universal rights and popular struggles for democracy had confronted elites with a profound question: How could they preserve their social, economic, and political advantages in an age when the idea of a privileged class was coming under mounting attack from below? This first Bernays understood the "public sphere" as contested ground and public relations as a historic response to the vocal demands of a conscious, and increasingly critical, public.

Yet as he described his life and his profession, I glimpsed another Bernays. This one saw the public as a malleable mass of protoplasm, plastic raw material that—in the hands of a skilled manipulator—could be manufactured at will. According to this Bernays, the public mind posed little danger and could be engineered through dexterous appeals to its instinctual and unconscious inner life. This Bernays was the paradigmatic "expert" in a world where "expertise" often refers to a scientifically trained individual's capacity to monitor, forecast, and influence the ideas and/or behavior of others.

This dichotomy characterized Bernays's thinking over a lifetime. In the pivotal years of the late 1940s, for example, Bernays evinced two dramatically dissimilar perspectives on the tasks faced by public relations specialists in a potentially hazardous postwar world.

At one end, in 1947, Bernays maintained that corporate public relations must answer to the ultimatums of a public that had—over the preceding decade and a half—become resolutely aware of its social and economic rights. Toward this goal, Bernays argued, "slogans" and "incantations" would be insufficient.

Business must champion and establish policies that would lead to stable employment; adequate old-age pensions; social security; and other forms of insurance, including group accident, sickness, hospital, and life. These concessions, Bernays understood, were necessitated by a public arena that is shaped, at times, by the ideas and actions of ordinary people and by the social expectations they bring to the historical stage. Embedded within this side of Bernays's thinking was an understanding that, willy-nilly, powerful institutions were not always able to govern the dynamics—or the origins—of public expression. The mobilizations of the 1930s had actively punctuated that fact.

At the same time as Bernays was recommending substantive programmatic proposals, however, he was also ordaining the "engineering of consent" as an indispensable instrument of rule. This Bernays was the painter of mental scenery, the fabricator of captivating "pseudo-environments" designed to steer the public mind furtively toward the agendas of vested power. He was a master of stagecraft, shaping "news" and "events" with a hidden hand. Beside the democrat stood the demagogue, a nimble master of illusions, a man who sought to colonize the public sphere on behalf of entrenched managerial interests.

It would be a misconception, however, to see Bernays's contradictions as particular to the man. The ambiguities of his perspective—the murky dissonance separating one who is *responding to* from one who seeks to *manage* the public mind—have marked the history of public relations throughout the twentieth century.

In the period between 1900 and the First World War, for example, the genesis of corporate public relations began as a reply to wide-spread public indignation at the prevailing practices of big business in the United States. Facing the muckraking publicity of progressivism and terrified by the articulate militancy of America's industrial workforce, large corporations began to employ public relations firms to reconcile the openly declared interests of business with the concerns and goals of a critical—albeit still primarily middle-class—public. In a variety of ways, public relations during this period attempted to provide factual argument and, at times, palpable actions that would answer antibusiness arguments and enunciate a commonality between the private enterprise system and the public interest.

During and after World War I, as progressivism waned and working-class militancy was crushed by a vicious program of repression, the complexion of PR began to change. Inspired by the propaganda successes of the wartime Committee on Public Information and fortified by theories of social psychology, corporate PR moved away from a "public service" ideal and increasingly aspired to stroke and cajole the public psyche. Throughout the twenties, a rapidly expanding legion of public relations experts embraced the conscious manipulation of symbols as the most effective strategy for appealing to the public mind. If, prior to the war, public relations had been fired by the apparition of an aware and discerning population—one that had vigorously influenced the boundaries of public discussion—the public was now being conceived as an unconscious organism, eminently susceptible to the mesmeric power of mass suggestion.

By the late forties, corporate PR had swung the other way. Chastened by a wave of mass mobilizations in the thirties and disciplined by social expectations that had come to the surface during the New Deal period, corporate public relations programs began to mouth New Deal values while advancing a welfare capitalist perspective. Recalling rampant public antagonism toward business throughout the Great Depression and concerned that it might burst forth anew as the war drew to an end, a growing number of corporations initiated pension funds, health plans, and other social security policies that an unprecedented number of Americans now understood to be a constitutionally guaranteed birthright. If the business sector didn't deliver on these promises, PR people reasoned, the public would turn once more toward their government, and the survival of "free enterprise" would be in jeopardy.

As American business flourished during the fifties and prosperity touched the lives of many heretofore "forgotten" Americans, the social emergency of the thirties began to disappear from public relations thinking. Coincidentally, the repressive impact of McCarthyism nursed the assumption that the public was becoming governable once again. In this climate, and emboldened by corporate control of a new and pervasive communications apparatus—television— new ways of thinking began to arise. Though they coincided—at least for a time —with welfare capitalist policies, these new ideas were built on the idea of a fragmentary and spectatorial public that could be swayed by images that were now being pumped, day and night, into each and every American home.

In the years since the 1950s, interactions between public relations and social history have persisted. During the 1960s and 1970s, public ultimatums began to emerge once again. Breaking the hush of the consensus of the fifties, corporate renditions of "the good life" and of the United States as the "land of opportunity" came under mounting scrutiny from within and outside American society. A multiplicity of voices, including those of the civil rights movement, the anti-Vietnam war movement, women's rights activity, and environmentalism, interrogated the values of a commodity culture and testified to the fact that many people were in exile in the "land of opportunity." Irreverent, noncommercial media also began to appear during this period—most notably "underground" newspapers, produced on a shoestring by journalistic fledglings uninstructed in the conventions of a business-dominated press. As these independent media spread throughout the country—reminding a generation that history was in their hands—habitual boundaries separating medium from audience were violated and redrawn.

As countercultural perspectives erupted, and in the face of mounting and diverse opposition, corporate PR thinking became defensive once more. Abandoning the certitude of the fifties, public relations experts now scrambled to address a public arena that seemed to be spinning out of control. "[W]e can preserve our freedom of enterprise only if it fulfills the aspirations of society," remarked Harold Brayman of DuPont in 1964. "We must learn," once again, "to adapt ourselves to the conditions that exist." To rise to the occasion, Brayman counseled, old ways of thinking would be ineffective. "One cannot fight in the jungles of Vietnam," he argued, "with battleships."

David Finn, of the forward-thinking firm of Ruder and Finn, helped to retrain PR thinking during this period. Citing emerging social movements, most of which were questioning the "white bread" homogeneity of corporate life,

Finn maintained that the overarching presence of "the corporate image" was not simply ineffective, but represented a fundamental public relations problem. One of a generation of PR men who came forward during the sixties, Finn argued that corporate public relations must shun the "party line" image of the corporation that had been so ardently assembled in the years after World War II. Corporate PR, he advised, must espouse and embrace the principles of diversity and self-determination that were—like it or not—gathering in the streets.

> What is wrong with the "party line" approach . . . is . . . the evils which come in the process of stifling individual initiative. It suggests that it is more important for the corporation to create an impression of monolithic unity than for individuals to express themselves freely.

As had been the case throughout much of the century, this shift in public relations thinking reflected the imprint of popular democracy. If practitioners help to "build respect for variety in public life, for the right of people to hold different opinions and to express them freely," Finn asserted, "I think public relations can thus become an integral part of the democratic process." To be effective, he warned, public relations people must be closely tuned to the political intonations in their work.

> Public relations should . . . be wary of the dangers inherent in conformity, and the fact that its work could create its own brand of "big brotherness" if it is not careful. Public relations should not permit itself to envy the propaganda advantages which totalitarian governments sometimes achieve through their monolithic control of communications. Instead it should learn to respect difference, dissension, conflict, and above all, individuality . . .

For about a decade, beginning in the mid-1960s, much public relations was in synch with Finn's remarks. As had been the case before, there was a need to adapt to changing social conditions. A prime example of this adaptation was the growing number of public relations people who discussed, as never before, the need to acknowledge the demands of the African American population in the United States.

"In the Negro community," wrote D. Parke Gibson, publisher of a newsletter focusing on marketing to African Americans, "the belief still exists, and it will for some time, that there is insincerity on the part of American corporations really to provide equality of opportunity to Negroes." To change this situation, Gibson proposed, companies must "[s]eek the advice of reputable Negro specialists in public relations in order to avoid the possibility of offending Negro Americans through well-meaning but wrong directed action."

James F. Langton, public relations officer of the Bank of America, offered similar counsel. The civil rights struggle, he argued, was an inevitable outcome of America's past. Corporations, he wrote in the *Public Relations Journal*, must sensitize themselves to the history of race relations in the United States.

> After a long and agonizing history of white oppression, white violence and white hate, the Negro today is in a state of revolt. . . . It's time we understood this history and, with understanding, come to realize that Negro hate is the mirror of White hate, and Negro violence a mirror of White violence.

As a start in the direction of redressing African Americans' grievances, he suggested, "There must be some aggressive employment programs designed to seek out and encourage trainable Negro applicants."

To some extent, such ideas were consonant with the history of public relations as an imperative corporate response to popular democratic mobilizations. Here, as had been true in the past, corporations—prodded by the federal government—worked overtime to inaugurate social programs while they flooded the pipelines of persuasion to broadcast a spiritual bond between corporate activities and the interests of diverse American communities.

The corporate recognition of American diversity, however, pointed in other directions as well. To some extent, it provided the core around which future approaches to the engineering of consent would be developed.

⋘◉⋙

Whatever else may be said of the social movements of the 1960s, it must be conceded that they were animated by an intensely democratic vision. Young radicals of the period dared to imagine a future world in which social injustices predicated on class, race, gender, and persuasion would be redressed and in which the *wretched of the earth* would be rewarded by a realm of unbounded possibility. At the heart of sixties politics, then, stood the glaring conflict between a democratic ideal of universal rights and tenacious social realities that were still premised on the denial of these rights to significant portions of the population, both at home and abroad. Whether it was African Americans or Chicanos, heterosexual women or gays, U.S. soldiers in the jungles of Vietnam or students on the campuses of American universities, each constituency called America to task, each challenged the nation to implement its democratic pledge. In widespread calls for "participatory democracy," a vision of society, administered collectively by—and according to the needs of—its various constituents, was gaining ground.

As public relations experts approached the tumultuous terrain, however, an ominous shift began to take place. If, at the grassroots level, divergent voices were challenging the society to meet its responsibility to all its people, the opinion-measurement industry began a parallel effort to render this diversity of voices into a set of manageable categories. Beginning in the late sixties and intensifying from the seventies onward, public opinions and behaviors began to be demographically factored into discrete analytical units, an instrumental array of "lifestyles" or "subcultures" to be studied and, once studied, predictably governed. As social or cultural patterns have shifted, of course, specific categories have changed, but the intent of these pigeonholes has remained constant: to provide useful attitudinal road maps that permit compliance professionals —PR experts, political consultants, social psychologists, merchandisers, advertising copywriters, and the like—to target particular groups in an idiom they will perceive to be their own. *Democracy* has given way to *demography* as the prevailing American faith.

❧◎❧

... As the trend has played itself out, an all-inclusive vision of democracy has been a casualty. While demographically specific approaches to the marketing of ideas is often pointed to as a sign of increased democracy—different groups of people hearing *what they want to hear*—it also enables the public relations establishment to summon opinions and generate messages that exacerbate hostilities between groups, heighten the prejudices of particular sectors of the population, and contribute to an increasingly fragmented—and hence more manageable—society.

Widely publicized *gains* for one demographic group—African Americans, women, gays, or people on welfare, for example—are simultaneously repackaged and advertised as being *losses* for another—whites, men, heterosexuals, or wage earners, for instance. In the process, the New Deal notion of "the people" as a diverse union with common democratic objectives has been demolished. If the New Deal vision of "the people" was convoked around the need to contain the ingrained rapacity of business interests, today popular antagonisms between groups have deepened, while unfettered corporate consolidation is flourishing. Amid carefully orchestrated publicity campaigns against progressive social initiatives, the idea of an inclusive America, along with a general commitment to *the common good*, has become fugitive.

This development was chaperoned by the publicity machine of Reaganism, which reinstalled corporate boosterism, free-enterprise politics, and self-righteous contempt for poor people as the rule of the day. If public institutions were once seen as the province of all people, today the term *public* (as in public education, public housing, public broadcasting, public assistance, and public health) is most often employed to characterize institutions that serve people who are deemed *undeserving* and *undesirable*. Amid a religious celebration of "free" market forces, America has become a society in the process of extinguishing democratic expectations that rose from the bottom up during the 1930s, expectations that informed the allegedly *golden age* of post–World War II prosperity.

Public relations has played a critical role in this change. Since the mid-seventies, corporate PR's defection from the idea of universal rights has been glaring. Citing the pretext of economic exigency, more and more corporations have diminished or dismantled the public policies—welfare capitalist programs—that, three decades earlier, were understood as a necessary response to public ultimatums. Simultaneously, image-management, spin-control, and astroturf organizing—reinforced by demographics and television—have provided the most visible rendition of public life....

Amid the flight from "liberal" values, the ideal of opinion engineering has again seized control of American public life. From the onset of Reaganism, we have witnessed the premeditated undermining of civil rights; the growing economic misery of vast, largely African American populations; and the rollback of opportunity as even a glimmer of a promise in many American communities. The United States is more starkly divided in terms of income than any other industrial nation, and the politics of the National Association of Manufacturers, once widely scorned for placing profit above all other values, is the rule of the day. All this is cavalierly reported as an ineluctable result of shifting public opinion—a euphemism for the triumph of a relatively small right wing that has donned the previously accessible mantle of "the people," while the identity of all others—the numerical majority—has been buried in a sinkhole of demographically reinforced "minority" status.

⋅⟨◉⟩⋅

Today, with a powerful machinery of opinion management deeply entrenched —and little coherent opposition heard from below—the meaning and realization of democracy have become more and more elusive. The extent to which power and influence are routinely employed to assemble "phantom publics" on behalf of any purpose challenges us to rethink the structures of social communication and to imagine again the ways by which democratic participation may be accomplished.

Some may argue, looking back on... history,... that present circumstances are transient—that, as in the past, the force of democratic expression will undermine and ultimately transgress the engineering of consent. For those who are used to looking at American history as a "pendulum" swinging back and forth between conservatism and liberalism, such an eventuality may seem preordained.

But if one examines other developments,... this interpretation is significantly flawed. Looking at the historical development of public relations as a force in American society, one sees that a consequential change has taken place, one that throws simplistic pendulum theories into question. Coinciding with recurrent swings between public relations as a response to democratic mobilizations and as an attempt to colonize the horizons of public expression, there has been a parallel development. Over the course of this century, while arenas of public interaction and expression have become scarce, the apparatus for molding the public mind and for appealing to the public eye has become increasingly pervasive, more and more sophisticated in its technology and expertise. Economic mergers in the media and information industries, in particular, are only reminders that though many are touched by the messages of these industries, fewer and fewer hands control the pipelines of persuasion.

At the dawn of a new millennium, particularly in the face of this communications imbalance, pivotal questions become more urgent:

- Can there be democracy when the public is a fractionalized audience? When the public has no collective presence?
- Can there be democracy when public life is separated from the ability of a public to act—for itself—as a public?
- Can there be democracy when public agendas are routinely predetermined by "unseen engineers?"
- Can there be democracy when public opinion is reduced to the published results of opinion surveys, statistical applause tracks?

- Can there be democracy when the tools of communication are neither democratically distributed nor democratically controlled?
- Can there be democracy when the content of media is determined, almost universally, by commercial considerations?
- Can there be democracy in a society in which emotional appeals overwhelm reason, where the image is routinely employed to overwhelm thought?
- What developments will emerge to invigorate popular democracy this time around? What will move us beyond prevailing strategies of power that are aimed at managing the human climate?...

In thinking about ways to reawaken democracy, we must keep in mind that the relationship between publicity and democracy is not essentially corrupt. The free circulation of ideas and debate is critical to the maintenance of an aware public. The rise of democratic thinking, in fact, cannot be explained apart from the circulation of pamphlets, proclamations, and other literary documents that provided a basis for public discussion and helped to transform once-heretical ideas into common aspirations.

Publicity becomes an impediment to democracy, however, when the circulation of ideas is governed by enormous concentrations of wealth that have, as their underlying purpose, the perpetuation of their own power. When this is the case—as is too often true today—the ideal of civic participation gives way to a continual sideshow, a masquerade of democracy calculated to pique the public's emotions. In regard to a more democratic future, then, ways of enhancing the circulation of ideas—regardless of economic circumstance—need to be developed.

We need to imagine what an active public life might look like in an electronic age. We need to discover ways to move beyond thinking of public relations as a function of compliance experts and learn to think of it as an ongoing and inclusive process of discussion. Ordinary people need to develop independent ways and means of understanding and airing public problems and issues and of acting on them....

Present inequities regarding *who has a say? who gets to be heard?* need to be corrected. The vast power of the commercial communications system today lies in its unimpeded control over the avenues of public discussion. For this situation to change, the public sphere—currently dominated by corporate interests and consciously managed by public relations professionals—must revert to the people.

Though camouflaged by business as usual, the capacity to make such a change happen is within sight. Ironically, the enormous authority of a business-centered worldview is derived from the fact that large corporations have been permitted to occupy and impose upon public properties—such as the broadcast spectrum—without paying any significant rent to the public. For a negligible licensing fee, private corporations harvest an incessant windfall of public influence.

If this practice was to change—if a fund to support public communication, for example, regularly received a fair rent from those who were permitted to exploit public properties commercially—funding for noncommercial venues of expression and for noncommercial arenas of public education would be plentiful. If 15 to 25 percent of all advertising expenditures in the United States were applied this way, the crisis in funding for public arts and education would evaporate. New visions would flourish. Locally based community communications centers—equipped with up-to-date technologies and opening new avenues for distribution—would magnify the variety of voices heard. Schools could more adequately prepare their students for the responsibilities of democratic citizenship.

POSTSCRIPT

Do Public Relations Practitioners Provide a Valuable Service to the Public?

Lukaszewski clearly enjoys his role as a public relations practitioner, and he makes no apologies for his work. Instead, he views public relations as a persuasive field, which has the power to be a "transformative" force that provides a valuable public service. His examples are drawn from his own experiences in working with clients who have special communication needs and who seek to influence the public through association with positive images and thoughts.

Ewen's description of the evolution of the public relations field also identifies some valuable services that have come about through the effective practice of public relations, but he balances two visions. The first is one in which public relations provides a valuable service to an increasingly critical public. The second is that of public relations professionals as mind managers, capable of manipulation and deceit.

As you read the following selections, consider whether or not the client that a public relations practitioner serves affects your judgment of whether public relations is good or bad. Also consider whether public relations serves members of the public or deceives them by influencing their opinions. Then, examine whether or not certain public relations firms have specialties, such as nonprofit organizations, for-profit Fortune 500 companies, or some other guidelines that influence how and what clients they are willing to support. Is it possible for any company to pick and choose its client base? How important is the profit motive to any public relations firm, and how is the firm's success measured?

Edward L. Bernays, whom Ewen cites extensively, is known as the father of public relations. Until his dying days, Bernays sought to have public relations practitioners trained in behavioral and ethical activities. He fought long and hard to have the study of public relations legitimated, and he wanted practitioners to be qualified by examination before they were allowed to practice. While Bernays's dreams of creating a profession that had important standards, codes of conduct, and ethics mirrors the type of career pattern a lawyer may take, his actual plans for a national, standardized test never fully materialized. As a result, as in many professions, there is a range of viewpoints and activities by the profession's members.

The public relations field remains large, and it offers many potential job opportunities for people who find that their own moral and ethical attitudes and behaviors can be accommodated. Schools that teach public relations skills and history continue to enroll larger numbers of students than ever before. Yet, it is still important to consider the various dimensions that accompany any influential field. In this manner, the types of questions raised by this selection could also be posed in connection with any other career in the field of communications.

One of the earliest books written about public relations is *Crystallizing Public Opinion,* by Edward L. Bernays (Boni & Liveright, 1923). One of Bernays's most often quoted articles is "Engineering of Consent," *Annals of the American Academy of Political and Social Science* (vol. 250, 1947). In addition to many articles and books authored by Bernays, Ray E. Hiebert has written an excellent book about the powerful public relations practitioner, Ivy Lee, titled *Courtier to the Crowd: The Story of Ivy Lee and the Development of Public Relations* (Iowa State University Press, 1966).

Over the years, several books have been written to explore specific public relations campaigns, many of which have to deal with political campaigns or specific products. Joe McGuiness's classic, *The Selling of the President, 1968* (Simon & Schuster, 1969) tells the story of the campaign between Richard Nixon and George McGovern. Kathleen Hall Jamieson's *Packaging the Presidency: A History and Criticism of Presidential Campaign Advertising,* 3rd ed. (Oxford, 1997) addresses the power of advertising in creating a political campaign.

From the perspective of specific clients and their public relations campaigns, perhaps one of the best books is Randall Rothenberg's *Where the Suckers Moon* (Knopf, 1994), focusing on the introduction of the Subaru automobile to the U.S. market.

There are also some influential journals and trade magazines that provide other dimensions of the fields of public relations and advertising. *Public Opinion Quarterly* is an academic journal that spans a variety of issues, *Public Relations Journal* is both an academic and a trade magazine, and *AdWeek* is tied to trends in contemporary advertising.

On the Internet . . .

Educause

This site contains summaries of new technology news from various publications as well as links to many other resources. This site is designed to facilitate the use of technology in teaching, research, and learning.

http://www.educause.edu

The Electronic Frontier Foundation

The Electronic Frontier Foundation (EFF) is a nonprofit civil liberties organization that is working to protect free expression and access to public resources and information online. It also works to promote responsibility in the new media.

http://www.eff.org

The Journal of Computer-Mediated Communication

This site has been maintained by the Annenberg School for Communication at the University of Southern California since 1995. Many issues are discussed in this electronic journal, including electronic commerce, law and the electronic frontier, Netplay, and designing presence in virtual environments.

http://www.ascusc.org/jcmc/

Yahoo International

This Yahoo service contains resources on different countries, providing information about media systems and media programming available around the world.

http://dir.yahoo.com/regional/countries/index.html

PART 6

The Information Society

*P*redictions of a world that is increasingly reliant upon media and communication technologies have generally provided either utopian and dystopian visions about what our lives will be like in the future. Now the ability to communicate instantly around the world has become a reality.

Recent media distribution technologies present new options of traditional ways of doing things. Although many are experiencing how electronic communication can change lives and the ways we work and communicate, many questions remain unanswered. What rights do individuals have concerning the accessibility of private information? Will new ways of communication change the way individuals interact? Will everyone have access to the services and technologies that enable more immediate information exchange? How will new technologies influence us as individuals?

- Can Privacy Be Protected in the Information Age?

- Does the Internet Have the Power to Transform Culture?

ISSUE 17

Can Privacy Be Protected in the Information Age?

YES: Simson Garfinkel, from "Privacy and the New Technology," *The Nation* (February 28, 2000)

NO: Adam L. Penenberg, from "The End of Privacy," *Forbes* (November 29, 1999)

ISSUE SUMMARY

YES: Journalist Simson Garfinkel discusses how today's technology has the potential to destroy our privacy. He makes the case that the government and individuals could take steps to protect themselves against privacy abuse, particularly by returning to the groundwork set by the government in the 1970s and by educating people on how to avoid privacy traps.

NO: *Forbes* reporter Adam L. Penenberg discusses his own experiences with an Internet detective agency, and he explains how easy it is for companies to get unauthorized access to personal information. He specifically describes how much, and where, personal information is kept and the lack of safeguards in our current system.

Privacy, or the legal right "to be left alone," is something we often take for granted until we feel that our privacy has been violated. In the following selections, Simon Garfinkel and Adam L. Penenberg discuss the range of privacy issues with which we now are faced, due to the computer's ability to store and match records for virtually any transaction we make using a computer. Data companies are emerging that have various standards about seeking the permission to save and sell personal information. While Garfinkel discusses how we could protect our privacy by drawing from already existing laws and statutes, Penenberg explains that many companies have avoided any prior legislation or standards to become information brokers.

This issue brings up questions of what privacy is, and what it means to us, but it also reminds us that as we use newer technologies, there are often unavoidable problems caused by and related to their use. The "transparency," or lack of obvious technological control, is apparent in uses of the Internet and in the ability of high-speed computers to match check numbers, driver's license numbers, and other identifying bits of information. For those who wonder why their names appear on certain mailings, why they are contacted by telemarketers, or how secure is their personal information, this issue will bring up questions and uncover some of the answers.

Survey research reveals that many people feel that their privacy has been invaded at some time and that concerns about privacy are growing. But there are also some disturbing studies to indicate that young people are far less concerned about privacy issues than their parents. Could it be that younger people have not yet experienced the potential situations for privacy invasion, or, are we seeing a social value, in this case the right to privacy, in some type of transition?

Garfinkel advocates a position on privacy protection that would return us to a time in history when government was much more proactive in protecting the rights of citizens and residents. If his theory is correct, many agree that it would not be very expensive for the government to ensure safeguards about this basic right. However, trends in government involvement in businesses seem to be leading away from government oversight and toward giving greater control to businesses to monitor their own actions. Many of the companies discussed by Penenberg operate with few standards or guidelines at all. When the government itself is one of the primary repositories for personal information, could it, or should it, take the lead in defining certain standards and criteria for the protection of the innocent? Furthermore, if control should be exercised, would it be best left to the federal government, state, or local legislators?

Perhaps one of the key issues behind the privacy dilemma is the question of how and what people can do if they find that their privacy is invaded. With so many laws and statutes on the books, the legal wrangling over questions of privacy can be expensive and difficult to challenge. Many times people do not know how much information has been gathered about them until they find that the information is wrong, and it causes a problem. Consider the person who knows that he or she always pays bills on time, but for some reason, a credit reporting agency finds him or her negligent. Consequently, his or her new car loan or credit card application is denied because of the incorrect records. What recourse should that person have, and how long would it take to correct any misinformation? How could that person find out what other records might be inaccurate?

One of the growing areas of privacy concern is the collection and appropriate distribution of medical information about a person. Is it right to let others know the status of someone's confidential medical records? Should the results of voluntary or required drug testing, pregnancy tests, or AIDS tests be available to employers or anyone else without written authorization of the person being tested? Can those confidential records be used to prevent someone from buying insurance, getting a job, or getting a driver's license?

There are many questions related to issues of privacy, and we will undoubtedly see the courts debating exact parameters of privacy and information control in the near future. For now, we all need to think of the related issues of privacy and keep searching for answers to these important questions.

Simson Garfinkel

 **YES**

Privacy and the New Technology

You wake to the sound of a ringing telephone—but how could that happen? Several months ago, you reprogrammed your home telephone system so it would never ring before the civilized hour of 8 AM. But it's barely 6:45. Who was able to bypass your phone's programming?

You pick up the receiver, then slam it down a moment later. It's one of those marketing machines playing a recorded message. What's troubling you now is how this call got past the filters you set up. Later on you'll discover how: The company that sold you the phone created an undocumented "back door"; last week, the phone codes were sold in an online auction.

Now that you're awake, you decide to go through yesterday's mail. There's a letter from the neighborhood hospital you visited last month. "We're pleased that our emergency room could serve you in your time of need," the letter begins. "As you know, our fees (based on our agreement with your HMO) do not cover the cost of treatment. To make up the difference, a number of hospitals have started selling patient records to medical researchers and consumer-marketing firms. Rather than mimic this distasteful behavior, we have decided to ask you to help us make up the difference. We are recommending a tax-deductible contribution of $275 to help defray the cost of your visit."

The veiled threat isn't empty, but you decide you don't really care who finds out about your sprained wrist. You fold the letter in half and drop it into your shredder. Also into the shredder goes a trio of low-interest credit-card offers. Why a shredder? A few years ago you would never have thought of shredding your junk mail—until a friend in your apartment complex had his identity "stolen" by the building's superintendent. As best as anybody can figure out, the super picked one of those preapproved credit-card applications out of the trash; called the toll-free number and picked up the card when it was delivered. He's in Mexico now, with a lot of expensive clothing and electronics, all at your friend's expense.

On that cheery note, you grab your bag and head out the door, which automatically locks behind you.

This is the future—not a far-off future but one that's just around the corner. It's a future in which what little privacy we now have will be gone. Some people call this loss of privacy "Orwellian," harking back to *1984*, George Orwell's classic work on privacy and autonomy. In that book, Orwell imagined a future in which a totalitarian state used spies, video surveillance, historical revisionism and control over the media to maintain its power. But the age of monolithic state control is over. The future we're rushing toward isn't one in which our every move is watched and recorded by some all-knowing Big Brother. It is instead a future of a hundred kid brothers who constantly watch and interrupt our daily lives. Orwell thought the Communist system represented the ultimate threat to individual liberty. Over the next fifty years, we will see new kinds of threats to privacy that find their roots not in Communism but in capitalism, the free market, advanced technology and the unbridled exchange of electronic information.

The problem with this word "privacy" is that it falls short of conveying the really big picture. Privacy isn't just about hiding things. It's about self-possession, autonomy and integrity. As we move into the computerized world of the twenty-first century, privacy will be one of our most important civil rights. But this right of privacy isn't the right of people to close their doors and pull down their window shades—perhaps because they want to engage in some sort of illicit or illegal activity. It's the right of people to control what details about their lives stay inside their own houses and what leaks to the outside.

Most of us recognize that our privacy is at risk. According to a 1996 nationwide poll conducted by Louis Harris & Associates, 24 percent of Americans have "personally experienced a privacy invasion." In 1995 the same survey found that 80 percent felt that "consumers have lost all control over how personal information about them is circulated and used by companies." Ironically, both the 1995 and 1996 surveys were paid for by Equifax, a company that earns nearly $2 billion each year from collecting and distributing personal information.

Today the Internet is compounding our privacy conundrum—largely because the voluntary approach to privacy protection advocated by the Clinton Administration doesn't work in the rough and tumble world of real business. For example, a study just released by the California HealthCare Foundation found that nineteen of the top twenty-one health websites have privacy policies, but most sites fail to follow them. Not surprisingly, 17 percent of Americans questioned in a poll said they do not go online for health information because of privacy concerns.

◦◉◦

But privacy threats are not limited to the Internet: Data from all walks of life are now being captured, compiled, indexed and stored. For example, New York City has now deployed the Metrocard system, which allows subway and bus riders to pay their fares by simply swiping a magnetic-strip card. But the system also records the serial number of each card and the time and location of every swipe. New York police have used this vast database to crack crimes and disprove alibis. Although law enforcement is a reasonable use of this database, it is also a use that was adopted without any significant public debate. Furthermore, additional controls may be necessary: It is not clear who has access to the database, under what circumstances that access is given and what provisions are being taken to prevent the introduction of false data into it. It would be terrible if the subway's database were used by an employee to stalk an ex-lover or frame an innocent person for a heinous crime.

"New technology has brought extraordinary benefits to society, but it also has placed all of us in an electronic fishbowl in which our habits, tastes and activities are watched and recorded," New York State Attorney General Eliot Spitzer said in late January [2000], in announcing that Chase Manhattan had agreed to stop selling depositor information without clear permission from customers. "Personal information thought to be confidential is routinely shared with others without our consent."

Today's war on privacy is intimately related to the recent dramatic advances in technology. Many people today say that in order to enjoy the benefits of modern society, we must necessarily relinquish some degree of privacy. If we want the convenience of paying for a meal by credit card or paying for a toll with an electronic tag mounted on our rearview mirror, then we must accept the routine collection of our purchases and driving habits in a large database over which we have no control. It's a simple bargain, albeit a Faustian one.

This trade-off is both unnecessary and wrong. It reminds me of another crisis our society faced back in the fifties and sixties—the environmental crisis. Then, advocates of big business said that poisoned rivers and lakes were the necessary costs of economic development, jobs and an improved standard of living. Poison was progress: Anybody who argued otherwise simply didn't understand the facts.

Today we know better. Today we know that sustainable economic development depends on preserving the environment. Indeed, preserving the environment is a prerequisite to the survival of the human race. Without clean air to breathe and clean water to drink, we will all die. Similarly, in order to reap the benefits of technology, it is more important than ever for us to use technology to protect personal freedom.

Blaming technology for the death of privacy isn't new. In 1890 two Boston lawyers, Samuel Warren and Louis Brandeis, argued in the *Harvard Law Review* that privacy was under attack by "recent inventions and business methods." They contended that the pressures of modern society required the creation of a "right of privacy," which would help protect what they called "the right to be let alone." Warren and Brandeis refused to believe that privacy had to die for technology to flourish. Today, the Warren/Brandeis article is regarded as one of the most influential law review articles ever published.

Privacy-invasive technology does not exist in a vacuum, of course. That's because technology itself exists at a junction between science, the market and society. People create technology to fill specific needs and desires. And technology is regulated, or not, as people and society see fit. Few engineers set out to build systems designed to crush privacy and autonomy, and few businesses or consumers would willingly use or purchase these systems if they understood the consequences.

⋅⟨◉⟩⋅

How can we keep technology and the free market from killing our privacy? One way is by being careful and informed consumers. Some people have begun taking simple measures to protect their privacy, measures like making purchases with cash and refusing to provide their Social Security numbers—or providing fake ones. And a small but growing number of people are speaking out for technology with privacy. In 1990 Lotus and Equifax teamed up to create a CD-ROM product called "Lotus Marketplace: Households," which would have included names, addresses and demographic information on every household in the United States, so small businesses could do the same kind of target marketing that big businesses have been doing since the sixties. The project was canceled when more than 30,000 people wrote to Lotus demanding that their names be taken out of the database.

Similarly, in 1997 the press informed taxpayers that the Social Security Administration was making detailed tax-history information about them available over the Internet. The SSA argued that its security provisions—requiring that taxpayers enter their name, date of birth, state of birth and mother's maiden name—were sufficient to prevent fraud. But tens of thousands of Americans disagreed, several US senators investigated the agency and the service was promptly shut down. When the service was reactivitated some months later, the detailed financial information in the SSA's computers could not be downloaded over the Internet.

But individual actions are not enough. We need to involve government itself in the privacy fight. The biggest privacy failure of the US government has been its failure to carry through with the impressive privacy groundwork that was laid in the Nixon, Ford and Carter administrations. It's worth taking a look back at that groundwork and considering how it may serve us today.

The seventies were a good decade for privacy protection and consumer rights. In 1970 Congress passed the Fair Credit Reporting Act, which gave Americans the previously denied right to see their own credit reports and demand the removal of erroneous information. Elliot Richardson, who at the time was President Nixon's Secretary of Health, Education and Welfare, created a commission in 1972 to study the impact of computers on privacy. After years of testimony in Congress, the commission found all the more reason for alarm and issued a landmark report in 1973.

The most important contribution of the Richardson report was a bill of rights for the computer age, which it called the Code of Fair Information Practices. The code is based on five principles:

- There must be no personal-data record-keeping system whose very existence is secret.
- There must be a way for a person to find out what information about the person is in a record and how it is used.
- There must be a way for a person to prevent information about the person that was obtained for one purpose from being used or made available for other purposes without the person's consent.
- There must be a way for a person to correct or amend a record of identifiable information about the person.
- Any organization creating, maintaining, using or disseminating records of identifiable personal data must assure the reliability of the data for their intended use and must take precautions to prevent misuse of the data.

◆

The biggest impact of the Richardson report wasn't in the United States but in Europe. In the years after the report was published, practically every European country passed laws based on these principles. Many created data-protection commissions and commissioners to enforce the laws. Some believe that one reason for Europe's interest in electronic privacy was its experience with Nazi Germany in the thirties and forties. Hitler's secret police used the records of governments and private organizations in the countries he invaded to round up people who posed the greatest threat to German occupation; postwar Europe realized the danger of allowing potentially threatening private information to be collected, even by democratic governments that might be responsive to public opinion.

But here in the United States, the idea of institutionalized data protection faltered. President Jimmy Carter showed interest in improving medical privacy, but he was quickly overtaken by economic and political events. Carter lost the election of 1980 to Ronald Reagan, whose aides saw privacy protection as yet another failed Carter initiative. Although several privacy-protection laws were signed during the Reagan/Bush era, the leadership for these bills came from Congress, not the White House. The lack of leadership stifled any chance of passing a nationwide data-protection act. Such an act would give people the right to know if their name and personal information is stored in a database, to see the information and to demand that incorrect information be removed.

In fact, while most people in the federal government were ignoring the cause of privacy, some were actually pursuing an antiprivacy agenda. In the early eighties, the government initiated numerous "computer matching" programs designed to catch fraud and abuse. Unfortunately, because of erroneous data these programs often penalized innocent people. In 1994 Congress passed the Communications Assistance to Law Enforcement Act, which gave the government dramatic new powers for wiretapping digital communications. In 1996 Congress passed two laws, one requiring states to display Social Security numbers on driver's licenses and another requiring that all medical patients in the United States be issued unique numerical identifiers, even if they pay their own bills. Fortunately, the implementation of those 1996 laws has been delayed, thanks largely to a citizen backlash and the resulting inaction by Congress and the executive branch.

꿈

Continuing the assault, both the Bush and Clinton administrations waged an all-out war against the rights of computer users to engage in private and secure communications. Starting in 1991, both administrations floated proposals for use of "Clipper" encryption systems that would have given the government access to encrypted personal communications. Only recently did the Clinton Administration finally relent in its seven-year war against computer privacy. President Clinton also backed the Communications Decency Act (CDA), which made it a crime to transmit sexually explicit information to minors—and, as a result, might have required Internet providers to deploy far-reaching monitoring and censorship systems. When a court in Philadelphia found the CDA unconstitutional, the Clinton Administration appealed the decision all the way to the Supreme Court—and lost.

One important step toward reversing the current direction of government would be to create a permanent federal oversight agency charged with protecting privacy. Such an agency would:

- Watch over the government's tendency to sacrifice people's privacy for other goals and perform governmentwide reviews of new federal programs for privacy violations before they're launched.
- Enforce the government's few existing privacy laws.
- Be a guardian for individual privacy and liberty in the business world, showing businesses how they can protect privacy and profits at the same time.
- Be an ombudsman for the American public and rein in the worst excesses that our society has created.

Evan Hendricks, editor of the Washington-based newsletter *Privacy Times*, estimates that a fifty-person privacy-protection agency could be created with an annual budget of less than $5 million—a tiny drop in the federal budget.

Some privacy activists scoff at the idea of using government to assure our privacy. Governments, they say, are responsible for some of the greatest privacy violations of all time. This is true, but the US government was also one of the greatest polluters of all time. Today the government is the nation's environmental police force, equally scrutinizing the actions of private business and the government itself.

At the very least, governments can alter the development of technology that affects privacy. They have done so in Europe. Consider this: A growing number of businesses in Europe are offering free telephone calls—provided that the caller first listens to a brief advertisement. The service saves consumers money, even if it does expose them to a subtle form of brainwashing. But not all these services are equal. In Sweden both the caller and the person being called are forced to listen to the advertisement, and the new advertisements are played during the phone call itself. But Italy's privacy ombudsman ruled that the person being called could not be forced to listen to the ads.

There is also considerable public support for governmental controls within the United States itself—especially on key issues, such as the protection of medical records. For example, a 1993 Harris-Equifax survey on medical privacy issues found that 56 percent of the American public favored "comprehensive federal legislation that spells out rules for confidentiality of individual medical records" as part of national healthcare reform legislation. Yet Congress failed to act on the public's wishes.

The Fair Credit Reporting Act [FCRA] was a good law in its day, but it should be upgraded into a Data Protection Act. Unfortunately, the Federal Trade Commission and the courts have narrowly interpreted the FCRA. The first thing that is needed is legislation that expands it into new areas. Specifically, consumer-reporting firms should be barred from reporting arrests unless those arrests result in convictions. Likewise, consumer-reporting firms should not be allowed to report evictions unless they result in court judgments in favor of the landlord or a settlement in which both the landlord and tenant agree that the eviction can be reported. Companies should be barred from exchanging medical information about individuals or furnishing medical information as part of a patient's report without the patient's explicit consent.

❧❦❧

We also need new legislation that expands the fundamental rights offered to consumers under the FCRA. When negative information is reported to a credit bureau, the business making that report should be required to notify the subject of the report—the consumer—in writing. Laws should be clarified so that if a consumer-reporting company does not correct erroneous data in its reports, consumers can sue for real damages, punitive damages and legal fees. People should have the right to correct any false information in their files, and if the consumer and the business disagree about the truth, then the consumer should have a right to place a *detailed* explanation into his or her record. And people should have a right to see all the information that has been collected on them; these reports should be furnished for free, at least once every six months.

We need to rethink consent, a bedrock of modern law. Consent is a great idea, but the laws that govern consent need to be rewritten to limit what kinds of agreements can be made with consumers. Blanket, perpetual consent should be outlawed.

Further, we need laws that require improved computer security. In the eighties the United States aggressively deployed cellular-telephone and alphanumeric-pager networks, even though both systems were fundamentally unsecure. Instead of deploying secure systems, manufacturers lobbied for laws that would make it illegal to listen to the broadcasts. The results were predictable: dozens of cases in which radio transmissions were eavesdropped. We are now making similar mistakes in the prosecution of many Internet crimes, going after the perpetrator while refusing to acknowledge the liabilities of businesses that do not even take the most basic security precautions.

We should also bring back the Office of Technology Assessment, set up under a bill passed in 1972. The OTA didn't have the power to make laws or issue regulations, but it could publish reports on topics Congress asked it to study. Among other things, the OTA considered at length the trade-offs between law enforcement and civil liberties, and it also looked closely at issues of worker monitoring. In total, the OTA published 741 reports, 175 of which dealt directly with privacy issues, before it was killed in 1995 by the newly elected Republican-majority Congress.

Nearly forty years ago, Rachel Carson's book *Silent Spring* helped seed the US environmental movement. And to our credit, the silent spring that Carson foretold never came to be. *Silent Spring* was successful because it helped people to understand the insidious damage that pesticides were wreaking on the environment, and it helped our society and our planet to plot a course to a better future.

Today, technology is killing one of our most cherished freedoms. Whether you call this freedom the right to digital self-determination, the right to informational autonomy or simply the right to privacy, the shape of our future will be determined in large part by how we understand, and ultimately how we control or regulate, the threats to this freedom that we face today.

Adam L. Penenberg  **NO**

The End of Privacy

The phone rang and a stranger cracked sing-songy at the other end of the line: *"Happy Birthday."* That was spooky—the next day I would turn 37. "Your full name is Adam Landis Penenberg," the caller continued. "Landis?" My mother's maiden name. "I'm touched," he said. Then Daniel Cohn, Web detective, reeled off the rest of my "base identifiers"—my birth date, address in New York, Social Security number. Just two days earlier I had issued Cohn a challenge: Starting with my byline, dig up as much information about me as you can. "That didn't take long," I said.

"It took about five minutes," Cohn said, cackling back in Boca Raton, Fla. "I'll have the rest within a week." And the line went dead.

In all of six days Dan Cohn and his Web detective agency, Docusearch. com, shattered every notion I had about privacy in this country (or whatever remains of it). Using only a keyboard and the phone, he was able to uncover the innermost details of my life—whom I call late at night; how much money I have in the bank; my salary and rent. He even got my unlisted phone numbers, both of them. Okay, so you've heard it before: America, the country that made "right to privacy" a credo, has lost its privacy to the computer. But it's far worse than you think. Advances in smart data-sifting techniques and the rise of the massive databases have conspired to strip you naked. The spread of the Web is the final step. It will make most of the secrets you have more instantly available than ever before, ready to reveal themselves in a few taps on the keyboard.

For decades this information rested in remote mainframes that were difficult to access, even for the techies who put it there. The move to desktop PCs and local servers in the 1990s has distributed these data far and wide. Computers now hold half a billion bank accounts, half a billion credit card accounts, hundreds of millions of mortgages and retirement funds and medical claims and more. The Web seamlessly links it all together. As e-commerce grows, marketers and busybodies will crack open a cache of new consumer data more revealing than ever before.

It will be a salesman's dream—and a paranoid's nightmare. Adding to the paranoia: Hundreds of data sleuths like Dan Cohn of Docusearch have opened up shop on the Web to sell precious pieces of these data. Some are ethical; some aren't. They mine celebrity secrets, spy on business rivals and track down hidden assets, secret lovers and deadbeat dads. They include Strategic Data Service (at datahawk.com) and Infoseekers.com and Dig Dirt Inc. (both at the PI Mall, www.pimall.com).

Cohn's firm will get a client your unlisted number for $49, your Social Security number for $49 and your bank balances for $45. Your driving record goes for $35; tracing a cell phone number costs $84. Cohn will even tell someone what stocks, bonds and securities you own (for $209). As with computers, the price of information has plunged.

You may well ask: What's the big deal? We consumers are as much to blame as marketers for all these loose data. At every turn we have willingly given up a layer of privacy in exchange for convenience; it is why we use a credit card to shop, enduring a barrage of junk mail. Why should we care if our personal information isn't so personal anymore?

Well, take this test: Next time you are at a party, tell a stranger your salary, checking account balance, mortgage payment and Social Security number. If this makes you uneasy, you have your answer.

"If the post office said we have to use transparent envelopes, people would go crazy, because the fact is we all have something to hide," says Edward Wade, a privacy advocate who wrote *Identity Theft: The Cybercrime of the Millennium* (Loompanics Unlimited, 1999) under the pseudonym John Q. Newman.

You can do a few things about it. Give your business to the companies that take extra steps to safeguard your data and will guarantee it. Refuse to reveal your Social Security number—the key for decrypting your privacy—to all but the financial institutions required by law to record it.

Do something, because many banks, brokerages, credit card issuers and others are lax, even careless, about locking away your records. They take varied steps in trying to protect your privacy. Some sell information to other marketers, and many let hundreds of employees access your data. Some workers, aiming to please, blithely hand out your account number, balance and more whenever someone calls and asks for it. That's how Cohn pierced my privacy.

"You call up a company and make it seem like you're a spy on a covert mission, and only they can help you," he says. "It works every time. All day long I deal with spy wannabes."

I'm not the paranoid type; I don't see a huddle on TV and think that 11 football players are talking about me. But things have gone too far. A stalker would kill for the wealth of information Cohn was able to dig up. A crook could parlay the data into credit card scams and "identity theft," pilfering my good credit rating and using it to pull more ripoffs.

Cohn operates in this netherworld of private eyes, ex-spooks and ex-cops, retired military men, accountants and research librarians. Now 39, he grew up in the Philadelphia suburb of Bryn Mawr, attended Penn State and joined the Navy in 1980 for a three-year stint. In 1987 Cohn formed his own agency to investigate insurance fraud and set up shop in Florida. "There was no shortage of work," he says. He invented a "video periscope" that could rise up through the roof of a van to record a target's scam.

In 1995 he founded Docusearch with childhood pal Kenneth Zeiss. They fill up to 100 orders a day on the Web, and expect $1 million in business this year. Their clients include lawyers, insurers, private eyes; the Los Angeles Pension Union is a customer, and Citibank's legal recovery department uses Docusearch to find debtors on the run.

Cohn, Zeiss and 13 researchers (6 of them licensed P.I.s work out of the top floor of a dull, five-story office building in Boca Raton, Fla., sitting in cubicles under a flourescent glare and taking orders from 9 a.m. to 4 p.m. Their Web site is open 24 hours a day, 365 days a year. You click through it and load up an online shopping cart as casually as if you were at Amazon.com.

The researchers use sharp sifting methods, but Cohn also admits to misrepresenting who he is and what he is after. He says the law lets licensed investigators use such tricks as "pretext calling," fooling company employees into divulging customer data over the phone (legal in all but a few states). He even claims to have a government source who provides unpublished numbers for a fee, "and you'll never figure out how he is paid because there's no paper trail."

Yet Cohn claims to be more scrupulous than rivals. "Unlike an information broker, I won't break the law. I turn down jobs, like if a jealous boyfriend wants to find out where his ex is living." He also says he won't resell the information to anyone else.

Let's hope not. Cohn's first step into my digital domain was to plug my name into the credit bureaus—Transunion, Equifax, Experian. In minutes he had my Social Security number, address and birth date. Credit agencies are supposed to ensure that their subscribers (retailers, auto dealers, banks, mortgage companies) have a legitimate need to check credit.

"We physically visit applicants to make sure they live up to our service agreement," says David Mooney of Equifax, which keeps records on 200 million Americans and shares them with 114,000 clients. He says resellers of the data must do the same. "It's rare that anyone abuses the system." But Cohn says he gets his data from a reseller, and no one has ever checked up on him.

Armed with my credit header, Dan Cohn tapped other sites. A week after my birthday, true to his word, he faxed me a three-page summary of my life. He had pulled up my utility bills, my two unlisted phone numbers and my finances.

This gave him the ability to map my routines, if he had chosen to do so: how much cash I burn in a week ($400), how much I deposit twice a month ($3,061), my favorite neighborhood bistro (the Flea Market Cafe), the $720 monthly checks I write out to one Judith Pekowsky: my psychotherapist. (When you live in New York, you see a shrink; it's the law.) If I had an incurable disease, Cohn could probably find that out, too.

He had my latest phone bill ($108) and a list of long distance calls made from home—including late-night fiber-optic dalliances (which soon ended) with a woman who traveled a lot. Cohn also divined the phone numbers of a few of my sources, underground computer hackers who aren't wanted by the police— but probably should be.

Knowing my Social Security number and other personal details helped Cohn get access to a Federal Reserve database that told him where I had deposits.

Cohn found accounts I had forgotten long ago: $503 at Apple Bank for Savings in an account held by a long-ago landlord as a security deposit; $7 in a dormant savings account at Chase Manhattan Bank; $1,000 in another Chase account.

A few days later Cohn struck the mother lode. He located my cash management account, opened a few months earlier at Merrill Lynch & Co. That gave him a peek at my balance, direct deposits from work, withdrawals, ATM visits, check numbers with dates and amounts, and the name of my broker.

That's too much for some privacy hawks. "If someone can call your bank and get them to release account information without your consent, it means you have no privacy," says Russell Smith, director of Consumer.net in Alexandria, Va., who has won more than $40,000 suing telemarketers for bothering him. "The two issues are knowledge and control: You should know what information about you is out there, and you should be able to control who gets it."

How did Cohn get hold of my Merrill Lynch secrets? Directly from the source. Cohn says he phoned Merrill Lynch and talked to one of 500 employees who can tap into my data. "Hi, I'm Dan Cohn, a licensed state investigator conducting an investigation of an Adam Penenberg," he told the staffer, knowing the words "licensed" and "state" make it sound like he works for law enforcement.

Then he recited my Social Security, birth date and address, "and before I could get out anything more he spat out your account number." Cohn told the helpful worker: "I talked to Penenberg's broker, um, I can't remember his name...."

"Dan Dunn?" the Merrill Lynch guy asked. "Yeah, Dan Dunn," Cohn said. The staffer then read Cohn my complete history—balance, deposits, withdrawals, check numbers and amounts. "You have to talk in the lingo the bank people talk so they don't even know they are being taken," he says.

Merrill's response: It couldn't have happened this way—and if it did, it's partly my fault. Merrill staff answers phoned-in questions only when the caller provides the full account number or personal details, Merrill spokesperson Bobbie Collins says. She adds that I could have insisted on an "additional telephonic security code" the caller would have to punch in before getting information, and that this option was disclosed when I opened my CMA [cash management account]. Guess I didn't read the fine print, not that it mattered: Cohn says he got my account number from the Merrill rep.

Sprint, my long distance carrier, investigated how my account was breached and found that a Mr. Penenberg had called to inquire about my most recent bill. Cohn says only that he called his government contact. Whoever made the call, "he posed as you and had enough information to convince our customer service representative that he was you," says Russ R. Robinson, a Sprint spokesman. "We want to make it easy for our customers to do business with us over the phone, so you are darned if you do and darned if you don't."

Bell Atlantic, my local phone company, told me a similar tale, only it was a Mrs. Penenberg who called in on behalf of her husband. I recently attended a conference in Las Vegas but don't remember having tied the knot.

For the most part Cohn's methods fly below the radar of the law. "There is no general law that protects consumers' privacy in the U.S.," says David Banisar, a Washington lawyer who helped found the Electronic Privacy Information Center (www.epic.org). In Europe companies classified as "data controllers" can't hand out your personal details without your permission, but the U.S. has as little protection as China, he contends.

The "credit header"—name, address, birth date, Social Security—used to be kept confidential under the Fair Credit Reporting Act. But in 1989 the Federal Trade Commission exempted it from such protection, bowing to the credit bureaus, bail bondsmen and private eyes.

Some piecemeal protections are in place: a 1984 act protecting cable TV bills; the 1988 Video Privacy Protection Act, passed after a newspaper published the video rental records of Supreme Court nominee Robert Bork. "It's crazy, but your movie rental history is more protected under the law than your credit history is," says Wade, the author.

Colorado is one of the few states that prohibit "pretext calling" by someone pretending to be someone else. In July James Rapp, 39, and wife Regana, 29, who ran info-broker Touch Tone Information out of a strip mall in Aurora, Colo., were charged with impersonating the Ramseys—of the JonBenet child murder case—to get hold of banking records that might be related to the case.

Congress may get into the act with bills to outlaw pretext calling. But lawyer Banisar says more than 100 privacy bills filed in the past two years have gone nowhere. He blames "an unholy alliance between marketers and government agencies that want access" to their data.

Indeed, government agencies are some of the worst offenders in selling your data. In many states the Department of Motor Vehicles was a major peddler of personal data until Congress passed the Driver's Privacy Protection Act of 1994, pushing states to enact laws that let drivers block distribution of their names and addresses. Some states, such as Georgia, take it seriously, but South Carolina has challenged it all the way up to the U.S. Supreme Court. Oral arguments are scheduled. . . .

As originally conceived, Social Security numbers weren't to be used for identification purposes. But nowadays you are compelled by law to give an accurate number to a bank or other institution that pays you interest or dividends; thank you, Internal Revenue Service. The bank, in turn, just might trade that number away to a credit bureau—even if you aren't applying for credit. That's how snoops can tap so many databases.

Here's a theoretical way to stop this linking process without compromising the IRS' ability to track unreported income: Suppose that, instead of issuing you a single 9-digit number, the IRS gave you a dozen 11-digit numbers and let you report income under any of them. You could release one to your employer, another to your broker, a third to your health insurer, a fourth to the firms that need to know your credit history. It would be hard for a sleuth to know that William H. Smith 001-24-7829-33 was the same as 350-68-4561-49. Your digital personas would converge at only one point in cyberspace, inside the extremely well guarded computers of the IRS.

But for now, you have to fend for yourself by being picky about which firms you do business with and how much you tell them. If you are opening a bank account with no credit attached to it, ask the bank to withhold your Social

Security number from credit bureaus. Make sure your broker gives you, as Merrill Lynch does, the option of restricting telephone access to your account, and use it. If a business without a legitimate need for the Social Security number asks for it, leave the space blank—or fill it with an incorrect number. (Hint: To make it look legitimate, use an even number between 10 and 90 for the middle two digits.)

Daniel Cohn makes no apologies for how he earns a living. He sees himself as a data-robbing Robin Hood. "The problem isn't the amount of information available, it's the fact that until recently only the wealthy could afford it. That's where we come in."

In the meantime, until a better solution emerges, I'm starting over: I will change all of my bank, utility and credit-card account numbers and apply for new unlisted phone numbers. That should keep the info-brokers at bay for a while—at least for the next week or two.

POSTSCRIPT

Can Privacy Be Protected in the Information Age?

Without a doubt, different cultures have various attitudes, laws, and values with regard to issues of personal privacy. In the United States, the definition of privacy has been handed down from the Supreme Court. Challenges to privacy often are debated in our highest court, and therefore, are influenced by legal precedent. New technology challenges the court to examine those precedents and see if a balance among the right to know, the right to privacy, and the technological capability to share information can coexist.

In many other countries, however, there are different cultural attitudes and concepts of what is "private" and what is not. Both the UN Declaration of Human Rights and the World International Property Organization (WIPO) have considered the right to privacy as a basic human need for all people. It is the role of governments then, to come up with national and regional policies to enforce these various beliefs with regard to their specific cultures. An excellent collection of issues such as these can be found in James R. Michael's *Privacy and Human Rights: An International and Comparative Study With Special Reference to Development in Information Technology* (UNESCO, 1994).

A number of studies further illuminate how broad a concept privacy may be for individuals. Ann Cavoukian's *Who Knows: Safeguarding Your Privacy in a Networked World* (McGraw-Hill, 1997) takes a practical approach toward understanding how we can control information about ourselves.

ISSUE 18

Does the Internet Have the Power to Transform Culture?

YES: Peter F. Drucker, from "Beyond the Information Revolution," *The Atlantic Monthly* (October 1999)

NO: Kevin A. Hill and John E. Hughes, from *Cyberpolitics: Citizen Activism in the Age of the Internet* (Rowman & Littlefield Publishers, 1998)

ISSUE SUMMARY

YES: Professor Peter F. Drucker outlines a history of social organization in relation to technology in order to put the "information revolution" into perspective. He compares the changes in our present and future lives to the introduction of the Industrial Revolution and reminds us that while social change often takes much longer than the term revolution suggests, the real impact of social change is often accompanied by more subtle shifts in our institutions.

NO: Professors Kevin A. Hill and John E. Hughes discuss the utopian and dystopian visions of the future and find, based upon empirical evidence, that neither scenario of the future is likely to occur. Instead, the actual practices involved with the Internet point to a future in which different social groups may influence the Internet's ability to effect change.

The term *revolution* suggests rapid change, but in the context of the history of the world, some revolutions have taken generations to come about. This is part of the thesis put forth by Peter F. Drucker, who is concerned about both the manifest and latent effects of social change, as caused by technology. According to his essay, past revolutions, like the Industrial Revolution, not only took years to spread, but many of the most important aspects of change occurred as indirect effects of the adoption of new practices that supported the spread of the Industrial Revolution. Drucker contends that the information revolution, like the Industrial Revolution, "has only transformed processes that were here all along." But still, the new processes, rather than technologies, are the ones that he believes have the most power for transforming our culture. Therefore, he concludes, electronic commerce will undoubtedly be the biggest component to the information revolution, and e-commerce will, in the end, triumph as the key to the information revolution.

Kevin A. Hill and John E. Hughes concern themselves more with how traditional institutions, like politics and democracy, will be transformed in the future. They take a similar position to Drucker's in the sense that they are less concerned about the technologies themselves than how they become used within specific contexts. Like many previous technological theorists, such as Lewis Mumford, Marshall McLuhan, Langdon Winner, and Neil Postman, their concern is focused on how technologies and systems become used in the everyday sense by various publics.

What is notable about these two selections is that all three authors use historical metaphors to make their arguments. While Drucker is more literal and evolutionary in the grounding of his position, Hill and Hughes take from the history of utopian and dystopian visions of the future to situate their study of how individuals actually use the services of the Internet. Furthermore, while Drucker answers the question of intercultural change by looking at the business practices of large institutions on a global scale, Hill and Hughes target social change within specific cultures.

Predictions of the future can often change over time, but the best way to understand the potential for change is to look at history. If communication is what binds us together as people, then technology is the means for us to create both stability and change within any social framework. When these frameworks overlap, we see culture evolving to reflect the myriad, and often unevenly unfolding, realities of evolution.

New technologies seem to be proliferating so quickly that we do not have time to evaluate their potential for change or even form judgments of whether such changes might be good or bad for us as individuals or groups. The topics covered in this selection require that we look at the "big picture" of social change and critically examine the world in which we live and the practices necessary for the future.

Peter F. Drucker  **YES**

Beyond the Information Revolution

T he truly revolutionary impact of the Information Revolution is just beginning to be felt. But it is not "information" that fuels this impact. It is not
"artificial intelligence." It is not the effect of computers and data processing on
decision-making, policymaking, or strategy. It is something that practically no
one foresaw or, indeed, even talked about ten or fifteen years ago: *e-commerce*
—that is, the explosive emergence of the Internet as a major, perhaps eventually *the* major, worldwide distribution channel for goods, for services, and,
surprisingly, for managerial and professional jobs. This is profoundly changing
economies, markets, and industry structures; products and services and their
flow; consumer segmentation, consumer values, and consumer behavior; jobs
and labor markets. But the impact may be even greater on societies and politics
and, above all, on the way we see the world and ourselves in it.

At the same time, new and unexpected industries will no doubt emerge,
and fast. One is already here: biotechnology. And another: fish farming. Within
the next fifty years fish farming may change us from hunters and gatherers on
the seas into "marine pastoralists"—just as a similar innovation some 10,000
years ago changed our ancestors from hunters and gatherers on the land into
agriculturalists and pastoralists.

It is likely that other new technologies will appear suddenly, leading to
major new industries. What they may be is impossible even to guess at. But
it is highly probable—indeed, nearly certain—that they will emerge, and fairly
soon. And it is nearly certain that few of them—and few industries based on
them—will come out of computer and information technology. Like biotechnology and fish farming, each will emerge from its own unique and unexpected
technology.

Of course, these are only predictions. But they are made on the assumption that the Information Revolution will evolve as several earlier technology-
based "revolutions" have evolved over the past 500 years, since Gutenberg's
printing revolution, around 1455. In particular the assumption is that the Information Revolution will be like the Industrial Revolution of the late eighteenth
and early nineteenth centuries. And that is indeed exactly how the Information
Revolution has been during its first fifty years.

The Railroad

The Information Revolution is now at the point at which the Industrial Revolution was in the early 1820s, about forty years after James Watt's improved steam engine (first installed in 1776) was first applied, in 1785, to an industrial operation—the spinning of cotton. And the steam engine was to the first Industrial Revolution what the computer has been to the Information Revolution—its trigger, but above all its symbol. Almost everybody today believes that nothing in economic history has ever moved as fast as, or had a greater impact than, the Information Revolution. But the Industrial Revolution moved at least as fast in the same time span, and had probably an equal impact if not a greater one. In short order it mechanized the great majority of manufacturing processes, beginning with the production of the most important industrial commodity of the eighteenth and early nineteenth centuries: textiles. Moore's Law asserts that the price of the Information Revolution's basic element, the microchip, drops by 50 percent every eighteen months. The same was true of the products whose manufacture was mechanized by the First Industrial Revolution. The price of cotton textiles fell by 90 percent in the fifty years spanning the start of the eighteenth century. The production of cotton textiles increased at least 150-fold in Britain alone in the same period. And although textiles were the most visible product of its early years, the Industrial Revolution mechanized the production of practically all other major goods, such as paper, glass, leather, and bricks. Its impact was by no means confined to consumer goods. The production of iron and ironware—for example, wire—became mechanized and steam-driven as fast as did that of textiles, with the same effects on cost, price, and output. By the end of the Napoleonic Wars the making of guns was steam-driven throughout Europe; cannons were made ten to twenty times as fast as before, and their cost dropped by more than two thirds. By that time Eli Whitney had similarly mechanized the manufacture of muskets in America and had created the first mass-production industry.

These forty or fifty years gave rise to the factory and the "working class." Both were still so few in number in the mid-1820s, even in England, as to be statistically insignificant. But psychologically they had come to dominate (and soon would politically also). Before there were factories in America, Alexander Hamilton foresaw an industrialized country in his 1791 *Report on Manufactures*. A decade later, in 1803, a French economist, Jean-Baptiste Say, saw that the Industrial Revolution had changed economics by creating the "entrepreneur."

The social consequences went far beyond factory and working class. As the historian Paul Johnson has pointed out, in *A History of the American People* (1997), it was the explosive growth of the steam-engine-based textile industry that revived slavery. Considered to be practically dead by the Founders of the American Republic, slavery roared back to life as the cotton gin—soon steam-driven—created a huge demand for low-cost labor and made breeding slaves America's most profitable industry for some decades.

The Industrial Revolution also had a great impact on the family. The nuclear family had long been the unit of production. On the farm and in the artisan's workshop husband, wife, and children worked together. The factory, almost for the first time in history, took worker and work out of the home and moved them into the workplace, leaving family members behind—whether spouses of adult factory workers or, especially in the early stages, parents of child factory workers.

Indeed, the "crisis of the family" did not begin after the Second World War. It began with the Industrial Revolution—and was in fact a stock concern of those who opposed the Industrial Revolution and the factory system. (The best description of the divorce of work and family, and of its effect on both, is probably Charles Dickens's 1854 novel *Hard Times*.)

But despite all these effects, the Industrial Revolution in its first half century only mechanized the production of goods that had been in existence all along. It tremendously increased output and tremendously decreased cost. It created both consumers and consumer products. But the products themselves had been around all along. And products made in the new factories differed from traditional products only in that they were uniform, with fewer defects than existed in products made by any but the top craftsmen of earlier periods.

There was only one important exception, one new product, in those first fifty years: the steamboat, first made practical by Robert Fulton in 1807. It had little impact until thirty or forty years later. In fact, until almost the end of the nineteenth century more freight was carried on the world's oceans by sailing vessels than by steamships.

Then, in 1829, came the railroad, a product truly without precedent, and it forever changed economy, society, and politics.

In retrospect it is difficult to imagine why the invention of the railroad took so long. Rails to move carts had been around in coal mines for a very long time. What could be more obvious than to put a steam engine on a cart to drive it, rather than have it pushed by people or pulled by horses? But the railroad did not emerge from the cart in the mines. It was developed quite independently. And it was not intended to carry freight. On the contrary, for a long time it was seen only as a way to carry people. Railroads became freight carriers thirty years later, in America. (In fact, as late as the 1870s and 1880s the British engineers who were hired to build the railroads of newly Westernized Japan designed them to carry passengers—and to this day Japanese railroads are not equipped to carry freight.) But until the first railroad actually began to operate, it was virtually unanticipated.

Within five years, however, the Western world was engulfed by the biggest boom history had ever seen—the railroad boom. Punctuated by the most spectacular busts in economic history, the boom continued in Europe for thirty years, until the late 1850s, by which time most of today's major railroads had been built. In the United States it continued for another thirty years, and in outlying areas—Argentina, Brazil, Asian Russia, China—until the First World War.

The railroad was the truly revolutionary element of the Industrial Revolution, for not only did it create a new economic dimension but also it rapidly changed what I would call the *mental geography*. For the first time in history human beings had true mobility. For the first time the horizons of ordinary people expanded. Contemporaries immediately realized that a fundamental change in mentality had occurred. (A good account of this can be found in what is surely the best portrayal of the Industrial Revolution's society in transition, George Eliot's 1871 novel *Middlemarch*.) As the great French historian Fernand Braudel pointed out in his last major work, *The Identity of France* (1986), it was the railroad that made France into one nation and one culture. It had previously been a congeries of self-contained regions, held together only politically. And the role of the railroad in creating the American West is, of course, a commonplace in U.S. history.

Routinization

Like the Industrial Revolution two centuries ago, the Information Revolution so far—that is, since the first computers, in the mid-1940s—has only transformed processes that were here all along. In fact, the real impact of the Information Revolution has not been in the form of "information" at all. Almost none of the effects of information envisaged forty years ago have actually happened. For instance, there has been practically no change in the way major decisions are made in business or government. But the Information Revolution has routinized traditional *processes* in an untold number of areas.

The software for tuning a piano converts a process that traditionally took three hours into one that takes twenty minutes. There is software for payrolls, for inventory control, for delivery schedules, and for all the other routine processes of a business. Drawing the inside arrangements of a major building (heating, water supply, sewerage, and so on) such as a prison or a hospital formerly took, say, twenty-five highly skilled draftsmen up to fifty days; now there is a program that enables one draftsman to do the job in a couple of days, at a tiny fraction of the cost. There is software to help people do their tax returns and software that teaches hospital residents how to take out a gall bladder. The people who now speculate in the stock market online do exactly what their predecessors in the 1920s did while spending hours each day in a brokerage office. The processes have not been changed at all. They have been routinized, step by step, with a tremendous saving in time and, often, in cost.

The psychological impact of the Information Revolution, like that of the Industrial Revolution, has been enormous. It has perhaps been greatest on the way in which young children learn. Beginning at age four (and often earlier), children now rapidly develop computer skills, soon surpassing their elders; computers are their toys and their learning tools. Fifty years hence we may well conclude that there was no "crisis of American education" in the closing years of the twentieth century—there was only a growing incongruence between the way twentieth-century schools taught and the way late-twentieth-century children learned. Something similar happened in the sixteenth-century university, a hundred years after the invention of the printing press and movable type.

But as to the way we work, the Information Revolution has so far simply routinized what was done all along. The only exception is the CD-ROM, invented around twenty years ago to present operas, university courses, a writer's oeuvre, in an entirely new way. Like the steamboat, the CD-ROM has not immediately caught on.

The Meaning of E-commerce

E-commerce is to the Information Revolution what the railroad was to the Industrial Revolution—a totally new, totally unprecedented, totally unexpected development. And like the railroad 170 years ago, e-commerce is creating a new and distinct boom, rapidly changing the economy, society, and politics.

One example: A mid-sized company in America's industrial Midwest, founded in the 1920s and now run by the grandchildren of the founder, used to have some 60 percent of the market in inexpensive dinnerware for fast-food eateries, school and office cafeterias, and hospitals within a hundred-mile radius of its factory. China is heavy and breaks easily, so cheap china is traditionally sold within a small area. Almost overnight this company lost more than half of its market. One of its customers, a hospital cafeteria where someone went "surfing" on the Internet, discovered a European manufacturer that offered china of apparently better quality at a lower price and shipped cheaply by air. Within a few months the main customers in the area shifted to the European supplier. Few of them, it seems, realize—let alone care—that the stuff comes from Europe.

In the new mental geography created by the railroad, humanity mastered distance. In the mental geography of e-commerce, distance has been eliminated. There is only one economy and only one market.

One consequence of this is that every business must become globally competitive, even if it manufacturers or sells only within a local or regional market. The competition is not local anymore—in fact, it knows no boundaries. Every company has to become transnational in the way it is run. Yet the traditional multinational may well become obsolete. It manufacturers and distributes in a number of distinct geographies, in which it is a *local* company. But in e-commerce there are neither local companies nor distinct geographies. Where to manufacture, where to sell, and how to sell will remain important business decisions. But in another twenty years they may no longer determine what a company does, how it does it, and where it does it.

At the same time, it is not yet clear what kinds of goods and services will be bought and sold through e-commerce and what kinds will turn out to be unsuitable for it. This has been true whenever a new distribution channel has arisen. Why, for instance, did the railroad change both the mental and economic geography of the West, whereas the steamboat—with its equal impact on world trade and passenger traffic—did neither? Why was there no "steamboat boom"?

Equally unclear has been the impact of more-recent changes in distribution channels—in the shift, for instance, from the local grocery store to the supermarket, from the individual supermarket to the supermarket chain, and from the supermarket chain to Wal-Mart and other discount chains. It is already clear that the shift to e-commerce will be just as eclectic and unexpected.

Here are a few examples. Twenty-five years ago it was generally believed that within a few decades the printed word would be dispatched electronically to individual subscribers' computer screens. Subscribers would then either read text on their computer screens or download it and print it out. This was the assumption that underlay the CD-ROM. Thus any number of newspapers and magazines, by no means only in the United States, established themselves on-line; few, so far, have become gold mines. But anyone who twenty years ago predicted the business of Amazon.com and barnesandnoble.com—that is, that books would be sold on the Internet but delivered in their heavy, printed form —would have been laughed off the podium. Yet Amazon.com and barnesand-noble.com are in exactly that business, and they are in it worldwide. The first order for the U.S. edition of my most recent book, *Management Challenges for the 21st Century* (1999), came to Amazon.com, and it came from Argentina.

Another example: Ten years ago one of the world's leading automobile companies made a thorough study of the expected impact on automobile sales of the then emerging Internet. It concluded that the Internet would become a major distribution channel for used cars, but that customers would still want to see new cars, to touch them, to test-drive them. In actuality, at least so far, most used cars are still being bought not over the Internet but in a dealer's lot. However, as many as half of all new cars sold (excluding luxury cars) may now actually be "bought" over the Internet. Dealers only deliver cars that customers have chosen well before they enter the dealership. What does this mean for the future of the local automobile dealership, the twentieth century's most profitable small business?

Another example: Traders in the American stock-market boom of 1998 and 1999 increasingly buy and sell online. But investors seem to be shifting away from buying electronically. The major U.S. investment vehicle is mutual funds. And whereas almost half of all mutual funds a few years ago were bought elec-tronically, it is estimated that the figure will drop to 35 percent next year and to 20 percent by 2005. This is the opposite of what "everybody expected" ten or fifteen years ago.

The fastest-growing e-commerce in the United States is in an area where there was no "commerce" until now—in jobs for professionals and managers. Almost half of the world's largest companies now recruit through Web sites, and some two and a half million managerial and professional people (two thirds of them not even engineers or computer professionals) have their résumés on the Internet and solicit job offers over it. The result is a completely new labor market.

This illustrates another important effect of e-commerce. New distribution channels change who the customers are. They change not only *how* customers buy but also *what* they buy. They change consumer behavior, savings patterns, industry structure—in short, the entire economy. This is what is now happening, and not only in the United States but increasingly in the rest of the developed world, and in a good many emerging countries, including mainland China.

Luther, Machiavelli, and the Salmon

The railroad made the Industrial Revolution accomplished fact. What had been revolution became establishment. And the boom it triggered lasted almost a hundred years. The technology of the steam engine did not end with the rail-road. It led in the 1880s and 1890s to the steam turbine, and in the 1920s and 1930s to the last magnificent American steam locomotives, so beloved by railroad buffs. But the technology centered on the steam engine and in manufacturing operations ceased to be central. Instead the dynamics of the technology shifted to totally new industries that emerged almost immediately after the railroad was invented, not one of which had anything to do with steam or steam engines. The electric telegraph and photography were first, in the 1830s, followed soon thereafter by optics and farm equipment. The new and different fertilizer industry, which began in the late 1830s, in short order transformed agriculture. Public health became a major and central growth industry, with quarantine, vaccination, the supply of pure water, and sewers, which for the first time in history made the city a more healthful habitat than the countryside. At the same time came the first anesthetics.

With these major new technologies came major new social institutions: the modern postal service, the daily paper, investment banking, and commercial banking, to name just a few. Not one of them had much to do with the steam engine or with the technology of the Industrial Revolution in general. It was these new industries and institutions that by 1850 had come to dominate the industrial and economic landscape of the developed countries.

This is very similar to what happened in the printing revolution—the first of the technological revolutions that created the modern world. In the fifty years after 1455, when Gutenberg had perfected the printing press and movable type he had been working on for years, the printing revolution swept Europe and completely changed its economy and its psychology. But the books printed during the first fifty years, the ones called incunabula, contained largely the same texts that monks, in their scriptoria, had for centuries laboriously copied by hand: religious tracts and whatever remained of the writings of antiquity. Some 7,000 titles were published in those first fifty years, in 35,000 editions. At least 6,700 of these were traditional titles. In other words, in its first fifty years printing made available—and increasingly cheap—traditional information and communication products. But then, some sixty years after Gutenberg, came Luther's German Bible—thousands and thousands of copies sold almost immediately at an unbelievably low price. With Luther's Bible the new printing technology ushered in a new society. It ushered in Protestantism, which conquered half of Europe and, within another twenty years, forced the Catholic Church to reform itself in the other half. Luther used the new medium of print deliberately to restore religion to the center of individual life and of society. And this unleashed a century and a half of religious reform, religious revolt, religious wars.

At the very same time, however, that Luther used print with the avowed intention of restoring Christianity, Machiavelli wrote and published *The Prince* (1513), the first Western book in more than a thousand years that contained not one biblical quotation and no reference to the writers of antiquity. In no time at all *The Prince* became the "other best seller" of the sixteenth century, and its most notorious but also most influential book. In short order there was a wealth of purely secular works, what we today call literature: novels and books in science, history, politics, and, soon, economics. It was not long before the first purely secular art form arose, in England—the modern theater. Brand-new social institutions also arose: the Jesuit order, the Spanish infantry, the first modern navy, and, finally, the sovereign national state. In other words, the printing revolution followed the same trajectory as did the Industrial Revolution, which began 300 years later, and as does the Information Revolution today.

What the new industries and institutions will be, no one can say yet. No one in the 1520s anticipated secular literature, let alone the secular theater. No one in the 1820s anticipated the electric telegraph, or public health, or photography.

The one thing (to say it again) that is highly probable, if not nearly certain, is that the next twenty years will see the emergence of a number of new industries. At the same time, it is nearly certain that few of them will come out of information technology, the computer, data processing, or the Internet. This is indicated by all historical precedents. But it is true also of the new industries that are already rapidly emerging. Biotechnology, as mentioned, is already here. So is fish farming.

Twenty-five years ago salmon was a delicacy. The typical convention dinner gave a choice between chicken and beef. Today salmon is a commodity, and is the other choice on the convention menu. Most salmon today is not caught at sea or in a river but grown on a fish farm. The same is increasingly true of trout. Soon, apparently, it will be true of a number of other fish. Flounder, for instance, which is to seafood what pork is to meat, is just going into oceanic mass production. This will no doubt lead to the genetic development of new and different fish, just as the domestication of sheep, cows, and chickens led to the development of new breeds among them.

But probably a dozen or so technologies are at the stage where biotechnology was twenty-five years ago—that is, ready to emerge.

There is also a *service* waiting to be born: insurance against the risks of foreign-exchange exposure. Now that every business is part of the global economy, such insurance is as badly needed as was insurance against physical risks (fire, flood) in the early stages of the Industrial Revolution, when traditional insurance emerged. All the knowledge needed for foreign-exchange insurance is available; only the institution itself is still lacking.

The next two or three decades are likely to see even greater technological change than has occurred in the decades since the emergence of the computer, and also even greater change in industry structures, in the economic landscape, and probably in the social landscape as well.

The Gentleman Versus the Technologist

The new industries that emerged after the railroad owed little technologically to the steam engine or to the Industrial Revolution in general. They were not its "children after the flesh"—but they were its "children after the spirit." They were possible only because of the mind-set that the Industrial Revolution had created and the skills it had developed. This was a mind-set that accepted— indeed, eagerly welcomed—invention and innovation. It was a mind-set that accepted, and eagerly welcomed, new products and new services.

It also created the social values that made possible the new industries. Above all, it created the "technologist." Social and financial success long eluded the first major American technologist, Eli Whitney, whose cotton gin, in 1793, was as central to the triumph of the Industrial Revolution as was the steam engine. But a generation later the technologist—still self-taught—had become the American folk hero and was both socially accepted and financially rewarded. Samuel Morse, the inventor of the telegraph, may have been the first example; Thomas Edison became the most prominent. In Europe the "businessman" long remained a social inferior, but the university-trained engineer had by 1830 or 1840 become a respected "professional."

By the 1850s England was losing its predominance and beginning to be overtaken as an industrial economy, first by the United States and then by Germany. It is generally accepted that neither economics nor technology was the major reason. The main cause was social. Economically, and especially financially, England remained the great power until the First World War. Technologically it held its own throughout the nineteenth century. Synthetic dyestuffs, the first products of the modern chemical industry, were invented in England, and so was the steam turbine. But England did not accept the technologist socially. He never became a "gentleman." The English built first-rate engineering schools in India but almost none at home. No other country so honored the "scientist"—and, indeed, Britain retained leadership in physics throughout the nineteenth century, from James Clerk Maxwell and Michael Faraday all the way to Ernest Rutherford. But the technologist remained a "tradesman." (Dickens, for instance, showed open contempt for the upstart ironmaster in his 1853 novel *Bleak House*.)

Nor did England develop the venture capitalist, who has the means and the mentality to finance the unexpected and unproved. A French invention, first portrayed in Balzac's monumental *La Comédie humaine*, in the 1840s, the venture capitalist was institutionalized in the United States by J. P. Morgan and, simultaneously, in Germany and Japan by the universal bank. But England, although it invented and developed the commercial bank to finance trade, had no institution to finance industry until two German refugees, S. G. Warburg and Henry Grunfeld, started an entrepreneurial bank in London, just before the Second World War.

Bribing the Knowledge Worker

What might be needed to prevent the United States from becoming the England of the twenty-first century? I am convinced that a drastic change in the social mind-set is required—just as leadership in the industrial economy after the railroad required the drastic change from "tradesman" to "technologist" or "engineer."

What we call the Information Revolution is actually a Knowledge Revolution. What has made it possible to routinize processes is not machinery; the computer is only the trigger. Software is the reorganization of traditional work, based on centuries of experience, through the application of knowledge and especially of systematic, logical analysis. The key is not electronics; it is cognitive science. This means that the key to maintaining leadership in the economy and the technology that are about to emerge is likely to be the social position of knowledge professionals and social acceptance of their values. For them to remain traditional "employees" and be treated as such would be tantamount to England's treating its technologists as tradesmen—and likely to have similar consequences.

Today, however, we are trying to straddle the fence—to maintain the traditional mind-set, in which capital is the key resource and the financier is the boss, while bribing knowledge workers to be content to remain employees by giving them bonuses and stock options. But this, if it can work at all, can work only as long as the emerging industries enjoy a stock-market boom, as the Internet companies have been doing. The next major industries are likely to behave far more like traditional industries—that is, to grow slowly, painfully, laboriously.

The early industries of the Industrial Revolution—cotton textiles, iron, the railroads—were boom industries that created millionaires overnight, like Balzac's venture bankers and like Dickens's ironmaster, who in a few years grew from a lowly domestic servant into a "captain of industry." The industries that emerged after 1830 also created millionaires. But they took twenty years to do so, and it was twenty years of hard work, of struggle, of disappointments and failures, of thrift. This is likely to be true of the industries that will emerge from now on. It is already true of biotechnology.

Bribing the knowledge workers on whom these industries depend will therefore simply not work. The key knowledge workers in these businesses will surely continue to expect to share financially in the fruits of their labor. But the financial fruits are likely to take much longer to ripen, if they ripen at all. And then, probably within ten years or so, running a business with (short-term) "shareholder value" as its first—if not its only—goal and justification will have become counterproductive. Increasingly, performance in these new knowledge-based industries will come to depend on running the institution so as to attract, hold, and motivate knowledge workers. When this can no longer be done by satisfying knowledge workers' greed, as we are now trying to do, it will have to be done by satisfying their values, and by giving them social recognition and social power. It will have to be done by turning them from subordinates into fellow executives, and from employees, however well paid, into partners.

Kevin A. Hill and John E. Hughes

 **NO**

Cyberpolitics

Computer-Mediated Heaven or Hell?

How is the Internet going to affect society? Reading through the growing number of works related to computers and politics, we see that most answers fall into one of two camps. Probably the larger camp belongs to the utopians, those who see computer networks as ushering in a new age of democratic politics. The other camp, naturally enough, has just the opposite prediction—computer networks will create a new age of conflict and misinformation. At the risk of oversimplifying their positions, we summarize below the basic ideas and beliefs of each camp.

For any democracy, information is an essential resource. On the one hand, one of the major failings of democracy is that so few people actually take part in the democratic process. In 1996 less than one-half of the eligible adult population voted in the presidential contest, and far fewer are involved in activities such as campaigning, writing letters, or circulating petitions. One of the reasons many pundits think the public fails to participate is that they lack sufficient information about the political process. Without basic knowledge about the government, how it works, and who runs it, people simply tune out. On the other hand, we have the simple fact that democracy thrives on information. Democracy requires leaders and, hopefully, the populace to discuss ideas and policies affecting the society. But deliberative, thoughtful discussion requires knowledge and informed discussants.

Enter the information superhighway. For utopian visionaries, the promise of nearly unlimited information delivered to your monitor in mere moments is the promise of a better democracy. The Internet, they contend, can help to make all of us more active and knowledgeable about government. In fact, these technologies make it possible to hold national town hall meetings in which the nation (or some sizable portion) meets possibly to debate and certainly to decide the issues of the day. For example, it is technologically possible (though currently prohibitively expensive) to attach a keypad to everyone's television so that during a televised "issues convention" we could each simply log our position—pressing 1 to vote yes, 2 to vote no. An even more sophisticated vision would be an on-line equivalent to CNN's "Talk Back Live," where the public watches the debate and e-mails, faxes, or calls in their opinions or questions. The experts and local audience discuss the comments and then a vote is taken. Either way, even today the technology is available to make such interactive democracy possible....

In his book *Data Smog*, David Shenk (1997) offers... [a]... critical assessment of electronic voting. He believes that the Internet will flood users with so much information that it will become impossible to sort the legitimate from the illegitimate, the good from the bad, and the accurate from the inaccurate. This position is based upon two central facts. First, the Internet is indeed full of information, perhaps too full. While utopians see this as liberalizing, Shenk's view is that this is constraining. After all, if a person cannot find the information he or she is seeking but instead finds false or misleading information, what good is the Internet? In fact, Shenk argues that the utopian idea of pure democracy through an electronic town hall is not only unworkable but also dangerous. The ninth of his thirteen "laws of data smog" reads, "The electronic town hall allows for speedy communication and bad decision-making." He sees the public as uninterested and intentionally uninformed. People are ignorant, he contends, because they do not care. And giving more power (via a town hall) to people who do not care about or understand the policies they debate is likely to be counterproductive. In short, those less optimistic about the effect of new media, including the Internet, see a world in which technology enables us to substitute data entry for thoughtful discussion and passive viewing for active participation.

Leaning Left or Right?

We need to address one other major aspect of computer-mediated political communication (CMC). Technologies may be neutral in and of themselves, but that does not mean their consequences are neutral. For example, computers do not care about rifts between labor and management, but it is clear that computers alter the need for and the definition of labor in our modern economy. Similarly, CMC need not help or hinder a particular ideology, but that remains a possible outcome....

Others have... found other types of new media to be dominated by conservatives and Republicans. Diana Owen (1996) concludes that talk radio listeners have a strong tendency to be Republican and conservative. Further, whether Democrat or Republican, talk radio listeners tend to be more ideologically extreme than non-listeners.

Do political activists who use the Internet also tend toward conservatism and ideological extremism? If so, why? We see three potential causes of ideological bias on the Internet. First, the Internet is largely the playground of highly educated, upper-income males. All three of these characteristics tend to promote a conservative ideology. Second, the Internet is an alternative to mainstream media, which are often perceived by Republicans as being biased against conservatives. Third, libertarians, as Shenk points out, find the culture of the Internet particularly appealing and so they, and those with similar beliefs, are over-represented on the Internet....

Questions to Answer

Is the Internet going to usher in a new age of democracy in the United States and throughout the world? Is the Internet dominated by libertarians and ideological extremists from both sides? Do flames dominate political discussion? What about other types of communication such as recruitment and information sharing? . . .

Internet Leviathan

On Rhetoric, Hyperbole, and the Greatness of Sliced Bread

The Internet is the biggest celebrity on Earth today. As with any flesh-and-blood celebrity, this interconnected series of computer networks is adored, hated, mistrusted, idolized, stereotyped, and misunderstood. It has the power to offer up vast amounts of information literally anywhere in the world where there is a working telephone line and electricity. A remote village clinic in Zaire can use a satellite up-link, a gasoline generator, and a simple computer to access vital World Health Organization databases in Geneva—a feat that could easily save the lives of dozens of people in the village. On the other hand, a small group of terrorists using the same technical setup and any freely available encryption software could maintain an undetectable worldwide network for years. With the good comes the bad, as with any new technology or human endeavor.

Almost anything people can do through the mail, over the phone, or face to face, they can do using the Internet. People have met spouses in America On-line chat rooms. They have bought hard-to-find motorcycle parts from someone on the other side of the nation who posted a classified ad in the Internet newsgroup *rec.arts.motorcycles.for-sale*. They have constructed Web pages devoted to highlighting human rights violations in obscure countries. On the other hand, while many people find spouses through chat rooms, a few child molesters have stalked potential victims this way. While many people can find good deals on items to purchase through on-line classified ads, others post solicitations for money that are scams. Finally, for every Web page concerned with human rights, there is probably another devoted to advancing a white supremacist cause.

These juxtapositions of acceptable and unacceptable, profane and sublime, legal and illegal, ethical and unethical, left wing and right wing, are all consequences of such a freewheeling, impossible-to-regulate communications medium as the Internet. Pundits, academics, and Internet users alike have remarked on some of these juxtapositions. For example, as the Web has made databases easier and easier to access by millions of people around the world, lawyers and Internet users have fretted about privacy concerns. Second, as the number of sexually oriented Web sites and Usenet newsgroups proliferated, the United States government passed the Communications Decency Act of 1996 in an attempt to protect children from exposure to such easily available materials. Immediately civil liberties groups filed suit against the law, and ultimately the Supreme Court unanimously declared the law unconstitutional. Third, investors have taken to the Internet like fish to water, owing to the ease with which one can research companies and their stocks on-line. At the same time, scam artists have arisen in chat rooms, in the newsgroups, and on Web pages, much to the bane of the FBI, the Secret Service, and state attorneys general.

What about politics? If there is a flip side to all the other activities on the Internet, how could politics possibly be immune? Viewing recent ads for Internet service providers and hardware manufacturers, not to mention several recent "how-to" books on the subject, one could easily believe that the Internet is inevitably going to bring all people together in harmony, make politicians more accountable to their constituents, and advance the causes of human rights and social justice generally. Certainly this is a possibility, but how is the Internet any different than fax machines, telephones, and door-to-door canvassing? Is e-mailing a complaint to one's congressperson any more effective than sitting down and writing a letter to her? Further, if the Internet is going to make it easier for human rights and citizen activist groups to organize, recruit members, and petition the government for redress of their grievances, does not the same logic apply to white supremacist groups, violent anti-government militias, the Ku Klux Klan, anarchists, communists, cults, and any single "nut" with an agenda? After all, it is just as easy for the Klan to put together a Web site as it is for the American Civil Liberties Union, the authors of this [selection], or an eight-year-old. Anyone with $149 Web page creation software can construct the slickest Web site one could imagine.

Many people would like to believe MCI's recent commercial—that on the Internet there are no races, there are no genders, there is no age, and there are no disabilities. Maybe the Internet will bring about an era of unprecedented human cooperation, as some people would like to believe. But logic and even a cursory use of any Internet search engine will illuminate parts of the Web, newsgroups, and chat rooms that are specifically devoted to advocating actions that are injurious to certain races, genders, ages, and disabilities. True, the Internet does carry with it the potential to create a global community that can influence politics for the better. But it also carries just as large a potential to tribalize the world. Many pundits worry that the Internet will create a world of people who do nothing but sit at home in front of their computer screens chatting away with people they will never meet. To these pundits, this is a gigantic step backward in human relations. The same thing applies to politics: many people believe the Internet will create a political utopia, or at least a sliver of utopia. Others worry that the Internet will make it easier to look up instructions for how to blow up federal buildings, make parcel bombs, and find the time and place for next week's Klan rally....

The Internet and the Future of Political Communication

It has been our position... that the Internet is a great thing. At the same time, we maintain that the Internet is merely an extension of the fax machine, the telephone, the postal system, the picket fence, and cable television in being a medium of political communications. Surely the Web is a publication medium and political space that has an immediacy and uncontrollability unparalleled in human communications. Having said that, political groups are *not* suddenly transformed in their thinking and practices when someone says in a staff meeting, "Hey! Let's put together a Web site!" Rather, the printed brochures, the handbills, the television commercials, and the other documents all get transformed into Web pages. These Web sites then join the stable of lobbying, information, and recruitment devices that interest groups rely upon in everyday life. The Internet is a supplement to political discourse, not a gigantic paradigm shift. As we have seen here, conservatives, libertarians, and to a lesser extent right-wing extremists have caught on to this idea quicker than others. Further, the Usenet discussion groups and various political chat rooms are venues in which people can talk to each other, exchange ideas and information, and hurl some choice insults.

We started with the research question, How does the Internet affect politics? We then proposed three hypothetical answers to this question. First, we thought that the Internet would be dominated by Republicans, conservatives, and libertarians.... Internet activists as a group are actually more *Democratic* and *liberal* than the public at large. If we had stopped with this analysis of the demographic and political profiles of Net users in general, we may well have abandoned the hypothesis that the Internet is conservative, Republican, and libertarian. [We have] demonstrated that the actual *content* of the Usenet newsgroups, chat rooms, and the World Wide Web's political areas is in fact dominated by conservative ideas. We have an apparent contradiction here: if the bulk of Internet activists are Democrats and liberals, how in the world can the Net's major venues be dominated by conservatives? After all, aren't these liberal, libertarian, and Democratic activists the very people posting messages, engaging in chats, and creating Web sites? Yes and no. While it is always a tricky proposition to compare aggregate and individual results in any analysis, we strongly believe that based on our empirical evidence, politics on the Internet is dominated by a relatively small, though vociferous and technologically savvy, conservative minority. While Internet activists as a group may not be overwhelmingly conservative, a conservative subset of those people is very active posting messages, engaging in political chats, and creating Web pages.

Second, we hypothesized that the Internet would encourage more confrontation of a personal nature than would a face-to-face meeting in "real life." On this score we did find that there was a substantial amount of "flaming" taking place in the Usenet discussion groups and in America Online's political chat rooms. However, in the presence of discussions about issues and the provision of political information, the majority of these written discussions were in fact civil. Therefore, those dystopians who fear that computer-mediated political communication will lead to a decline in civility need not lose sleep.

Third, we proposed... that the Internet would be more open to non-mainstream groups and points of view than would be the traditional media or other venues of political discussion in real life.... A large portion of the postings written in Usenet newsgroups about American politics were explicitly anti-government, as were the chats on America Online.... As for the rest of the world, ... as the level of democratization in a country decreases, the number of anti-government postings about that country on the Usenet increases. Left-wing and right-wing fringe discussion of American politics is absolutely more prevalent on the Internet than it would be in the mainstream print or broadcast media. Likewise, people seem to be more willing to express anti-government feelings against repressive governments on the Usenet than they could comfortably do in the streets of many capital cities worldwide....

Will the Internet Transform Politics?
Or Will Politics Transform the Internet?

The utopians propose that as more and more people connect to the Internet and engage in political conversation, governments will become more accountable to the people, direct citizen input into the political process will become ubiquitous, and viable on-line political communities will form. Conversely, the dystopians fear that such direct democracy will amount to nothing more than mob rule and rash decision making, and that the flood of information provided by the Internet will wash up a large share of outright misinformation that does nothing but obscure sensible political dialogue. Some people fervently hope that computer-mediated political communication will make the world a smaller place, serving to break down ethnic, geographic, age, and gender barriers. Of course, there are also people who fear that, as the Internet grows in size and takes on more users, people will flock to specialized sites and newsgroups, thus furthering the tribalization of the world. The one idea that utopians and dystopians share is that, for better or worse, the Internet will fundamentally alter the political landscape of the United States if not the entire world. The bulk of analysts agree that political and societal change are the *effect*, and the Internet is and will be the *cause*.

This logic of cause and effect at first blush is unassailable. Any new technology often generates hopes and fears, and the twentieth century in particular is full of examples of how technology has changed society. The invention of the atomic bomb and the intercontinental ballistic missile fundamentally changed the logic of global warfare. Television and radio changed the ways in which people communicate with each other, and how government reaches its citizens. The Hubble Space Telescope has served to alter our understanding of the far reaches of the cosmos. Even farther back in modern history, Galileo's tiny refractor served to change our view of Earth's place in the universe and solar system. It is logical, then, that so many pundits and scholars have proposed that the Internet will be another technology that will alter politics, society, and interpersonal relationships. There are always people who fear the changes that new technologies bring in daily life and even in our worldviews. These dystopians were behind the censuring of Galileo, and the same logic probably applies to the United States government's rash attempts to control data encryption and the putative spread of pornography on the Internet.

... [O]ur major finding, is that the Internet is not going to radically change politics. Rather, we see cause and effect in a different way. As more and more people log on and participate in the Net's political forums, politics and society will *change the Internet*. This belief is not only grounded in our data here, but also offers us an opportunity to join the utopians and dystopians in some rank speculation. Right now, politics in cyberspace is undoubtedly the playground of conservatives, libertarians, and those with some kind of anti-government senti-ment. However, it is not our contention that the Internet itself has made these people conservative, libertarian, or anti-government. On the contrary, these early days of the mass Internet have merely attracted these groups of people because they feel that the government and the traditional media are not listen-ing to them. The open, anarchic nature of the Internet naturally attracts the disaffected, who can play on a level field with everyone else. After all, anyone with Net access can post Usenet messages, engage in political chats, and create a Web site. Conservatives, libertarians, and those on the fringes of the spectrum feel shut out by traditional politics and the media. As such, they have been the first to flock to the Internet's political areas. Our strong suspicion is that as more and more people get Internet access, the differences between real life populations and the Internet's population will diminish. Simply put, the Net's uniqueness will become diluted, particularly in the United States.

In the early days of public opinion polling, the *Literary Digest* confidently predicted that the Republican Alf Landon would trounce President Franklin D. Roosevelt in the election of 1936. This bold prediction was based on a mail questionnaire the magazine sent to millions of telephone subscribers and au-tomobile owners. Of course the poll was woefully wrong because only a rel-ative handful of people owned telephones or cars at the height of the Great Depression. The telephone subscribers were a biased sample of the American population: they were substantially richer, and thus far more Republican, than society at large. Does this mean that public opinion analysts no longer rely on the telephone to conduct random sample surveys? Absolutely not; anyone who has sat down to dinner only to be interrupted by a marketing or political survey knows this. The telephone has revolutionized public opinion polling, primarily because over 98% of the American population can be reached this way relatively cheaply and quickly. Telephone owners are no longer a small, biased sample of the American population; almost everyone now owns a telephone.

We believe that in the next few years, enough people will have access to the Internet to essentially dilute the political and demographic differences be-tween the connected and the unconnected. As the demographic and ideological uniqueness of Net users decreases, the current conservative, anti-government, and libertarian bouquet of the Internet will merge into one shared by society at large. . . .

We found very little data to support the supposition that the Internet changes people's minds politically. Rather, reading Web pages seems to be an act of self-selection; people go on-line to find out more information about a subject, not to be transformed. Likewise, debate and information-based discus-sion in the Usenet newsgroups and political chat rooms serves to reinforce pre-existing ideological positions, not to change them. Currently a large chunk of the on-line population engaging in these activities are conservative, libertarian, and anti-government. There is nothing inherent about the Internet that dictates this will always be the case.

Many Internet old-timers will probably agree with our arguments here that the Internet will not change people as much as people will change the Internet politically. Back in the "old days" when the Internet was the warren of tech-heads and academics (circa 1990), the Net was in essence a tekkie and egghead playground. But with the advent of widespread Net access, particularly through the commercial services like America Online, the Internet has become increasingly diversified and commercialized. Anyone reading Usenet newsgroup titles in 1992 or 1993 would have seen some new groups like *alt.flame.aol* or *alt.newbies.die.die.die.* These were (and are) places where the old-timers could complain about the newfangled Internet, and how it was being ruined by "newbies." Many people rued the flood of new Internet users as an unwelcome dilution of the "true" character of cyberspace as a place where only computer programmers came to exchange ideas. Of course a large proportion of the Internet's newsgroups, Web sites, and FTP servers are *still* devoted to more tech-minded pursuits. Just because newcomers created millions of new Web pages and tens of thousands of newsgroups, the older parts of the Net did not disappear. In the near future, we believe that more and more liberals and moderates will log on to the Internet, and create another wave of Web sites, newsgroups, and chat rooms. That day is not here yet, and politically the Internet is *still* the domain of conservatives, libertarians, and to a lesser extent right-wingers. But it will not remain so for long, although of course the conservatives, libertarians, and right-wingers are not going to leave the Net. Rather, the Internet will grow to accommodate new users.

Globalization or Tribalization?

The utopians believe that computer-mediated political communication will serve to not only facilitate grassroots democracy, but will also bring people all across the world closer together. Functionally, the Internet cannot help but to do the latter. A link in a Web page can just as easily point to a Web site in Australia or Brazil as it can to a page hosted on a site down the street. A Usenet newsgroup devoted to the politics of Singapore can be read and posted to by people in Singapore, of course, but an Internet user in Zimbabwe or the United States or Canada can also read this group and write messages for it. Real-time chat on the Internet can involve a live text-based conversation between people with Net-connected computers anywhere on the planet (or in orbit when the space shuttle is there, since it also has the capability to hook into the Internet). Globalization of communications via the Internet is a reality.

But does the technological potential for such communication necessarily mean that people flung over the four corners of the globe will be more understanding of each other? The same potential for uncivil flaming in newsgroups and scandalous Web pages that impugn someone's integrity also are part and parcel of this globalization. The authors have seen Web pages in Norway devoted to extremely offensive jokes aimed at blacks. Likewise, a hot topic of conversation in the newsgroup *alt.politics.french* is insults hurled back and forth across the English Channel between people in Britain and France. Just as the Web allows (even makes inevitable) fringe right- and left-wing American groups a worldwide forum, it can encourage "virtual" ethnic and nationalist conflict. Simply because people can talk to each other regardless of distance does not mean they will cooperate. Indeed, the studies of computer-mediated political communication... predict that such disembodied communication will almost always be less civil than face-to-face conversation.

On the other hand, the dystopians should not garner too much fear of a world gone mad solely because of the Internet. This communications medium does allow right-wing Cuban-American organizations in Miami to hurl insults at the Cuban government, while the latter does the same to the former with its official web page. Such an exchange, while sometimes heated and unseemly, does serve an educational function for anyone interested in Cuban politics or the mechanisms of propaganda. Further, this exchange is a classic illustration of free speech on the part of Cuban exiles, and government advertising by the Castro regime. We believe that the Internet per se is benign in regard to globalization. It is simply another communications technology that serves to not only bring people "closer together," but also to allow insulting each other. We [observed] that the Internet is sacred *and* profane. A medium as truly gigantic as the Internet is inevitably going to contain a little bit of everything. While we are not confident that any natural force is going to serve to balance out each point with an equal counterpoint in cyberspace, we do not see any reason that malignant communications will hold sway over beneficial political missives on the Net.

Pundits worry publicly that the Internet will destroy society as we know it, obliterating the concept of common public spaces and fundamentally changing human interaction for the worse. These people are essentially in fear of increasing tribalization and a societal disconnectedness. The Internet will turn us all into geeks cowering in some dark corner of the basement, basking in the soft glow of a computer monitor rather than chatting with our neighbors over picket fences. Further, the argument goes, the Internet leads to dangers such as the posting of bomb recipes or the proliferation of pornography. The same arguments have been used in the past about cable television. Who has not heard the phrase "500 channels and nothing is on"?...

We are not denying that the Internet has a huge potential to change our political interactions with each other and established political institutions. Rather, our final belief after analyzing all this empirical data is that people will mold the Internet to fit traditional politics. The Net itself will not be a historical light switch that turns on some fundamentally new age of political participation and grassroots democracy. On the other hand, computer-mediated political communication is not going to destroy society as we know it and lead to mob rule.

POSTSCRIPT

Does the Internet Have the Power to Transform Culture?

We often concern ourselves with the superficial issues of change. What is "information"? What is a "revolution"? We may be better off asking what the impact of the information or revolution might be on our daily lives. Additionally, how can responsible laws and practices be created that have the power to influence not only privacy but consumer behavior? How integral are the changes brought about by computers and the Internet to our economy? How do our attitudes and beliefs, such as a utopian or dystopian view, cloud the way we evaluate social change and make judgments about the future?

While this issue focuses primarily on the power of the Internet as a tranformative technology and system, it reminds us of every other major new technology that had the potential to change social relations. Marshall McLuhan has said that every time we have a new medium of communication, there are many people who warn that the technology will be evil and have negative social effects. The Luddite movement of the mid-1700s witnessed bands of people who smashed the machinery of the early Industrial Revolution, fearing that their lives would become irrevocably altered if those machines were allowed to change current practices.

Similarly, the telegraph, telephones, film, radio, and television all have histories that reflect concerns for the way these technologies could change society. Perhaps the irony is that only after the change can the effects of change be evaluated completely.

There are many texts that expand on the ideas presented in this issue. The early work of Lewis Mumford, such as *The Myth of the Machine,* which comprises *Technics and Human Development* vol. 1 (Harcourt, Brace & World, 1967) and *The Pentagon of Power,* vol. 2 (Harcourt, Brace, Jovanovich, 1970), discusses the relationship of technology and social change so effectively that other authors have followed Mumford's approach. A more contemporary author who follows the same reasoning is Jeremy Rifkin, who has written a number of texts, notably, *Time Wars: The Primary Conflict in Human History* (Simon & Schuster, 1987) and *Biosphere Politics: A Cultural Odyssey from the Middle Ages to the New Age* (HarperCollins, 1991).

Other, more contemporary publications include Alan L. Porter and William H. Read, eds., *The Information Revolution: Current and Future Consequences* (Ablex, 1998), Gail E. Hawisher and Cynthia L. Selfe, eds., *Global Literacies and the World-Wide Web* (Routledge, 2000), and Hamid Mowlana's *Global Communication in Transition: The End of Diversity* (Sage, 1996).

Contributors to This Volume

EDITORS

ALISON ALEXANDER is professor and head of the Department of Telecommunications in the Grady College of Journalism and Mass Communication at the University of Georgia. Prior to becoming department head, she was a faculty member for 11 years at the University of Massachusetts. She received her Ph.D. from Ohio State University, her M.A. from the University of Kentucky, and her B.A. from Marshall University. She was editor of the *Journal of Broadcasting & Electronic Media* from 1989–1991. She is past president of both the Association for Communication Administration and the Eastern Communication Association. She has served on the board of directors of the Broadcast Education Association. Dr. Alexander's research examines audiences and media content, with a focus on media and the family. She is the author of over 40 book chapters, reviews, and journal articles. She is coeditor of *Media Economics: Theory and Practice*, 2d ed. (Lawrence Erlbaum, 1997).

JARICE HANSON is a professor in the Department of Communication at the University of Massachusetts and associate dean of the College of Social and Behavioral Science. She received a B.A. in speech and performing arts and a B.A. in English at Northeastern Illinois University in 1976, and she received an M.A. and a Ph.D. from the Department of Radio-Television-Film at Northwestern University in 1977 and 1979, respectively. She is the author of *Connections: Technologies of Communication* (HarperCollins, 1994) and coauthor, with Dr. Uma Narula, of *New Communication Technologies in Developing Countries* (Lawrence Erlbaum, 1990). Her research focuses on technology, policy, and media images.

STAFF

Theodore Knight   List Manager
David Brackley   Senior Developmental Editor
Juliana Gribbins   Developmental Editor
Rose Gleich   Administrative Assistant
Brenda S. Filley   Director of Production/Design
Juliana Arbo   Typesetting Supervisor
Diane Barker   Proofreader
Richard Tietjen   Publishing Systems Manager
Larry Killian   Copier Coordinator

AUTHORS

THE AMERICAN CIVIL LIBERTIES UNION (ACLU) is an advocacy organization dedicated to the preservation of individual rights as outlined in the Bill of Rights. It is involved in litigating, legislating, and educating the public on a broad array of issues affecting individual freedom in the United States.

GEORGE J. ANNAS is the Edward R. Utley Professor of Law and Medicine at Boston University's Schools of Medicine and Public Health in Boston, Massachusetts. He is also director of Boston University's Law, Medicine, and Ethics Program and chair of the Department of Health Law. His publications include *Judging Medicine* (Humana Press, 1988) and *Standard of Care: The Law of American Bioethics* (Oxford University Press, 1993).

BEN H. BAGDIKIAN has been a Washington bureau chief and foreign correspondent, an assistant managing editor of *The Washington Post*, and dean of the Graduate School of Journalism at the University of California at Berkeley. He is the author of *The Media Monopoly*, 6th ed. (Beacon Press, 2000).

RUSS BAKER is a freelance writer based in New York City who often writes on issues of media and press policy.

MICHAEL A. BANKS is the author of 40 books, including *The Internet Unplugged: Utilities and Techniques for Internet Productivity... Online and Off* (Information Today, 1997) and many magazine articles for the general and computer press. He writes about Internet criminals and privacy threats and how to protect against them.

SAM BROWNBACK (R-Kansas) is active in a number of legislative areas, including music violence and its impact.

JOHN E. CALFEE is a resident scholar at the American Enterprise Institute in Washington, D.C. He is a former Federal Trade Commission economist, and he is the author of *Fear of Persuasion: A New Perspective on Advertising and Regulation* (Agora, 1997).

MICHELLE COTTLE is a staff editor for *The Washington Monthly,* for which she occasionally writes key features.

JOSEPH R. DiFRANZA is an M.D. in the Department of Family Practice at the University of Massachusetts Medical School in Fitchburg, Massachusetts. He and his colleagues have written several articles on the effects of tobacco advertising on children.

LEONARD DOWNIE, JR., is executive editor of the *Washington Post*.

PETER F. DRUCKER is a professor at the Claremont Graduate School who has authored over 30 books on management and social change. His most recent book is *Management Challenges for the 21st Century* (HarperInformation, 1999).

STUART EWEN is professor of media studies at Hunter College in New York City. He also teaches history and sociology at the City University of New

York Graduate Center. His book, *All Consuming Images* (Basic Books, 1988), provided the basis for the award-winning PBS series, *The Public Mind.*

JIB FOWLES is professor of communication at the University of Houston–Clear Lake. His previous books include *Why Viewers Watch* (Sage Publications, 1992) and *Advertising and Popular Culture* (Sage Publications, 1996). His articles have also appeared in many popular magazines.

RUSSELL J. FRACKMAN is an attorney who specializes in litigation involving the areas of entertainment, copyright, and trademark.

ROBERT N. FREEMAN is a media concentration research project manager at the Columbia Institute for Tele-Information.

SIMSON GARFINKLE is a columnist for *The Boston Globe* and fellow at the Berkman Center for Internet and Society at Harvard Law School. He is author of *Database Nation: The Death of Privacy in the 21st Century* (O'Reilly & Associates, 2000).

MICHAEL GARTNER, former president of NBC News, is editor of the *Ames Daily Tribune,* a daily newspaper near Des Moines, Iowa. His 36-year-long career in print journalism includes 14 years with the *Wall Street Journal.* He received a J.D. degree from New York University and is a member of the bar associations in New York and Iowa.

JAMES W. GENTRY is a professor in the Department of Marketing, College of Business Administration, at the University of Nebraska–Lincoln. He received his Ph.D. from Indiana University.

DONALD GRAHAM is the publisher of the *Washington Post.*

MARJORIE HEINS is the former director and staff counsel to the American Civil Liberties Union Arts Censorship Project. She is the author of *Sex, Sins, and Blasphemy: A Guide to American Censorship,* 2d ed. (New Press, 1998) and *Not in Front of the Children: "Indecency" in History, Politics, and Law* (Hill and Wang, 2001).

DALE HERBECK is a professor at Boston College, where he heads the Debate Program. He is active in the National Communication Association and has written many scholarly articles on media and politics.

KEVIN A. HILL is assistant professor of political science at Florida International University.

PAUL M. HIRSCH is a professor at the Kellogg School of Management at Northwestern University. He is the author of many articles on management practices and mass media organizations. His research interests include organization theory and media industries.

PETER HUBER is an attorney who has coauthored three books, *Federal Telecommunications Law* (Little, Brown, 1992); *Federal Broadband Law* (Little, Brown, 1995); and *The Telecommunications Act of 1996* (Little, Brown, 1996).

JOHN E. HUGHES teaches at Monmouth University, where he is an assistant professor of political science.

KATHLEEN H. JAMIESON is dean of the Annenberg School of Communications at the University of Pennsylvania. Her most recent book is *Everything You Think You Know About Politics... And Why You're Wrong* (Basic Books, 2000).

WILLIAM E. KENNARD graduated with an A.B. in communications from Stanford and then attended Yale Law School. He was named as chair of the Federal Communication Commission by President Clinton in 1997.

S. ROBERT LICHTER is president of the Center for Media and Public Affairs in Washington, D.C., and editor of the online magazine *Newswatch*. His books include *The Media Elite* (Hastings House, 1990) and *Good Intentions Make Bad News: Why Americans Hate Campaign Journalism* (Rowman & Littlefield, 1996).

JOSEPH LIEBERMAN, is a senator (D) from Connecticut and a vice-presidential candidate in 2000.

JAMES E. LUKASZEWSKI, APR, fellow PRSA, is a specialist in crisis and litigation communications management and one of the most prolific authors in public relations today. He is a guest columnist or member of the editorial board for *PR News, Public Relations Quarterly, pr reporter, PR Tactics,* and *Ragan's Public Relations Journal.* He is the author of several monographs and books. In cooperation with the Public Relations Society of America, he released three new books on crisis communications issues, including *War Stories and Crisis Communication Strategies: A Crisis Communication Management Anthology,* 2d ed. (The Lukaszewski Group, 2000); *Crisis Communication Planning Strategy: A Crisis Communication Management Workbook,* 3rd ed. (The Lukaszewski Group, 2000); and *Media Relations Strategies During Emergencies: A Crisis Communication Management Guide,* 3rd ed. (The Lukaszewski Group, 2000). Visit his Web site at www.e911.com.

MARY C. MARTIN is an assistant professor in the Department of Marketing, Belk College of Business Administration, at the University of North Carolina at Charlotte. She received her Ph.D. from the University of Nebraska–Lincoln.

WILLIAM G. MAYER is assistant professor of political science at Northeastern University and was a fellow of the Harvard Center for Ethics and the Profession in 1995–1996. His most recent book is *In Pursuit of the White House 2000: How We Choose Our Presidential Nominees* (Seven Bridges Press, 2000).

HORACE NEWCOMB is the F. J. Heyne Centennial Professor in Communication at the University of Texas–Austin. He is the editor of *Museum of Broadcast Communications Encyclopedia of Television* (Fitzroy Dearborn Publishers, 1997).

ELI M. NOAM is director of the Institute for Tele-Information and a professor of finance and economics at Columbia University's Graduate School of Business.

THOMAS E. PATTERSON is chair of the Department of Political Science at Syracuse University's Maxwell School of Citizenship. His publications include *The American Democracy* (McGraw-Hill, 1998).

ADAM L. PENENBERG writes for *Forbes*. He is a journalist who writes on issues of privacy and security.

KATHA POLLITT, a poet and an essayist, is associate editor for *The Nation*. Best known for her book of poetry, *Antarctic Traveller* (Alfred A. Knopf, 1982), she has also written about the legal and moral ramifications of important social practices and decisions.

NEIL POSTMAN, founder of New York University's Program in Media Ecology, is a professor of media ecology and chair of the Department of Communication Arts at New York University in New York City, where he has been teaching since 1962. He has published 18 books and over 100 articles for the scholarly and popular press on media, culture, and education, one of which, *Amusing Ourselves to Death* (Viking Penguin, 1985), has been translated into eight languages and has sold 200,000 copies worldwide. In 1986 he received the George Orwell Award for Clarity in Language from the National Council of Teachers of English.

W. JAMES POTTER is a professor of communication at Florida State University. He has conducted research on media violence and has served as one of the investigators on the National Television Violence Study. Recent books include *Media Literacy* (Sage, 1998) and *An Analysis of Thinking and Research About Qualitative Methods* (Lawrence Erlbaum, 1996).

LARRY J. SABATO is director of the Center for Governmental Studies at the University of Virginia in Charlottesville and author of numerous books, including *Feeding Frenzy: How Attack Journalism Has Transformed American Politics* (The Free Press, 1993).

RUTH SHALIT is associate editor of *The New Republic*. She specializes in media organizations and social issues.

PAUL SIMON (D-Illinois, retired) is currently director of the Public Policy Institute and faculty member at Southern Illinois University. As senator, he spearheaded the drive to curb television violence.

MARK STENCEL is politics editor for Washingtonpost.com and coauthor, with CNN's Larry King, of *On the Line: The New Road to the White House* (Harcourt Trade Publishers, 1993).

ANDREW SULLIVAN is a journalist and writes for *The New York Times Magazine*.

ELIZABETH WEISE writes for *USA Today*. She is also coeditor of *Wired Women: Gender and New Realities in Cyberspace* (Seal Press, 1996).

Index